ADOBE WALLS

ADOBE WALLS

The History and Archeology of the 1874 Trading Post

By T. Lindsay Baker *and* Billy R. Harrison

Foreword by B. Byron Price

TEXAS A&M UNIVERSITY PRESS, *College Station*

Library of Congress Cataloging-in-Publication Data

Baker, T. Lindsay.
    Adobe Walls : the history and archeology of the 1874 trading post.
    Bibliography : p.
    Includes index.
    ISBN 1-58544-176-7 (pbk.)
    1. Adobe Walls Site (Tex.)   2. Adobe Walls, Battle
of, Tex., 1874.   I. Harrison, Billy R.   II. Title.
F394.A25B34   1986   976.4'815   85-40045

Manufactured in the United States of America
Fourth printing, 2003

Contents

Figures

Maps

Tables

Foreword

F ROM events like the 1874 Battle of Adobe Walls spring heroes and legends. Visions of outnumbered defenders battling overwhelming odds and of underdogs fighting to preserve home and freedom have always appealed to Americans. They are the stuff of high drama and the grist of novels and motion pictures. For all its epic qualities, however, the Adobe Walls story has not inspired movie moguls since 1914, when there was talk in the Panhandle press that a photoplay based on *The Life and Adventures of "Billy" Dixon* might be made. Heralded as the thing "that would put the Texas Panhandle on the map," the project apparently never was completed.

Ironically, except in *The Hide Hunters*, a 1973 novel by Lewis B. Patten, and more recently in Elmer Kelton's *The Wolf and the Buffalo*, the events surrounding the fight scarcely have stirred the novelist's pen. The same cannot be said of historians, who in a plethora of works have recorded even minute details of the battle. Many of these studies have freely mixed the truth with romanticism and folklore. Almost all have dealt with the subject from a limited perspective. Only a few writers have examined the events of 1874 within the broader context of regional and national affairs or have examined the historical roots of the cultural conflict that brought the warring parties to the field of battle. Even fewer have attempted to document the social aspects and material culture of the buffalo hide trade, as has been done so effectively with the fur trappers of the early nineteenth century.

This study attempts a more comprehensive view of the Adobe

Walls saga. It combines new data and fresh interpretations with elements of the story previously explored in depth. Moreover, this work also is intended as a case study illustrating the manner in which evidence obtained from a historic archeological site may be combined with a traditional historical narrative in an interdisciplinary approach. The cordial cooperation for several years between historian T. Lindsay Baker and archeologist Billy R. Harrison and the resulting manuscript is proof that such a course is not only feasible but also highly desirable.

B. Byron Price

Director
Panhandle-Plains Historical Museum
Canyon, Texas

Introduction

O CCUPIED for only six months, the 1874 Adobe Walls trading post was the center of buffalo hunting in Texas during its first year. As the white hunters decimated the great Kansas herd for skins, they began moving southward across the Arkansas and Cimarron rivers into the Texas Panhandle, where the bison still were plentiful. With the hunters came merchants, who selected a site on the Canadian River in northern Texas for a commercial enterprise. They would buy hides from the hunters and sell them supplies in return. Established in March, 1874, the post constructed by the traders was three months later the object of a massive Indian attack. Although the handful of whites withstood the onslaught on June 27, the continued hostility of the Indian tribes during the subsequent weeks forced most of them to retreat to safer territory back in Kansas. The post itself was abandoned by its last white occupants in August, 1874, and remained unoccupied for the next century.

In 1975 the Panhandle-Plains Historical Museum began a systematic archeological excavation of the 1874 Adobe Walls site. The fact that it had lain virtually undisturbed for a century meant that the artifacts found were recovered from an 1874 time capsule. The excavation, supervised by Curator of Archeology Billy R. Harrison, continued for five seasons, resulting in a precise study of the major structures at the site, their contents, and their precise locations. The recovered artifacts and the written records of the excavation are housed at the Panhandle-Plains Historical Museum. Concurrent with the archeological work at Adobe Walls, Curator of Agriculture and Technology T. Lindsay Baker conducted a detailed examination of the historical sources relating to the Adobe Walls site. Baker traveled to archives throughout the western United States, as well as in the District of Columbia, searching for obscure documents and rare published accounts concerning the history of the post.

This book presents the results of the excavation of the Adobe Walls trading post combined with a narrative history of the site that is based on both documentary and archeological evidence. Throughout this project the archeologist and the historian have collaborated, often daily, to interpret not only the objects recovered but also the sometimes cryptic and often contradictory written sources.

In writing this book, the authors have endeavored to prepare a case study to serve as a model for the examination of similar historic archeological sites. They have used one form for note citations in both the historical and archeological sections. Likewise, a unified bibliography lists both historical and archeological materials. Both types of sources have been used freely in the two sections.

The completion of a project of this magnitude would have been impossible without the help of many interested individuals, businesses, and organizations. All those involved in the effort are worthy of the greatest appreciation the authors can offer.

The Panhandle-Plains Historical Society, the Texas Historical Foundation, and the Amarillo Area Foundation shared the financial burden for this project and provided constant encouragement. Electricity was contributed for the archeological field camp by the North Plains Electrical Cooperative of Perryton, Texas; the power provided the much-appreciated convenience and comfort of ice and refrigerated food storage during the excavation.

The owners of the Turkey Track Ranch, which surrounds the Adobe Walls site, graciously allowed the field party to camp on their property and provided much-needed water. Ranch personnel watched over the excavation site during the absence of the archeologists, provided valuable information about the surrounding area, assisted in relaying messages, and in many ways helped to relieve camp monotony.

Over a period of several years, field and laboratory volunteers donated many hours to the Adobe Walls project. Special thanks go to James Word; Thomas and Sandra Alexander; Susan Bradshaw; Ray and

Margaret Thompson; the late Roy Thompson; Mark Caine; Rodney Glover; Meg Nelson; Walter Riddlespurger; Inga Rapstine; Bob, Gay, Clayton, and Deedra Smith; Edward Lane; Marsha Hall; Paula and Reba Day; Voni Kone; George and Pearl Collier; Keith Taylor; James Jeffress; Gene and Ruth Maples; and Dick Stotts.

Fourteen months of archeological field work were spread over five successive seasons, and numerous people were involved. Regular crew members became citizens of the Adobe Walls community from two to three months each year as a permanent camp was set up. The round trip to the nearest town, either Spearman or Stinnett, was sixty miles, and the field crew was isolated in its camp on the grassy meadow at the Walls. Among those 1970s citizens of Adobe Walls, we are grateful in particular to Edwin Kiser, Nicholas Petruccione, Michael Wehrman, Candace Collier, Dena House, and Charles Rivas for their help. Two members deserve special credit for their guidance and help donated to the effort. Henry and Jo Smith of Amarillo gave their time freely during all phases of this project. Jo reconstructed all the glass and ironstone artifacts, in addition to helping with field work on weekends. Henry worked full time in the field, in the laboratory, and in the final preparation of the archeological section of this book. In no way can we express sufficient thanks for their unselfish contributions.

Particular thanks are due the members of the staff of the Cornette Library, the Geosciences Department, and the Killgore Archeological Research Center of West Texas State University, not to mention the generous assistance and great patience of the staff members from the Panhandle-Plains Historical Museum. Victoria Taylor-Gore of the museum exhibits department should be singled out for her help, especially her patience in preparing the artifact illustrations and reconstructed views of buildings and of objects recovered within them.

Archivists and librarians in all parts of the United States assisted in the research that accompanied the excavation of the Adobe Walls site. The authors would like particularly to note the contributions of the following institutions holding documentary materials relating to the history of the post: Texas State Library, Research Center of the Panhandle-Plains Historical Museum, Kansas State Historical Society, Oklahoma Historical Society, Colorado Historical Society, Idaho State Historical Society, Library of Congress, National Archives, Denver Public Library, Beinecke Library of Yale History, Boot Hill Museum, Kansas

Heritage Center, Boston Public Library, Society for the Preservation of New England Antiquities, Western History Collections of the University of Oklahoma, Curatorial Library of Colonial Williamsburg, Inc., Amarillo Public Library, Hutchinson County Library, El Paso Public Library, Fort Worth Public Library, San Antonio Public Library, Southwest Collection of Texas Tech University, Texas Tech University Library, Daughters of the Republic of Texas Library, Witte Memorial Museum, Marriott Library of the University of Utah, Genealogical Department of the Church of Jesus Christ of Latter Day Saints, Field Museum of Natural History, Lowie Museum of Anthropology, Special Collections of the University of Wyoming, U.S. Army Field Artillery and Fort Sill Museum, Colorado Division of State Archives and Public Records, Nita Stewart Haley Memorial Library, and Barker Texas History Center of the University of Texas. Special thanks go to the following descendants and relations of 1870s Texas Panhandle buffalo hunters and merchants who generously opened family records for our use: Mrs. Mabel Bennett, Mrs. Frank Irwin, Mrs. Dora Dixon Coble, Mr. Robert Jones, and Mrs. Fred U. Leonard. Towana Spivey, curator of Fort Sill Collections at the U.S. Field Artillery and Fort Sill Museum, provided a most helpful critical review of the archeological section of the manuscript.

Finally, the authors would like to thank the three directors of the Panhandle-Plains Historical Museum under whom the excavation and research leading to the preparation of this book were conducted. The idea for excavating the site was developed and the work was initiated under the administration of James A. Hanson. The preparation of concurrent historical research and the completion of the excavation were done during the directorship of William C. Griggs, himself a historian of the great buffalo hunt. The final manuscript preparation was done with the sage advice and support of Director B. Byron Price. Without the support from these three men, this study in its present form would not exist.

ADOBE WALLS

PART 1
History

CHAPTER 1

The Hide Men Come to
Adobe Walls

---

*I can make a great deal more money at this than anything I ever
went at before.*
—J. Wright Mooar.

Iɴ these brief words J. Wright Mooar, who might be called the father
of the great buffalo hunt, described the motivation of most hide men.[1]
From 1871 until the end of the decade, professional hunters using specialized firearms systematically killed tens of thousands of bison for
their skins, a commodity for which there had grown a ready market in
both the eastern states and Europe. Beginning in Kansas and spreading
northward and southward, the hunters swept the plains clear of the
shaggies, leaving the way open for cattlemen, who followed close at
their heels.

Initially the buffalo skin trade was an almost exclusive preserve of
the Indians. The native Americans killed the bison for their own needs
and to secure skins to trade with the white men. A commercial boom
in Indian-killed and -prepared buffalo *robes*, skins tanned with the hair
intact, began in the 1830s. Such trade had begun growing two decades
before. As early as 1815 about 26,000 robes were being shipped down
the Missouri River, and a decade later more than 184,000 annually
were reaching New Orleans alone. Buffalo robes purchased from the
Indians and bartered by traders continued to sell strongly through the
middle of the nineteenth century. The southwestern plains represented an important source of Indian-prepared buffalo robes, one of
the most significant traders in the region being Bent, St. Vrain and

Company, operators of Bent's Fort on the Arkansas River in what today is southeastern Colorado. In the 1830s and 1840s thousands of Indian-killed and -tanned robes were funneled through this large adobe trading post on the Santa Fe Trail and then freighted to Saint Louis and other points to the east.

Even before the middle of the nineteenth century a few Americans were engaged in buffalo hunting, some for sport and some for meat. An increasing market developed for buffalo meat to feed railway construction crews and others, drawing the attention of hunters like "Buffalo Bill" Cody, George and Matthew Clarkson, and William Mathewson. It was not until the early 1870s, however, that the great buffalo hunt actually began.

Untreated buffalo *hides*, as opposed to the tanned, fur-covered robes, at first had little commercial value. The meat hunters left them to rot on the prairies. They must have sat around their campfires wishing they could find a profitable outlet for the wasted skins. The answer came in 1870, as hide dealers began buying hard, dried "flint" hides to be made into leather. Initially the technology for making usable leather from the soft and spongy buffalo hides was found only in Europe. Soon, however, the trade secrets reached America, and tanneries on both sides of the Atlantic began processing the heretofore unwanted hides into leather.[2]

From the outset of the commercial hunting William Christian Lobenstine, a Leavenworth, Kansas, dealer in leather and hides of all kinds, was a commanding figure in the buffalo hide trade. A native of Germany and a veteran of the California Gold Rush, he stimulated perhaps the first truly large-scale hunting of bison for their hides.[3] During the winter of 1871–72 he received an order from an English tannery for five hundred hides and passed the order on to Charles Rath, a Kansas merchant and trader who operated a substantial buffalo meat-hunting outfit. The order, however, was too large for Rath to handle by himself, so he asked a Vermont Yankee, Josiah Wright Mooar, to assist him. Mooar killed fifty-one more bison than were needed and, not knowing what else to do with the extra hides, shipped them to New York City, where his brother-in-law, a commission merchant, found a buyer at $3.50 a hide. After paying his shipping and other related expenses Mooar realized a return of just over $139. Soon thereafter the buyer, a Pennsylvania tanner, placed an order for two thousand more hides, and from these beginnings the great buffalo hunt began in earnest.[4]

The buffalo hunters were as diverse as the societies that had produced them. They were Americans and immigrants, cultured and illiterate, honest and criminal. One unifying element among them was the fact that they saw hunting the bison for their hides as a means of supporting themselves, although the occupation held dangers both from their quarry and from rival hunters, the Plains Indians.

Modern popular opinion and portrayals to the contrary, a substantial proportion of the professional hide men were reputable citizens. Typical examples were James and Robert Cator, two English brothers who immigrated to America in 1871 in search of employment. After sailing from Liverpool and landing at New York City, they made their way to the West, where they felt the opportunities for economic advancement were the most propitious. They traveled by train to Dodge City, Kansas, where they planned to become farmers, but they found that they lacked the necessary capital. Of the available means of livelihood, buffalo hunting seemed to offer the greatest promise, so in the winter of 1871–72 they joined the hunt.[5]

Although the brothers' correspondence to their family has not been preserved, they did carefully keep the letters they received, and these letters sent from across the Atlantic provide valuable insights into not only the Cators' activities but also the buffalo hunt in general. Their father, a naval officer stationed at Hull in Yorkshire, wrote to 'them, for instance, that "you seem at last to be well in with the Buffs" and "it must be a grand sight to see such an immense mass of animal moving about." Worried about his sons' safety after reading in his British newspapers accounts of Indian unrest on the Great Plains of North America, he warned them, "You will have to keep a look out for your scalps. I am not afraid of them openly[,] but sneaking up, when you are asleep. I hope you have plenty of dogs about your camp."[6] Their mother, expressing concern for her two "darling boys," asked the brothers to "give up this Buffalo hunting—so precarious as it is," suggesting that they "leave off hunting amongst those horrid 'Indians'" and "take a farm somewhere in a more *civilized place* & be out of danger." Probably realizing that she would go unheeded, she wondered what her boys looked like in the wilds of the American West, asking, "tell me if you both have *Whiskers & Beards*."[7]

Another man who considered himself a reputable hunter was J. Wright Mooar, the Yankee who played an active part in the early development of the buffalo hide trade. A native of Pownal, Vermont, he worked in a textile mill and as a streetcar conductor in Chicago before he became a professional hunter on the Kansas prairies. He and his brother, who joined him from New York, formed a partnership, Wright doing the hunting and John Wesley Mooar the marketing. They began their enterprise at Dodge City, the early center of the trade, and expanded southward as the nearby herds began diminishing. Men who enjoyed the finer pleasures in life, they drew a distinction between two kinds of hunters.[8] As J. Wright Mooar recalled in 1928, "On the buffalo range there were two classes of people, just like there are two classes in any other pursuit of life."[9] Although he obviously saw himself as a member of the better class, Wright Mooar knowingly employed fugitives from justice as members of his hunting outfits. Once, he recollected, "We had eleven outlaws hired. I remember some of them. They were good fellows. They stayed with us. We never had any preachers with us. . . . You never saw one of those fellows that was lazy. They was good hands when they hired out to work. None of them bothered any of our stuff."[10]

One of the men belonging to "the other class" of hunters on the buffalo range, in the opinion of J. Wright Mooar, was "Brick" Bond. Born in New York State, Orlando A. Bond moved to Minnesota and then to Dodge City, where he was nicknamed "Brick" because of his brick-red hair.[11] Bond employed a ten- to sixteen-man hunting outfit composed, according to Wright Mooar, of "outlaws and rustlers . . . a hard bunch." Even in later years Mooar related that "'Brick' Bond's bunch of bushwhackers would have killed" anyone who crossed them. Bond and his crew had an almost violent encounter with a party of soldiers from Fort Dodge. Bond confronted the sergeant and six men as they were passing through Dodge City, boldly asking them what they were doing in town, and when the sergeant replied that they were looking for horse thieves, Brick flew into a rage, "talked pretty tough," and so threatened and frightened the soldiers that the sergeant and his men "pulled out up the river to find the safest place for the night."[12]

Some of the buffalo hunters spread fear and dread among the frontier population, both Indian and white. One of these was Henry Born, known to most as "Dutch Henry." The son of German immigrant parents in Wisconsin, he had by the early 1870s become a familiar personage on the Kansas buffalo range. Reputedly sparked by the refusal of an army officer at Fort Lyon, Colorado, to aid him in apprehending a party of Cheyenne Indians who had stolen stock from his hunting outfit, Born himself became one of the most feared of all the professional horse thieves on the central plains. Specializing in Indian- and government-owned horses and mules, he raided throughout the region, his name becoming a household word on the prairies.[13] Of Henry Born the *Daily Denver Tribune* in 1879 declared: "There are very few people at all acquainted with the crime calendar of the West who have not heard of 'Dutch Henry,' who has ranged in his depredations all along the western slope. . . . He is known to all who own large herds of horses or mules, and is known only to be dreaded." The Denver editor continued, Born "has been shot and cut from top to toe, from Dakota to Texas, but [is] still the same reckless and powerful man he was in the beginning. He seems to be entirely devoid of fear. . . . He is a fine shot and uses the lasso to perfection."[14] The opinions of the Colorado newspaperman were seconded by the editor of the *Dodge City Times*, who reported to his readers, many of whom knew Born, that "Dutch Henry is the most noted horse thief on the border—has stolen more horses, been captured oftener, wounded oftener, broken jail oftener, and has been through more thrilling adventures than any other man in the west. His name is a by-word in Kansas; and it is earnestly hoped that he will be brought to justice."[15] The justice never came, as Henry Born repeatedly escaped his captors to spend his last years peacefully living beside a trout lake in the Colorado Rockies.[16]

The morals of most of the buffalo hunters lay somewhere between those of Dutch Henry and Brick Bond and those of men like the Cator or Mooar brothers. One such person was William Dixon, known to most as Billy Dixon. When speaking of the two classes of hunters, J. Wright Mooar said Dixon was "with this other class, though he was a rather better man than the outfit he ran with," adding significantly, "though he was of that stripe."[17] Others minced no words in describing the hardened hunter. Jordan Edward McAllister knew him as one of the numerous Kansas hide men operating in the Texas Panhandle in 1874 and perhaps exaggerated in declaring that "Billy Dixon was the meanest man among them."[18] Many people acquainted with Dixon's dark complexion and long dark hair thought he was part Indian, but this was not the case.[19] He had been born in West Virginia in 1850 and was orphaned at an early age. His family sent him to live with an uncle in Missouri, but he tarried there only briefly before moving into Kansas, where by 1865 the teenager had become a teamster.[20]

J. Wright Mooar, who became well acquainted with Billy Dixon during the 1870s, came to respect him. After being orphaned, according to Mooar, Dixon was "throwed into this western country alone," but he always "carried his mother's picture until that fight him and the soldiers had [with the Indians] at the Buffalo Wallow [on September 12, 1874], and he lost his mother's picture there." Mooar said that the U.S. government tried to recover the picture from the Indians but never succeeded. He continued, "I never knew he had such a picture, but it turned out that he carried [it] everywhere from the time he was fourteen years old, always had it with him and he looked at it secretly. That told me more about the real man than volumes of anything else could."[21]

With the large-scale slaughter of bison being conducted on the Kansas plains through 1872 and 1873, the numbers of shaggies were so depleted that the hide men were forced to look farther afield for the beasts. When construction of the Santa Fe Railway stopped at Granada, Kansas, in 1872, hundreds of men were thrown out of work, and many of them joined the buffalo slaughter. During the winter of 1872–73 perhaps more bison were killed than in all previous seasons combined. According to Billy Dixon as many as 75,000 bison were taken within a sixty- to seventy-five-mile radius of Dodge City alone. Dixon recalled, "The noise of the guns of the hunters could be heard on all sides, rumbling and booming hour after hour, as if a heavy battle were being fought."[22]

To keep the big freight wagons filled with hides and moving back and forth between their scattered camps and Dodge City, the principal market, the hunters spent more time on the range but killed fewer and fewer animals. They had to find a new supply or turn to other occupations. Enjoying their lives in the open perhaps as much as their profits, increasing numbers of men decided to go south in search of herds as large as those that once roamed Kansas.[23]

In 1873 a few Dodge City hide hunters made trips into No Man's Land, now known as the Oklahoma Panhandle, and farther south into the Texas Panhandle. Many did so with trepidation, mistakenly believing they were trespassing onto the legal hunting preserve of the Comanche, Kiowa, Cheyenne, and Arapahoe Indians, most of whom were supposed to be living on their reservations in the Indian Territory. The No Man's Land was that in fact—a territory under federal control but not apportioned exclusively to either the Indians or the whites. The Texas Panhandle, belonging to the state of Texas, the only state in the Union that retained ownership of its public lands, was open to whoever wished to go there. Confusion over the jurisdiction in these areas stemmed from a widespread but mistaken belief that the 1867 Treaties of Medicine Lodge had reserved them as a hunting ground for the Indians. By the terms of the treaties the Indians were permitted to hunt on the federally owned plains south of the Arkansas River and east of the reservations "so long as the buffalo may range thereon in such numbers as to justify the chase," but legally so was anyone else.[24]

Always seemingly a few steps ahead of most of the buffalo hunters, J. Wright Mooar with another hunter named John Webb made an exploring trip across the strip of No Man's Land into the Texas Panhandle as far south as the Canadian River in July, 1873. Traveling on horseback and carrying no supplies other than a sack of salt, ammunition, and their firearms, they passed over the "neutral strip" and rode down as far as the divide between the Canadian River and Palo Duro Creek. They then traveled west to the breaks of the Blue River before returning to Dodge City. What Mooar found, in his words, was "buffalo, a solid herd as far as we could see, [and] all day they opened up before us and came together again behind us."[25] The two men had found what they were searching for. Other men also explored the prospects for hunting in the Texas Panhandle during 1873, among them the two Cator brothers and Billy Dixon, the latter also finding what he described as "a vast wilderness, inhabited by game—truly a hunter's paradise."[26]

Influenced by the prevailing notion that No Man's Land and the Texas Panhandle were legally reserved to the Indians and hesitant to venture there with a full hunting outfit, J. Wright Mooar and another hunter, Steele Frazier, went to confer with Col. Richard Irving Dodge, the post commander at Fort Dodge, Kansas. They bought new suits of clothes, rode the half-dozen miles from Dodge City to the post, and strode into his outer office to inform the orderly that they wished to see the commander. The orderly replied that the colonel was busy and could not see them, but Mooar insisted that he tell his superior that there were two buffalo hunters to see him. To the surprise of perhaps both the hunters and the orderly, Colonel Dodge ushered out his other visitors and asked the two men in. Mooar and Frazier asked him what his attitude would be if the hunters passed south into what they thought was Indian territory to ply their trade, but the officer initially avoided answering. Instead, he questioned them thoroughly about what Mooar had found on his trip, about the vast herds of bison he had seen, about the hunters' methods, and about the profits they earned. Finally, at the end of the interview, Mooar again posed the question he had come to ask. No longer evasive, Colonel Dodge replied, "Boys, Boys! If I were a buffalo hunter, I would hunt where the buffalo are." [27]

Not only the Mooar brothers but also many other hunting outfits began drifting down into the Texas Panhandle in late 1873, but they met one significant obstacle. The nearest market for their hides was still in Dodge City, more than 150 miles away, yet it was the nearest railroad point to the Texas Panhandle hunting grounds, far closer than any comparable shipping points to the south and east in Texas. The time, expense, and danger involved in freighting wagon trains loaded with hides to Dodge City caused many hunters to have second thoughts about moving their operations into the Panhandle. [28]

The marketing problem was solved by Alexander Charles "Charlie" Myers, one of the largest of the Dodge City merchants, [29] and his partner, Frederick J. Leonard. [30] The businessmen proposed to establish a trading post in the middle of the new buffalo range if the hide men would continue hunting year-round in the Panhandle. Needless to say, the hunters were pleased. At the new post they could sell their hides and buy supplies, have a blacksmith repair their wagons, have hot meals served to them, and carouse and drink with the other hunters in camp. According to Billy Dixon, Myers and his partner agreed to put in the trading post if the hide men going southward would haul the merchants' goods at "a liberal freight rate" to a jointly chosen location. The storekeepers in turn agreed to sell their merchandise at Dodge City prices. The hunters seemingly could not lose, for on their journey to the Panhandle their wagons would be mostly empty anyway, in anticipation of the hides they hoped to gather. Only time would tell whether the Panhandle prices would remain as low as those in Dodge. [31]

Fig. 1. Two skinners removing the hide from a bloated bison carcass. (Photograph by L. A. Huffman. Courtesy Panhandle-Plains Historical Museum.)

Fig. 2. A rick of "flint" hides awaiting rail shipment from Dodge City. (Courtesy Panhandle-Plains Historical Museum.)

Fig. 3. A Dodge City hide yard showing buffalo hides drying and being pressed into bales for rail shipment, with a mound of bison bones being stacked in the background. (From *Harper's Weekly*, April 4, 1874, p. 307.)

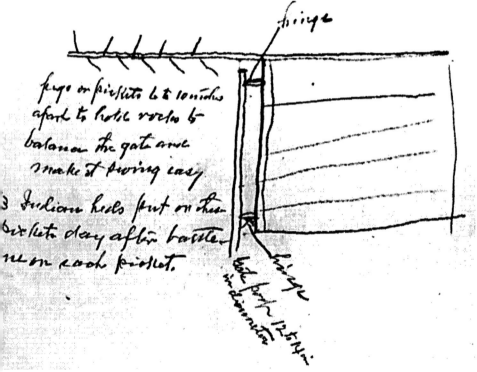

Fig. 4. The gateway leading into the hide yard at the Myers and Leonard store at the Adobe Walls trading post; sketch prepared in 1922 during the visit of Andrew Johnson and Orlando A. "Brick" Bond to Adobe Walls. (Courtesy Kansas State Historical Society.)

Fig. 5. William Dixon at Fort Elliott, Texas, in 1876. (Courtesy Kansas Collection, Kenneth Spencer Research Library, University of Kansas.)

Fig. 6. (*left*). James N. Hanrahan. (Courtesy Idaho State Historical Society.);
Fig. 7. (*right*). Orlando A. "Brick" Bond. (Courtesy Boot Hill Museum, Inc.)

Fig. 8. (*left*). Charles Edward "Dirty Faced Ed" Jones. (Courtesy Panhandle-Plains Historical Museum.); Fig. 9. (*right*). Judge Emanuel Dubbs. (Courtesy Panhandle-Plains Historical Museum.)

Fig. 10. (*left*). "Dutch Henry" Born. (Courtesy Mrs. Mabel L. Bennett.); Fig. 11. (*right*). Josiah Wright Mooar. (Courtesy Panhandle-Plains Historical Museum.)

Fig. 12. *Left*, Olive King Dixon; *center*, James H. Cator; and *right*, Mrs. James H. Cator at the site of the Adobe Walls trading post. (Courtesy Panhandle-Plains Historical Museum.)

Fig. 13. (*left*). Charles Rath. (Courtesy Boot Hill Museum, Inc.); Fig. 14. (*right*). Tom Nixon. (Courtesy Boot Hill Museum, Inc.)

Fig. 15. (*left*). Lemnot I. Wilson. (Courtesy Panhandle-Plains Historical Museum.); Fig. 16. (*right*). James Langton. (Courtesy Boot Hill Museum, Inc.)

Fig. 17. (*left*). Frederick J. Leonard. (Courtesy Mrs. Margaret L. Pollock.); Fig. 18. (*right*). William Barclay Masterson. (Courtesy Panhandle-Plains Historical Museum.)

Fig. 19. (*left*). Andrew Johnson. (Courtesy Boot Hill Museum, Inc.); Fig. 20. (*right*). John Thomson Jones, alias Cheyenne Jack and Antelope Jack, ca. 1874. (Courtesy Robert Jones.)

Fig. 21. Frank D. Baldwin. (Courtesy Panhandle-Plains Historical Museum.)

By the spring of 1874 dusty little Dodge City was but two years old, yet already it was an aging belle, appearing to be past her prime. The great Kansas buffalo herds had been decimated, the business places in the community had lost their hustle and bustle, and the men and women in the town had started moving on to places that offered better opportunities. The plans to shift some of the Dodge City trading operations to Texas, however, seemed to breathe life back into the frontier settlement. Charlie Myers and Fred Leonard placed orders for substantial amounts of new merchandise, and everybody was talking about making real money again from the hide trade.

In March a wagon train of hunters, merchants, and hangers-on assembled, all of them planning to migrate to the Texas buffalo range. They did not know exactly where they were going, but they hoped that bison would graze by the thousands there. One in the caravan, Emanuel Dubbs, was one of the few hunters engaged in large-scale commercial buffalo hunting for meat, and he had just returned from a selling trip to Kansas City and points east. He broke with his practice of hunting only in the cooler months of the year and fitted up teams of oxen and mules to pull his big wagons down into Texas. Another member of the train was James N. "Jim" Hanrahan, whom Billy Dixon characterized as "a typical frontiersman, who hunted buffaloes on a large scale." The other hide men were glad to see him, for they knew the Irishman to be "a man . . . who had lots of nerve and knew all the ins and outs of frontier life."

The hunters had pumped money into all the local stores to buy last-minute supplies because, as Billy Dixon recalled, "we would be far from a railroad. We had no idea when we would get back to civilization." He added significantly, "A lot of fellows at Dodge thought that maybe we might never get back."

The long train of wagons, which Dubbs estimated to number about a hundred, slowly creaked out of Dodge City on a now-forgotten day in March, 1874. All the vehicles were heavily laden with the hunters' own supplies combined with the goods for Myers and Leonard's projected store. J. Wright Mooar estimated the worth of the merchants' stock to be about fifty thousand dollars. Both partners accompanied the expedition to supervise the construction of the store once a satisfactory location was found.

On the first day out they reached Crooked Creek, where they

spent the night. They continued on the second day to the Cimarron River, another camping spot with running water. Billy Dixon remembered this part of the trip as being quite disagreeable: "In the brakes of the Cimarron we had the hardest kind of pulling, as there was lots of sand and the country rough." The fourth day brought the long train to Beaver Creek, in the middle of No Man's Land. The more timid souls undoubtedly already were becoming nervous about Indians, but none were seen. The next night found the caravan at the mouth of Palo Duro Creek; here members of the group began seeing the camps of other hunters who had preceded them. Dixon saw his friends, the Cator brothers, and he recollected the time when he first saw them at Hays, Kansas: "They had just arrived from England, and were still wearing knee breeches and buckles." He chuckled to himself as he thought about how their clothes had amused the local population. Farther south the caravan pushed, its members being determined to locate the best buffalo country. They struck Moore's Creek at its head and followed it downstream to the Canadian River, where they camped the sixth night out. Disappointed at the grazing conditions in the area, which were much drier than usual, they moved on down the Canadian to a point already known to some of the hunters as the Adobe Walls.[32]

The site the hunters and merchants chose for their trading post was located about two miles north of the main course of the Canadian River on a broad, open meadow. For centuries this part of the river had been used as a crossing point, for much of the rest of the river is walled in by steeply eroded banks. At Adobe Walls two creeks form tributaries on the north and a third on the south, giving a comparatively smooth and gradual grade for Indian travois (wheel-less carts made of crossed poles) or white men's wagons crossing from the plains on the north. The meadow, with a shallow underflow of water from the two streams on the north side of the river, to this day grows luxuriant in the natural prairie hay that provided fine grazing for the merchants' and hunters' stock. In addition, springs broke out of the sides of the valley to give the hide men fresh, cool drinking water. Sufficient timber for constructing buildings was readily available along the creeks and on the banks of the river into which they fed. A contemporary noted that "the Canadian River passes through the Llano Estacado, its almost innumerable tributaries affording most pleasant,

well-sheltered valleys with abundant timber, excellent water and grazing." The Dodge City men had found one of the finest of these valleys.[33]

The location that the traders and hunters chose for their building
was toward the center of the meadow, a location that would allow
them a broad field of action for their long-range buffalo hunting guns
should they have to defend either the post or their horses from ma-
rauding Indians. The place was so ideal for a post that more than one
U.S. Army officer recommended it for a military subdepot.[34]

Only about a mile south of the place that the merchants and hunters chose were the crumbling remains of a much older building that
gave the place the name Adobe Walls. Most of the hide men puzzled
over the origins of the walls. Seeing that the remains consisted of sun-
dried adobe bricks, most of the white men from Dodge concluded that
they had been built at some unknown date by either Spaniards or
Mexicans. Sam Smith, one of the hunters who came south in 1874, decided that they were "the ruins of an old mission once occupied by
Spanish friars,"[35] and Dubbs speculated that they were "the remnant of
broken down and decaying Adobes, possibly constructed by Mexicans."[36] Andrew "Andy" Johnson, who became an important figure in
the history of the 1874 trading post and who arrived on the scene
about a month later than the initial party, supposed that the adobe
structure had been "built and used by Indian traders from New Mexico, as quantities of beads and other trinkets were dug up within the
inclosure."[37] The trader theory was supported by Lt. Frank D. Baldwin,
who saw the ruins in August, 1874, and who noted in his diary that
"from the best information I can get[,] this place was built many years
ago by the Mexicans, and for the purpose of establishing a tradeing
[*sic*] post from which point they could trade with the Indians." He
based his conclusion on the fact that such traders from New Mexico
"are still in this section of the country and pack their goods on burros
and it is from this source that the wild and savage foe procure the major part of their war supplies."[38]

The men who guessed that the walls had been built by traders
from New Mexico were the closest to the truth, for the rubble they
found was in fact the remains of a trading post established about thirty-
five years earlier by the firm of Bent, St. Vrain and Company, the founders and operators of Bent's Fort on the Santa Fe Trail. Charles and Wil-

liam Bent and their partner, Ceran St. Vrain, had sent a party of men to the Canadian River about 1840 to found a subtrading post. The Comanche, Kiowa, and Apache Indians were reluctant to trade at their main facility on the Arkansas River because their traditional enemies, the Cheyenne and Arapahoe tribes, inhabited the region. To remedy the situation the company established the Canadian River post, but the hostility of some of the roving bands soon forced its abandonment. From then on, its bare adobe walls stood peacefully, their solitude broken only by occasional passing Indians or white men.[39]

The gaunt walls of the Bent trading post witnessed in 1864 one of the fiercest Indian battles in the history of the American West, an encounter of California and New Mexico volunteers and Ute auxiliaries under Col. Kit Carson with a much larger force of Comanche, Kiowa, and Kiowa-Apache warriors. The purpose of the expedition dispatched from Fort Bascom, New Mexico, was to punish these tribes, which had been harassing commerce on the Santa Fe Trail, a critical communication and supply link between the U.S. military forces in New Mexico and the rest of the United States during the Civil War. Attacking a village upstream from the old Bent site, the troops followed the fleeing Plains Indians down the valley, only to discover additional villages. The resistance of the unexpectedly numerous warriors was strong, and it was probably only the effects of Carson's two howitzers that prevented the annihilation of his force. During the battle his men used the adobe ruins as a combination hospital and horse corral before they moved back up the river to destroy the one village they had overrun and then return to their base of operations in New Mexico.[40]

Myers and Leonard in March, 1874, began directing construction efforts immediately upon arrival at the spot they had chosen for their store. The hunters and members of their outfits who could be convinced to stay for a few days and help were paid to do the manual labor, but most were too eager to examine the surrounding country to linger and dig holes or cut timber. Dubbs stayed at the fledgling post only five days before packing up supplies for himself and his skinners and heading south. "While all this hammering and pounding and digging was going on," Dixon remembered, "I started with three companions and rode the country" to the south and east for about fifteen days, hoping to be the first to spot the buffalo in their annual migration northward.[41]

As soon as Myers and Leonard determined where the trading post would be built, they asked two professional teamsters, Charles Edward "Dirty Faced Ed" Jones[42] and his partner Joe Plummer,[43] to mark a trail from the Adobe Walls back to Dodge City. This would be the route the freight wagons would follow to carry hides to Dodge and return with goods and merchandise to sell in the store.[44] A number of teamsters, among them Jones, John Wesley Mooar, and a man named Warren, either supplemented their incomes from hunting or worked exclusively at hauling freight between the trading post and Kansas. As Jones recalled in later years, "I hauled more than one-half of the wood [cut lumber] that built the Adobe Walls. It was all hauled in two four-mule teams. Mine worked all the time."[45]

The March wind was still fresh for both the men who remained at the trading post and for those who had begun scouting the country. The chill air and the consequent desire for shelter may have added to the energy the men devoted to erecting Myers and Leonard's buildings. Though their establishment was generally described as being only a "store," the two Dodge City merchants in fact planned and built a complete trading post complex. Surrounding it was a picket corral, sometimes confusingly called a "stockade," made by digging a trench about two feet deep and a foot wide and placing in it upright cottonwood logs about four to eight inches in diameter. The enclosure was about two hundred feet wide and three hundred feet long. Dixon, who was present while some of it was being built, recalled that the rough timbers were hauled from Reynolds Creek on the south side of the Canadian, a distance of about six miles. The corral served as a hide yard, a protected area for livestock, and a general storage area.[46]

Various accounts describe the pickets of the corral fence as standing between seven and ten feet high, but Lt. Frank D. Baldwin, who saw the corral in August, 1874, estimated more precisely in his diary at the time that they extended "8 feet above ground." He also recorded that the corral fence was "loop holed four feet above the ground" every so often to provide for its defense. A large gate of an unusual design was erected on the east side of the corral. The gate was balanced on a single large vertical cottonwood timber sunk deeply in the ground. A crosspiece at one end supported the gate proper, and its other end served as a counterbalance. The end of the crossmember was fitted with about a dozen wooden pegs six to ten inches apart to hold heavy rocks. Such an arrangement allowed one man to swing the portal open or closed with ease.[47]

Inside the corral were three buildings composing the remainder of the Myers and Leonard trading post complex. All were located along the periphery of the corral so that their outer walls formed part of the rectangular "stockade." At the northeast corner of the corral the builders erected the store. From the archeological evidence it is known that they dug a one-foot-wide trench that formed a rectangle seventy feet long and twenty feet wide in which they placed pickets for the walls. These pickets were different from those in the corral fence. Instead of using only large, trimmed individual logs next to one another, the builders placed smaller vertical poles on either side of the trench in an alternating pattern. After the workmen filled the trench, they began filling the spaces between the cottonwood pickets with a moistened dirt mixture containing more clay than the loam upon which they erected the building. The front of the store faced the east, away from the corral, and this side of the building bore a porchlike appendage supported on wooden poles. It must have been a cool place to relax in the summer heat. The front also had a large double door, and the back had a smaller three-foot portal fitted with a heavy wooden door. Although there probably were others, glass windows certainly existed on the south and west sides. One of the men who witnessed part of the construction and knew the store when it was completed noted that "the roof [was] made of straight poles, the ends resting upon a center log, called a ridge log. Then the top [was] closely covered with fine brush, and earth put on top of that."[48]

The interior of the Myers and Leonard store was divided into two parts, a smaller storage area at the north end and a large open sales room at the south end, the latter having direct access from the outside through both doors. Along the east side of the sales room was a wooden counter mounted on posts, floored beneath with cut lumber; at this counter the traders sold smaller items of merchandise. At the north end of the counter stood a large corn bin, and nearby was a large balance-type scale, probably used to weigh the grain and other bulk products such as lead and gunpowder that were sold by the pound. Other furnishings included tables and chairs, kerosene lamps, and an assortment of packing crates. Seth Hathaway, a Kansas hide man, bought some of his supplies from Myers and Leonard; he recalled visiting the store: "I entered the house and found it was in two rooms. . . . [in the large room] was a counter across one side, behind which was kept the smaller stores, while . . . [in the smaller area] was stacked flour, bacon, corn meal, horse feed, lead and other things for which the hunters found use, and which Meyers [*sic*] traded for hides."[49]

Completing the Myers and Leonard complex were a mess hall and an adjoining stable. These buildings were located in the southwest corner of the corral, its pickets forming parts of their walls. In the extreme corner was the kitchen, measuring twelve by twenty-nine feet; two of its walls helped form the corral. This room housed a large cast-iron cookstove, tables or counters, and cooking utensils. Myers and Leonard employed an old man named Keeler as their cook; in this room he prepared the meals for the store personnel as well as for the hunters, skinners, and teamsters who drifted in and out of the post. It is uncertain whether Keeler stored most of his food in the kitchen or in the store building, but it is known that he used crockery to keep some food items in the preparation area. Water was convenient in a shallow well just outside the door to the kitchen. Adjoining this room to the north was a second room, most likely associated with the kitchen. This enclosure, twenty-five by eighteen feet, was open on the east side. Here, possibly, Keeler fed his customers.

Surprisingly, the hide men at Adobe Walls ate meals not from tin plates or wooden bowls but from imported white English ironstone dishes. Besides being heavy and durable, they also were pleasing to the hunters, skinners, and freighters, many of whom undoubtedly had most of their meals in the field using few utensils other than their hunting knives.[50]

The final structure in the Myers and Leonard trading post was its stable. Few written accounts of the post mention it, and then only in passing, perhaps because observers considered it merely part of the corral. One visitor to the store complex, however, did note that it provided stabling for forty horses. Extending north along the west corral fence from the mess hall area, the stable was seventy feet long and twenty-six feet wide. Along its length four sets of cottonwood posts were set in the ground, apparently to support a light brush roof on either side of a center aisle. The posts also may have divided the area into stalls. Cut-lumber feed troughs extended along the outer sides of the length of the structure so that the animals housed there could be fed conveniently.[51]

After Myers and Leonard's buildings were completed but before the heat of the summer began, the partners made one significant structural addition to their trading post: the construction of circular picket bastions at the northeast, northwest, and southeast corners of the complex. The pickets, like those in the corral fence, were set in trenches in single rows without daubing, but they were both thicker and taller than those in the fence. The bastions themselves seem to have been either unroofed or covered only with light thatching.[52]

While Charlie Myers and Fred Leonard were shifting a portion of their commercial operations to the Texas Panhandle and building their new trading post, their competition was not standing by idly. The other principal mercantile establishment at Dodge City in 1874 was the firm of Charles Rath and Company, an equal partnership of Charles Rath[53] and Robert Marr Wright.[54] As soon as the buffalo hunters' talk of moving to the Panhandle reached their ears, the two businessmen began thinking about how they might retain their trade. In February, Robert Wright went to confer with Col. Richard Irving Dodge, the same army officer whom J. Wright Mooar had gone to see a year before, to determine if there were any legal restrictions that might prevent his firm from moving some of its commercial dealings to the Panhandle.[55] The firm of Charles Rath and Company certainly did not intend to lose their portion of the hunters' business to Myers and Leonard just because they were the first to expand into Texas.

The establishment of another store, however, represented a financial strain on both Rath and Wright, so they took an additional partner, a handsome young Irishman named James Langton.[56] Each member of the new partnership contributed one-third to the venture in Texas, although Langton did not become a part in the Rath and Company Dodge City dealings.[57] Hot on the heels of Myers and Leonard, the three men in spring, 1874, began ordering additional merchandise and arranging for transportation to haul it to the Texas plains.

About a month after the initial caravan of merchandise set off for the Panhandle, a second began forming in dusty little Dodge City. This one, almost exclusively composed of Rath and Company vehicles, was manned by four men who would remain at the new store as well as by teamsters and others who would help to build it once they reached the site. Sometime after the middle of April, wagons hauling goods worth an estimated twenty thousand dollars slowly creaked out of Dodge, crossed the Arkansas River, and headed down what already was becoming a worn trail into the new buffalo country.

About the beginning of May the Rath and Wright train reached the place its drivers and passengers had been hearing about. The big, open, green meadow must have been a refreshing sight to the traders and teamsters after several days of rolling over the broad plains and struggling through the brakes in the valleys that crossed their path. Charles Rath himself had decided to accompany the party to Texas so that he could supervise the construction of the new store, leaving Robert Wright behind to attend to their business interests in Dodge.[58] Rath brought with him one of his most reliable employees, a Swedish immigrant named Andrew Johnson, whom the hide men in Kansas knew best as "The Swede" or "Andy the Swede." Johnson would remain at the post for the next three months and perhaps to his own surprise would become one of the most important people in its history.[59]

On arrival at Adobe Walls, the Rath and Company party set up tents and began erecting their building. Not nearly so extensive as the Myers and Leonard complex, the Rath and Company facility was to consist of store, corral, and outhouse. Instead of using the picket construction their competitors had chosen, the Rath and Company crew erected a sod store building. This was an architectural form very common in Kansas during the 1870s, and it was quite natural for the Dodge City merchants to adopt it when they moved their operations south.

To secure the necessary sod blocks, the workmen used a special plow made by Patrick Ryan, the first blacksmith in Dodge City. It probably saw earlier service in the erection of buildings in Dodge. Designed to cut about three to five inches beneath the surface of the ground and parallel with it, the plow sliced up strips of sod that were then cut into proper lengths for building blocks. The blocks were carried to the building site, where they were laid into walls without the use of mortar.[60] Andy Johnson, who helped build the Rath and Company store, later recalled: "We hitched a yoke of oxen to a breaking plow and began to turn sod which we used in constructing our building. . . . It was 20 feet by 70 feet, with walls 3 feet thick at the bottom and 1½ feet feet thick at the top."[61] Johnson's recollections fifty years after the event were remarkably good, for evidence at the site shows a building that measured about twenty-two and one-half feet by fifty-nine feet. The remaining wall base averaged very nearly the three-foot thickness that he remembered.[62]

The Rath and Company store was divided into three rooms. Northernmost was the kitchen, for Rath, Wright, and Langton competed with Myers and Leonard not only in merchandise sales but also in the restaurant trade. Here Mrs. Hannah Olds, the only woman who came to the trading post as a permanent employee, prepared meals for the transients passing through the camp and for the Rath and Company personnel. She came to Adobe Walls with her husband, William, a man in poor health, who also was a company employee. The pair previously had operated a boardinghouse at Dodge City. The kitchen contained the Olds's cookstove, shelving, and all the crockery, utensils, and china needed to prepare and serve food to large groups of men.[63]

South of the kitchen was a sales room smaller than that in the Myers and Leonard store, as Rath and Company did not have so large a stock of merchandise. This room had two of the three doors in the building, one on the east and the other on the west leading to the corral area; a third door opened from the kitchen to the west. In the east wall of the sales room workmen dug a fireplace and lined it with pieces of sandstone. The extreme southwest corner of the store was partitioned into a room measuring ten feet by ten feet, which most likely provided quarters and some privacy for Hannah and William Olds.[64]

Sometime after the store construction was finished but before the heat of summer, a rectangular sod bastion was added to its southeast corner. It measured nineteen feet by eighteen feet on the outside, and its walls abutted the store walls rather than being interlaced with them, as were the building corners. In this bastion Johnson later dug a well so that the people inside could have water without having to walk to the distant springs to get it.[65]

The roof of the Rath and Company store consisted of cut-lumber planks supported at their upper ends by a heavy cottonwood ridgepole the length of the building and at their lower ends by the walls themselves. The builders then covered the plank roof with a layer of sod to give the store a comparatively weatherproof covering. Some accounts state that the roof was made from cottonwood logs and brush covered with sod, but evidence both from archeological remains and from a sworn statement by Charles Rath indicates the use of cut lumber, which of course had to be hauled from Dodge City.[66]

Work went remarkably fast on the Rath and Company store, and by May 20 the building was sufficiently along that Charles Rath felt that he could return to Dodge City. With him on the return trip went most of the men brought along to erect the store. Only Johnson, Mr. and Mrs. Olds, and George Eddy, the bookkeeper, were left behind as paid employees.[67] Two weeks later Langton, part owner of the store and the man selected to be its manager, reached the new trading post.[68]

After the Rath and Company store was completed, the builders moved out of their tents and occupied the building. Then they began working on two auxiliary structures, a sod corral fence and a privy. West of and adjoining the store they marked an outline for a corral approximately fifty-five feet wide by eighty-five feet long. They began laying sod blocks to build its walls, but for some reason they never finished the job. Even during store construction they had been selling goods from their freight wagons and buying hides, and perhaps business had grown so heavy that they decided not to take the time to finish the corral. It was Johnson's job to attend to the horses morning and evening, and probably Langton felt that the animals were all right under the Swede's care even without a corral. The greatest fear concerning livestock was theft by Indians, and the men had not seen a single red warrior.[69]

Beyond the projected corral more than two hundred feet west of the store stood a wooden outhouse. Mentioned in only a few written accounts of the trading post, it appears to have been some type of picket structure with an opening on the north end of its east wall. Since no such buildings are known to have been associated with the Myers and Leonard store, it is possible that this facility was erected at the Rath and Company store mainly for the convenience and modesty of Hannah Olds.[70]

Two more buildings, a saloon and a blacksmith shop, were constructed, completing the Adobe Walls trading post. The saloon generally is credited exclusively to James N. Hanrahan, the same man who as a hunter had accompanied the Myers and Leonard caravan to Texas in March. In reality, the saloon business was a profit-sharing venture of Hanrahan and Charles Rath. As he had with James Langton, Rath drew into his commercial efforts another person to contribute capital. When the two men made their agreement to collaborate is not known, but when Charles Rath returned to Dodge City in late May, 1874, he began to assemble building materials and liquor stock for a saloon. Jim Hanrahan may very well have accompanied Rath, for he was back in Dodge City in early June. On June 5 he departed again for the Panhandle, arriving there a few days later.[71]

The new saloon was built by Andy Johnson and others about half-way between the two general merchandise stores; it resembled that of Rath and Company in its sod construction. With walls three feet thick at the base and tapering toward the top and with dimensions of twenty-three feet by thirty-nine feet, the structure had a three-foot-wide doorway at each end and at least one glazed window on the south wall. In 1922 Johnson and "Brick" Bond, who frequented the trading post, remembered its having two windows on each long side. Most descriptions of the saloon state that the walls were provided at intervals with openings through which firearms might be fired in the event of an Indian attack. The roof of the saloon was supported on a large cottonwood ridgepole running the length of the building, with perhaps one vertical support toward its center. On either side of the doorways at each end stood timber posts that undoubtedly helped support the ridgepole so that all of its weight would not rest on the sod walls. Whether the earthen covering on the saloon roof lay on sawed lumber planks or on poles and brush has not been determined for certain.[72]

A final structure completing the Adobe Walls trading post was its blacksmith shop. Freight wagons were essential to the establishment and operation of the post. These vehicles, sometimes pulled two and three in tandem by long teams of draft animals, not only carried the merchandise and supplies to the trading post but also hauled the hides back to Dodge City, where they were loaded on railway cars for shipment to the East. Although durable and heavily built, the wagons required periodic maintenance and repairs, as the trail to and from Kansas was indeed rough. This is not to mention the obvious requirement for properly shod horses, mules, and oxen. Broken-down wagons or lame animals represented more than mere delay and annoyance—they could cause a fatal accident for both teamsters and passengers if Indians were about. To keep the wagons rolling, Thomas O'Keefe opened his blacksmith shop.

Measuring twenty-four feet by twenty-one feet, O'Keefe's simple building stood thirty-five feet, or about a third of the way, north of the saloon toward Myers and Leonard's store. O'Keefe built his shop from timber pickets but differently than had the workmen who erected Myers and Leonard's structures. Instead of using trenches to hold his vertical pickets, the enterprising blacksmith dug four deep postholes at the corners of the structure and placed stout posts in them. Then he ran split log members connecting the tops and bottoms of his posts to form a sort of channel into which he placed numerous vertical pickets. After this work was done, sand was placed both inside the floor area and around the outside edge of the walls to help support both sides of the lower crossmembers as well as the lower ends of the pickets.

O'Keefe left the gaps between the pickets open, perhaps to keep the shop cooler while he was working at the forge. It may have been for the same reason that he oriented his building so that its front faced more northeasterly than the other structures at the trading post. When the front and side doors were open, the prevailing southwesterly winds ventilated the shop. Evidence suggests that instead of using a sod-covered roof, he chose instead some form of brush or thatch, a questionable decision for a building where fire would be used almost daily. O'Keefe placed his forge in the southeast corner of the completed shop, as shown by substantial accumulations of coal and iron slag. In the northwest corner he excavated a circular pit. When it was filled with water he could use this depression to set iron wagon tires on wooden wheels and to quench hot metal from the forge.[73]

Daily life at Adobe Walls proved to be agreeable, pleasant, and profitable for both the traders and the hunters. The merchants and their employees began a brisk trade with the hide men almost immediately, despite the fact that the great southern herd of bison had not yet reached the Canadian River on its annual migration northward. A late spring in 1874 probably had retarded its movement. Hunters encountered and dispatched only scattered groups of buffalo bulls and cows. These early kills nevertheless enabled the merchants to begin building what soon would grow into huge ricks of dried "flint" hides behind their stores.[74]

By the middle of June, 1874, when Fred Leonard returned from a trip to Dodge City, he found Adobe Walls a very busy place. He recollected, "We were receiving a thousand buffalo hides a day and selling lots of goods." His estimate of business was confirmed by the Dodge City press, which reported wagons filled with hides rolling into town from the Canadian.[75]

William Barclay "Bat" Masterson, later to become a famous lawman, was on the scene at the time. According to Johnson, he worked as a skinner for Dixon, and according to Leonard, was one of his employees.[76] About twenty years later Masterson recalled that around the Rath and Company store the hides were "dried and piled in piles of 40 and fifty, already [*sic*] for shipment, piled up all around the store, from 30 to 100 feet."[77] Andy Johnson, who worked in the Rath hide yard, estimated that by late June his firm alone had bought between thirty-five thousand and forty-five thousand hides. J. E. McAllister, who visited the post in the same month, remembered seeing a rick of hides nearly a hundred yards long and ten feet high.[78] When Seth Hathaway first came to the trading post about the same time and viewed it from some distance, "The first idea I had was that there was a small settlement out there in the wilderness, one hundred and fifty miles from any town." He continued, "On getting closer, what I first took for houses turned out to be piles of buffalo hides stacked up and ready to be hauled to the railroad."[79] Adobe Walls had indeed become the buffalo hide entrepôt.

Hides were the principal medium of exchange at the trading post, the merchants keeping records on how many the hunters brought in and the value of supplies they purchased. James H. Cator probably best expressed the terms by which the hunters in the Panhandle understood the value of their bison skins: "The hides were just the same as dollars. You had to keep account of them just the same as money. You traded them for provision[s] just the same as money, bought things with them just like money."[80] The only known receipt covering the sale of hides at Adobe Walls indicates that on June 20, 1874, Rath and Company was paying $2.00 for bull hides and $1.10 for buffalo cow hides.[81] Later, however, repeated testimony from hunters and traders who bought and sold at the post reports that the going price in the summer of 1874 was $2.15 for bull hides and $1.15 for cow hides.[82]

Much light can be shed on the lives of the hide men by examining records of what they purchased with their hides at Adobe Walls. Fortunately, the two Cator brothers saved the receipts from their days as hunters, and a handful of these represent their dealings at the trading post in the Panhandle. The heaviest purchases were for ammunition and foodstuffs. Hunting supplies bought in substantial volume included gunpowder, lead, cartridges, and primers, as well as small quantities of such goods as patch paper and gun oil. Bulk food purchases generally consisted of flour, baking powder, bacon, sugar, and coffee, with the occasional addition of food items like canned tomatoes, soup, and fruit; fresh peaches; crackers; tea; salt; pepper; pickles; dried apples; and syrup. Among the articles of clothing that appear in the receipts from Adobe Walls are trousers, shirts, shoes, and socks. The hunters purchased a great variety of miscellaneous supplies, including chewing tobacco, bottles of bitters and gin, matches, rope, knives, inexpensive eating utensils, wolf poison, axle grease, and bars of castile soap. For their teams the hunters bought large amounts of corn as feed, as the dry spring and summer of 1874 had left only poor grazing.[83]

From the Cators' receipts it is possible to determine the differences in prices between goods purchased at Adobe Walls and back in Dodge City. Although Myers and Leonard reportedly told the hunters that they would charge them Dodge City prices for their merchandise, in reality the cost of freight to Texas was added to most items. Interestingly, Rath and Company seems to have attempted to undercut Myers and Leonard in pricing many articles of merchandise. The mark-up in prices was most evident on foodstuffs, which were both heavy and bulky to transport. Bacon that sold for fifteen to eighteen cents a pound at Dodge cost sixteen to twenty cents at Adobe Walls; flour that cost a nickel a pound in Dodge cost between six and a half cents and seven cents at the trading post. Sugar sold for fourteen to twenty-five cents a pound in Kansas, and interestingly it was competitively priced at Adobe Walls, the cost varying from just over fourteen cents a pound to twenty cents a pound. Tea also was marked competitively at $1.00 to $2.00 a pound in Texas, whereas it sold for $1.50 to $1.75 at Dodge. Coffee, on the other hand, always was higher in Texas. At the Dodge City stores it went for twenty-eight to thirty-six cents a pound, but at Adobe Walls it always was more expensive at forty to forty-five cents. One of the hunters' luxuries, chewing tobacco, also cost more in Texas. A one-pound plug in Kansas cost sixty cents to $1.00, but in the Panhandle trading posts the hunters paid $1.25 for the same plug.

Hunting supplies likewise were more expensive at Adobe Walls. Gunpowder that sold in Dodge City for forty-four cents a pound cost the hunters fifty-two to sixty cents a pound, but without it they could not hunt the buffalo. Lead also was higher, costing only twelve to thirteen cents a pound in Kansas but from fourteen to fifteen cents a pound in Texas. For their animals during the dry summer of 1874, the hide men had to buy corn, another heavy and bulky item that came to the trading post by wagon. In Dodge City it cost twenty-two to twenty-five cents a hundredweight, but because of the transportation costs it took twenty-eight to thirty-five cents to buy the same hundredweight of grain in Texas.

Although food and shooting supplies at Adobe Walls cost more after a 150-mile trip from Kansas, clothing prices were about the same in both places. Because these lighter and less bulky goods were not so expensive to ship, the merchants did not mark them up so much. Work trousers costing $1.40 in Dodge cost the hunters $2.00 in Texas, but socks were about the same, costing fifty cents at Adobe Walls and fifty to sixty-six cents a pair at Dodge City, probably depending on the material and quality.[84]

The records of purchases by the buffalo hunters suggest what their diet must have been like, but these documents do not tell the whole story. Coupled with the men's reminiscences, however, they help reconstruct at least partially how the hunters, skinners, and teamsters in the Panhandle ate. Clearly, wild game was an important part of their meals,[85] but it was supplemented by bacon, which not only gave them a different flavor but also provided grease for preparing other foods.[86] The large volumes of flour[87] and baking powder[88] the hide men purchased undoubtedly were used to prepare biscuits or yeast powder bread,[89] to which some of them added syrup.[90] Surprisingly, the hunters bought canned fruits, vegetables, and soup, which cost them between fifty cents and a dollar a can,[91] but they must have enjoyed the taste well enough to pay such prices. Fresh peaches and plums and dried fruit also were popular. Humorous stories are told of Panhandle hunters who did not know how to prepare dried apples and who used too many of them, ending up with whole cauldrons filled with the stewed fruit.[92] Occasionally a hunter would cook up a pot of beans[93] or pick a mess of wild greens,[94] and some of the tins of canned tomatoes probably were used in stew.[95] Popular condiments included crackers[96] and pickles.[97]

Hot meals were available to anyone at the trading post who could afford the average price of about a dollar a day.[98] The most popular hot drinks were coffee[99] and tea,[100] substantial amounts of which the merchants sold at Adobe Walls, together with rather large amounts of sugar.[101] Hunters also regularly consumed liquor, especially whiskey. Billy Dixon remembered that among the hide men "whisky-drinking was a pastime or diversion in which few men did not indulge." In fact, the man who did not drink alcohol might even be considered deviant by the others. Frank J. Brown was one of the minority who did not drink, "so consequently," he recalled years later, "I was not counted a good fellow by the crowd who hung around Hanrahan's Saloon." Often whiskey is mentioned in accounts of evenings in the saloon at the trading post,[102] but it was by no means the only alcohol available. Other drinks included beer from the Brandon and Kirmeyer brewery in Leavenworth, shipped by rail to Dodge City and then by wagon to the Panhandle,[103] and a variety of bitters. The latter were beverages, usually alcoholic, containing medicinal herbs giving them a bitter taste. Most often they were consumed by individuals with stomach or digestive problems; many of the varieties were laxative. Both archeological evidence and store receipts document bitters use at the trading post.[104] In addition to buying alcohol in the saloon, customers could also buy it over the counter in at least one of the stores, for Myers and Leonard did a good business in gin.[105]

Smokers and chewers abounded among the hide men in the Panhandle. Written references document hunters smoking cigars at the trading post, and archeological evidence shows that many of the hide men bought smoking tobacco and crumbled it into inexpensive but decorative clay pipes with bowls shaped like birds' claws or men's heads.[106]

Health problems genuinely concerned some of the hunters and skinners, miles and days away from the nearest medical treatment. Most of the men had some knowledge of first aid, but illness and injuries plagued many of them. H. H. Raymond, a Dodge City hunter who was an intimate friend of such hide men as Emanuel Dubbs, Bat Masterson, and Andy Johnson, kept a record of his bout with an infected knee. "[I] stuck [a] nail in my knee last night. pained me so did not sleep at all." Four days later he noted in his diary that his leg hurt so severely that he had to come into camp. The next day he wrote, "Leg pained me so very bad [I] had to stay in camp. I slept none last night. . . . Jim got some drug to put on my leg." Two days later he reported that his leg was somewhat better and that he had made himself a bunk of "hollow cottonwood snags." Raymond needed further medication, and the next day he noted: "I staid in camp. my leg pained me all night and all day. . . . Jim went down to Obrians to get some lineament for me at eve." In a few days the injury had begun healing enough that the hide man could finally jot down in his little pocket notebook: "I went out and helped skin buffalo today. . . . leg great deal better . . . helped Jim peg and pile hides." [107] So far from relief, a simple toothache could represent pure misery. James H. Cator suffered from one in 1874, and his father, on hearing from brother Robert about the malady, wrote, "We were sorry to hear poor 'Jim' had tooth ache. . . . It is a nasty thing and quite upsets a man & makes him feel not worth a straw." [108]

The number of medicine bottles, not to mention bitters containers, found at the site of the Adobe Walls trading post reinforces the documentary evidence concerning health problems on the buffalo range. Among the medicinal products the hide men are known to have used at the post were Frederick Brown's Essence of Jamaica Ginger, a remedy for diarrhea, "incipient cholera," and like ailments; H. T. Helmbold's Fluid Extracts; Hamlin's Wizard Oil; and Merchant's Gargling Oil, which came from Lockport, New York. [109]

Injuries like the one suffered by H. H. Raymond sometimes were of mysterious origin, and some hunters preferred not to discuss how they were hurt. In 1927 J. Wright Mooar recollected an occasion in autumn, 1874, when Billy Dixon found his way into his camp with an injury.

> We were camped at a big tree off from Adobe Walls in 1874 and I was there by myself. I looked up and saw a man coming into camp and recognized him as Dixon. I walked over to the wagon, picked up my gun, and slipped a cartridge into it. He walked into camp and I asked him what he wanted. He unloaded his, walked over and set it against the wagon, and came back. He wanted to know if I was the only one there, and said that he wanted me to do a favor for him. He pulled up his trousers and showed me a bullet hole through his calf. We always kept a little first-aid

outfit; so I washed the wound with some Castile soap, put some salve in which there was some Carbolic on it, bandaged it up with linen, and sewed the bandage on. He got up, shouldered his gun, and said:

"I don't care for anybody to know how I got that."

He walked off without limping or flinching. I never knew how he was shot and I never told this until he was dead.[110]

What did the hide men look like as they worked on the buffalo range? Certainly most of them were dirty, for swimming offered the only opportunity for bathing. None of the hunters, however, mention swimming as a frequent activity. Nevertheless, they did buy soap. Castile soap, made from olive oil and sodium hydroxide, appears in their store receipts and reminiscences. Skinners were especially dirty. The hunters had the "clean" job of shooting the animals, but the skinners worked almost daily with bison carcasses, some putrified. Covered with blood, fat, and the animals' parasites, the men must have had body odors that defy imagination. It was truly a filthy lifestyle.[111]

Although the hunters bought a variety of garments, the most popular were bibless denim "overalls," the nineteenth-century term for work trousers. J. Wright Mooar later recalled that the buffalo hunters dressed in the manner of all working men of that period and region.[112] Wide-brimmed hats protected the men's faces and necks from the weather and could be used to signal distant hunters. Reflecting on the hide men's headgear, Mooar related that he used a large cowboy style himself because it helped camouflage him as he approached bison for the kill: "Well, I got down on my hands and knees and crawled and had a big white hat that was the same color as the ground and I could get closer to them."[113] The men who frequented Adobe Walls most often wore shirts and trousers, sometimes with suspenders. Some of the men wore drawers and undershirts. As for footwear, some preferred boots and others, shoes.[114]

Buffalo hunters in the Panhandle wore their hair uncut as a mark of their profession. One man related that when he first entered the Hanrahan saloon, he saw a number of noted hide men at the bar, all of whom "wore their hair long, combed down with the ends falling like shawls over their shoulders." His description fits perfectly a photograph of Billy Dixon made in 1876 (fig. 5), when he was a civilian scout for the army. The editor of the *Dodge City Times*, who saw Dixon passing through the town in September, 1877, reported with a touch of humor that "his hair is something less than nine feet long, and his general appearance indicates his calling."[115]

The hide men of Adobe Walls engaged in many recreational activities besides drinking; one of the most popular was horse racing. Before the great southern herd of bison reached the Walls in spring, 1874, the hunters had time on their hands and often raced their horses. Dixon noted that many of the men prided themselves on the fleetness of their mounts. Joe Plummer, who helped mark the trail from the trading post back to Dodge City, owned one of the fastest animals, a gray mare he raced for both pleasure and profit.[116]

Target shooting was also a popular sport among the professional hunters, who were proud of their marksmanship. The first time Seth Hathaway approached Adobe Walls, "nothing of special interest occurred on the trip until I got within a few miles of the place when I heard sounds as though a fight was going on." Coming closer, he discovered that the warlike sounds he had heard were men "trying their new Sharpe's [*sic*] 50 calibre . . . rifles by shooting at different objects at a hundred to a thousand yards distance." After he had looked around the post and had found nothing more exciting to do, he too went outside and took part in the shooting.[117] According to Dubbs, "There was a hill or small mountain at a distance of 800 yards from . . . the store building, and about half way up its steep acclivity was a table rock and just above it against the side of the cliff a white chalky substance . . . the hunters for amusement used to shoot at it for a mark, some one having stepped the distance which . . . was just 800 yards."[118]

The hide men found storytelling to be another enjoyable diversion, especially around the campfire or in the cool shade on a hot afternoon. Hathaway remembered the men's sitting around whiling away their time by boasting how many bison they had killed, "swapping lies with one another." The stories told by men in the Myers and Leonard caravan to Texas in March, 1874, must have been especially vivid, for Billy Dixon remembered them more than thirty-five years later. He recalled in particular the tales from a number of Civil War veterans in the party who told "endless stories of desperate battles that were greatly to our liking."[119]

Most of the hide men loved playing cards and gambling despite the prospect of quickly losing the proceeds of months of work. Teamster Charles E. Jones reputedly lost everything he owned one evening in Dodge. Dixon described him as "very close and stingy" and as never having been known to gamble. He had saved up about two thousand dollars in cash plus "a lot of buffalo hides on hand ready to sell" when a girl in a gambling hall persuaded him to try his luck at the roulette wheel. Jones won at first, but in the end he lost all his money in a single night.[120]

Music played a surprisingly prominent role in the lives of the hide men. Dixon recalled that "there were always fiddlers in a crowd like ours, perhaps an accordeon [*sic*], and a dozen fellows who could play the French harp." The musicians would play on their own or to accompany singers. When there were no musical instruments, the hide men would sing without them. The musicians also played so that the hunters might dance. To make the dancing easier, the men would peg out an especially large, dry buffalo bull hide, which, according to one hunter, gave "a much better footing for dancing than might be supposed," as they were "stiff enough and hard enough to respond in the liveliest way to jigging." On one occasion Billy Dixon and his crew came into their camp on the buffalo range to find one of the skinners, Mike McCabe, dancing by himself on a dry hide. "He was giving all the fancy steps and dancing as if a full orchestra were playing." As soon as McCabe saw that he was being watched from a distance by the rest of the outfit, "he stopped dancing, and seemed chagrined," but no one seemed to mind. They all knew that he had just been entertaining himself to break the monotony.[121]

The hide men seem to have been especially sensitive to Hannah Olds's presence at the trading post. Almost without exception they respectfully referred to her as "Mrs. Olds."[122] For her pleasure some of the men captured a mustang colt that had become separated from its mother and had mingled with the stock belonging to the hunters and traders. Being too young to feed on grass, the colt, named Inez, was nurtured by Hannah Olds on bread and sugar and became the pet of the settlement. It even wore a "blanket" she sewed together from old flour sacks.[123]

Domestic animals at the post other than draft animals included a coyote, a partly domesticated crow, and an assortment of dogs. Some of the canines, like Billy Dixon's setter, Fannie, belonged to individuals. Others apparently had the run of the post, begging food wherever they might find it. The crow had been captured by one of the hunters and brought to Adobe Walls, where, finding an inexhaustible supply of grain in the stores, it lingered to fly from building to building, chattering away.[124]

Darkness brought quiet to the trading post. Most of the people who stayed up did so in the dim light of Hanrahan's saloon, where drinking and carousing usually continued until late. Most of the hunters, skinners, and teamsters slept in the open, either in bedrolls or on hides on the ground or in wagons, but the merchants and a few of the transients slept inside the buildings. As the summer temperatures rose, more of the men slept outdoors for comfort. Dixon recollected that it was the custom in the buffalo country for the men to sleep outdoors. Another hide man recalled that "a buffalo hunter never slept inside when on a hunt," such a thing being considered "foolish and not according to tradition," but a few did prefer the luxury of roofs over their heads.

When the trading post was first established, the merchants posted guards at night for protection against Indians, but after the buildings were erected this practice was abandoned. No one expected Indians to disturb the tranquillity of the post unless it was to steal stock. By early June, however, some of the men at Adobe Walls had begun to change their minds about the lax security.[125]

On June 11 word reached Adobe Walls that two hunters, Dave Dudley[126] and Tommy Wallace,[127] had been attacked four days earlier in their camp about fifteen miles southeast of the trading post. The incident occurred while the men's partner, Joe Plummer, was hauling a load of hides to Adobe Walls. As was later learned, a war party of Kiowas led by Lone Wolf and including High Forehead, Boy, White Goose, Teeth, Good Talk, Wise, Kicking, Buffalo with Holes in His Ears, Man Who Walks above the Ground, and Bear Mountain had surprised the two men in camp and killed them on the spot. On finding his partners' bodies disfigured and the camp destroyed, Plummer galloped toward Adobe Walls to spread the alarm and to solicit help in burying his men.[128]

Before Plummer reached the trading post, however, he came upon Frank Maddox's surveying party engaged in locating land along the Canadian River for the Houston and Texas Central Railway Company.[129] William Benjamin Munson,[130] one of the surveyors, remembered the incident: "We . . . had about finished [the survey] when we were met one evening by a man who approached us on horseback at great speed. We hailed him and he advised us that his comrades . . . had been murdered while he was away with a load of hides at Adobe Walls. . . . He asked us to go with him to bury his comrades[,] which we did. We found them terribly mutilated, their skulls broken open and the brains removed and the cavity filled with grass, their hearts cut out, and stakes driven through their bodies pinning them to the earth, and the bodies otherwise horribly mutilated."[131] J. E. McAllister, who also was in the country at this time, saw the two corpses, noting that the warriors had pulled Wallace's clothes off, "cut his insides out, and his ears, nose, fingers, and toes off"—truly a gruesome sight even for hardened frontiersmen.[132]

The surveyors helped Plummer bury the men and then, as Munson recalled, "We at once closed up our survey work and that night made a forced march until long after dark so that our camp would not be known to the Indians," who had watched the burial from a distance. Heading back toward Camp Supply in present-day northwestern Oklahoma, where they had started, they met E. C. Lefebre and John H. Talley, federal deputy marshals of the state of Kansas who had been authorized to operate in the Cheyenne and Arapahoe Reservation and surrounding country. Indian agent John D. Miles had asked them to scout toward the west to investigate reports of war parties in the area. The surveyors told Lefebre and Talley about what they had seen, and "at the advice of the party we returned with them." The addition of two armed marshals did not solve the problems of the surveyors, for the war party continued to trail them as they retreated eastward, attacking their camp on the evening of June 11. Munson recalled the events: "The next day after a long march and drive we made camp at the head of the north fork of the Canadian River on the branch known as Wolf Creek. When supper was almost ready, many of the men having fallen asleep, being worn out with the hard day[']s march, we were suddenly awakened by the whiz of bullets and the discharge of guns." They were attacked by an unknown number of Indians, some of whom circled "among our stock trying to make them break loose so they could steal them." Hesitant to fire toward their own horses, they did succeed in shooting one warrior's mount, apparently demonstrating to the Indians that "it was too hot for them." They disappeared into the approaching darkness with two of the white men's horses. Munson recalled, "The next day we landed at Camp Supply, being thankful that we had gotten in before a large body of Indians had made their appearance in the country."[133] This was only a taste of things to come.

The same day Dudley and Wallace were killed, other Indians attacked James N. Hanrahan and his teamsters, who were trekking down the trail from Dodge City to Adobe Walls with a load of alcohol to sell in the saloon. They had left two days before and encountered the warriors at Sharp's Creek, about seventy-five miles below Dodge. The irate teamsters reported that the red warriors had come upon them as they rested their horses and had stampeded the stock by discharging their weapons. It was probably the party's salvation that the Indians did not know the contents of their wagons, for they satisfied themselves with stealing all but one of the men's horses. The stranded party remained on the stream overnight and until the middle of the afternoon of the next day when another outfit including A. C. Myers and S. S. Van Sickel came along and helped move their goods on down to the trading post.[134]

By the time that the Hanrahan and Myers outfits reached the trading post, further disturbing reports had come in. John Thomson Jones, an Englishman known variously as "Antelope Jack" and "Cheyenne Jack,"[135] and W. Muhler, a German known to most of the hide men as "Blue Billy,"[136] were killed in their camp not far from the Canadian. Anderson Moore, their partner, came into the trading post with the news, telling everyone that the two men had been surprised by unidentified Indians, murdered, and terribly mutilated. The press in Dodge City reported that John Jones "was found with his legs and arms stretched to their utmost, and pinned to the ground . . . [by] a stake through his body" and noted that "decency forbids us stating the particulars" of Muhler's disfigurement. It was more than a week before a group of hide men from the trading post went out to bury the two unfortunate hunters, and during the interval rain had washed their bodies down the creek by which they had been camping. Their remains were never found.[137]

J. Wright Mooar and his hunting outfit had a number of encounters with Indians in May and June, 1874, enough to convince them to leave the Panhandle until things simmered down. Mooar's crew at this time consisted of himself, Mart Galloway,[138] Phillip Sisk,[139] Lem Wilson,[140] Dave Campbell,[141] and John Hughes.[142] The outfit headed out from the trading post in early May, going first down the Canadian to the mouth of Red Deer Creek and then up that stream southward to the head of the Washita, moving on the middle Washita to Gageby Creek. There they saw their first party of red men, but they "would not accept an invitation to come in" and soon disappeared. The next morning a party of warriors, perhaps the same ones seen the day before, charged into the hunters' camp from the south, clinging to the sides of their galloping horses. Awakened by the clatter and yells, John Hughes sat up in his bedroll, grabbed his buffalo gun, and fired a bullet through one of the Indian horses into its rider. The remainder of the war party took cover in a thicket and fired on the camp from there. Although it was still dark, the hide men could see the flashes of the Indian guns, and they used their big Sharps rifles to best effect. The heavy fire drove the warriors from cover, but two of them rode back by the camp swinging low from their ponies to retrieve a fallen comrade.

Undaunted, the Mooar outfit crossed the North Fork of the Red River the following day and camped on its Salt Fork. There they found the bison migrating northward in great numbers, and in a matter of ten days they took 666 hides. Wright Mooar sent Phillip Sisk back to Adobe Walls to pick up brother John Wesley Mooar and others to haul the hides into the trading post. John Wesley Mooar, Charles E. Jones, and a man remembered as Warren were at this time freighting between Dodge City and Adobe Walls, fully aware of the unrest among the Indians. Back at Dodge, Jones had asked Warren if he intended to return to the Panhandle for more hides, whereupon Warren said, "No, if you and Mooar are fools enough to go down among the Indians, you can go, but I am going to stay at home." Jones replied, "If you are born to be killed by Indians, you would be killed by Indians if you went to New York. That wouldn't make any difference."

Mooar and Jones then loaded their wagons with merchandise for the traders and headed back down the trail to Texas. After hearing the stories of war parties related by the traders and hide men at Adobe Walls, Jones returned to Dodge, leaving John Wesley Mooar, who expected to hear some word from his brother. The next day Sisk came in from the buffalo range to request help in hauling hides from the Mooar camp on the Salt Fork of the Red River back to the trading post.

John Wesley Mooar returned with Sisk to the camp, where another encounter occurred. The two brothers were eating lunch on top of a wagonload of hides when J. Wright spotted a large party of war-riors about a mile away examining the hunters' tracks, the red men as yet not having seen the wagons in the distance. Since the hide men's teams were grazing and drinking at a water hole quite some distance away, Lem Wilson and Phillip Sisk, whose guns were fouled from heavy shooting, started on foot for the animals. In time the Indians saw the wagons and began charging toward them. With the warriors and blow-ing a bugle was a black man, whom the hide men presumed to be a de-serter from the U.S. Cavalry. A superbly skilled marksman, Wright Mooar placed a curtain of fire in front of the approaching warriors. "Those Indians came right to the barrage I laid there and stopped. They saw that was a threat; not to cross the line." Meanwhile, Sisk and Wilson had rounded up the teams and hitched them to the wagons, and the hide men set off toward Red Deer Creek as fast as they could go. Just after the fleeing hunters crossed that stream a thunderstorm intervened, filling the channel to overflowing and delaying the pursu-ing Indians.

Delayed again three days later by the flooded Canadian near Adobe Walls, the hide men were again set upon by the Indians, who boldly rode through their camp galloping past the cook fire, knocking over the pans and coffeepot, prompting Wright Mooar later to recol-lect with humor that a "lively time was had by all." The next morning John Webb arrived from the Myers and Leonard store with forty-eight yoke of oxen and two big Murphy wagons with seven-foot wheels to help the Mooars haul their cache into the post. The teamsters and hunters reached the north bank after some difficulty and made camp for the night.

Bouts with the Indians still were not over. As Wright Mooar re-called, "supper was in preparation, when a whooping band of redskins dashed through camp, shooting right and left. They got a warm recep-tion." No hunters were hurt, and the warriors recovered their casu-alties from the field. The next morning, June 11, the Mooar outfit fi-nally reached Adobe Walls, where they learned of the fate of Dudley and Wallace and of John Jones and Muhler. Things had finally grown too hot for the Mooar brothers, so they and their outfit set out for Dodge City. Eight miles away from the trading post they met a haggard Charles E. Jones on his way south with a load of ammunition and fire-arms belonging to the merchants. He had driven ninety miles without sleeping or unharnessing his mules. Stopping only long enough to un-load his cargo, Jones turned around and with only a five-hour rest started back for Dodge, catching up with the Mooar party the next day.

At Palo Duro Creek the Mooar outfit met Isaac Scheidler,[143] whom the hunters knew as Ike, a teamster who was headed toward the Walls with a load of supplies and merchandise. John Webb called out pro-phetically, "Ike, you hurry back, or the Indians will get your scalp." As they proceeded northward, the Mooars next met a hunting party headed by a man named Burr, who reported that they had clashed with a war party the day before on the Cimarron River. Wright Mooar remembered that one of the members of the group was a young man named Billy Tyler to whom Burr remarked, foreshadowing later events, "You are going to fall early in this war." Finally, on June 29 the Mooar party reached Dodge City safely and there learned that Mr. Warren, true to Charles E. Jones's fatalistic remark a few days before about being "born to be killed by Indians," had been slain and scalped just outside Dodge.[144]

The raids on hide men in the Panhandle were by no means all that occurred during June, 1874. On the twenty-fourth of the month the mail carried by troops from Camp Supply to Fort Dodge was attacked by a party of about forty Indians, mostly Comanches and Kiowas, who were bested in the encounter, losing four of their number.[145] The day before, the two Cator brothers only a few miles from the trading post saw Indians in the vicinity of their camp but did not suspect that they were on the warpath. The next morning they found their mules miss-ing, their ropes having been cut during the night.[146] Also about this time Frank J. Brown's outfit had an uneventful encounter with the red men. Had Brown not surreptitiously moved his camp, it might have been attacked and become the scene of another gory massacre.[147] The Emanuel Dubbs outfit was not so lucky. While Dubbs was away from camp at the mouth of Barton Creek on Sadler Creek looking for lost stock, his three men were surprised, killed, and brutally mutilated. Thirty years later the old hunter recollected that on his return, "A sight met my eyes that even now after all these years makes me shudder. At first, I thought the camp was deserted, . . . [but] on a closer look I dis-covered under the last rays of the setting sun, that the tongue of the lead ox wagon was propped up with an ox yoke and across the tongue in a spread-eagle fashion was the naked body of one of my men. Even from where I lay, I could see that he had been tortured to death." Dubbs lingered no longer in the area, sensing that he was being watched, and he fled toward Adobe Walls.[148]

Even with reports like these coming into the trading post almost daily, most of the hide men were not very concerned. James W. McKinley later remembered that even though "these facts seemed a little suggestive[,] the older plainsmen did not think it forboded a general outbreak. . . . we might be called upon occasionally to give up a few scalps, [but] this was no evidence that the Indian was on the war path. . . . The hunters were not being disturbed."[149] After all, they thought, no Indians would ever attack a place with so many white men and big guns as Adobe Walls.[150]

CHAPTER 2

Seeds of Unrest Flower into Violence

We saw somebody coming on the prairie crying one day and we said, "There he is, Quanah!"
—Iseeo.

T HE winter months of 1873 and 1874 were bad times for the southern Plains tribes, times of great unrest that in the following spring and summer would break into open warfare between them and the increasingly dominant white men.[1] The nomadic tribesmen had agreed to reside on reservations set aside for them in the Indian Territory, and from that vantage point they saw the continuing destruction of the buffalo herds from which they had drawn sustenance as far back as they could remember. Tribesmen who stayed on the reservations, trying to follow the "white man's road," received only inferior and infrequent rations—poor encouragement—while among them came numerous whiskey peddlers, whose goods caused a deterioration of the moral fiber of their entire populations. At the same time bands of well-organized professional white thieves mercilessly preyed on the Indian horse herds, taking the stolen animals to Kansas where they were sold in almost complete safety. Times were bad, and as events would unfold they became worse.

The most important factor contributing to the unrest was the hunting of the professional hide men, who systematically destroyed the commissary of the nomadic plainsmen. The extent of the destruction was well described by Gen. Nelson A. Miles in March, 1875: "The bison, which has from time immemorial furnished the Plains Indians

their food, shelter and raiment, is fast disappearing and will soon become extinct. . . . Some idea of their destruction may be gathered
from the fact that a half-million hides have been shipped from a single
station this season, and a thousand men [are] employed in the business. During the past three years the vast herd has diminished one-
fourth."[2] Federal authorities could do little to curtail the decimation of
the herds, for they had control or at least partial control of events only
in the Indian Territory, an area too small to supply sufficient buffalo for
the Indian needs. The Indians believed that the Great Spirit had created the bison especially for their use, for their tepees, clothing, cra-
dles, and shields, not to mention their diet. They even used the hooves
as material from which to fashion spoons, dishes, and powderhorns,
the long shaggy hair for lariats, the sinew for "thread" and bowstrings,
and the bone for tools. The red men realized that the annihilation of
the herds meant the destruction of their lifestyle, but even while the
hunt was proceeding at its incredible pace, most of the bands remained at least nominally at peace.[3]

Many white men, perhaps the majority of them on the frontier,
felt that the cause of the Indian unrest lay in the nature of the red men
themselves. Gen. Nelson A. Miles reported to a superior that violence
was the natural product of a people "accustomed from childhood to
the wild excitement of the chase or conflict with some other hostile
tribe, [who were] taught that murder is noble and labor demeaning."
He stated that the reservation existence gave the former nomads "an
indolent, listless life, the very foundations for vice and crime."[4] The
hide men, more biased in their view, believed that the warriors raided
and made war for their own material benefit. John Wesley Mooar wrote
to his sister in July, 1874, after the unrest of the Plains tribesmen had
broken into general raiding, that such violence was an effort to secure
more liberal annuities from the federal government. He declared,
"One old Cheyenne Chief says he has got to have 30 bbls. of sugar to
make him peaceable." Mooar continued, expressing popular senti-
ment, that "I think it is about time the government quit paying black-
mail and give them a dressing."[5] The hunters who had fallen victim to
the warriors were even more vehement. Their attitude is evident in
the remarks by Emanuel Dubbs, three members of whose crew were
killed by Indians in the Texas Panhandle in 1874: "They are a lazy,
dirty, lousey, deceitful race. True manhood is unknown, and they hold

their women in abject slavery. . . . They are the only race of people under the sun that cannot be reclaimed by Christianity, and civilizing influences. The old adage 'The only good Indian is the dead Indian' is not very poetical, but it is true." The hide men hated the Indians and hoped to see them exterminated.[6]

The professional horse thieves agreed with the hide hunters. Making their headquarters either in Dodge City or on the Great Bend of the Arkansas, they raided principally in the Indian Territory between the Cheyenne and Arapahoe Agency and the Kansas border, Kansas being considered "safe" country in which to market their stolen stock. Although Comanche, Kiowa, Arapahoe, and Cheyenne herds were raided, the Cheyennes seem to have suffered the most. There were federal deputy marshals operating in the Indian Territory to control the lawlessness, but their efforts were hampered by a lack of manpower and juries reluctant to indict, convict, or pass heavy sentences on whites charged with crimes against the Indians.

The most prominent horse thief operating in the Indian Territory was William A. "Hurricane Bill" Martin, although other white badmen raiding the Indian herds in the area included Jack Gallagher and Robert Hollis. In early March, 1874, Martin's band swept down on the herd of Little Robe, the most prominent of the Cheyenne chiefs, taking forty-three horses. The chief and members of his band set out in pursuit, but being poorly mounted the Indians were unable to catch up with Martin, who had stolen their best horses. Not far from his camp Little Robe was joined by his son, Sitting Medicine, and several other young men. Giving up the chase, Little Robe returned to camp, but his son and others over his protests continued the hunt.

Unable to locate their own stolen animals, Sitting Medicine and the other young men decided to revenge their loss by stealing horses in Kansas. On the return trip, however, they met a group of troops under Capt. Tullis Tupper, who gave pursuit, recovered the stock, and injured two of the warriors, including Sitting Medicine. The raiding party returned without further trouble to the reservation on April 16, and within a month Sitting Medicine had recovered from his wound, but the damage was done. The incident split the Cheyennes into two groups. One of them, led by Whirlwind, White Shield, and Stone Calf, remained at the agency, still hoping to preserve peace, but the other, under Grey Beard, moved out onto the plains, isolating the more compromising members of the tribe. In March, 1874, Little Robe's horses were reported to have been "exposed for sale on the streets of Dodge City" at the same time that Myers and Leonard's first caravan of wagons was preparing to leave for Adobe Walls. It is possible that several of the men in the party rode some of the Indians' horses into Texas.[7]

Whiskey peddlers also operated illegally in the Indian Territory, carrying diluted rotgut liquor directly into the camps of the red men. The whiskey drove the Indians crazy. The warriors traded whatever they could find—robes, horses, anything—for the whiskey that numbed them so that they could hardly hunt. Some of their families nearly starved as a result. One white man working among the Cheyennes as a legitimate trader reported that "whisky is more plentiful than good water and all hands in the vicinity are nearly continually drunk." Yamparika Comanche chief Quirt Quip confirmed the reports, declaring that many of his warriors were intoxicated much of the time and that "they have a great many hearts, would make up their minds at night for one thing and get up in the morning entirely changed."[8]

Insufficient government rations intensified hunger on the reservations. Those red men who stayed at the agencies were poorly rewarded, for winter and early spring, 1874, were especially wet, making it difficult for teamsters to deliver the foodstuffs allotted the reservation Indians. Nelson A. Miles described the sad situation, noting that "they have been for weeks without the bread-ration—and their year's allowance of food is exhausted in six or seven months." All this privation was suffered at the very same time that their traditional food supply, the bison, was being exterminated by the white men almost beneath their noses, and precisely at the time of the year when the grass was growing green and the young men yearned to take the war trail.[9]

Although food was scarce on the reservations, firearms and ammunition were abundant. There seemed no way for the authorities to control the flow of arms. While agents at one reservation might restrict the sale of guns, powder, and lead, the commodities were readily available from traders at other reservations or from whiskey peddlers. When, for instance, the sale of arms to the Cheyennes was temporarily stopped because some of their young men had come in with a herd of stolen ponies, the unconcerned warriors simply acquired what they wanted from the Osages farther east. W. M. D. Lee and Albert E. Rey-

Fig. 22. Quanah with two of his wives. (Courtesy Panhandle-Plains Historical Museum.)

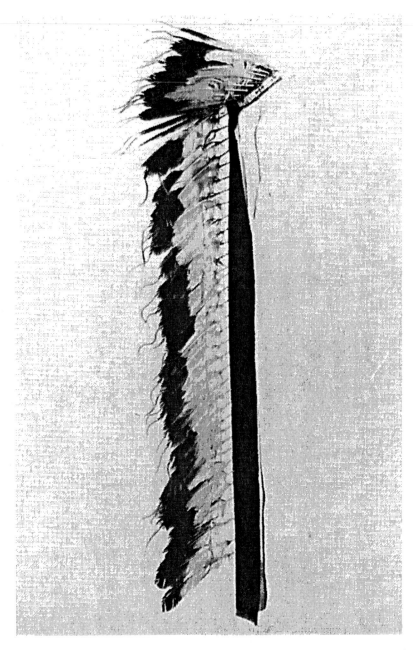

Fig. 23. The bonnet that Quanah wore in the 1874 Battle of Adobe Walls and later gave to Gen. Hugh Scott. (Courtesy Lowie Museum of Anthropology, University of California, Berkeley.)

Fig. 24. Isatai (second from right) with his family. (Courtesy Panhandle-Plains Historical Museum.)

Fig. 25. Lone Wolf. (Courtesy Smithsonian Institution.)

Fig. 26. Yellowfish, the last Comanche survivor of the 1874 Battle of Adobe Walls. (Courtesy Panhandle-Plains Historical Museum.)

Fig. 27. *Left* (standing), Isatai, and *right* (seated), Quanah. (Courtesy Panhandle-Plains Historical Museum.)

Fig. 28. Orlando A. "Brick" Bond and Andrew Johnson in 1922 at the site of the 1874 Battle of Adobe Walls. (Courtesy Kansas State Historical Society.)

Fig. 29. Visitors standing in line for the barbecue dinner at the 1924 fiftieth-anniversary celebration of the 1874 Battle of Adobe Walls. (Courtesy Panhandle-Plains Historical Museum.)

Fig. 30. A group of cowboys attending the 1924 fiftieth-anniversary celebration of the 1874 Battle of Adobe Walls. (Courtesy Panhandle-Plains Historical Museum.)

Fig. 31. Dedication of the Indian monument at the Adobe Walls battleground on October 19, 1941. (Courtesy Panhandle-Plains Historical Museum.)

nolds, licensed traders at the Cheyenne and Arapahoe Agency, may very well have been a source of firearms. Although they received from the tribesmen about thirty thousand buffalo robes worth about $150,000 between March 1 and May 31, 1874, they reported rather small sales of 238 pounds of powder, 456 pounds of lead, 30,000 caps, and 2,000 rounds of fixed ammunition. Some of the figures must have been juggled, for the reported sale of ammunition was exceedingly low in contrast to the large volume of robes. The extent of the illegal trade was illustrated by James M. Haworth, the Comanche and Kiowa agent, who in May, 1874, reported, "I cannot get any direct or possibive [*sic*] information as to the sale of arms but am certain somebody has been doing it extensively as a great many of the Indians are armed with the latest improved Pistols and guns with large amounts of fixed ammunition to suit them." Three months later Lt. Frank D. Baldwin of the U.S. Army complained that "today the Indians are armed as well as any soldier was in 1872 and so slight is the difference between their arms and those now in the hands of the troops, that we may say as well as the U.S. Troops of today."[10]

It may indeed have been to the advantage of the traders operating legally in the Indian Territory for the warriors to vent their rage on the hide men decimating the bison farther to the west. As long as the buffalo hunters operated only out of Kansas, they presented a minimal threat to the merchants on the reservations, who earned much of their income from the buffalo robes bartered from the Indians. After the Dodge City men moved their commerce into the Texas Panhandle, however, the situation changed. Rath, Myers, and the others who established stores at Adobe Walls soon eliminated the commercial advantages that Lee, Reynolds, and the other merchants on the reservations had enjoyed in trading for Indian-killed and -tanned buffalo robes. If the licensed traders in the Indian Territory could foment trouble for those on the Plains by providing arms to potential raiders, the competition might at least be threatened if not completely swept aside.[11]

Into this volatile situation came a catalyst—a young Comanche medicine man, Isatai.[12] Although little is known about his early life, his career undoubtedly was shaped by events that took place far away from him near the Rio Grande in December, 1873. At this time a combined Comanche and Kiowa raiding party was returning from Mexico with several captives and a herd of stolen horses when they encountered troops under Lt. Charles E. Hudson. In a hot fight that followed on a misty, overcast day, the soldiers killed nine of the thirty warriors and recovered fifty animals. Among the dead were Isatai's uncle, as well as both the favorite son and a nephew of Kiowa chief Lone Wolf. Isatai swore vengeance on the whites for his uncle's death, and he began a systematic effort in winter and spring, 1874, to organize a huge war party to satisfy his craving for white scalps.[13]

A skilled magician, Isatai in a matter of months secured a following among not only the Comanches but also the Kiowas and southern Cheyennes. The agent for the Comanche and Kiowa tribes in 1874 reported that the new "prophet" claimed miraculous healing powers and even the ability to raise the dead. The medicine man predicted that a comet then visible in the sky would disappear within five days, which it did, and he also accurately foretold a severe spring and summer drought. Isatai told his listeners that he had ascended to the abode of the Great Spirit "high above that occupied by the white man's Great Spiritual Power" and that the Indian deity had empowered him to wage war successfully on the hated whites. To demonstrate those abilities he reputedly belched forth wagonloads of cartridges only to swallow them again. He claimed the power to prevent the white men's guns from firing and assured skeptics that even if they did shoot, the bullets would pass through the warriors' bodies without leaving any mark or injury. Many warriors believed. Others questioned, but all were hopeful.[14]

Isatai began making the rounds of the various Comanche bands and then turned his attention to the camps of the Kiowas, Cheyennes, and Arapahoes. With him on some of these visits was another young Comanche named Quanah, later known as Quanah Parker. He was the mixed-blood son of a chieftain named Pe-ta and his captive white squaw, Cynthia Ann Parker, who had been taken as a child by raiders in 1836.[15] At the time Quanah was virtually unknown, and although he had never led any notable war parties, he too thirsted for white scalps. His nephew had been killed on the Double Mountain Fork of the Brazos River not long before, and he felt the loss deeply.[16]

Quanah and Isatai seriously began recruiting warriors to join their war party in late spring. Thirty years later Quanah recalled his efforts: "I work one month. I go to Noconie Comanche camp on head of

Cache Creek—call in everybody—I tell him about my friend kill him in Texas. I fill pipe—I tell that man, You want to smoke—he take pipe and smoke it. I give it to another man—he say I not want to smoke—if he smoke pipe he go in warpath[;] he not hand back. God kill him, he afraid." [17]

For seventy-five years Comanches had occasionally visited the annual Sun Dances of the Kiowas and for almost a quarter-century had been exposed to a similar religious phenomenon practiced by the Cheyennes. Isatai saw that by holding a sun dance for all the Comanche bands he might forge them into a solid front against the white men. The great chiefs of the tribe had never succeeded in gathering in one place all the scattered Comanche bands, but Isatai with his inflammatory rhetoric succeeded where they had failed. When visiting Comanche camps, Isatai pointed out how the Wichitas, Caddos, and other sedentary bands had declined in power and influence because they endeavored to follow the "white man's road." He predicted the same fate for the Comanches if they did nothing to avert it, and he called for them to unite under his powerful protective medicine to drive the whites from the Plains so that the buffalo would return in their former numbers and the tribe would again flourish.

The Comanche bands began gathering sometime in May at a point on the Red River near the mouth of Sweetwater Creek. Although there are numerous published accounts of the great Comanche Sun Dance, it is difficult to recreate precisely what happened there. Several writers have described the 1874 event in the same terms used by anthropologist Ralph Linton in a 1935 article on Comanche sun dances, as there were small such rites both before and after the great assembly in spring, 1874. It can be assumed, however, that the bands began assembling a few days before the planned ceremonies. The first four days of the dance were devoted to preparations—construction of a large brush-and-timber lodge in which the dance itself would be held, killing of a buffalo bull to be stuffed and placed atop the structure, and a visit by a group of mud-covered warriors acting as clowns to provide comic relief.

Important preliminary rites preceded the actual dance. One was the construction and destruction in a sham battle of a mock fort that strikingly resembled the buffalo hunters' trading post at Adobe Walls with its stockade corral. After the military exercise in which the enemy was destroyed, all the tribal members returned to the medicine lodge, the men going inside to begin three days of dancing. The warriors moved day and night to the sound of a huge drum played by several old men, taking neither food nor drink for the whole time and reaching a fever pitch of excitement.[18]

Everyone at the Comanche Sun Dance knew that war would be made, but on whom and when? Isatai and Quanah wanted specifically to avenge the deaths of their relatives, but they did not get their way. According to several Comanches who were there, "Quanah first spoke about going out on the expedition before Isatai arrived at [the] gathering. Isatai arrived & said he had power . . . to prevent [our] enemies['] guns from going off, so they gave him the leadership."[19] Quanah remembered the events in this way:

> . . . they ask me, "when you go on warpath?" and I say maybe tomorrow maybe next day. . . . I see old man Otter Belt & White Wolf and lots [of] old men and they said[,] "You pretty good fight[er] Quanah—but you not know everything. We think you take pipe first against White buffalo hunters—you kill white men [and] make your heart feel good—after that you come back [and] take all young men [and] go Texas warpath—then I say to Otter Belt and He Bear, you take pipe yourself [and] after that I take all young men & go [on] warpath [to] Texas and they say all right— Esati [Isatai] make big talk that time—God tell me we going [to] kill lots white men—I stop the bullets in gun—bullets not penetrate shirts—we kill them just like old woman.[20]

Thus the elders of the tribe decided that their first target would be the hated hide men in the Panhandle, not whites farther to the south where Quanah's nephew and Isatai's uncle had been slain. The two young warriors were satisfied, however, and the next full moon, which would come in late June, was chosen as the time for the attack.

After the ceremonies concluded, Isatai and Quanah began visiting Kiowa, Cheyenne, and Arapahoe camps to recruit warriors. Iseeo was in one of the Kiowa villages when Quanah came there carrying a pipe and asking the location of the chief's lodge. Iseeo pointed toward his uncle's tepee, whereupon "he went to the left of the door all around the outside of the lodge, entered and sat down in the back of the lodge." Soon the chief appeared and called in all his young men. Quanah said, "My nephew was killed . . . [and] his body is lying on the ground in Texas. I want to get even. I am coming looking for you. I give you this pipe to smoke." Iseeo later recollected that everyone heard the Comanche, and all the young men watched to see if the chief would accept the offer. The Kiowa leader answered, "I am not afraid of that pipe. But hold up. Wait until all the old men hear about it—if they say good—I will smoke it." Then Quanah went to the elders, but as Iseeo recalled, "they were afraid of that pipe." Thus only a few Kiowas joined the growing war party, but enough to represent the tribe. Most of Lone Wolf's warriors were probably still gone on a long, fruitless trip back to the Rio Grande to recover his son's and nephew's bodies. By early summer, however, they were back in their old hunting grounds in time to join the huge war party that was forming.[21]

The two young Comanches had much better luck among the Cheyennes. Together with other Comanche warriors, they met with the members of this tribe at their annual sun dance at the head of the Washita River. The Comanches gave a great feast for the Cheyenne chiefs and leaders of the "soldier bands," asking them to join in the inspired war against the buffalo hunters, who were only about forty miles away. Isatai told the assembled warriors that they would catch all the hide men asleep and club them to death. Impressed with the medicine man's reputation and his arguments, many accepted the pipe. After the sun dance was over, a large party of Comanche and Kiowa warriors demonstrated in front of the Cheyenne camp, Isatai again assuring the new members of the war party that the white men's guns could do them no harm.[22]

The Arapahoes by 1874 had become comparatively peaceable and accustomed to the reservation life, but the oratory of Isatai and Quanah stirred a number of them to join the party, not as participants but as observers. They wanted to see whether Isatai's medicine was as strong as he had claimed. They may very well have exercised the best judgment of all concerned.[23]

The main war party probably started forming at the large Cheyenne encampment near the head of the Washita River. The Indian raiders knew that the "white men's houses" had been built somewhere on the Canadian, and Isatai and Quanah believed that this settlement would be the best place to begin the campaign to drive the hide men from the range. The party set out toward the Canadian, the leaders leaving early in the morning and stopping at noon for the others to overtake them. Several bands of warriors arrived late, but others forged ahead, eager to start picking off individuals or small groups of hunters. Lone Wolf's party of Kiowas, just returned from the Rio Grande, had reached the Texas Panhandle by the first week of June and already killed hunters Dudley and Wallace. More depredations followed throughout the next two weeks.

Meanwhile, seven scouts were dispatched from the main body to find the post and to ascertain the strength of its defenders. Quanah recalled:

> Well pretty soon we move nearer . . . pick 7 men [who] go look for White men[']s houses on Canadian . . . old man White Wolf go with them—they gone all night—Next day a man watching from little hill call out here they come and we run out & see scout circle 4 time[s] to the right and we know they find houses . . . everybody make a long line . . . old man Black Beard in the middle[;] then seven scouts came up in single file in front [of] old man Black Beard. he say, tell the truth—what did you see—and 1st scout say "I tell you true, I see four or five log houses[.] I see horses running around," and all seven scouts say the same thing— Black Beard say, "all right pretty soon we kill a white man."

That same day the war party set out again, this time about eleven o'clock in the morning, drawing even closer to the white men's houses. They must not have been too far away, for they rode for only about five hours before stopping. Quanah later reported that the party paused to "put saddles & blankets in trees & hobble extra ponies—make medicine[,] paint faces[,] put on warbonnets." They then continued along the Canadian, riding in fours until finally crossing over to the north bank. Paralleling the river and leading their horses most of the way to escape detection, the party stopped once more "pretty near a red hill near a little cr[eek] where [the] houses were." It was time to rest again, this time through most of the night, in preparation for the fight that would come very early the next morning. Quanah remembered: "He Bear say 'dismount[,] hold lariats in hand—I call you [to] mount again[']—some go to sleep[,] some smoke tobacco and talk until He Bear and Tabananica call." When two old Comanches revisited the scene of these events in 1939, one of them, Yellowfish, pointed toward a high bluff west of the trading post site and said, "We shot some buffalo over there the day before and stopped and cooked them," so there must have been at least some food on hand as the warriors lounged in the moonlight on the night of June 26, 1874. Some of the experienced men rested well, but others were too nervous and stayed up all night talking and fretting over their arms or war paint. For some it was a first raid, and they were perhaps the most excited. It was to be the first time under fire for both Yellowfish and his friend, Timbo, and as the elders had thought that the latter was not old enough to participate in the fight, he had not been given any of Isatai's protective medicine war paint.

Early in the morning while it was still quite dark, the warriors on the bank of the Canadian began stirring. They and their ponies quietly continued up the river until almost daylight. They were finally able to make out the rude outlines of the hide men's buildings, almost too far away to see in the gloom.[24]

The Battle of Adobe Walls

It was a case of every fellow for himself and "get" as many Indians as possible.
—Andy Johnson.

T HE night of Friday, June 26, 1874, was not very different from any other night at Adobe Walls. The usual complement of traders and their employees were there, together with Billy Dixon, his hunting outfit, and several other hide men who had come in from their camps. Most of the merchants bedded down at their regular hour, but the hunters, skinners, and a few others stayed up past midnight having a general good time in Jim Hanrahan's saloon. He and Dixon were making final plans for a combined hunting trip, for Hanrahan had skinners but no hunters on his payroll, and Dixon needed help for his outfit. The saloon keeper's men were to leave with Dixon's crew for the buffalo range the next morning. In return for their services Hanrahan would receive a percentage of the hides.

The twenty-sixth had been a hot summer day, the drought of 1874 being at its peak, and the night was quite sultry. All the doors and windows of the buildings were wide open to catch any breeze, though most of the men chose to sleep under the stars. Dixon recalled, "Outside could be heard at intervals the muffled sounds of the stock moving and stumbling around, or a picketed horse shaking himself as he paused in his hunt for young grass. In the timber along Adobe Walls Creek to the east owls were hooting." The members of the war party just a few miles away were hearing similar sounds.

One by one the hide men found their bedrolls. After picketing his horse, Dixon lay down beside his wagon not far from Tom O'Keefe's blacksmith shop, the bright full moon shining in his face. He placed his Sharps rifle at his side between the blankets to protect it from the dew and drifted off to sleep. Two teamsters walked to their wagon just outside the Myers and Leonard corral and there fell into a deep slumber. A number of men laid out their bedrolls inside the nearby corral, and a few chose spots within the buildings. Even though Andy Johnson and some others had spotted three or four unidentified figures on a distant hilltop in the twilight, no one was alarmed. Perhaps the intermittent raiding by small parties of Indians had lulled the hide men into feeling that there would be no general outbreak of violence.[1]

Because the sod covering on the roof of Hanrahan's saloon had been too thin to turn rain, on Friday, June 26, a few men had placed a thicker earthen covering atop the building. They apparently put too much on it, placing unexpected strain on the cottonwood ridgepole that ran the length of the building. This seemingly unrelated event affected everything that followed.

About two o'clock on the morning of Saturday, June 27, the inmates of the saloon heard a loud crack like the report of a rifle. Jim Hanrahan jumped up and cried that the ridgepole was breaking, and he warned everyone to leave the building. Well-circulated horror stories of collapsing sod-covered roofs trapping or killing Kansas homesteaders undoubtedly spurred some to depart. But not all in the dram shop were worried. One later recollected that he was more irritated than frightened: "We lay for some time trying to sleep and the dirt kept falling." Finally, Hanrahan roused everyone and ordered Mike Welsh and Oscar Shepherd, two of his employees, to climb on top of the roof and shovel off some of the new sod to lessen the weight on the beam. Other men searched for a timber to prop up the ridgepole from inside the building. The repairs were accomplished by the light of the stars, the moon having set at about 2:00 A.M., approximately the time the beam split.

The activity at the saloon did not awaken everyone at the trading post. Others, temporarily roused, simply went back to sleep. Johnson, for instance, concluded that it was too early for him to get up and attend to the Rath livestock, and he returned to bed, barring the door of the store behind him. Hanrahan rewarded with free drinks the few men who stayed up to help him save the saloon roof.[2]

While the hide men repaired the roof or prepared to set off for the buffalo range, the Indians were on the move. After their rest of several hours on the north side of the Canadian, the war party formed a long line and continued upstream toward the trading post. Getting closer, the warriors dismounted and led their horses. Only the stars illuminated their way until about four o'clock, when the eastern sky began showing signs of the rising sun. By this time the warriors were in position. They could not see a sign of life in the distance and thought that Isatai was indeed right—they would be able to kill the unsuspecting white men as they slept. Quanah recalled, "Pretty soon we make a line—the chiefs try to hold young men back[;] go too fast—pretty soon they call out, 'all right, go ahead,' we charge down on houses in wild charge—threw up dust high." Little did they know that the hide hunters had been aroused by the cracking ridgepole two hours before.[3]

Among the hide men who remained awake was Billy Dixon, who had planned to leave on the hunt early that morning. About half an hour before sunrise, at four-thirty, Jim Hanrahan sent one of his employees, William "Billy" Ogg, to bring in the horses for his and Dixon's wagons. In 1898 Dixon recalled the next minutes this way: "One of Hanrahan's men had gone after the horses some two or three hundred yards. Presently he came running back and I heard the Indians yell and they came rushing up with our horses in front of them. I grabbed my gun and fired one shot [before] I retreated into Hanrahan's." Yellow-fish, excited by his first attack on the white man, later vividly remembered seeing the brilliant flash from a single hide man's gun in the semidarkness.[4]

Billy Ogg and Billy Dixon spotted the movement in the distance at almost the same time, but Dixon being closer to the buildings was the first to raise the alarm; Ogg ran in breathlessly only a few moments later. The warriors on the fleetest steeds headed for the hide men's horse herd, driving it before them, and at first Dixon and the others who were up thought that this was the Indians' goal. They soon knew better.[5]

Probably half of the traders and hide men were asleep when the screaming warriors descended on Adobe Walls. Only at the saloon, where Dixon's and Hanrahan's men were preparing to leave, was there any activity. Acting instinctively if not rationally, Dixon paused to tie his horse to his wagon, leaving himself barely enough time to get inside the sod saloon before the warriors engulfed it. Just behind him sprinted Billy Ogg, who had won his race with death. Most of the hide men were in one stage or another of dishabille, gun belts strapped around their waists, firing their weapons as if their lives depended on it—and they did. The initial charge was directed toward the center of the trading post, but the fire from the saloon divided it in half. As the mounted formation split, Oscar Shepherd, Hanrahan's bartender, cried out in pleasant recollection of social evenings at Dodge City, "Gents to the right and ladies to the left!"[6]

The flanking fire of the hide men in the saloon was the salvation for those in the other two stores. To the south they could protect three sides of the Rath and Company store, which stood in the open, and to the north they could cover most of the south side of the corral fence at the Myers and Leonard complex, even though the unoccupied blacksmith shop blocked part of their view. Fighting at all three buildings for the first few minutes was at close quarters. In all the buildings the defenders blocked the doors and windows with whatever was at hand, while thick sod walls afforded them substantial protection.[7]

Side arms, not rifles, saved the day during these initial minutes as the warriors, both on horseback and on foot, crowded around the buildings in the semidarkness, shooting through the windows and doors at the occupants. Quanah and other attackers even climbed on the roofs of some buildings to make openings through which they might shoot. Some of them flattened themselves against the building walls where the white men were unable to see and shoot at them. This worked well until the defenders made additional loopholes through which to fire.

Dixon recalled later that "they did their utmost to break in the doors of the saloon, but our constant firing finally drove them away." Several warriors backed their horses up to the doors and tried vainly to break them in with the weight. One warrior attempted to force one of the doors by throwing a wooden barrel at it. Occasionally a door might be cracked open slightly, and one of the warriors remembered seeing Quanah throw his lance through one of the breaches into the darkness within.[8]

The Battle of Adobe Walls was a different experience for the people in each of the three buildings. Individuals hardly knew what was going on in their own buildings during the first heat of battle, and they came to know of events in other structures only from people who had fought in them. Consequently, one must cautiously evaluate stories of the fight, relying more on the accounts of particular events that came from people who could have seen them.

The first minutes of the fight in the Rath and Company store were, if anything, more confused than those in the saloon. It seems that everyone there had been sound asleep. The first thing they heard was blacksmith Tom O'Keefe kicking on the door from the outside and shouting, "Open the door and let me in . . . the Indians are coming!" O'Keefe had been dozing near his shop when he heard Dixon's warning. Grabbing his blankets, he ran barefooted to the Rath store, where James Langton, clad only in his underwear, opened up to let him in. Just on his heels ran Sam Smith, also in his underclothes, with his gun in one hand and cartridge belt in the other. He too had been sleeping in the open. Already inside were Hannah and William Olds, manager Langton, and his bookkeeper, George Eddy. Together with Andy Johnson they formed the complement in the Rath and Company store, the smallest number of whites in any of the three buildings.

The Indians were within gunshot of the store by the time the door closed behind O'Keefe and Smith. Although Langton had in stock a number of new guns and about eleven thousand rounds of fixed ammunition, there was not a single professional hunter in the group. Some of the inmates became so excitedly helpless that they later were unable to account for what they did. James Langton and several others were so overcome by the excitement that they became nauseated, the store manager himself later admitting that he "parted with his supper of the night before." Fortunately, Johnson retained his composure, hurriedly barricading the door with bags of grain. He later recalled being sprayed with kernels of corn as an Indian bullet passed through one of the sacks.

As was the case at the saloon, side arms were the salvation of the Rath store defenders during the first few minutes. Each man stationed himself at a window and did what he could to fight from there. Johnson remembered emptying his revolver at the enemy even before blocking the doors. "There could be no organized resistance," he went on. "It was a case of every fellow look out for himself and 'get' as many Indians as possible."[9]

Accounts of Hannah Olds's participation in the fight differ. Most writers, including Johnson, agree that she courageously stayed by her

husband's side, handing him ammunition or loaded guns, but significantly all accounts except Johnson's come from people who were in
other buildings.[10] One version of the battle, published about 1915 and
based in part on James Langton's memories, differs considerably.

> Poor Mrs. Olds fainted. . . . Kind hands poured water on her face until
> she revived. When she recovered her sense, the realization of the predica-
> ment in which they all were, and particularly the awful fate that awaited
> her, if they were overcome, so overpowered her that she tried to commit
> suicide. She set up a series of yells and screeches in her fright, that the
> Indians outside must have thought that they were killing one another to
> save themselves from butchery. Strong hands prevented her from doing
> violence to herself, but there was no way to prevent her screeching, and
> the only thing to do was to give her freedom to screech until she became
> exhausted.[11]

Gunfire in the direction of Hanrahan's saloon first alerted the inmates of the Myers and Leonard store to the attack. Fred Leonard and
Bat Masterson were lying in their bedrolls inside the company corral
when the charge began. Masterson jumped up and ran for the saloon,
while Leonard reached for his cartridge belt and six-shooter; with
boots in hand he made for the back door of his store. Closing it behind
him, he turned to break open a sealed case of Sharps rifles in his north
storeroom. About a dozen men quickly found their way into the store,
and the new weapons together with others on hand allowed Leonard
to arm all but two of the men with the powerful firearms. Revolvers
were needed now, for by this time the warriors were already swarming
all around the store and its adjoining corral.

The Myers and Leonard store complex, it will be remembered,
had three bastions, one at the corner of the store and two at corners of
the corral, and for a time the hide men tried to use them in the defense
of the compound. But, as Fred Leonard wrote to his partner, A. C.
Myers, four days later, "the bastions . . . were useless." The store building itself proved difficult to defend, for the Indian bullets passed easily
through the earth and picket walls. Wherever a hide man might choose
to fight, he had to pile up sacks of grain, packing crates, or anything
else that would afford protection. But the fact that the walls were thinner than those of the other two buildings gave the Myers and Leonard
fighters one advantage. The mud chinking between the vertical posts
had not yet seasoned hard, so it was easy to make gunports wherever

they were needed. Since at one time, according to Fred Leonard, there were as many as 150 warriors around his store alone, the hide men needed this advantage. Some of the fighting at closest quarters occurred at this northernmost of the buildings, one of the battle participants recalling, "So close would they come that we planted our guns in their faces and against their bodies through the portholes."[12]

The corral was more of a liability than an asset to the defenders of the Myers and Leonard complex. Efforts to place men in the corral corner bastions failed, and the entire open area was left unprotected. Fred Leonard just after the fight reported that the Indians "rode around up to the corral and got off their horses, and fought as brave as any men I ever saw." The stockade sheltered the attackers as they stood or crouched behind the big pickets and killed all the stock in the compound and sniped at the white men in the store building. Johnson once said that the Myers corral was "of more protection to the Indians than it was to the white men"; another time he declared, "If you ever build a place to withstand an Indian attack, don't build your stockade like we did."[13]

Indians hidden by the corral probably killed one of the hide men. According to one version, Billy Tyler and Fred Leonard were attempting to run from the store to one of the bastions when the intense fire from the Indians behind the corral pickets forced them to turn back. As Tyler entered the doorway, he was shot by an assailant hidden behind the corral fence.[14] On one occasion Billy Dixon remembered that Tyler "was shot through an improvised embrasure," but another time he stated that "just as Tyler was entering the door of the . . . store, he turned to fire, and was struck by a bullet that penetrated his lungs."[15] Leonard's brother, relating the story he had heard, in 1911 stated that Tyler was shot at the back door to the store after having run into the corral to close the big gate just south of the building.[16] An article published three years after the fight claimed that Tyler died when he was "shot in the left side of the neck while in a sitting position, looking out at the stockade gate," having been the target of a warrior who was scarcely fifteen feet away.[17] Other sources claim that Tyler's death wound came as he attempted to drag a wounded Indian through the door to the store, an opinion voiced by Robert M. Wright, who certainly knew the stories from the battle participants.[18] Several other people associated with the trading post declared that Tyler was killed in an unsuccessful attempt to run from the Myers and Leonard store to the saloon.[19] Whatever the circumstances, Tyler fulfilled the prophecy of a few days before when a comrade had warned him that he was "going to fall early in this war."[20]

The fighting at close quarters lasted only about half an hour, but it was the time of the greatest danger for the white men. Had the Indians been better organized and concentrated their effort at individual buildings rather than along a broad front, they might very well have succeeded in taking the post.[21] A very important factor in the failure of the initial assault was the warriors' astonished discovery that Isatai's medicine—which was supposed to prevent the hunters' guns from firing—was of no value. They were shocked and disheartened to see their comrades fall one after the other, killed by the men they had expected to club to death in their sleep.[22]

Each of the hide men had his own memories of the first minutes. Fred Leonard, for instance, recalled that "I killed one Indian that I know of, and I don't know how many more, as I was shooting at them with my 40 at from forty to sixty yards."[23] Seth Hathaway remembered:

> The Indians were about one hundred yards from the house when the hunters turned loose their guns. At the first fire a number of horses and riders went down. We had no time to see anything more, for they were on us in a flash and for the next few minutes, which seemed like hours, it was each man for himself.
>
> The house soon filled up with smoke, and as of course every chink was closed but the loopholes, it became stifling in the place, and every man perspired freely. Now and then there was a shout from a hunter as his shot told, and words of encouragement were exchanged.[24]

The story of the first few minutes at the Battle of Adobe Walls as presented was the accepted one for almost sixty years, until all of the principal participants in the fight were dead, when J. Wright Mooar presented a substantially different account. Whether his story is true or not, it does shed interesting light on certain aspects of the days preceding the fight and thus deserves attention.

Feeling that he had some responsibility to keep his story confidential as long as battle participants survived, in 1927 Wright Mooar suggested to historian J. Evetts Haley that he did not agree with the standard account of the fight given in the *Life and Adventures of "Billy" Dixon*, written by Dixon's widow, Olive, and based on his recollections. According to Mooar, "The ridgepole in the house did not crack that night, as is claimed in his book, and some time I am going to tell about that."[25] Half a dozen years passed, however, before Mooar did indeed tell his version of the story, to the Reverend James Winford Hunt, who edited Mooar's reminiscences in 1932 for publication in *Holland's* magazine. In 1939 Mooar gave even more details in an interview with J. Evetts Haley, Earl Vandale, and Hervey Chesley.[26]

According to Mooar the ridgepole incident was only a trick devised by Jim Hanrahan to awaken the hunters on the morning of the twenty-seventh because he had received a secret warning that an attack was coming. The story goes that Hanrahan or his new partner, Dixon, fired a gunshot about two in the morning to arouse the hunters before the attack and that Hanrahan continued giving them free drinks to keep them from going back to bed. Mooar declared that Hanrahan had learned a few days before from Amos Chapman,[27] a government scout who lived with the Cheyennes and who had visited the trading post, the exact date and time of the impending assault. Because the hide men distrusted Chapman, with his ties to the reservation Indians, and suspected him of being a spy for either the Indians or the government, Hanrahan purportedly "smuggled" him out of the trading post in John Wesley Mooar's wagon. In this way the Mooar brothers learned of the "secret warning" and were able to leave the Panhandle in time to avoid the hostilities.[28]

Although a number of later authors have accepted Wright Mooar's version seemingly without question, it offers a number of problems. First of all, when Chapman visited Adobe Walls he was not alone but had with him James E. McAllister,[29] an employee of traders W. M. D. Lee and A. E. Reynolds. McAllister related the events as he remembered them:

> I and Amos Chapman were at Adobe Walls two days before the fight took place in 1874. I was working for Lee and Reynolds at Fort Supply, I[ndian] T[erritory], running a bull train. Amos was a government scout. . . . Two men had stolen a couple of horses from Lee and Reynolds and Amos and I were following them across the plains. We ran upon the men on the head of Wolf Creek, but didn't catch them and we thought they would be by Adobe Walls. We made for that place but the two men whom we were after did not go by there. We followed them across the Panhandle to Fort Bascom, N.M., but never caught them. . . .
>
> The Indians around Fort Supply would be in to the fort every day, and

they told us that they were going down to Adobe Walls and kill the buffalo hunters. When we passed there we told the hunters what the Indians had said, and that they were coming, but they wouldn't believe us. They weren't even looking for them when they came.[30]

Obviously, McAllister and Chapman did warn the hide men, but it certainly does not seem to have been any secret. Further, Wright Mooar claimed that the message was delivered to just three men at the post: Hanrahan, A. C. Myers, and Charles Rath. Myers and Rath, however, had already returned to Dodge City by that time and only Hanrahan remained at Adobe Walls.[31]

Another difficulty with the Mooar account of the "secret warning" is the fact that the hide men in and near the trading post were already well aware of the Indian danger all around them. They had heard firsthand of some of the attacks, murders, and mutilations, and they accepted the fact that there was increased danger. When A. C. Myers returned to Dodge City on June 19, he reported to the press that "the Indians are more than plenty" and that the men at the post knew that "there are one thousand lodges encamped within forty miles," an apparent reference to the Cheyennes gathered for their annual medicine dance. Myers declared that "there are quite a large number of hunters in that locality and they are 'red hot' to pitch into the Indians," continuing that he "never saw a set of men so eager for a fight—so anxious to exterminate the whole race of Indians, as the hunters now on the Canadian are." These hide men did not need any warning—all they wanted was Indians to kill.[32]

Although most evidence weighs against J. Wright Mooar's claim that Amos Chapman delivered a secret warning and that the ridgepole incident was set up by James Hanrahan, some sources support his proposition. Mooar himself had seen the saloon being erected and declared that its ridgepole was too stout to crack under the weight of the sod. "You and I both couldn't pull that down," he remarked to historian J. Evetts Haley. Billy Dixon and others examined the beam the day after its supposed cracking, and they could find nothing wrong with it. The original manuscript for the *Life and Adventures of "Billy" Dixon* contained the statement: "It has been told that the ridge pole broke. As a matter of fact, when the ridge pole was examined afterwards, it was sound and firm." Probably because these two sentences contradicted the rest of the story, editor Frederick S. Barde in 1913 struck them and they never reached print in the two published versions of the book.[33] The questions about the roof remain, and the mystery may never be solved.

Sometime early in the fight the two Scheidler brothers met their deaths in their wagon just north of the Myers and Leonard corral. Jacob Scheidler, an employee of Brick Bond and known to everyone as "Shorty," had just arrived with a load of hides from Bond's camp on Palo Duro Creek. Shorty planned to wait at the Walls for his brother, Isaac, who was on the way down with a load of merchandise for the Rath store. Isaac, known to all at the post as "Ike," came in on the evening of the twenty-sixth and with his brother's help unpacked his goods and loaded up hides to carry back to Dodge City. Hoping for an early departure the next morning, they slept in one of the wagons with their big, black Newfoundland dog.[34]

Events surrounding the death of the two German teamsters are almost as clouded as those concerning Billy Tyler's only a few feet away. According to a few accounts, one of the brothers was awake at the time of the attack. He ran toward the Myers and Leonard store but turned back when he saw that his brother was still asleep in the wagon. These versions state that he was killed in the open just outside the door to the store, one source noting that a hide man stepped out to pick him up and carry him inside. The other brother was killed while still in the vehicle, his body being found later "partly dressed, laying alongside the wagon, cut in a terrible manner."[35] Most accounts of the brothers' deaths, however, state that they were stranded in their wagon outside the corral by the screaming horde of warriors, who at first never suspected that they were inside. After a few minutes they were discovered and quickly put to death, their wagon being pilfered for its contents.[36]

Some of the attackers also recalled the Scheidlers' death, and their reminiscences agree that, in Quanah's words, "we killed two white men in [a] wagon." Timbo, at the time just a teenager, was nearby, and he also recalled that the wagon at the extreme north end of the trading complex stood quietly while the warriors focused their attention on the stores. "Though there were Indians all around it," he related, "none of them knew that there was anyone in the wagon." Finally, one of the mounted Comanches, a warrior named Cheyenne, rode up and raised the wagon sheet with the end of his bow. His interest incurred a muzzle blast from one of the Scheidlers' guns, a shot sealing their fate. In a matter of moments, Timbo remembered, the warriors riddled the wagon cover with spears, arrows, and bullets until the Scheidlers breathed no more.[37] Billy Dixon said later that for the remainder of the fight the warriors "flaunted the bloody scalps of the poor Shadlers [*sic*] with devilish glee."[38] Not only were the two brothers killed and scalped, but their big black dog put up such a stiff defense of his masters' bodies that the warriors likewise dispatched him and took a long scalplike strip of hide from his side.[39]

A handful of accounts concerning the attack on the Scheidler brothers also mention the death of a mysterious "Mexican teamster" or "bull-whacker," perhaps one of their employees. Some say that he was killed in his camp near the Scheidler wagon and others that he was on the way to awaken the brothers when he was overtaken and murdered. His identity, if he ever existed, remains unknown.[40]

About half an hour after the initial assault, the Indians withdrew and altered their strategy; now, they turned to skirmishing, occasionally charging individual buildings. During this phase of the battle, which lasted until the middle of the day, the warriors maintained a constant barrage of gunfire on the trading post while groups of them assaulted one building after another. Some of the warriors circled the houses on horseback, clinging to the leeward sides of their mounts and shooting from under their necks, while others attempted to creep nearer the houses for sharpshooting. For the latter braves, the big stacks of buffalo hides and the Myers and Leonard picket corral provided helpful cover. By this time, however, the white men were better prepared for them and were able to withstand the more concentrated assaults. In one such charge, about twenty braves tried to force the door at the Rath and Company store, James Langton noting afterward that "if they had done this when they first came, we wouldn't have lasted a minute."[41]

Even a small sampling of participants' recollections of the battle conveys a feeling of what it must have been like. During a lull in the fighting, one splendidly dressed young warrior charged toward the Rath and Company store, leaping from his horse as he approached the building. With incredible courage he ran up to the side of the store, pushed his revolver through one of the loopholes in the sod wall, and emptied it into the interior of the store. Fortunately for the occupants, the bold act only filled the store with smoke. The warrior, however, was wounded in the back by one of the defenders and paralyzed. He lay crumpled against the south wall of the structure, where the inmates could hear but not see him without exposing themselves to Indian fire.[42] According to Johnson, "He was helpless and could not get away. He constantly called to his father who was in a ravine some distance away to the south. His father would not show himself . . . but he was shouting directions to his son. They made so much noise that one of the hunters went to the window to shoot the boy and put an end to the conversation. As soon as the boy saw the gun at the window he drew a revolver and shot himself."[43]

From his vantage point inside the Hanrahan saloon, Dixon noticed what appeared to be an Indian who had taken cover behind one of the ricks of buffalo hides behind the Rath and Company store. From the saloon the brave could be seen, but he was completely hidden from the defenders inside the store. Dixon described what followed:

> About 75 yards to the rear of the store was a large pile of buffalo hides, and while the fight was in progress I noticed an Indian horse standing by it, and could see the head dress or feathers of an Indian, as though he were hugging very close to the hides. I fired at his feathers, and he dodged around to the other side of the pile; this brought him within range of the guns from Rath's house, and he was forced to dodge back again. In this manner we kept him in hot water about ten minutes. Then I fired at his horse, which dropped at the crack of the gun.
>
> I could then see the Indian a little plainer, or rather could tell better where he was standing, behind the pile of hides, by his head feathers. I was shooting a buffalo gun, known as Sharp's big fifty. Guessing at his position as well as I could, I fired right through the hides at him. I must have scorched him, for he immediately broke from his hiding place, ran about 15 steps, and then dropped in the grass. He gave a short yelp like a coyote at every jump.[44]

This must have been one of Billy Dixon's favorite stories in later years, for it appears in most of his accounts of the fight. His widow, Olive, even wrote to her editor, Frederick Barde, that she had "often heard . . . Mr. Dixon . . . tell about shooting at the Indians behind the buffalo hides and how the Indians finally went zig zag fashion yelling like a coyote."[45]

As the battle progressed through the morning, increasing numbers of red men fell under the gunfire from the three buildings. Many of the injured or dismounted braves attempted to reach the comparative safety of the tall grass at a point about halfway between the piles of buffalo hides behind the stores and the low hills toward the west. Near the post, however, their prospects for rescue were not nearly so great. The warriors hidden behind the ricks of hides and the corral fence repeatedly requested covering fire from those stationed in the tall grass. Warriors injured or killed often were recovered from the field of battle by other mounted braves, who rode up to them and pulled them up onto the animals or dragged them to safety. Jim Hanrahan in later years expressed his respect for the courage of the rescuers, declaring that they "showed traits of character that would be worthy of emulation by any race or color of men, exposing themselves freely to save their comrades." Dixon remembered one rescue in which a warrior on a white horse raced toward a fallen brave. The latter jumped up behind his rescuer, and they started at full speed for safety when one of the hide men's guns cracked. The bullet struck the horse, breaking one of its hind legs. As blood streamed down the horse's leg, both Indians began whipping the animal, which lurched and staggered on three legs to carry them away.[46]

One of the Indians injured in the fight was Quanah himself. As is the case with the shootings of Billy Tyler and the Scheidler brothers, there are almost as many versions of Quanah's injury as there are tellers of the tale. Generally reliable sources state that he lost his horse to white gunfire and took shelter behind either a rock or a buffalo carcass, where he was struck, probably by a ricochet bullet, between his shoulder blade and his neck. For a time his arm was paralyzed, and he was badly stunned. In time, however, he made his way to comparative safety in a plum thicket, where he was picked up by mounted warriors.[47] Other accounts of the battle from white sources identify Quanah as having been shot in the stomach or breast in front of either the saloon or the Myers and Leonard store. Since he was unknown to the whites at the time, the veterans probably just added him to their latter-day stories of the fight to make them sound better to listeners.[48] As an old man, Charles Goodnight, who knew the Comanche chief, related to J. Evetts Haley that Quanah had told him that his life had been saved in the battle when a bullet was deflected by the buffalo powder horn that he wore swinging from his shoulder. The pioneer rancher also quite interestingly wrote to Olive K. Dixon in 1913 that Quanah once had told him that Billy Dixon was the man who shot him, a distinction Dixon himself never claimed and one he probably did not deserve.[49] In his interview with Hugh Scott in 1897, Quanah tersely reported only that "I got shot in the side."[50]

The injury to Quanah, wherever he suffered it, definitely affected the course of the battle. From that time on, the warriors fell back from the trading post to snipe at the buildings. Even then, they were at a disadvantage, for the range of the buffalo hunters' guns far outdistanced their own.

As time passed, the prowess of the professional hunters became an increasingly important factor in the outcome of the battle, and their place in the folklore of the Texas Panhandle was ensured. These men were accustomed to shooting bison from long distances. They used firearms especially designed for killing big game, and many of them loaded their own cartridges, thus knowing precisely the distance their weapons could reach. Moreover, shooting matches at the post regularly featured targets ranging from several hundred to a thousand yards away. Even in the East at the Creedmore rifle range on Long Island, perhaps the finest range in America at the time, international competitions were held with similar Sharps rifles in which thousand-yard shooting was considered ordinary. To evaluate the reports of marksmanship exhibited at Adobe Walls, all these factors must be considered. The men who later became famous for their shots were engaged in an activity similar to their professional work. They were truly in their own element.[51]

Numerous accounts discuss the hide men's shooting at a distant group of Indians who were holding a council of war after the failure of their initial assault. Perhaps the earliest version of the incident was published in 1888 and was based on information a newspaper reporter obtained in an interview with Dixon. The hide man related that after the Indians had failed to overwhelm the post, they withdrew about three-quarters of a mile to plan further strategy. "All the hunters were armed with the long range guns that had just come out," Dixon remembered, "so while they were standing there having a council the hunters began to pick them off and killed a great many before they could get out of range." Other versions of this story say that one chief was killed and that Isatai's pony was shot, hit in a place that was not covered by his protective medicine paint. Sam Smith, who was in the

Rath and Company store at the time, witnessed the incident and reported: "One chief fell from his horse and the medicine man's horse was killed. This broke up the council." The death of Isatai's horse demoralized the warriors, who now realized that no supernatural power would help them in their fight with the hated white men.[52]

After the attackers had been driven back some distance from the buildings, the defenders in Hanrahan's saloon discovered that they were running low on ammunition. They decided to send men to the stores on either side for more. Masterson chose to go to Myers and Leonard's building, while Hanrahan and Dixon went to Rath's amid a hail of ineffective gunfire from the distant warriors. Once Hanrahan and Dixon reached Rath's building, the defenders begged Dixon to stay. There were only six men in the store, not one of them a professional hunter, and besides, they argued, they had Hannah Olds to protect. Dixon agreed to remain, and while in the store he performed another long-remembered feat of marksmanship.[53]

Against the west-facing door in the kitchen at the north end of the Rath store, the defenders had stacked up a huge pile of corn and flour sacks and other supplies and merchandise. As there was a transom over the portal, Billy Dixon clambered over the pile, with .50-caliber Sharps rifle in hand to take a look outside. In an area about eight hundred yards away at the base of a line of low hills where the grass was tall, he could see something crawling. Leveling his rifle, he carefully took aim and shot. The recoil of his weapon was so great that the hunter tumbled down from his perch atop the pile of sacks and goods, knocking down a washtub and some eating utensils. Johnson, who was there at the time, remembered that "we thought him dead, but he was all right and soon got back on the sacks and finished his shooting." Taking aim again, Dixon fired a second time at the moving object but missed. "I . . . was provoked at seeing the bullet kick up the dirt just beyond the object," he remembered. On the third shot, however, Billy made his mark, for the object moved no more. After the fight he went out to see what he had been shooting at and found "a dead Indian lying flat on his stomach, . . . naked, save for a white cloth wrapped round his hips" and with one knee broken by a gunshot. In another account Dixon recalled, "He had crawled a quarter of a mile with shattered knee before I killed him."[54]

The Indians told their own stories of the hunters' skill as marksmen. Co-hay-yah, one of the Comanche participants in the fight, in the 1930s remembered the shooting: "Buffalo hunters were bad. . . . They sure killed us out. . . . Buffalo hunters had awful long range. Sometimes we wouldn[']t be thinking of it & they would kill our horses. . . . No wonder they could kill the buffalo!" Another Indian reported that a group of braves was riding along on horseback "trying to devise some means of rescuing their dead" when "suddenly, and without warning or apparent cause, one of the warriors fell from his horse dead." His companions dismounted to see what had happened, finding that a bullet had passed through his skull. The wind was blowing and the hide man's rifle was fired from such a distance that the braves had been unable to hear the report when it fired.[55]

Timbo remembered the death of a different brave in an incident that seems equally remarkable. After regrouping on the leeward side of the hills to the northwest of the trading post, Timbo and a number of his comrades started back over the low mounds toward the white men's houses for another assault when one of the warriors toppled from his mount. The Comanche remembered that the white men were not able to shoot so well toward the west because there were not so many openings in their buildings on that side, but that he had seen them "digging at the chinks in one of the houses." He continued, "I guess a white man poked his rifle through there and took good aim, for he dropped him dead, shot squarely through the back. We got his body and dragged it behind the hill." Of such shooting in the battle, Quanah once remarked to Charles Goodnight, "They killed us in sight and out of sight."[56]

Of all the marksmanship exhibited during the Adobe Walls fight, one shot has entered the folklore of the region.[57] This is Billy Dixon's "long shot" three days into the siege, a shot that struck a warrior an estimated three-quarters of a mile away. Though the distance was equaled by other shots in the battle, this incident is most difficult for historians to verify. Accounts of most of the other feats of marksmanship in the battle were printed as early as the 1880s, but no versions of the famed long shot ever reached print until after the first decade of the twentieth century. Dixon never claimed to have made it.

The story, as retold many times, relates that on the third day of the siege Billy Dixon saw a party of about fifteen Indians on the side of the bluff east of the trading post and decided to see if he could hit any of them. "I took careful aim and pulled the trigger," he is reported to have said in recounting the experience to his wife. "We saw an Indian fall from his horse," the others dashing for cover. A few moments later two warriors returned to recover the body of their comrade. Dixon's biography itself states that "a number of exaggerated accounts have been written about this incident" and that it was "what might be called a 'scratch' shot." Only one paragraph is devoted to it.[58]

One of the earliest written accounts of this famous long shot comes from Willis Skelton Glenn, a hide hunter who knew several of the men who had fought at Adobe Walls. Because his version of the incident is one of the first ever to have been recorded, it merits attention.

> . . . the white men had guns of all kinds. The Indians going back the same direction they came, quite a number were assembled on a little knoll some 1400 yards distance, thinking themselves safe. . . . These hunters with their sharp shooting rifles, did their best to dislodge these Indians. Finally one fell, and the rest ran away much surprised at such a long range shot. Each one of the hunters claimed the shot and it was hard to tell who had done the work. They argued for a day or so, when some of the bolder men decided to go back to the hill and examine the Indian, and they found him shot in the back. As they could not see the edges of the lead, one of them said, "We will see who hit him" and out with his knife and took out the bone the ball was in and returned to camp, and it proved to be the new Sharp's [*sic*] #45 that had been sent there for trial.[59]

When the first accounts of the famed long shot appeared, knowledgeable people began to question them. Not doubting that the shot was made, J. Wright Mooar in 1927 declared that Dixon "was not the man who killed the Indian on the hill."[60] W. S. Carter, who spent much of his boyhood in the Adobe Walls area in the 1880s and 1890s and who carried mail while Dixon was postmaster in the vicinity, remembered that "old Billy Dixon's wife claimed that at the fight Billy killed an Indian a quarter of a mile away. I have my doubts about that . . . Billy himself told me that he 'shot at' an Indian that far away but he wasn't even sure he had hit him let alone killed him."[61] Even the location of the Indian when allegedly killed is in question. Some of the first accounts of the incident from early in this century state that the distance of the shot was about 800 yards; Glenn stated 1,400 yards. The first edition of Olive K. Dixon's *Life and Adventures of "Billy" Dixon* in 1914 reports 1,200 yards; a surveyor measured the distance in 1924 and stated that it was 1,028 yards; and the second edition of Dixon's biography in 1927 reports 1,538 yards. Obviously after the passage of years no one knew where the Indian supposedly fell.[62]

One of the most intriguing episodes in the history of the Adobe Walls fight is the story of the black bugler who fought with the Indians. As with most tales associated with the battle, it has many variations, but from the tangled net of stories one common thread appears. Throughout much of the fight the white men inside the buildings heard in the distance the sound of bugle calls. At first some of them must have thought that it heralded the arrival of a troop of cavalry, but they were sorely disappointed when no soldiers appeared and the mysterious bugling continued. Some of them erroneously believed that various calls directed the warriors' movements, a fact later denied by one Comanche participant, who stated that "the calls were unnoticed by the Indians."

The black bugler undoubtedly was a deserter from the U.S. Cavalry. Quanah even went so far as to relate to Hugh Scott that "one of the Comanches killed was a yellow nigger painted up like other Comanche[s;] he left a nigger soldier company." A few writers have suggested that the bugler was the famous Kiowa chief, Satanta, who also blew a bugle, but at that time the famed chief was ill at Fort Sill, and he did not participate in the fight.[63]

Sometime before the middle of the day, while the warriors were still charging toward the stores en masse, the men at the Myers and Leonard store heard the sound of tomahawks chopping through the bottom of the Scheidler brothers' wagon, which by this time had been turned on its side. The white men could tell that a party of warriors was attempting to break through its floor to steal belongings from the vehicle. Fred Leonard, Charley Armitage, and "Dutch Henry" Born punched more chinking from between the vertical poles in the north wall of the store to get a better look. From their vantage point they could see five braves at work on the far side of the wagon. Sticking their buffalo guns through the new loopholes, they let fly three big chunks of lead. All passed through the wagon and each struck its target. At this point a sixth figure sprang from inside the overturned wagon, a trumpet slung across his back. According to most accounts, Armitage then took a rifle from Leonard and, as Bat Masterson related, "plunked a big forty-calibre bullet through him, and he bugled no more."[64] Another version of the story attributes the death of the black bugler to Dutch Henry Born, who had tired of listening to the bugle calls and declared, "I'm going to shoot that damned nigger the first chance I get." When Born's shot made its mark, he exclaimed to the others, "I got the damned nigger, boys, that will end that music."[65]

Many of the accounts of the Battle of Adobe Walls present as fact an incident that originated in fiction. This story recounts the brave dash by "Old Man" Keeler, Fred Leonard's cook, through a hail of Indian bullets to cross the open corral from the Myers and Leonard store to pump a bucketful of water for the relief of the dying Billy Tyler. The story was told many times by R. C. Crane, one of the early promoters of the West Texas Historical Association, who based his narratives on an otherwise generally reliable article published in *Pearson's Magazine* in 1908. Crane's status as an official in the historical organization gave his stories credence.[66] The origin of the tale, however, as best can be ascertained, was the fictional biography of Bat Masterson, *The Sunset Trail*, written by Alfred Henry Lewis and published in 1905.[67]

Although certain aspects of the battle that took place on June 27, 1874, are well detailed, others are clouded by conflicting evidence or missing altogether. It is not known how many white men took part in the fight. Probably the smallest estimate to come from a battle participant is fifteen; other white participants in the fight remembered as many as twenty-eight defenders.[68]

Ascertaining how many Indians were involved in the attack on Adobe Walls is equally difficult. As the years passed the reported numbers grew to the point that some accounts published in this century suggest that a horde of warriors swarmed over the trading post, outnumbering the hide men forty- to sixty-to-one. The reports of Indian strength recorded just after the fight are probably the most reliable. Four days later, for instance, Leonard wrote to his partner, A. C. Myers, that the trading post had been attacked by 200 warriors, a number repeated by Lt. Frank D. Baldwin in his diary for August, 1874, noted by Gen. Nelson A. Miles in his memoirs, and remembered by S. S. Van Sickel, a hunter who came in just after the fight. Lt. Col. J. W. Davidson at Fort Sill on July 7, 1874, reported from information he had secured from interpreters and scouts that an estimated 200 to 250 warriors had participated in the battle.[69]

As time passed, the estimated number of Indian participants grew. For most of his life Billy Dixon reported to journalists and others that he remembered between three hundred and five hundred attackers,[70] but when his widow prepared his biography for publication she and her editor decided that there were between seven hundred and a thousand.[71] Several battle participants, including James Langton and Andrew Johnson, in later years reported between four hundred and six hundred attackers,[72] and many late nineteenth- and early twentieth-century narratives of the fight fixed the figure between five hundred and seven hundred warriors.[73]

Some astronomical figures for Indian strength have been presented, most having no basis in fact. In 1876 when he was delivering buffalo hides to be tanned by Indians at the Cheyenne and Arapahoe Agency, J. Wright Mooar visited with Chief Whirlwind of the Cheyennes, a participant in the fight, who claimed that there were fifteen hundred warriors in the attack. Surely the old man was exaggerating.[74] Other outlandish estimates include nine hundred from participant Sam Smith, who fought in the Rath store,[75] around one thousand from Rath and Company employee George Curry,[76] more than one thousand from Frank Smith, who came into the post just after the fight,[77] and fifteen hundred from Willis Skelton Glenn, a hide man who was not in the fight but who knew many of the men who were.[78] One popular writer even went so far as to state fancifully that six thousand warriors swooped down on the post![79]

Problems also abound in even approximating the number of Indian casualties. Reports of Indian bodies left near the buildings vary from a low estimate of seven to an exaggerated total of twenty-seven. The lowest figure comes from Seth Hathaway, who left the post the night after the fight and probably before additional corpses were discovered by the defenders.[80] Several witnesses to the battle and its aftermath, as well as initial reports of the fight in two Kansas newspapers, state nine dead Indians lay on the ground, a figure also noted by Gen. Hugh Scott in the marginal notes appended to his interview with Quanah in 1897.[81] The figure eleven also appears in a substantial number of early accounts of the fight, including a report by Lt. Col. J. W. Davidson from Fort Sill on July 7, 1874, a telegram from Charles Rath and A. C. Myers to the governor of Kansas on July 8, 1874, and Lt.

Frank D. Baldwin's diary for August, 1874.[82] The next widely reported number of Indian bodies lying near the buildings is thirteen, a figure noted by Billy Dixon in some accounts and by both S. S. Van Sickel and W. C. Cox, hunters who came into Adobe Walls shortly after the battle.[83] Other versions state that fourteen to twenty-seven dead warriors were found after the fight.[84]

The total number of braves killed in the fight is even more difficult to gauge. Most estimates range from a dozen to thirty. Quanah, perhaps minimizing the losses, in 1897 stated that "the white men killed six Comanches, 4 Cheyennes and some Arapahoes."[85] Comanche and Kiowa agent J. M. Haworth on September 1, 1874, reported to his superiors that the Cheyennes had lost five warriors, the Comanches six, with one more dying later from wounds he suffered in the fight, a total of a dozen. George Bent thought that these figures were about right.[86] This estimate of Indian losses is confirmed at least in part by a mid-1930s interview with several Comanche battle participants.[87] Historian Wilbur Sturtevant Nye, on the basis of his interview with Indian participants, reported about fifteen killed and a large number wounded.[88]

Most of the white men who fought in the battle thought that they had killed about thirty warriors. Leonard, when he wrote his first letter from the trading post four days after the fight to report the battle, told A. C. Myers in Dodge City that "about 25 or 30 Indians were killed; we found 11."[89] A report of the battle published in the Topeka *Commonwealth* only eleven days after the fight noted about thirty dead braves, the same total that Cheyenne interpreter Ben Clark reported to Gen. Hugh Scott in about 1897. This figure also appears in Gen. Nelson A. Miles's memoirs, giving it further credence.[90] Charles E. Jones in 1876 learned from Spotted Wolf, an Arapahoe chief, who raised "fingers on both hands three times and then five fingers on one hand," that there were thirty-five braves killed.[91]

From this point the estimates of Indian casualties rise considerably, probably reporting more deaths than occurred. A hide man who was in the relief party, for instance, reported the deaths of "over *40* Indians & one nigger";[92] Johnson estimated forty-five;[93] Hathaway sixty;[94] Coulter in the first historical account of the fight in 1877 reporting seventy;[95] Dixon in his earliest known reminiscences "at least seventy-five warriors;[96] Masterson "over eighty killed";[97] Fred Leonard, who in 1874 reported only twenty-five to thirty dead, in later life stating either eighty-two or eighty-four;[98] his brother noting about one hundred "killed and wounded";[99] and another Masterson account declaring that there were "fully 100 . . . shot dead or badly hurt," a figure supported by Rath and Company employee George Curry.[100] The highest total comes to us by way of J. Wright Mooar from Cheyenne chief Whirlwind, who told Mooar in 1876 that either 115 or 150 warriors were killed, an estimate undoubtedly as exaggerated as his claim for 1,500 warriors participating in the fight.[101]

More than just the bodies of braves were left on the field of battle. Several hide men remembered discovering blood-soaked cloths and even amputated limbs in the surrounding area. Johnson noted that he saw "a good many bloody bandages around there on the hills," Dixon adding that "at one place, a lot of clothing, such as moccasins, leggings, blankets, etc., had been cut up and destroyed." He speculated "that many of the Indians had died of their wounds, and their effects were destroyed because they could not be carried off."[102]

Isatai, after the Indians finally retreated about the middle of the afternoon, was utterly disgraced. The huge war party that was supposed to emerge victorious had been forced to retreat from the field of battle to nurse its wounds and attend to its dead. According to certain versions, a group of Cheyennes wanted to whip or even kill Isatai. Other braves prevented the retribution by declaring that he was already so disgraced that no further punishment was necessary. Differing accounts report that the medicine man ran away "before they got to him." Looking back on the events later in the century, Quanah remembered that one of the warriors taunted Isatai: "What's the matter [with] you[r] medicine . . . you [have] 'pole cat medicine.'" This derogatory remark may have referred to Isatai's excuse that his supernatural power had been broken by the action of a Cheyenne brave who had killed a skunk on the way to the attack. The medicine man lived near Fort Sill at least as late as 1912, and by the 1940s the Indians in the area remembered him as "that comical fellow."[103]

About four o'clock on the afternoon of the twenty-seventh, one of the hide men in the saloon, "Bermuda" Carlyle, ventured outside to pick up an Indian trinket that had attracted his attention. The attackers had retreated so far away that no warriors shot at him. One after another the white men emerged from their shelters, communicating for the first time with the inmates of the other buildings. Despite the three deaths at the Myers and Leonard store complex, many defenders seemed to be interested more in picking up Indian artifacts as souvenirs of their encounter with the red men than in mourning. The whites began stripping the dead Indian bodies that lay close to the stores, retrieving warbonnets, weapons, shields, quirts, kerchiefs, bridles, and a number of scalps. When, for example, Billy Dixon removed a silver-mounted bridle from the carcass of an iron-gray Indian pony, he discovered "a scalp . . . evidently . . . taken from the head of a white woman, the hair being dark brown in color and about fifteen inches in length . . . lined with cloth and edged with beads." [104]

The hunters in time carried their trophies back to Dodge City, and a handful of them have survived to this day. Andy Johnson picked up a number of relics, among them a quirt handle, a red printed kerchief, a silver armband, and a rawhide shield. In 1904 he sold the shield to James Mooney, noted turn-of-the-century ethnologist, who at the time was collecting artifacts for the Field Museum in Chicago, where the shield remains today. [105] Then, three years before his death in 1925, Johnson gave Olive K. Dixon his quirt handle, armband, and kerchief for donation to the Panhandle-Plains Historical Museum in Canyon, Texas. [106]

Other Indian artifacts from Adobe Walls remained in Indian hands and were carried by their owners back to the Indian Territory. A few of these objects, among them the fine warbonnet that Quanah wore in the fight (see fig. 23), eventually reached public depositories. He gave the headdress to his friend Hugh Scott sometime in the 1890s, and from him it passed through the hands of private owners until it reached the Lowie Museum of Anthropology at Berkeley, California, in 1901. [107] Several of Isatai's personal belongings, including his buffalo-horn headdress and ceremonial shield and lance, were acquired from his grandson in 1963 and now are a part of the ethnology collection of the Panhandle-Plains Historical Museum. [108]

After the white men had rifled the clothing and belongings of the warriors they had killed, they turned to attend to their own dead. Billy Tyler's body still lay inside the Myers and Leonard store; those of the two Scheidler brothers were on the outside where they had fallen. A few of the hide men took shovels and dug a common grave not far from where Ike Scheidler's wagon lay on its side at the north side of the corral. They then blanketed the three corpses, carried them to the pit, and quickly buried them without ceremony.[109]

The Battle of Adobe Walls had ended.

Who Was Really There?

---

*I would appreciate it very much if you would write me and give
me the names of every man that was in the fight with a Noterys
[sic] Seal . . . so it will go into the History of the State correct.
There are so meny [sic] Imposters who claim to have been there.*
—J. Wright Mooar to Andy Johnson, January 20, 1923.

No one really knows precisely which men defended themselves
from Indian attack in the 1874 Battle of Adobe Walls.[1] The number of
white participants in the fight has been reported to be as few as fifteen
and as many as thirty. Certain individuals are known without question
to have been there on the twenty-seventh of June, but for others documentation or even positive identification is either lacking or questionable. The hide men who were there did not all know each other, one
noting, for instance, that "I have heard since that Bat Masterson was in
the fight but I did not know him then." Further confusing matters is
the fact that numerous hide men came into the trading post for safety
in the days immediately following the battle, and some of them either
claimed or later were said to have participated in the fight. This clearly
was the case of hunter Frank J. Brown, who by his own statement
came into the post after the fight but who is listed on a monument at
the site as having been one of the white defenders. Finally, during the
1910s and 1920s a number of persons falsely claimed participation in
the famous battle. Most of them were probably lonely old men who
indeed had been on the frontier and who enjoyed the attention their
often repeated stories and flights of fancy received. These men ranged
from a former chief of police in Texas to a street peddler in California.
This chapter will examine the lives of the white men who either were

or claimed to have been at the trading post during the celebrated fight.[2]

Charley Armitage, an Englishman and a friend of the Cator brothers in the Old World, was one of the several foreign-born defenders of the Adobe Walls post. Billy Dixon remembered that he worked as one of his skinners during the weeks immediately preceding the battle and described him as "an agreeable fellow." Several battle participants credit Armitage with having killed the black bugler, but curiously a number of twentieth-century accounts list his name as Harry instead of Charley, and he is so listed on the monument at the battle site.[3]

Henry Born, who described himself as "known to some as Dutch Henry," is listed in most accounts of the battle as one of the white participants, a claim he himself made. He was a native of Manitowac, Wisconsin, having been born there in 1849, the son of German immigrant parents. After he fought at Adobe Walls, Born became a professional horse thief and made his name well known on the Plains. In the 1880s he headed for Colorado, where he discovered and shared in the initial wealth of the Happy Thought Mine at Creede. Perhaps with part of this money, he settled in later years beside a beautiful trout lake in the San Juan Mountains above Pagosa Springs. At what came to be known as Born's Lake, he and his wife had four children, and Born became a respected citizen of the area. His last surviving daughter wrote to the author about his last years: "Very few times of his past life was talked of at home. It seems it was another time and world and one he wished to forget. For the first 7 years they lived at the lake, he did not even have a gun in the house. He said he had all of the killing that he wanted." Dutch Henry continued living peacefully high in the Rockies until his death there on January 10, 1921.[4]

James Campbell is noted as having fought in the Battle of Adobe Walls only in twentieth-century sources. His name first appears in Edward Campbell Little's generally reliable article on the fight published in 1908, and it is repeated in Olive K. Dixon's biography of her husband. Apparently the only participant to have had any recollections of him was Fred Leonard, who in the 1920s remembered that Campbell had fought in the Myers and Leonard store and that he had been given Billy Tyler's gun after the latter was shot. No record of his activities after the fight have been located.[5]

James "Bermuda" Carlyle appears in some of the earliest accounts of the battle, and Dixon remembered him as the first person to venture from the buildings after the battle to pick up relics from the bodies of dead warriors. He was a member of the first large party of hide men to depart the trading post after the battle, but there are no later references to him in Kansas.[6] It has been speculated that the "James Carlyle" of Adobe Walls was the same person as the "Jim Carlyle" who was killed in November, 1880, when a posse attempted to arrest Billy the Kid and members of his gang at the Greathouse and Keck Ranch near White Oaks, New Mexico. Frank Collinson, who knew this same Carlyle in western Texas, reinforces the story. He related that the Carlyle who was shot had worked earlier on the buffalo range and at one time had classed hides for some of the Dodge City and Indian Territory buyers. He remembered Carlyle as "a good hide man" and as "a fine, quiet man, not the least inclined to be a gunman."[7]

William "Billy" Dixon became one of the most famous men who fought at Adobe Walls. He also became renowned for his participation in the September 12, 1874, Battle of Buffalo Wallow, in which six soldiers and scouts defended themselves against an overwhelming number of attacking Indians. For his heroism in this encounter Dixon received the Congressional Medal of Honor, which today is part of the collections of the Panhandle-Plains Historical Museum. Dixon served Gen. Nelson A. Miles as a civilian scout and later guided early surveying parties in the Panhandle. In 1894 he married Olive King, a young schoolteacher who a year earlier had come to the Texas Panhandle from Virginia, and their first home was his log cabin less than a mile from the site of the Adobe Walls fight. For a while Dixon even served as master of the Adobe Walls, Texas, post office. After a few years Dixon and his family moved to Plemons, Texas, and then on to Cimarron County, Oklahoma. It was here at the age of sixty-two that he became ill with a cold and succumbed to pneumonia on March 9, 1913; he was buried with Masonic rites at Texline, Texas. After his death Olive K. Dixon in 1914 published the first edition of her husband's biography based on information he had given her. She issued a second edition in 1927, a work that for many years was the standard account not only of his life but also of the Battle of Adobe Walls.[8]

George Eddy, the bookkeeper at the Rath and Company store, is another participant about whom little is known. Although most twentieth-century accounts show the spelling of his name as Eddy, other variants include Ebey, Enby, and Ebs, and no one knows which is correct. One account reports him as the person who shot the courageous warrior who stuck his hand through one of the loopholes in the wall of the Rath store to empty his revolver inside the building. No information has been found to document his life either before or after his tenure as a bookkeeper at the trading post.[9]

"Frenchy," whose name appears as one of the battle participants on the monument at Adobe Walls, is reported to have been in the fight by only one bona fide participant, Billy Dixon. Fred Leonard, who was also on the scene, argued that he "did not arrive until the morning of the fourth day after the fight." Dixon's statement may be more reliable, for Frenchy was the cook in his hunting outfit and one might expect him to know if his employee was there.

Frenchy's true identity can only be presumed. The most notable Frenchy on the buffalo range in the mid-1870s was James S. French, who used "Frenchy" as his alias. A white whiskey trader and occasional outlaw, he dressed like an Indian at times and frequented the Cheyenne camps. This man was the subject of a July 11, 1874, report in the *Leavenworth Daily Commercial*, which noted that "a white man called 'Frenchy,' who has been living right among the Cheyennes for two years," had been driven away "by irate red men." Leonard remembered the Frenchy at Adobe Walls not as being James S. French, but rather as Frenchy Bernard. Further complicating matters is the fact that during the 1870s a tramp known as "Frenchy" lived for some time in Dodge City, his activities often being noted in the local press. Thus, who Frenchy was or whether he actually was in the fight may never be known.[10]

James N. Hanrahan, who operated the saloon at Adobe Walls, is one of the most interesting figures in the history of the trading post. Reportedly a native of Pennsylvania, he had come west and settled at Dodge City about the time of its founding in 1872, and by 1874 he had a reputation as a seasoned frontiersman. He seems always to have taken an active interest in public affairs, and when Ford County was organized with Dodge City as its county seat in 1873, Hanrahan was appointed by the governor of Kansas to serve with Charles Rath and another local citizen as its initial county commissioners. When in the same year the first election was held in Ford County, Hanrahan was elected its first representative to the Kansas state legislature. After he learned of the plans to establish a trading post in the Texas Panhandle, Hanrahan sold his interest in a Dodge City saloon to his partner, Mose Waters, and joined with his friend Charles Rath in building and operating the saloon at Adobe Walls.[11]

Hanrahan led the first large party of hide men who left the Texas trading post after the battle, returning to Dodge City, but he did not remain there for very long. His name next appears several hundred miles to the west, in Lake City, Colorado, where in 1877 he was elected the Democratic candidate for Hinsdale County sheriff. Taking office on January 9, 1878, he served until his resignation on April 3, 1879.[12] His whereabouts for the next several years are unknown, until he resurfaced again in politics, this time in Idaho. He represented Custer County as a Populist in the Third Legislature of the state of Idaho, from 1895 to 1896. Hanrahan retired to Lost River and then Blackfoot, Idaho, where he died about the time World War I was ending in Europe.[13]

Seth Hathaway presented very convincing arguments to substantiate his participation in the 1874 Battle of Adobe Walls. His detailed description of the trading post, which generally agrees with archeological evidence, indicates that he knew the post when it was in operation, and his account of the battle not only supports most of the standard accounts but also elaborates on certain aspects of the fight. Although no other men who were there list Hathaway as a participant, this may be explained in part by the fact that he stated that he and Dutch Henry Born, who also appears in only a few listings, left the post at ten o'clock on the night after the battle to warn other hunters of the Indian danger. After reaching his own camp on the buffalo range, Hathaway returned directly to Dodge City rather than going back to the trading post. Thus, none of the other hide men who came in from their camps for protection offered by the trading post saw him there or heard his stories of the fight. Significantly, none of the verified participants disputed his claim to having been there, as was the case with most impostors.[14]

Andrew "Andy" Johnson, known as "Andy the Swede," was one of the most important of all the participants in the battle, but not because of any commanding role that he played, for no man could hold such a distinction in a fight in which it was "every man look out for himself," as Johnson stated it. Rather, it is because he lived longer than most of the Adobe Walls defenders and presented in quality and volume some of the best firsthand accounts available on the history of both the trading post and the battle.[15] Even when under pressure from old friends, Johnson refused to stretch the truth when testifying in legal suits filed in the 1890s over financial losses resulting from the fight.[16]

Andy Johnson was born at Engelholm, Sweden, on August 15, 1845, and at the age of twenty-four he left his home for the United States. After tarrying a while in Ohio, he removed to Dodge City about 1872. There he worked for several years for Charles Rath stacking buffalo hides, caring for livestock, and, as one of his associates noted in his diary for 1873, unloading and weighing boxcar loads of foodstuffs like corn and potatoes. At Adobe Walls, Andy oversaw the Rath and Company hide yard and livestock and worked around the store. He built most of the Rath store and the saloon with his own hands. He remained at the trading post until it was relieved a month after the fight and then returned with the merchandise and hides to Dodge City.

In later years Andy Johnson operated a restaurant and managed a retail liquor store, among other occupations, but he worked mainly as a blacksmith. One of his blacksmith shops stood at the location of the old Standard service station at the corner of Second and Trail streets in Dodge. In the early twentieth century, when the old board sidewalks in the city were being replaced by brick and concrete, Johnson bossed a cement crew. Many of the sidewalks he built are still in good condition and bear the letters "A. J." stamped in the concrete, a silent testimony to the quality of his workmanship. Andy returned to the site of the Adobe Walls trading post in 1922 and then again in 1924, when he was a featured guest at the fiftieth-anniversary celebration of the fight. A year later in June he passed away, his remains being interred at the Maple Grove cemetery in Dodge City.[17]

"Old Man" Keeler worked as the cook at the Myers and Leonard store complex and is known today primarily for his heroic but fictional dash for a bucket of water to relieve the thirst of the dying Billy Tyler. Very little is known about this man, whom western writer Stuart N. Lake identified in a 1951 letter to W. S. Campbell as "William Keeler." "I have been told," Lake related, "that Billy Keeler was one of the craftiest and most courageous Indian fighters and buffalo hunters that the Plains country knew. I have been told, also, that he died down around

old Fort Griffin but that information was about sixth-hand hearsay." This was more, however, than anyone else knew. Although the participation in the fight of "an old man named Keeler" was noted as early as 1877, none of the men who were there seem to have known him by any name other than "Old Man Keeler." Fred Leonard recollected only that on the morning after the fight Keeler prepared a breakfast of coffee, yeast powder bread, and fried buffalo meat for the men at his store. No one seems to have remembered or known any more about this elusive character.[18]

James Langton managed the Rath and Company store at the trading post and was an undisputed participant in the fight. Born in 1853, he was a native of Ireland, having been brought by his parents to Milwaukee, Wisconsin, as an infant. As an adult, he sought his fortune in the West, moving to Dodge City at least as early as 1872. When Charles Rath and Robert M. Wright decided to establish a branch house in the Texas Panhandle in spring, 1874, they took Langton in as a one-third partner in the new venture, and he served as its on-site manager. He remained at the trading post for the month following the battle, supervising the loading of merchandise and hides that were returned to Dodge City when the traders abandoned their stores.

Back in Kansas, James Langton turned to stock raising, a pursuit he followed through the next decade, and then he returned to merchandising. In 1877 he purchased a half-interest in the post sutler's store at Fort Dodge in partnership with his old friend, Robert M. Wright. Not long thereafter the local press reported that "since Mr. Langton's connecting with the sutler's store, times have been pretty lively at this place. A billiard table and card table have been put up and are largely patronized by the boys." By 1882 Langton and Wright also were jointly operating a meat market and by 1888 Langton had become co-owner of the Langton Hardware Company and partner with William G. Sherlock in a sewer contracting business.

In 1889 James Langton left Dodge City, his home for more than fifteen years, moving briefly to Rock Springs, Wyoming. Then he moved again, this time to Salt Lake City, where he founded the Langton Lime and Cement Company and became a wealthy man. In 1913 at the age of sixty, while on an outing in Mill Creek Canyon near Salt Lake City, he drove his automobile off the approach to a highway bridge and was killed instantly. Thus a man who had survived the Indian attack at Adobe Walls lived to a ripe old age before becoming a victim of the automobile.[19]

Henry Lease is mentioned in many accounts of the history of the trading post as one of the battle participants, but the only person there during the fight who asserted his participation was Dixon. Leonard stated that Lease did not come into the trading post from his camp on the buffalo range until the morning of the fourth day after the fight. Some versions of the Adobe Walls story credit him with having carried the first message from the trading post to Dodge City after the battle, a message written by Fred Leonard. Since Leonard ought to have known about Lease if indeed he was the messenger, evidence more strongly suggests that Henry Lease was not a participant in the fight. Even so, his name is chiseled in the granite of the battle monument.[20]

Frederick J. Leonard, co-owner with A. C. Myers of one of the stores at Adobe Walls, is one of the major characters in the history of the trading post. He was born in London, England, on November 24, 1849, but well before the Civil War his family had immigrated to America, settling at Lawrence, Kansas. He was a resident of that city at the time of the famous Quantrill raid. By the early 1870s he had moved westward to Dodge City, where he formed his business partnership with Myers. When he and Myers established their branch mercantile store at Adobe Walls, Leonard assumed its management. He stayed on the scene after the June 27, 1874, battle until the relief party arrived to remove the traders' merchandise and hides to Dodge City.

Back in Kansas, Fred Leonard for a few years operated one of the most popular restaurants in Dodge City. A report in the local newspaper noted that "his restaurant is finely furnished in table ware, cutlery, &c . . . [and] furnishes the finest [foods] the market affords." The article continued that "the most fastidious palate or epicure can satiate their appetites at his board [where] Mr. Leonard furnishes fresh oysters in season, and he serves them up in every style." Fred Leonard, considered to be among "the best people" in Dodge City, clearly was prominent socially. Contemporary reports repeatedly note his participation in organizing and conducting dances, balls, and other social affairs for which "his natural gifts and experience" were greatly admired.

In 1879 Leonard left Dodge City for another part of the state, and then in 1883 he moved to Salt Lake City. There he sold real estate, stocks, and bonds; served as county tax collector; and operated as a mining broker before becoming the manager of the Cullen Hotel in about 1910. He remained there until his death from arthritis at the age of seventy-eight on August 4, 1928.[21]

Mike McCabe was a hide skinner who worked for such outfits as those of J. Wright Mooar, James and Robert Cator, and Billy Dixon, being one of the latter's men at the time of the famous battle. With flaming red hair and a fiery temper, McCabe was a moody person. "Mike would fight at the drop of the hat," Dixon recalled, and "would sulk for weeks at a time over a fancied wrong." Because of this temperament, most of Mike's friends knew him as "Cranky" or "Fighting" McCabe. He was a compulsive gambler, Billy Dixon remembered: "There was something he had to get out of his system, and after he had been purged he was ready to resume his old ways. . . . A single night at the card table in Dodge City generally wound up McCabe's ball of yarn, and at once he was ready to return to the buffalo range without a complaint. . . . There was not a lazy bone in his body, and I never had a better hand." J. Wright Mooar had similar memories of Cranky McCabe. After he and his crew had come into Dodge City from a hunting trip, "Mike celebrated our return . . . by getting on a protracted spree, and was left at Dodge." Receipts for goods purchased indicate that after the fight at Adobe Walls, Mike McCabe became a skinner for the Cator brothers, but there are no references to him after that.[22]

James W. McKinley, fortunately for historians, was one of the participants who felt that he had witnessed history and subsequently recorded his reminiscences. His typescript account of the fight is one of the few such valuable sources.[23] No one who fought at the trading post seems to have had very much to say about James McKinley, but he was definitely a member of the first party of hide men who departed the post for Dodge City in July, 1874. Later in the summer he participated in the Lyman's Wagon Train Fight, his narrative of that encounter being one of the few firsthand accounts available. After the Indian troubles were over, McKinley settled in the Texas Panhandle, where he lived until the first decade of the twentieth century. Because of health problems, however, he traveled to the mineral water baths at Hot Springs, Arkansas, where, as a friend later recalled, he "was found dead in a bath tub March 1910."[24]

William Barclay "Bat" Masterson is probably the best known of all the white men who fought at Adobe Walls. He had been a hunter and skinner working out of Dodge City before he headed south to Texas in spring, 1874. Exactly what he was doing at the trading post is uncertain, for Johnson remembered him as one of Dixon's skinners and Leonard noted that he was an employee at the Myers and Leonard store. Whatever the case, when the Indians attacked, Masterson ran to the saloon and fought from there except for a brief foray from that building to the Myers store to bring back ammunition. Some accounts state that he was the youngest white man in the fight. He also was a member of the first large party of hunters to leave the post for Dodge City in July, 1874. Masterson served as a scout for the U.S. Army in the subsequent campaign in the Panhandle, but it was in Dodge, his home before the fight, that he remained for the next few years, serving as sheriff there during the heyday of the Texas cattle drives. He later left Dodge City, engaging in several different occupations, including promoting professional sporting events and dealing in liquor, but he became best known in later years as a journalist in New York City, where he died in 1921.[25]

Fred Myers appears in a number of the early accounts of Adobe Walls as one of the participants who fought at the Myers and Leonard store. Although circumstantial evidence suggests that he may have been a relation of store co-owner A. C. Myers, this has not been proved. In the first message from the trading post after the battle, Leonard noted that "Fred Myers killed two Indians." J. Wright Mooar almost fifty years after the battle wrote to Johnson about his recollections, reporting that Fred Myers was one of the party that John Wesley Mooar recruited at the Myers and Leonard store to help move their hides across the flood-swollen Canadian River only a short time before the fight. Despite all this documentation, very few twentieth-century accounts of the Adobe Walls story even mention Fred Myers. His name does not appear on the monument at the battle site, and no data have been located to shed light on his activities after the merchants abandoned their stores in the Panhandle.[26]

Billy Ogg, one of Jim Hanrahan's employees and probably a skinner, was one of the first white men to spot the Indians charging toward the Adobe Walls trading post. Most accounts of the first moments in the fight state that Billy Dixon raised the alarm, but Dixon himself disagreed repeatedly by giving the distinction to Ogg. Unfortunately, the hide man's actions at the beginning of the fight are all that is known of him, other than the fact that he returned to Dodge City in July, 1874. No further details of his life have been found.[27]

Thomas O'Keefe was the blacksmith at Adobe Walls. Little is known about this man except that he participated in the battle. He was sleeping in the open when awakened by the alarm that the Indians were coming, and he dashed to the Rath store, awakening its inmates with his cries to open up and with the sound of his bare foot kicking the door. O'Keefe fought in that building during the engagement, and then a month later he returned to Dodge City with the first large party of hunters to go there from the Walls.[28]

Hannah and William Olds served as cook and clerk, respectively, at the Rath and Company store and were present at the time of the battle. The married couple had operated a boardinghouse at Dodge City before coming to Texas. One early twentieth-century account cites William Olds as having come from Warsaw, Missouri, but this has not been confirmed. After the battle and following the accidental death of her husband, Mrs. Olds returned to Dodge City, and there were no further references to her.[29]

Isaac and Jacob Scheidler, better known to the hide men and to history as "Ike" and "Shorty," were the two teamsters who were killed outside the store buildings early in the fight on June 27, 1874. Little is known about these two men except that Fred Leonard's brother knew them in Neosho County, Kansas, before the battle and that Dubbs reported them as having been cousins of his wife. They had undertaken employment as teamsters on the plains because one of them suffered from tuberculosis and they hoped that a life in the open air would help cure his disease. Although accounts vary concerning the circumstances of their death at the hands of the Indians, there is no question that their bodies were found by the other hide men after the fight and that they were buried in a common grave with Billy Tyler on the north side of the Myers and Leonard corral. Their remains lie there today, and a tombstone was erected on the site in 1924.[30]

Oscar Shepherd was James Hanrahan's bartender at the Adobe Walls trading post, but little else is known about him. He is cited by some as being one of the two men whom Hanrahan sent atop the saloon to remove sod and decrease the weight on the ridgepole early on the morning of the fight. Dixon remembered that he secured the .50-

caliber Sharps rifle that he used during most of the battle from Shepherd, who was a poor marksman. About two weeks after the fight he joined the first large group of hide men leaving the post, arriving back in Dodge City on July 17, 1874, and nothing more is known of his life after this time.[31]

Frank Smith and *Sam Smith*, men whose names often are confused in accounts of the fight, may indeed have been the same person. They are listed as separate individuals in John Coulter's pioneering 1877 article on Adobe Walls, strong evidence that there were two Smiths. Leonard reported a Frank Smith as one of his employees, and many years later, in June, 1928, when a man by this name died in Brooklyn, New York, he was reported to have claimed participation in the fight.[32] Sam Smith's name appears even earlier, in a July, 1874, list of hide men who had left the trading post and arrived in Dodge City. More bona fide participants remembered there being a Sam Smith in the fight than recalled anyone named Frank Smith, among them Johnson and Dixon, both of whom are generally reliable sources. Then, in 1909 Edgar Rye edited and published in his book, *The Quirt and the Spur*, the reputed first-person reminiscences of Sam Smith's participation in the battle. The distinction between the two men might be clear had not an article been published in the *Hutchinson* (Kansas) *Herald* in 1929, which reported that "the last survivor" of the Battle of Adobe Walls, "Frank Smith, sometimes known as 'Sam' Smith," had some time before died in Brooklyn, information the author had secured from Olive K. Dixon. It is unlikely that more will be known about these two men—or one man—who clearly must have been in the fight.[33]

Edward Trevor is noted briefly in several accounts, among them those of Dixon and Leonard, as having fought in the Myers and Leonard store. Leonard remembered him as being the only person in the store not armed with a buffalo gun. No records concerning his life either before or after the battle have been located.[34]

William "Billy" Tyler was a teamster at Adobe Walls at the time of the fight. An 1874 report of the battle stated that he was an employee of Charles Rath, but much later Leonard stated that he was one of his employees. Since all accounts of the fight place Tyler at the Myers and Leonard complex, the evidence suggests that he was indeed an employee of that firm. Tyler had been on the buffalo range at least since 1872, and then in August of the following year Dodge City hide man

H. H. Raymond noted in his diary that he had "fixed my belt to hold 45 cartridges with some buck skin Billy Tyler gave me." Although the circumstances of Tyler's death are clouded by conflicting reports, it is certain that his body was removed to the north side of the Myers and Leonard corral to be buried with those of the two Scheidler brothers.[35]

Hiram Watson is yet another participant in the battle about whom very little is known. The early twentieth-century accounts of the fight state that he accompanied Billy Ogg on his way to bring in the horses early on the morning of the fight, but the report is not confirmed by additional sources. Other than the information that he fought from the saloon, none of his activities during the fight was remembered or recorded by any participant. With the exception of one brief notation that he was a member of the first large party of hide men who left Adobe Walls for Dodge City in July, 1874, we know nothing of his later life. More than twenty years later Gen. Hugh Scott at Fort Sill noted that "Watson, the driver at [Fort] Sill was in his wagon [at Adobe Walls] 400 yards from the store, was waked up by his employee who thought that he heard wolves—they was the Indians coming & [the two white men] barely got into the store 100 yds ahead of the Indians." Thus, in the 1890s Hiram Watson must have worked as a driver at Fort Sill. As late as 1945 an account of the Adobe Walls battle written by one James A. Watson, who claimed to have been the Watson in the fight, was published in a popular national magazine.[36]

Mike Welsh was another of James Hanrahan's employees, probably a skinner. Most accounts of the ridgepole incident state that he was one of the men who went atop the saloon roof to remove some of the sod. Reports of the Adobe Walls fight published in 1874 and 1877 give his surname as Welsh, the spelling used by Leonard and in this work. Most twentieth-century versions of the story, however, show it as Welch, apparently based on the spelling used in the 1908 article on the battle written by E. C. Little. No references to Welsh after he returned to Dodge City from Adobe Walls in July, 1874, have been found.[37]

These men, with perhaps one or two exceptions, most likely did take part in the 1874 Battle of Adobe Walls. In addition, however, a remarkable number of other people later claimed to have participated in the fight. Still others were falsely placed there by various writers. Ascertaining who fought requires careful sifting of fact from fiction, but as most of the impostors made mistakes in their accounts, they can be separated from the bona fide participants.

Dr. G. H. Branham of Menard, Texas, is typical of the men who in old age claimed to have fought at Adobe Walls. In 1937 Rupert Norval Richardson, authority on the history of the Comanche Indians, secured an autobiographical sketch of Branham, who claimed to have been one of the handful of whites at the trading post at the time of the battle. According to Branham, he had time to make his horse lie down beside a wall and to tie its feet "so he could not get up" before the horde of warriors descended on the stores. Branham then related that he and four other men, all later killed, successfully left the protection of the buildings to kill the black bugler at some distance from the post. Such notions are fanciful.[38]

John J. Clinton of Abilene, Texas, was one of the best known of the Adobe Walls impostors. As the chief of police in the Texas town, he had the respect of the local citizens, who seemed to believe his tales without question. As early as 1916 Clinton was claiming to have fought at Adobe Walls, telling such stories as his joining Billy Dixon, Billy Tyler, and the two Scheidler brothers in hiding themselves in a wagon in order to ambush and shoot the black bugler. Of this man J. Wright Mooar declared, "There are so meny [*sic*] imposters who claim to have been there . . . one man in particular, J. J. Clinton of Abilene, Tex[as]. I have contradicted his acts several times but as I was not there that day of the fight . . . what I know . . . don[']t am[oun]t to anything as evidence." Wright Mooar was justified in his efforts, for undoubtedly John J. Clinton was not in the fight.[39]

R. S. Davis was perhaps the most entertaining of all the impostors. He was a peddler on the streets of Fresno, California, in the mid-1920s, selling "a cure for the tobacco habit on Mariposa street." Perhaps as a means of retaining the attention of his audiences long enough to sell them his patent medicines, he told incredible, exciting stories about his purported exploits on the frontier. Davis, for instance, claimed that he had become a Texas Ranger at thirteen years of age and that as a Ranger he was one of twenty-seven whites who in one day killed ninety-seven Indians at Adobe Walls. At the end of the second day after the fight, Davis stated, the hide men were rescued when "General McKenzie [*sic*] arrived with a mounted troop of 320 men." The peddler concluded his tale this way: "When the excitement was over

McKenzie returned to 'Dobe Wall and inquired who had commanded our boys. Well, I had, and it happened that at the time I was known on the border as 'Napoleon Bonaparte' Davis, so one of the rangers spoke up: 'It was "Napoleon" over here, General.'"[40]

Emanuel Dubbs, who in the late 1870s became a prominent Texas Panhandle citizen, all his older years asserted that he had fought at Adobe Walls. Among all the men who claimed this distinction, in Dubbs it is the most difficult to separate fact from fiction. A Civil War veteran of the Union army, he was one of the early Dodge City buffalo hunters who specialized in hunting bison for their meat. This he cured and sold at settlements in eastern Kansas. After the buffalo herds were decimated, he began operating a combination dairy parlor and beer garden on Duck Creek near Dodge. Later in the 1870s he moved permanently to his old hunting grounds in the Texas Panhandle, and in 1878 he was elected the first county judge of Wheeler County. Dubbs lived until 1929, much of this time serving as a Disciples of Christ minister, and through many of these years he claimed to have fought in the famous 1874 battle.

Emanuel Dubbs was indeed a buffalo hunter in the Texas Panhandle during summer, 1874. His published description of the Adobe Walls trading post is sound and in accord with most other authentic accounts. Where his story seems to go astray is in his claim to have come into the post on the night before the battle, having fled Indians who had destroyed his camp and killed his men, an event that apparently did take place. Dubbs reported in his published reminiscences in 1909 that he was eating breakfast at the Walls when the Indians attacked, but here he cuts short his account of the battle. His explanation is that "when I commenced writing these reminiscences I only agreed with Mr. Hart to furnish about five thousand words, and as I have written more than that now, I cannot go farther into this history." In reality he probably did not know any more to say about the actual fight, for he continued to write page after page about other aspects of his life.

What Dubbs did write about the Battle of Adobe Walls must have been based on what he knew from his own experiences there before and after the engagement and from men who did participate in the fight. Historian J. Evetts Haley characterized Dubbs as "an honest, if long-winded man." Andy Johnson was more candid. When a member of the audience at the 1924 fiftieth-anniversary celebration of the Adobe Walls fight asked him if Dubbs had fought in the battle, Andy answered, "No, I think he was in Dodge City at that time." Not a single man who was in the fight remembered Dubbs as having been there. Frank Collinson, who knew many of the participants, was not so polite as Johnson. In a letter to western artist Harold Bugbee discussing Dubbs's published account, he declared, "I pronounced it a damed [*sic*] lie when it came out." The overwhelming evidence indicates that Emanuel Dubbs was not in the fight.[41]

A *Mexican teamster* is mentioned in passing in several accounts of the battle. Johnson related in 1911 that such a person had been sleeping in the wagon with the two Scheidler brothers and awakened and ran to the Myers and Leonard complex before the Indians surrounded the post. Robert M. Wright, co-owner of one of the stores, noted in 1913 that "a Mexican bull-whacker" had been killed at the same time the two brothers were slain. Another version of the story stated that the Mexican teamster met death at the hands of the attacking warriors after he ran back from the store to awaken the Scheidler brothers. Further confusing matters is the report from Fred Leonard in 1923 that on the night after the battle "a Mexican named Juan, who had spent the day in hiding while the furious fighting was going on," sneaked back to the post under the cover of darkness "and was accorded security in the camp." From these conflicting reports, all coming from or purportedly based on the remembrances of battle participants, we simply do not know whether the Mexican participated in the fight or even if he existed at all.[42]

Moccasin Jim is listed in John Coulter's pioneer article on Adobe Walls published in 1877, the first known account of the fight as a historical incident. Since the name does not appear in any version of the story coming from men who were there, it was most likely an erroneous addition to the generally quite reliable Coulter account.[43]

W. K. Myers of Cottonwood Falls, Kansas, was another of the better known impostors. He claimed to have been cooking his breakfast at Adobe Walls when the Indians attacked, and in later years he presented a fairly accurate story of the battle, although he varied from fact in several places. His most obvious misconception was that the defenders of the stores "could easily fight off the Indians," a statement quite far from the truth, for in the first minutes of the battle the hide men came very near to being overwhelmed. In response to a question about W. K. Myers, in 1935 Olive K. Dixon wrote to author Joseph Masters that "I would not want to get up a discussion on the subject," continuing that "all I have to say is that it is too bad that Mr. Myers waited until all the rest of the participants were dead before he made himself known." [44]

John Otterby, who also called himself *Chief Lean Elk*, presented one of the most entertaining stories of fictional participation in the fight. A Cheyenne Indian, he claimed to have left his band and to have drifted southward into the Texas Panhandle, where he became a skinner for a buffalo hunting outfit. He asserted that the hide men gathered at the trading post for a conference before the battle, and that at this time "I was at the Adobe Walls with the buffalo hunters when they had their fight." It is difficult to imagine the hide men at the Walls tolerating the presence of an Indian before the fight, and certainly not during it. Otterby's stories clearly were a figment of his imagination. [45]

Scott Miller is listed as a participant in the 1874 Battle of Adobe Walls in an account published in about 1915 that was supposedly based on information provided by men who were there. The garbled account of his part in the fighting relates that it was Miller who first blazed away at the attacking Indians in the semidarkness on the morning of the twenty-seventh, "spitting out death and demoralization from the mouth of his buffalo gun upon the savages as they madly careened around the place on their wiry ponies." There definitely was a hide man in the Panhandle named Scott Miller, for he is noted in a fragmentary financial account kept by the two Cator brothers for February, 1878, and is noted by a historian as having been a cowboy on the LX Ranch around 1880. Only one version of the story lists him as one of the defenders of Adobe Walls. [46]

Henry Wert (Wertz) is listed in John Coulter's 1877 article on the battle as having fought there. He was noted in 1874 as having been a member of the first party of hide men to leave the trading post for Dodge City, and because he came into Dodge from the post Coulter probably assumed that he had been in the fight and mistakenly included him as one of the defenders. No other accounts mention his name. [47]

In addition to these individuals, who either themselves claimed or were claimed by others to have been in the Adobe Walls fight, a number of other persons are listed in sketchy or questionable accounts as having been among the defenders. These men include "Blinky Jack," [48] A. J. Chappell, [49] a man named Clark, [50] a man named Cunningham, [51] "Spotty" Dunlop, [52] George May, [53] Fred W. Schmalsle, "Wall-Eyed" Bill Sellew, George Steel, a man named Tripp, J. E. Woods, Ira Wing, [54] and M. K. Wyatt. [55] None of them are known to have been participants.

Having analyzed the question of who really was at the Adobe Walls trading post at the time of the famous battle, we now turn to examining the history of the events that transpired there after the end of the fighting on the afternoon of June 27, 1874. This is a part of the Adobe Walls story never before examined in detail. Most writers simply assumed that after the fight the post was abandoned and that the traders and hide men retreated to Dodge City, having been driven from the Panhandle. Although in time the white men did abandon their "houses on the Canadian," the events that unfolded there in summer and autumn, 1874, are much more complex than appear on the surface. In fact, the events at Adobe Walls after the fight are among the most interesting of its history.

CHAPTER 5

Adobe Walls after the Fight

---

*We have been attacked by Indians, and corralled since June
27th, . . . but I am willing to stay if I can get sufficient men to
guard the place. . . . All men are of the opinion that the Indians
are waiting for reinforcements, and then give us another rattle.*
—Fred Leonard to A. C. Myers, July 1, 1874.

T HE traders and hide men at Adobe Walls on the evening of June 27
had no idea what havoc they had wreaked on Isatai and Quanah's
plans.[1] The demoralized warriors realized that the medicine man's
claims to power were baseless. Even though some members of the
huge war party remained in the area for several days nursing their
wounds and occasionally taking shots at the trading post, they made
no concentrated assaults. Believing that the warriors were waiting for
reinforcements to come from the Indian Territory, the hide men fortified their positions at the post and awaited attacks that never came.
In the meantime they dispatched messengers to Dodge City with pleas
for help. The military authorities in Kansas, however, refused to send
relief, so the Dodge City merchants were forced to organize their own
party of frontiersmen and teamsters to come to the aid of the trading
post that they supposed was still under siege.

By the time the hide men had pilfered their souvenirs from the
bodies of the dead Indians nearby and buried Billy Tyler and the
Scheidler brothers, darkness had begun to descend on Adobe Walls.
Fearing a night attack, they retreated to the two stores, abandoning the
saloon building. Fred Leonard later remembered that "nearly everybody became panicky and nearly all went down to Langton's[,] which
was a large adobe [sod] building [and] I had a hard time keeping six

men with me." From that night of nervousness, James McKinley remembered years later that one of the guards alarmed and awakened
the entire post by shooting at what he thought was a warrior creeping
toward one of the buildings. "It was a dog and the sentry made a good
shot," he recalled. Billy Dixon was one of the many fighters who had
nightmares. "I dreamed all night, the bloody scenes of the day passing in
endless procession through my mind—I could see the Indians charging
across the valley, hear the roar of guns and the blood-curdling war-
whoops, until everything was a bewildering swirl of fantastic colors
and movements."[2]

The few men who had spent the night at the Myers and Leonard
store were met in the morning with the fragrance of breakfast being cooked by "Old Man" Keeler. Fred Leonard remembered that he
cooked up a heaping meal of hot yeast powder bread and fried buffalo
meat with a big pot of coffee, "all of which was relished by the hungry
Indian fighters, who had no time to eat the previous day."[3]

At first light a few Indians began shooting at the buildings from
some distance, but the fire was ineffectual, and most of the hide men
paid it little notice. They did, however, begin to consider the desolation and destruction that surrounded them. All about them the hunters
saw dead stock. Every horse, mule, and ox had been driven away by
the attackers or killed. Even Hannah Olds's pet colt had been shot with
arrows. Mingled with the dead animals were the bodies of fallen warriors, who the evening before had been stripped of most of their re-
galia by the hunters. Already the stench from the decomposing animal
and human flesh was growing; it would become worse.

Inside the stores things were almost as bad. During the fight merchandise had been piled up against doors and windows, as well as
against the picket walls of the Myers and Leonard store, and many
goods not removed from place had been knocked or shot down during
the battle. Broken glass from bottles and windows was everywhere. In
both stores canned goods had been burst by bullets, the food inside
running out over the shelves and down the walls. The weather was
hot, and the sticky mess drew flies by the hundreds. Everything was in
shambles.[4]

Probably the worst problem for the hide men and merchants was
morale. All of them feared another, even larger attack. Many wanted
to leave the post for Dodge City and safety, but the fear of the Indians

still about and lack of horses forced them to remain where they were. Nerves were on edge. Most of the hide men thought the warriors were busy scouring the surrounding country, killing their friends and partners in their camps on the buffalo range. Fortunately, most of the camps were well to the west, and the majority of the hunters and skinners were spared, but the men at Adobe Walls did not know this. A gloom fell over the defenders, depression that deepened with the accidental death of another of their small party.[5]

Only shortly after the battle the inmates of the two stores began to fortify their positions. As one precaution, the defenders established lookout posts atop the buildings where the men might more easily spot approaching attackers. While standing guard on the roof of the Rath store, William Olds observed a party of warriors some distance away. Calling out excitedly, he started climbing down the rough wooden ladder that reached from an opening in the roof to the floor of the store. Billy Dixon, perhaps after hearing the cry of alarm, entered the room. "I saw Olds coming down the ladder with his gun in hand," he later recalled. "A moment later his gun went off accidentally, tearing off the top of Old's [*sic*] head. At the same instant Mrs. Olds rushed from an adjoining room—in time to see the body of her husband roll from the ladder and crumple at her feet, a torrent of blood gushing from the terrible wound." William Olds died instantly, the gunshot having entered just below his chin and having passed entirely through his skull, scattering his brains about the room in a grisly fashion. The hide men and traders did all in their power to comfort Hannah Olds, but as one writer early in this century noted, "It was hard to bear the burden of his loss with the evidence of the accident before her." That day another grave was added to those already at Adobe Walls, and the pall fell more heavily over its defenders.[6]

Even before they began fortifying their positions, the hide men at Adobe Walls struggled to remove the decomposing animals and Indians lying near the buildings. James H. Cator, who came into the post shortly after the fight, described the scene.

> Right on the west of Mr. Rath's buildings were the hides, and below, two Indians lay there dead. Right at the next building, which was the saloon, . . . I do not think more than twenty five or thirty yards [away], five Indians lay dead. A little further west of them there was another Indian lying shot right through the knee. He was dead. On the east side of

A. C. Myers' building one Indian lay dead. Some of them that had been lying close to the buildings had been drawn away. On the north side of Myers' building another Indian was dead. . . . There were dead horses lying all about. . . .

The Cheyennes have their hair long, they do not trim it, but braid it with little pieces of ribbon, and are very careful of it, more so than the others. A number of those were lying there. . . .

Some [of the dead warriors were] in blue blankets, some red, some naked; nothing on at all but a breech clout. Some of them had a kind of light grayish robe thing on, with spots on it. . . .

[Their warbonnets] looked like a scalpthing [*sic*]—fitted close to the head, with long tail feathers stic[k]ing out. When it was doubled up these were inside, they fitten [*sic*] right in, but when it was opened out the feathers stuck straight up.[7]

Each person at the trading post had his own memories of the animal carcasses and Indian bodies. Dixon remembered the "high carnival" that the hide men's pet crow held as it flew from one carcass to another. The stench remained the most indelible of Johnson's recollections. Much later in life he still remembered with distaste that the day after the fight the smell grew so bad that the hide men began to roll the putrifying animals, now bloated by the heat, onto dry buffalo hides and to pull them some distance away. Most accounts report that the men placed them in a large pit and buried them.[8]

While this was going on, the first of the hide men from the buffalo range had started coming into the trading post for safety. Many of them had heard the sound of distant gunfire the day before and presumed that a fight was going on, but others paid no attention, thinking that it was only the sound of other hunters at work.[9]

For the week to ten days after the battle, more hunters and skinners abandoned their camps on the plains and in the stream valleys to seek refuge at the stores. Initially, the movement was just a trickle of men and animals, but by July 1, Fred Leonard could report that there were enough men at the post to "stand off 500 Indians" and that his corral was filled with stock. Warnings, at first carried by men on foot, had been sent to the hide men in their camps as soon as the fight was over.[10] James Cator in 1892 recalled that "the night of the 28th, a man came in from the Walls . . . and told us the place had been attacked and we had better come in." While he, his brother, and their crew were gone, the Indians sacked their camp.[11]

Frank J. Brown left an especially vivid account of the events surrounding his outfit's return to safety at Adobe Walls. Hearing the sound
of heavy gunfire from the direction of the trading post and knowing
that Indians were in the vicinity, they assumed that a big fight was under
way. Fearing that their lives were in danger if they remained at their
camp, Brown and his men decided to return to Adobe Walls by way of
the plains rather than by following their usual route along the Canadian River valley. When on the next day they sighted the Walls from
the bluffs above, the Brown crew members could see that Indians
were all over the surrounding hills. They had no choice except to pro-
ceed. "The Indians were thick on every side but I noticed they kept
out of range of the guns from the stockade," Brown later recalled. The
outfit formed at the top of the escarpment, a man driving each wagon
and others at the sides on horseback, all with guns and ammunition
ready. "We started 'likity split' down the hill," Brown said. The men at
the post and the Indians both spotted the wagons and horsemen about
the same time, the marksmen at the Myers and Leonard store firing at
the warriors as they tried to head off the approaching hide men. Finally, a party of hunters rode out from the trading post to meet the
Brown outfit and accompany it to the stockade corral. As the Indians
fell back, Brown recalled: "We whipped up our horses and went in on
the run. The men had the gate open. If they hadn't come to meet us
and shot so well from inside, I don't believe we'd ever made it." [12]

Not all the hide men returned to Adobe Walls. Several parties,
such as those of Seth Hathaway, Jim Lane, and George Ray, upon hearing of the attack on the trading post returned directly to Dodge City.
Others like the Dick Bussell crew decided that their pocketbooks
were more important than their scalps. They remained on the plains
despite the Indian danger, but they definitely were in the minority. [13]

The men stranded at the trading post had waited for other hunters to come in before they attended to the bodies of the Indians. They
presumed that they would be able to use the horses of the new arrivals
to pull away the bodies, but the men from the outlying camps apparently had other ideas. Instead of drawing away the remains of the
dozen or so braves who had fallen near the buildings, the hardened
hide men severed the heads and used them to decorate the crosspiece
that supported the big gate to the Myers and Leonard corral. The
heads were scalped and then stuck on the wooden pegs holding the

rocks that counterbalanced the weight of the portal. W. C. Cox, one of the hide men who participated in the grim proceedings, later remembered that "we pitched out their headless bodies like you would a dead dog's." The remains lay there for at least the next three years, for in 1877, J. Phelps White visited the site and there found "the skeletons of some twelve or fifteen Indians out behind the houses where the boys had dragged and left them." The scene must have been grisly indeed, for many years later "Brick" Bond, a hunter who had sought refuge at the trading post, remembered that "they were a hideous looking sight, for they looked like they had been laughing when their heads were cut off." [14]

The Indians lingered in the area around Adobe Walls for about a week. During these several days there was occasional skirmishing by both sides. When the Cator brothers' outfit came into the Walls, for instance, it exchanged gunfire with a war party at a range of about four hundred to five hundred yards, with no casualties on either side. On the day after the fight, according to Johnson, a party of warriors passed within sight of Adobe Walls driving a herd of loose horses, perhaps animals stolen from outlying hunters' camps. There were just enough Indians in the area to make the men at the stores apprehensive about returning to their isolated camps. [15]

By the fourth night after the battle, the evening of July 1, 1874, the traders decided to try to send a messenger from Adobe Walls through the hostile territory to Dodge City. His message, recorded in the Kansas press and even fully reprinted in the *New York Times*, was twofold. The letter, written by Frederick J. Leonard to his partner, A. C. Myers, reported the battle and besieged state of the trading post and asked that a relief party be sent to remove the merchandise from its perilous position, exposed to attack and destruction by the Indians. Leonard reported, "The hunters are sick of hunting so they say, and are apt to leave without a moment's warning," leaving the goods unprotected. He continued, "If you can get an escort of 60 men, send [A. J.] Anthony's, or all of the horse teams you can get." If the hostilities subsided and the hunters went back to the buffalo range, manager Leonard added, he would send another courier with the message that he would stay on the scene to continue his commerce with the hide men. [16]

Both Billy Dixon and J. Wright Mooar remembered Henry Lease as being the courier. George Bellfield, a German-born hide man, supplied the horse, which the courageous Lease led away in the dark at the end of a forty-foot lasso. The moon was still full as he made his way on foot south to the Canadian, where he mounted and quietly rode upstream several miles before heading northward across the plains toward Dodge City. Traveling only at night to avoid detection, he arrived at Dodge City on Sunday, July 5. Most of the hide men back at the Walls probably doubted that Lease would make it through alive. Perhaps these concerns led them to dispatch another courier two or three days later. He was probably the same man that Sam Smith remembered as being named Reed. He made his way safely across the plains to arrive in Dodge on July 8 with a message that the post was still under siege.[17]

There is no question that the two couriers were paid for risking their lives, but the reports of the payment are contradictory. Andy Johnson on various occasions recalled that a man was paid either $150 or $200 to carry the message. Robert M. Wright later reported that "our manager down there, Langton . . . gave them [two messengers] two hundred dollars to ride up to Dodge," indicating that the messengers divided the money, whereas Langton himself remembered that "we paid . . . two men to carry the news" at a cost of $250.[18]

Even before the hunters had begun deserting the buffalo range for the comparative safety of Adobe Walls, the defenders at the post had begun fortifying their positions in the two stores. Besides adding loopholes at appropriate locations, they eventually constructed fortified observation posts atop the two structures. Johnson described these lookouts as "another wall on top of our buildings so that we might be better able to protect ourselves from attack." Holes were cut in the roofs to provide access by ladders from the interior, one of these being the one on which William Olds fumbled and shot himself.[19] The Myers and Leonard complex had a well near its mess hall in one corner of the corral, but the source of water for the Rath store was a spring six hundred or seven hundred yards away. Consequently, Andy Johnson excavated a shallow well inside the store to give its defenders a supply of water should they again be attacked.[20]

As the hide men came in from the range, all of them wanted to sleep inside the protection of the store walls. Within a week there were between one hundred and two hundred men at the two stores,[21] one of the Rath employees remembering that "they . . . made their beds on the floor, on the counters—every place in the building. One

man made his bed by the well." While on guard duty one night, Andy
Johnson was surprised, as was everyone else in the store, to hear the
sound of water splashing. Obviously someone had fallen into the well.
Johnson recalled with a touch of humor: "I went to the well and asked,
'What's the matter.' He started swearing and cursing and said, 'I could
kill the man that dug this well,' I was the one . . . but you can see that
he did not kill me."[22]

As another means of making their positions more secure, the hide
men set about tearing down the huge stacks of buffalo hides that stood
at each of the stores. They had provided shelter for the attacking Indians during the fight, and the men at the post feared that the warriors
would use them again should another attack come. One of the Rath
and Company men would later recall, "When the hunters came in,
they wanted to know why the stacks were torn down. We told them
that we had had a little Indian trouble."[23] About twenty years after the
battle, the merchants who had owned the stores at Adobe Walls filed
suits in the U.S. Court of Claims for the recovery of the losses they had
suffered at the hands of the Indians, and a major portion of their claims
was for hides lost. In the suits the traders declared under sworn oaths
that the Indians, not the hide men, had torn down the stacks of hides
during the fight and that the skins were ruined by heavy rainfall—and
this in a summer that was known for its drought. Clearly, they did
more than stretch the truth in their efforts to secure compensation.[24]

While the work to fortify the stores was under way, Andy Johnson,
perhaps for the sake of morale among the men, made a flag. Taking
several Indian blankets from the many strewn on the ground, he sewed
them together to make a field and then from a red blanket cut a big
five-pointed star, placing it in the center "as a symbol of the Lone Star
State." George Bellfield, one of the first hunters to abandon his camp,
saw it from the distance as he approached the trading post. He thought
that the traders were playing some sort of joke and remembered re-
marking to his crew, "Dem fellers think day's damn smart, alretty."
Then Bellfield started seeing the dead horses strewn about and, put-
ting the whip to his own animals, he came into the post at a dead run.[25]

The hunters continued coming into Adobe Walls for their own
safety, but after the Indians had disappeared from the immediate neigh-
borhood, many hunters decided that they would be better off returning to Dodge City. The merchants at the post had stopped buying

hides, as they had no means of removing them to Dodge, so the hunters had no place to sell their skins other than the Kansas market. This placed the traders in a difficult position, for they still needed the hide men, or at least some of them, to stay at the post to help defend their merchandise and accumulation of hides. The problem became most serious just before July 13.

On that day a large party of hide men led by former saloon keeper James N. Hanrahan departed the post. No word had been heard from Dodge City after the two messengers had been dispatched there, and the hide men were itchy to get back to Dodge. They were afraid that both couriers had been caught and slain by the Indians and that as a result no one even had heard of the fight.

Billy Dixon, a member of the group, remembered the trip in some detail. From the trading post the hide men went up Short Creek to the plains, traveling to the west of the main trail to avoid any war parties that might be watching the usual route, and they reached the head of Palo Duro Creek the evening of the first day. The second day they rode to San Francisco Creek, where they found the badly mutilated and decomposed body of Charlie "Dublin" Sharp, Henry Lease's partner. They buried the body at the crossing and then on the third day continued on toward the northeast, camping that night on Crooked Creek, where they felt themselves safe from Indian attack. The fourth day, July 17, saw their arrival in Dodge City, where Dixon recalled that "the whole town turned out to see us . . . everybody . . . anxious to learn the particulars" of the fight.[26]

The traders convinced a number of men to remain at the post until relief arrived from Dodge City. Although only a few actually received wages for standing guard, most were offered free room and board as encouragement to stay on the scene. Both Charles Rath and James Langton later claimed in their damage suits that together with Fred Leonard they housed and fed a large number of men, but Johnson, who in the sworn depositions was a more reliable witness, reported that they retained only between twenty-five and seventy-five men. The average cost of board at the Walls was a dollar a day, so the merchants did have a substantial outlay to keep the men around, but they felt it was worth the expense. Otherwise, they might have lost their whole stock. S. S. Van Sickel was one of the hunters who remained at the post, as he recalled, "to protect the merchants, and give them a chance to get transportation to Dodge City." Another man who stayed at the post later remembered lingering there "after the big fight, to help guard the stuff."[27]

An unexpected event occurred on the eve of the Hanrahan party's departure. Sometime after the fight Bat Masterson had borrowed from Hannah Olds her husband's buffalo gun. It was better than his, and everyone thought that it would be good for him to have it close at hand should the Indians appear again. When Mrs. Olds learned that Masterson would be leaving for Dodge City, she sent a message to Fred Leonard at his store, asking him to recover the gun for her.

From this point in the story there are two somewhat contradictory accounts. Billy Dixon witnessed the events as they unfolded and remembered that a man named Frank Brown came to Hanrahan's from the Myers and Leonard store to collect the gun, which Bat wanted to keep until the next morning. Hanrahan said that he would be responsible for the firearm, but Brown was insistent, making "a few mistakes in his language in discussing the matter." Dixon reported that "Brown crowded matters until Hanrahan grabbed him by the neck, shook him as a bulldog would a rabbit, and then threw Brown out of the saloon" with the words, "Get out of my building, you ———!" The saloon keeper then drew his gun, but bystanders intervened and reasoned with him not to go any further. After the near violence, Masterson on the next morning did return the gun.[28]

Frank J. Brown, one of the men involved, remembered the incident differently. According to his reminiscences, he and Fred Leonard together walked to the saloon and gave Masterson a note from Hannah Olds requesting the return of her husband's gun. When Masterson reportedly told Leonard, "I have charge of this gun. You go on and attend to your own business and I'll attend to mine," Brown interrupted, "Well, Batt [*sic*], by what right do you claim the gun?" The denizens of the barroom then turned on Leonard and Brown, striking the former and forcing him out the door and then jointly beating Brown in one corner of the saloon. He finally was pushed through one of the windows, only to return through the same opening with a revolver in each hand. Halfway through the window he was met with a buffalo gun pointed squarely at his head and was again pushed outside. For a couple of hours an armed standoff reportedly took place, the Hanrahan and Masterson crowd inside and the Brown and Leonard party outside, the latter group shooting "every time anyone of Batt's crowd stuck his head out." In the end, according to Brown, the men inside showed a white flag on the end of a gun barrel and surrendered Olds's rifle.[29]

Whatever the story, the irate participants somehow settled their argument, for Frank Brown and two of his men joined the Hanrahan party, which included both Masterson and Dixon, and departed for Dodge City around July 13.[30]

Unknown to the men at Adobe Walls, both of the couriers had safely reached the town. It was not so simple a matter, however, to organize a caravan of heavy freight wagons with armed guards to trek 150 miles over the plains to the relief of the post. Charles Rath, Robert M. Wright, and A. C. Myers joined forces in the task, making arrangements with A. J. Anthony, who owned a large freighting operation, to provide wagons and teamsters.[31]

The Dodge merchants sorely wanted a military escort, and to secure one they addressed several requests to Thomas A. Osborn, the governor of Kansas. Two of their messages have been preserved, although not their first petitions. On July 8 they telegraphed to him in Topeka the news that the second courier had arrived and that the post was still besieged, asking "if you can[']t send us troops, send fifty needle guns as we must get them out."[32] The governor was already at work trying to rouse the army to action, but he had to deal with Gen. John S. Pope, commander of the Department of the Missouri at Fort Leavenworth. Pope was quite unsympathetic toward the hide men, seeing them as members of the same class of white men as those who sold whiskey and stole horses in the Indian Territory. On the eighth, the general wired the governor that "I have no men to send down to the unlawful trading Posts in the Indian Country south of Dodge without endanger[ing] the safety of honest & respectable Frontier settlers in Kansas." Pope continued, "It is presumed that as soon as the Buffalo hunters now defending these illegal trading Posts are willing to abandon the Goods, they can get away as easily as their messengers can."[33] It is interesting as a sidelight to learn that Pope himself was later reprimanded for his actions by his superior, Gen. Philip H. Sheridan, commanding the Military Division of the Missouri. Sheridan wrote to Pope from Chicago on August 21, 1874: "You should have sent [aid] to the relief of the hunters or traders closed in at Adobe Wells [*sic*]," he de-

clared, adding that "no odds what may have been the character of
these men, they were in distress, & T[he]y came near being all mas-
sacred, and they had the legal right to hunt or trade at that point for it
is in Texas. . . . and . . . you should have used the troops for the protection of life and property wherever it might have been." [34]

Governor Osborn informed the Dodge City merchants of his failure but did supply them with a limited number of arms. On July 9 he
telegraphed a message to the railway agent at Dodge informing him
that he should expect the arrival of twenty-four carbines and ammunition to be delivered to the merchants, who would post bond in the
amount of one thousand dollars for their safe return.[35] By this time the
traders in southwestern Kansas had already arranged for twenty wagons with teamsters, and they set about securing a party of armed
guards to accompany the ox train south to the Walls. The wagon train
owner, A. J. Anthony, was to receive three cents a pound for all goods
returned to Kansas, but was himself to pay his own men and provide
them with food. The guards, organized under the command of Tom
Nixon, numbered between fifty and sixty, James Langton remembering
fifty-nine. They were paid and fed by the merchants, who gave them
forty dollars a month plus board.[36] Delay followed delay as the merchants waited in vain for word on a military escort. Monetary consid-
erations undoubtedly played an important part in their thinking. If the
army provided the escort, it would cost the traders nothing; otherwise
they would have to pay for it themselves.

Finally, on Thursday, July 16, the relief party started out from
Dodge City. It is ironic that just the next day James Hanrahan's party
arrived in the city. Somehow the two groups passed on the trail without seeing each other, probably because the hide men on the way
north were avoiding the main route. With the big wagons slowly lum-
bering along, their drivers and guards especially sensitive to the danger of Indian attack, it took several days for the Dodge City caravan to
reach the trading post, arriving there about July 22 or 23.[37]

The relief that the long-stranded traders and hide men felt when
they saw the ox-drawn freight wagons rumble into view across the big
open meadow can only be imagined. The arrival of the wagons, however, meant work for everyone at the Walls—the complete disman-
tling of the commercial venture. In determining what they would
carry back to Kansas, Langton and Leonard as managers selected the
most valuable merchandise and equipment to be loaded first. Thou-

sands of buffalo hides, Andy Johnson estimating between thirty-five thousand and forty thousand from the Rath store and Fred Leonard estimating about eight thousand from his store, were packed on the wagons. Only the heaviest bull hides and rejects were left behind. Since the twenty wagons in the relief column could not carry everything, Langton and Leonard contracted with the hide men at the post to use their vehicles as well. By the time the party was ready to leave, the train numbered between forty and fifty wagons. It departed the almost deserted trading post near the end of July, perhaps the twenty-ninth, and arrived in Dodge City on August 5.[38]

Although they had removed their merchandise from Adobe Walls, the traders left their options open by making arrangements with a handful of hide men to guard the post and to prevent its destruction by the Indians. The merchants felt that if the Indian unrest subsided, they might be able to return to their stores and renew the commerce they had enjoyed before the fight. Accounts vary on the number of men who stayed behind, one knowledgeable person reporting only nine, Leonard remembering twenty-six, and other men who were on the ground at the time suggesting intermediate numbers. To encourage the men to stay there, the traders left a supply of food—bacon, corn, flour, and the like—to last for five or six months. The guardians remained there into the month of August without seeing a single warrior, but they became discouraged. Their intention had been to hunt buffalo while using the buildings as their headquarters, but the herds at the time had become dispersed.[39]

Meanwhile, the U.S. Army was preparing for a fall campaign against the southern Plains tribes. The Adobe Walls fight and the preliminary raids on hunters in the area had been the catalyst, but numerous depredations had followed in June and July, and the cry rose along the frontier for an effort to force the tribesmen back to their reservations. During the military action that followed, known variously as the Red River Campaign, the Indian Territory Expedition, and the Buffalo War, numerous army units passed through the Adobe Walls area, most of them stopping at the post.[40] The first of these soldiers came in mid-August, 1874, their commander being Lt. Frank Dwight Baldwin.[41]

The hide men remaining at the trading post were both surprised and pleased when their old friends Billy Dixon and Bat Masterson appeared outside the buildings on the afternoon of August 18. They had become scouts for the army, only two of the many hunters who had entered military services as guides. Such men knew the country better than just about anyone else. Lieutenant Baldwin, realizing that his troopers and Delaware Indian scouts would probably come in after dark, had sent Dixon and Masterson ahead to tell the hide hunters that friends, not foes, would be approaching after night fell.

The pair found a number of men at the buildings. They learned that the hide men had not ventured far from the post and that they were discouraged over the lack of bison in the vicinity. "The boys cooked me a hot supper and I was telling them stories of the outside world when the soldiers arrived about 9 o'clock," Dixon recalled. The water level in the Adobe Walls Creek was so low from the drought that the troopers camped in a mesquite flat on nearby Bent's Creek just north of the ruins of the Bent trading post, where they could water their horses more easily.[42]

Dixon remembered that Lieutenant Baldwin had not recently seen much mounted service and was very tired and saddle-worn by the time he reached camp, but by the next morning he was feeling much better. About nine-thirty in the morning, after he had finished his breakfast in camp, the officer and four of his men started for the trading post. "I had proceeded about half a mile when I heard the yells of the wild Indians who were in persuit [*sic*] of 5 men who belonged at the stockade, two of them mounted and three in a wagon," Baldwin recorded. The hide men had been out about three miles from the buildings either picking plums or hunting (the accounts vary), and they had been surprised by a party of about fifteen warriors, who immediately attacked them. The men in the wagon and one on horseback, Tobe Robinson, successfully made their way back to the stockade corral at the Myers and Leonard store, but the other horseman, a hunter named George Huffman, was lanced and scalped by his attackers. Lieutenant Baldwin that evening wrote further in his diary: "They [the Indians] had run very close on my little party who had opened [fire] on them, [and] we made our way to the stockade through a shower of bullits [*sic*]." Baldwin then returned to his camp, gathered more men, and followed the war party for about a dozen miles "over the worst kind of sand hills" but succeeded only in capturing a few ponies.[43] Returning to Adobe Walls about five o'clock in the afternoon, Baldwin's command spent an uneventful night at the trading post, not desiring to camp in the open while hostile bands roamed the area. During the evening of the nineteenth, the hide men at the Walls held a council in which they decided to leave the post completely, joining Baldwin's party to return to the settlements. "I don't know but that it is the best thing they can do," the officer noted in his diary. Even so, he questioned their wisdom in leaving behind sufficient supplies to have lasted them two more months. Earlier he had offered to give them whatever ammunition they might need to defend themselves. Thus, the twenty-two men then at Adobe Walls left the place entirely, ending its history as an inhabited site. After this, the only people at Adobe Walls would be occasional visitors. The commercial venture in the Panhandle had ended.[44]

After the hunters and Lieutenant Baldwin's detachment departed Adobe Walls on August 20, no white men were known to have passed by the site for about two weeks. Few hide hunters were active in the area, which had become a battleground. On September 7, 1874, however, Lt. Henry Joseph Farnsworth of the Eighth U.S. Cavalry visited the abandoned post with a party of soldiers. Discovering a large amount of corn in one of the stores, the officer appropriated about 5,500 pounds for the use of his troops. He found the buildings in fair order, describing them in some detail. He interestingly commented that "the Ranch is admirably located and constructed for defense against Indians—displaying considerable skill, [and] why it should have been abandoned I cannot understand, [for] 20 resolute men could hold it indefinitely." After collecting the forage, Farnsworth and his men continued on their way.[45]

No more white men came to Adobe Walls until late October. By then, the Indians had returned, wreaking their vengeance on the buildings the whites had left behind. At the Rath store the doors and windows were ripped from the walls and stacked with other burnable materials on the floor. Inside the Myers and Leonard store the raiders ignited a pile of combustible objects, including wooden barrels, furniture, and a wheel-less wagon box. Just south of the store another wagon box was burned, while the warriors piled some of the remaining buffalo hides on the pickets of the corral fence. The fat in the skins helped the pickets burn easily. The blacksmith shop was burned down with little trouble. Only the saloon survived the destructive efforts of the warriors.[46]

Precisely when the Indians razed the buildings is unknown, but when Maj. Charles Elmer Compton visited the site about October 20, one of his scouts, Billy Dixon, noted that "the walls were still smoking." Compton's detachment of troops camped within sight of the deserted and destroyed post, the soldiers, Dixon recalled, picking up "everything that they could find in the hunt for souvenirs." In the trees on the south side of the Canadian, the troopers soon discovered the blanket-wrapped bodies of some of the Indians killed in the June battle. Dixon remarked that "the soldiers threw away the bones and carried off the blankets."[47]

It was on this October visit that Dixon found his long-lost setter, Fannie. "Her appearance affected me greatly, as . . . she had disappeared with the other dogs the day of the fight, and I was sure that she had been killed by the Indians or had wandered away and starved." After Dixon and the soldiers had patted and fed the dog, she disappeared briefly, only to return "with something in her mouth and . . . wagging her tail." Billy later reminisced: "When we saw what she had brought to us every man grinned and was as tickled as if he were a boy. Fannie had brought a fat, bright-eyed little puppy in her mouth . . . dropping the little fellow gently on a pile of bedding." Later the setter appeared with three more puppies, which Dixon speculated had been fathered by the Scheidler brothers' Newfoundland dog before the fight. He later recalled that "when we pulled out, Fannie and her babies were given a snug place in the mess wagon."[48]

Compton's command left the still-smoldering trading post only a few hours before Thomas McFadden and J. Frederick, two civilian scouts, arrived.[49] McFadden kept a diary vividly describing his daily activities. The men were following Compton, attempting to catch up with him to deliver a packet of dispatches, when they found the buildings "in ruins of fire still burning . . . a more uncanny looking place . . . hard to conceive." McFadden remembered seeing "on the remaining pickets of what once was a corral . . . exposed fourteen human skulls, the remains of the Indians who had been killed here in June by the hunters." Apparently the gate to the corral had been either torn down or destroyed and the heads moved from its crosspiece to several fence pickets. Curiously, the Indians had not removed the skulls. The two men soon found Compton's trail and followed it northward.[50]

The Cator brothers also visited Adobe Walls shortly after its destruction by the Indians. James H. Cator later described the scene: "It looked like the wagons and things left had been put around the place and set fire to . . . you could see corn charred together like, all sticking together . . . the sacks had been opened and it wasted and burned. The ground was white where the bags of flour were cut open and scattered all over the ground, and it had been wet and pasted like by rain. . . . There were remnants of the hides, some scattered around there, as if some had been piled up and burned."[51] Other visitors about the same time recorded similar observations, Bat Masterson remembering that "the last time I was there in October, 1874, everything was destroyed, all the buildings, etc., at Adobe Walls, and all the stockades had been burned down."[52] J.J. Long, an army teamster at the time, recollected seeing the post destroyed by fire but still remaining on pickets of the corral fence "some skulls of Indians, twelve or thirteen perhaps."[53] It was truly a scene of death and desolation.

Groups of white men continued to visit Adobe Walls throughout the fall and winter of 1874. Lt. Henry J. Farnsworth returned to the site in the first week of November but left no record of having actually examined the ruins. Moving southward to McClellan Creek on November 6, he encountered "at least 100 Cheyennes well mounted and in full fighting trim." The lieutenant's force of twenty-eight troopers fought them from one-thirty in the afternoon until nightfall, killing at least four of the braves and perhaps more, with the loss of one of his men.[54] Also in November, hide hunter John R. Cook passed by the site.[55] The last of the known white men at the Walls that year were Eighth Cavalry troopers under Capt. Charles A. Hartwell. They moved out from a camp near the ruins of the post on November 28, thereafter encountering "a party of forty to fifty mounted Indians" near Muster Creek. After a successful fight in which two warriors were left dead on the field and two others were seen falling from their mounts, Hartwell returned to the Walls on December 2 before continuing on his way.[56]

After 1874 and for the next century only curiosity seekers and an occasional cowboy working cattle in the area would visit Adobe Walls. In time, however, the fight would become a famous incident in Western history, drawing massive crowds to numerous celebrations held on the anniversary of the battle. Indians also would return to erect their own memorial to warriors' lives lost in the fight.

CHAPTER 6

Adobe Walls since 1874

After a night in this place we could not resist the opportunity to visit the old Dobe Walls battle grounds, . . . There is nothing there any more except the old mounds of dirt . . . where the buildings stood.—R. B. Quinn to Frederick S. Barde, January 6, 1911.

THE years immediately following the abandonment of the Adobe Walls trading post saw some limited activity by buffalo hunters in the vicinity followed by the entry of the cattlemen. The herds of bison in 1875 were not so thick as before, perhaps as a result of the activities of the professional hunters in the preceding year. Yet a few hunting outfits did work in the region during the winter of 1874–75, some of them remaining there until it became unprofitable to hunt.[1]

One of the crews that drifted down into the Panhandle was that of George A. Simpson. He and his outfit had been hunting in southeastern Colorado, and they decided to move into Texas in December, 1874. His was an unusual crew, for he had with him his wife, sister-in-law, and mother-in-law. Although women were not unknown in the hide camps, their presence was definitely exceptional. Simpson later recalled that once when they were camped near Adobe Walls a party of Indians briefly harassed his family while the men were out hunting. The three women were greatly frightened, but one of them had the presence of mind to run to a nearby knoll and signal to a small group of soldiers who were nearby. Heavily outnumbered, the six troopers recommended that the women "move down into camp with them, to feed the chief and his family, and to turn our horses out with their herd." Simpson later recalled that "it seemed that the whole tribe belonged to the chief's family and our food soon began to get scarce, so we had to tactfully find an excuse to leave them."[2]

Another hide crew operating in the Panhandle at this time was that of George W. Brown, who moved southward from Kansas in February, 1875. They passed the abandoned Adobe Walls trading post before encamping for the hunt on Red Deer Creek. He sent one of his men with a wagon about half-filled with dry hides to Dodge City for supplies, but the employee absconded with the team and vehicle, leaving the outfit stranded on the plains. Returning on foot to Adobe Walls, they found hunter George Bellfield camped. Because the Brown crew had eaten nothing but buffalo meat for about three weeks, Bellfield invited them to camp with him and to have a good meal. After feeding and sheltering the haggard party overnight, Brown directed them to a store that had just opened on Palo Duro Creek to the north. There they bartered hides for supplies and a team of horses, finally getting back to Dodge City in the spring of 1875.[3]

Not everyone was so successful in finding bison in the Panhandle. About 1875 or 1876, James E. May, who at the time was working on a ranch in southwestern Kansas, made a trip to the region with several other cowboys. They hoped to recover some horses that had disappeared from the ranch and to kill some bison for the meat and skins. May recollected that he and his men found neither the buffalo nor the horses.[4]

During the 1870s and 1880s, large numbers of sheep appeared in the Texas Panhandle, many belonging to sheep ranchers from eastern New Mexico. The sheepherders in time were forced out by the cattle raisers, but for a while they ranged over the site of the former trading post. W. H. Hull was an eighteen-year-old in 1879 when he herded sheep for several months around Adobe Walls. He later wrote to Andy Johnson that "while herding sheep, I picked up about a pint of bullets from the ground around there, fired during the battle."[5]

From the 1880s until the time of World War I, Adobe Walls remained isolated. The headquarters of the Turkey Track Ranch was established near the site about a decade after the fight, and in 1887 an "Adobe Walls, Texas," post office was established, but there never was any community in the area, only the ranchers and their employees.[6] A handful of individuals went to examine and poke around the ruins of the trading post, but for the most part these persons already were in the area and seemingly had nothing better to do. Such a visitor was U. G. Vanderwork, who as a boy of seventeen made the trip from Dodge City to Adobe Walls in 1883 to participate in a roundup. Much later he recollected that when he and his friends went to see the ruins of the hide men's post, they found still lying on the ground "human skulls and human bones scattered over the plains near Adobe Walls."[7]

About that time Billy Dixon settled near the trading post, becoming postmaster of Adobe Walls, Texas, in 1887. W. S. Carter, at the time a teenager, helped his father deliver the mail for Dixon. He reminisced that "Billy Dixon was postmaster. My father and him ordered stuff—anything and everything—from Montgomery Ward. This stuff came by express to Canadian and we took it to Adobe Wall[s] and sold it."[8]

Other people had different memories of Adobe Walls. Alexander Schneider, later a well-known Panhandle hotel operator, came to the region in 1886. He once noted that at the time "we had to vote at Adobe Walls" and that "at election time we had a barbecue, whiskey, and everything, and it took us about three days to cast our votes."[9]

The Adobe Walls site was not altered dramatically until 1914. That year Olive K. Dixon, widow of battle participant William Dixon, published the first edition of her biography of her husband. Entitled the *Life and Adventures of "Billy" Dixon of Adobe Walls, Texas Panhandle*, the book was the first to tell the general public the story of the Adobe Walls trading post and battle. After this, the trading post was increasingly considered a historic site to be visited and revered. As early as 1914, there was discussion concerning the production of a motion picture based on the story of Billy Dixon's life and his participation in the battle. Before a decade had passed plans also were afoot to convert the battle site into a memorial park and even to reconstruct the buildings as they had appeared at the time of the fight, an idea that persisted for many years.[10]

A visit to the site in December, 1922, by two old-timers from Dodge City spurred further interest in Adobe Walls. One of them was Andy Johnson, the Swedish immigrant who had helped erect the buildings and who had fought in the 1874 battle, and the other was former hunter "Brick" Bond, who had come into the trading post only shortly after the fight had ended. Accompanied by a historically minded Dodge City resident, Tom Stauth, they spent most of Sunday, December 3, at the ruins of the trading post.

While at Adobe Walls the two veterans pointed out to Stauth and about twenty local residents the locations of the graves of William Olds and of Billy Tyler and the Scheidler brothers. With shovels in hand, they and others dug down, locating both burial places, which in the intervening years had become lost. The first grave uncovered was that of William Olds. They found the crumbled remains of the wooden coffin that Johnson at the Rath store had made for his friend's remains. The press noted that "the bones were in good condition, although the body had been placed there 48 years ago." The men then uncovered the burial place of Billy Tyler and the Scheidler brothers, located at the opposite end of the site. From the grave they removed a knife that Johnson and Bond remembered as having belonged to Tyler.

After spending most of the day at the battleground, Stauth, Johnson, and Bond drove to Miami, Texas, to see Olive K. Dixon. They were unexpected guests, but Mrs. Dixon later wrote to a friend that she was "simply *delighted*" to see them, adding that "with the exception of my husband I had never seen and I never hoped to see one of the survivors of the historic battle." The Kansas visitors spent the evening in the Dixon home, during which time Mrs. Dixon made arrangements for the two old men to address assembled pupils at the Miami school auditorium. The next morning during the chapel period the students gathered to hear introductory comments by Olive Dixon and the local district judge, followed by extemporaneous remarks from the two former hide men. The local newspaper reported that "both the old gentlemen were given a rousing welcome by the pupils and the talks were vigorously applauded," Olive Dixon later remembering that "this attention pleased the old men very much." After the assembly the Dodge City party started back to Kansas, but the public exposure they had brought to the Adobe Walls site would bear fruit for several years to come.[11]

Within a few months promoters launched several projects related to the old trading post. A coordinating meeting was held at the battleground in June, 1923. Little known today, this conference and celebration had a profound influence on events in the history of the site for the next decade. About seven hundred people from all parts of the Texas Panhandle assembled on Thursday, June 14. The Canadian River was high, and because of the transportation difficulties, Mayor F. P. Reid of Pampa arranged for teams to pull the wagons or automobiles of those stranded in the mud.

The program opened at ten-thirty in the morning, Mayor Reid

presiding. Those in attendance considered the erection of monuments at the battle site, the organization of an association to promote the construction of a bridge across the Canadian near there, and the formulation of specific plans for a fiftieth-anniversary celebration the next year. Speakers during the day included C. T. Herring, president of the Tri-State Exposition in Amarillo; G. C. Edwards, a state highway department representative; T. F. Turner, president of the Panhandle-Plains Historical Society; and local officials. That night the majority of the participants camped out, the local press reporting that "many cars brought tents and [their] occupants are sleeping in the open, making the trip serve as an outing or brief vacation." Discussions continued on Friday the fifteenth, ending with a rodeo following the serious business.

Several developments resulted from the 1923 meeting. A committee was formed with Olive K. Dixon as secretary-treasurer to solicit donations and have a large stone monument made to mark the site of the 1874 battle. Initial plans called for a twenty-five-foot granite marker bearing a marble plate listing the names of the defenders in the fight. The committee also was authorized to have small granite markers made for the graves of William Olds and of Billy Tyler and the Scheidler brothers.

During the meeting the Adobe Walls Highway Association was formally created to promote the construction of a major bridge across the Canadian near Adobe Walls. Because the closest bridges were either the 1916 structure at Canadian or the "Amarillo Bridge" about thirty miles north of that city, local residents strongly felt the need for an all-weather crossing nearer their area. Mayor Reid of Pampa, a long-time promoter of the bridge, was elected president of the association, and local committees were formed for ten of the surrounding communities, some of them as far away as Guymon and Amarillo. Another committee was created to coordinate plans for the fiftieth-anniversary celebration of the battle. F. P. Reid also was selected to chair this committee, with Olive K. Dixon serving as secretary. Anniversary planning was conducted under the auspices of the Panhandle-Plains Historical Society.[12]

For a year the members of the various planning committees made arrangements for speakers, publicity, and scores of other details. As might be expected, one of the most active of all the members was Olive K. Dixon. While secretary-treasurer of the monument committee, she almost singlehandedly raised the one thousand dollars needed to prepare and erect the battlefield marker and the two gravestones. Donations came in by mail from many states but most came from patrons on the southern Great Plains. One of the larger gifts was the fifty dollars given by the Sweetwater, Texas, theatrical producer Harley Sadler. By late spring Mrs. Dixon was going personally from town to town to solicit donations to the fund. A press report in April noted, for example, that she had "spent the afternoon in Panhandle and received contributions of $28.00." The one thousand dollars required for the markers was a substantial amount of money in 1924; such a sum at that time could purchase three new Ford automobiles. Meanwhile, Mr. and Mrs. W. T. Coble, owners of the Turkey Track Ranch, donated to the Panhandle-Plains Historical Society the actual site of the trading post where the stones would be placed.

Work began on the battlefield monument in May, but in the interim the design for the marker had been changed after the committee members had learned that the high water table and soft soil in the meadow at Adobe Walls would preclude the erection of as large a marker as they initially had planned. Instead, a shorter rectangular pattern was chosen. Olive Dixon wrote in May, 1924, that "some think the monument as it will be now [will be] much prettier than the tall one and more like other monuments erected on battlegrounds."[13]

The final list of speakers for the celebration included Thomas F. Turner as president of the Panhandle-Plains Historical Society, Mayor F. P. Reid of Pampa, Olive K. Dixon, Professor L. F. Sheffy of West Texas State Teachers College, Andy Johnson of Dodge City (who was one of the handful of surviving battle participants), and J. A. Cotton of Snyder, Texas, a veteran of the Eighth Cavalry.[14] As early as January, 1923, Olive K. Dixon had started writing to Andy Johnson, first to secure his consent to attend the celebration and then to be certain that he did not change his mind. The effort, however, was well worth her time, for Johnson did attend the anniversary and was a center of attention during the festivities.[15]

The arrangements committee also undertook an ambitious advertising campaign to inform the public of the upcoming festivities. J. Lindsay Nunn of the *Amarillo Daily News* secured the interest of other editors in the region and successfully placed the reports of the celebration plans before readers throughout the Panhandle and surrounding area. In addition, the committee printed thousands of hand-bills that read in part, "Don't miss the big celebration . . . [of the] 50th anniversary of the famous frontier Battle of Adobe Walls in which a few white men fought so valiantly against an overwhelming number of Indians." Bundles of these announcements were sent to towns all over the southern Great Plains. Announcements listed the expected speak-ers, among them "Andrew Johnson of Dodge City, Kansas, (who fought in the battle in 1874) [who] will address the audience and promises to relate some history which has never been published," and promised other entertainments, including musical performances and horse races. Visitors should "come prepared to camp out" and "bring cakes and other food if you wish, but barbecued beef, bread and coffee will be furnished free to all who come." [16]

On the evening of Thursday, June 26, 1924, the crowds began ar-riving at the ruins of the old trading post. People came in automobiles, in wagons, on horseback, and even by airplane, dramatically illustrat-ing the rapidly changing times in which they lived. Lloyd M. Brown as a boy attended the celebration and remembered his father's driving their "490" Chevrolet over a plank roadway made of two-by-twelve boards across the sands of the Canadian River. Early arrivals enjoyed dancing to the music provided by a "colored orchestra" from Ama-rillo, although the formal program did not start until about mid-morning on Friday, the twenty-seventh. The estimated two thousand participants listened to speeches, saw the monument unveiled, en-joyed rodeos and horse racing, and ate a free lunch of barbecued beef from twenty head of stock donated for the occasion, plus bread, pick-les, and coffee. During and after the meal, music was provided by the West Texas State Teachers College Band. [17]

Many old-timers came for the event, one of the largest single as-semblages of Panhandle pioneers ever gathered together. Among the men associated with the history of Adobe Walls were not only Andrew Johnson and "Brick" Bond, but also lawman Bill Tilghman, a former hide hunter; J. Wright Mooar and James H. Cator, buffalo hunters turned ranchers; James E. McAllister, who had accompanied Amos Chapman to Adobe Walls just before the fight; and Jim Barbour, who had been a member of the Adobe Walls relief party. [18]

Participation in the festivities was difficult for some of these aged veterans of the frontier. One of the older celebrants soon thereafter wrote to Johnson to say that being there "was Hell on 'old stagers' & I got mine. You were so much in demand. . . . Hope your legs are all right." [19] Jim Barbour also wrote to Andy just after the anniversary, "hope you are feeling young as [a] yearling, well and y[ou] take care of your self, for the trip . . . was a strain on you both physicaly & mintly [*sic*]." [20]

Barbour was correct, for Johnson bore perhaps the greatest strain of all the old-timers because he had been called upon to speak before an estimated two thousand listeners. The thought terrified him. One of his friends in Dodge City, journalist Heinie Schmidt, later recalled that Johnson had asked for help in writing his speech. At the time Johnson lived in a two-room frame house just south of Boot Hill on old Front Street in Dodge City. Schmidt called on him there one evening to gather information for the talk, recalling later that "we used a large box of matches keeping Andy's pipe going and the lamp lighted." Finishing their work about two o'clock in the morning, Schmidt started for home, Andy still wearing his house slippers to accompany him part of the way. When the journalist parted with him, he turned to ask if there was anything else Andy had forgotten. Andy replied only, "Heinie, put lots of roses in it." The next morning when Johnson, "Brick" Bond, and Tom Stauth set off for Texas to attend the celebration, Andy was dressed as he had never been before—new suit, shoes, white shirt, bow tie, and a big black hat. [21]

Andrew Johnson woke up before his friends on the morning of June 27 and startled them by calling out, "Get up boys. We were up a lot earlier than this fifty years ago this morning." He was to give his talk that day and already was nervous. A newspaper reporter from Amarillo recorded Johnson's stay and comments in considerable detail, describing him as "a comparatively small man. His hair is almost white, his face has the appearance of leather. . . . He is not bent and feeble but is erect and active." The journalist found Johnson's eyes intriguing: "His eyes are a steely blue and though they have seen 79 summers they have not lost their lustre. They have a kindly beam. . . . Yet, when he begins to tell you of the incidents that occurred fifty years ago, his eyes lose their kindly look, they harden and get cold and it is easy for one to know how it was that Andy Johnson and 27 other men . . . withstood the onslaught." Andy Johnson was the star of the celebration and probably above all it was he the visitors remembered most. [22]

After the 1924 celebration, people continued occasionally to visit the Adobe Walls battleground to see the site and to view the new monument, but no large ceremonies were held there for five years. Then in 1929 the ruins became the scene of another large gathering, this time to reinter the remains of Billy Dixon. After his death in 1913 he was buried at Texline, Texas, but after the closing of the 1924 events, his widow was determined to see her husband's remains transferred to the place he had helped make famous. In early 1929 she began organizing efforts for another commemorative ceremony as part of the reinterment.

Dixon's remains were removed from Texline and escorted to Adobe Walls by parties of reserve military officers and Boy Scouts. The day was extremely hot, but the ceremonies began promptly at two o'clock on the afternoon of June 27, 1929, with a flag raising followed by Masonic rites and the reburial inside the ruins of the Rath and Company Store. The grave was marked by a large granite tombstone, which remains at the site.[23]

For a decade, hundreds and perhaps thousands drove to the ruins to examine the monuments and puzzle over what the trading post was like when it was inhabited. At least two small ceremonies were conducted at nearby Borger to mark the anniversary of the battle, but no major events were held at the site.[24]

One significant occurrence during the 1930s, however, was to bear fruit later. As early as 1931 plans were being considered for the four remaining Indian participants in the 1874 battle to return to the place where they had fought. Nothing immediately came of the plans, and during the next half-dozen or so years, two of these survivors passed away. Finally, in 1939 a trip from Oklahoma to the Texas Panhandle was arranged for the last two survivors. They found a warm welcome from everyone they met. After walking over the ground where they had fought sixty-five years before, the pair of old Comanches, Timbo and Yellowfish, together with several younger tribesmen were guests of honor at a special dinner given for them at the Turkey Track Ranch headquarters. That afternoon the party drove from Adobe Walls to Canyon, Texas, to view the exhibits at the Panhandle-Plains Historical Museum. On the way the Indians and their white hosts stopped to allow two younger Comanches to confer with representatives at the Borger Chamber of Commerce. This left the two old men alone in the car with history professor L. F. Sheffy from Canyon. Dr. Sheffy had observed, at least to his satisfaction, that neither of them spoke English with any fluency, so with a great number of gestures he expressed to them, "Borger have heap-big houses and no horses." After a moment of silence one of the old men replied in perfect English, "Well, we sure had plenty of horses when we were here last!"

The party continued on to the museum in Canyon, where a mounted buffalo captured their attention. The local press noted that "they silently gazed at it for several minutes" before turning to look at a plaster of paris figure of an Indian nearby. They inspected exhibits of Indian artifacts and then burst out in laughter, to the surprise of everyone. The two old men had spotted in one of the glass cases some photographs of Indian warriors, and among them they saw one of their friends and former battle participants, a brave named Yellow Horse, which they found exceedingly amusing. Upon leaving the museum, the old Comanches consented to being photographed, but only on the condition that all understood that they were on a "friendly mission," and then they departed for home in Oklahoma.

Although few white people paid attention at the time, one of the principal reasons for the Indians' visit to the Texas Panhandle in 1939 had been to ascertain whether they might erect a monument of their own at Adobe Walls. Learning that there was no opposition to their plan, they went home to wait until an appropriate opportunity presented itself.[25] The wait was not long.

By early 1941 plans were already under way for staging what would be called the Adobe Walls Indian Ceremonials at Huber Stadium in Borger, not far from the battle site. Comanche, Cheyenne, and Kiowa Indians from Oklahoma joined forces with the Hutchinson County Fair Association to present a pageant portraying the history of Adobe Walls as well as performances of tribal dances. On the third day of the pageant, October 19, the Indians planned to conduct rites at the battleground and to unveil a monument in memory of their dead in the battle.

An advance party of Indians appeared at Borger in April to make preliminary arrangements. The performers did not begin arriving until early October, with the bulk of the party coming in just days before the scheduled opening. The event was advertised statewide on radio and in newspapers, and to promote attendance from the Panhandle region caravans of Borger citizens and costumed Indians visited surrounding communities on the weekend before the pageant. Finally the "Adobe Walls Indian Ceremonials," directed by noted theatrical producer and playwright Mark Hamilton, opened on the evening of Friday, October 17, followed by performances the next two evenings.[26]

On Sunday, October 19, the Indians drove from Borger to Adobe Walls and there performed their rites before four thousand to five thousand whites, who watched in the distance. After preliminary dances, Yellowfish, a Comanche who as a teenager had fought the buffalo hunters at the site, directed the dedication of the Indian monument. With a Cheyenne chief on one side and a Kiowa on the other, he read from the marker the names of the braves who had fallen before the guns of the whites in their effort to drive the hide men from their hunting grounds. A reporter noted that "tears rolled down the weather-beaten cheeks of the older Indians." The services ended with a prayer and further dances to the pounding of tribal drums.[27]

Since the 1941 dedication of the Indian monument at Adobe Walls, the site has seen no more massive gatherings. Although the promoters of the Borger pageant had hoped that the affair would become an annual event, World War II intervened, diverting attention overseas.[28]

Most of the visitors since World War II have been like journalist Frank Tolbert, who came to Adobe Walls in the 1970s. He and a party of friends drove to the site one June morning in two Jeep station wagons laden with picnic supplies and ice chests filled with soda pop and beer. As often still happens with tourists wanting to visit the Walls, they became lost while passing through the wheat fields on the plains that skirt the edge of the Canadian River valley. After regaining their bearings, they followed the winding dirt road down to find the barely discernible outlines of the buildings and the monuments erected years before. They were intrigued by the 1941 marker inscriptions listing the Indian dead, names like Stone Teeth, Wild Horse, and Spotted Feather. After looking around, like most tourists they had their picnic lunch and then returned to civilization.[29]

Not until 1975 was there renewed historical activity at Adobe Walls. A team of archeologists under the supervision of Billy R. Harrison, curator of archeology at the Panhandle-Plains Historical Museum, in that year began a systematic five-year excavation of the trading post. This effort, described and discussed in the second half of this book, helped not only to reconstruct the lifestyle of the men at Adobe Walls but also, and perhaps more importantly, to shed light on the lives of all the hide men.[30]

PART 2
Archeology

CHAPTER 7

The Setting

T HE 1874 Adobe Walls trading post was built on a broad meadow on the north side of the Canadian River in the north central portion of the Texas Panhandle. The Canadian flows in a generally easterly direction across the region, cutting a valley as wide as fifteen miles and draining a considerably larger area. The long and often rugged slopes on both sides of the valley are dissected by thirty or more tributaries, of which Adobe and Bent creeks are typical examples. It was between these two streams that the merchants chose to build their post, at a spot located on a broad alluvial flat 2.9 miles north of the confluence of these two tributaries with the Canadian.[1]

The site lies in Hutchinson County within the Houston and Great Northern Railroad Survey No. 9, Block G, recorded on certificate number 5/831.[2] It is located at 35°53' north longitude and 101°25' west latitude, as shown on the U.S. Geological Survey 7.5-minute scale Adobe Creek, Texas, Quadrangle Map, and is recorded as site number 41HC1 by the Texas Archeological Research Laboratory. The site is 16.25 miles at 74° east of north from the nearest town, Stinnett, the seat of Hutchinson County. It may be reached via automobile by traveling 15.9 miles north from Stinnett on state highway 207, thence 5.9 miles east on paved Farm-to-Market Road 281, and thence 12.2 miles in a meandering southerly and southeasterly direction on an unnamed, unnumbered, partially paved, and partially graded county road. The former trading post is within the boundaries of the present-day Turkey Track Ranch 1.4 miles south of the ranch headquarters. The location of

Fig. 32. Archeological field party members excavating the bastion at the Myers and Leonard store during summer, 1979. (Photograph by T. Lindsay Baker.)

the Bent's earlier 1840s trading post and of the 1864 battle between Kit Carson's military expedition and the Plains Indians lies 1.2 miles south of the 1874 site.[3]

Extending southward from the 1874 Adobe Walls site, the Quaternary alluvial floodplains of Adobe and Bent creeks merge with the broader floodplain bordering the north side of the wide, sand-clogged channel of the Canadian. This level floodplain is broken only by tree-lined stream channels and a low mound topped with residual Potter gravels. South of the river one sees juniper-dotted slopes of Tertiary sediments of the Ogallala Formation, which gains elevation above the floodplains toward the Llano Estacado Escarpment. Adobe Creek, about three-quarters of a mile east of the site, is bordered along its east bank by erosional remnants of Permian red beds of the Quartermaster Formation. These remnants rise steeply approximately one hundred feet in elevation and are topped by broad mesas. Farther to the north, the valley of Adobe Creek quickly is lost to view in the rising slopes of the Canadian River valley. The interfluvial divide between Adobe and Bent creeks west of the Adobe Walls site is formed by a Permian projection covered with Tertiary aged sand from the Canadian. The divide is dotted on its east slope by seep springs that create a broad marsh area between the archeological site and the divide. Immediately north of the springs is a small, isolated, gravel-topped ridge.

The buffalo hunters' trading post site is situated on a small elevated area composed of Lincoln series soils surrounded by a larger area of Sweetwater series soils. The composition of the Lincoln soils is grayish-brown, calcareous, loamy, fine sand approximately fourteen inches thick. Beneath the Lincoln soils one finds the light yellowish-brown loamy, fine sand of the Sweetwater soils, which extends to a depth of sixty inches or more. These soils in parts of the floodplain are subject to flooding one to three times a year, although the inundation usually lasts only about one to five hours. The depth of the water table varies from thirty-six to sixty inches below the surface. Today one finds four seep springs at the base of the interfluvial divide west of the site, and these very likely may have been flowing springs during the occupancy of the trading post.[4]

The Lincoln and Sweetwater soils with available moisture support a plant-life community of tall and middle height grasses and forbs plus

Fig. 33. East across the site of the 1874 Adobe Walls trading post toward the Adobe Creek valley. (Photograph by Billy R. Harrison.)

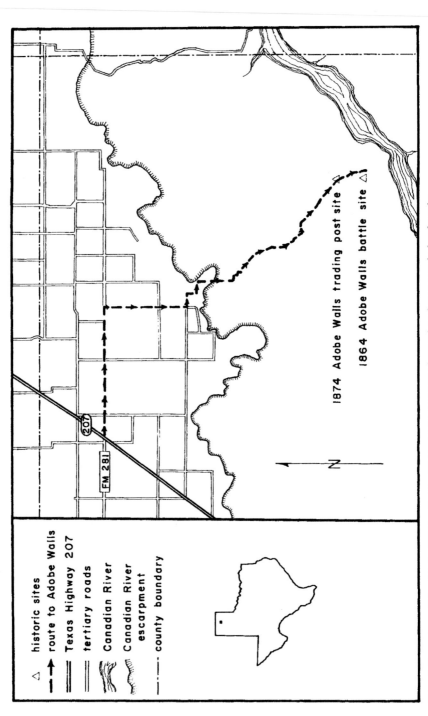

1874 Adobe Walls trading post site

1864 Adobe Walls battle site △

N

207

FM 281

Map 1. Location of the Adobe Walls site in reference to current physical and man-made landmarks.

a limited range of trees and shrubs. Wild plums and grapes are abundant. This plant community, coupled with a sufficient water supply, provides a habitat for domestic livestock and a wide range of wildlife. The natural fauna found in the area today include deer, antelope, rabbit, turkey, quail, pheasant (an introduced fowl), dove, many nongame birds, and several species of reptiles and fishes. The combination of playa lakes on the plains above the site, man-made ponds, and present-day grain fields attracts large numbers of migratory ducks, geese, and cranes. The common predators are the bobcat, kit fox, red fox, and coyote. Among the extinct fauna are the bear, beaver, lobo wolf, bison, and prairie chicken.[5]

CHAPTER 8

Overview of the Site and Field Work

T HE boundaries of the Adobe Walls trading post site are almost impossible to set. The site reasonably might include the entire area from the Canadian River to the Turkey Track Ranch headquarters and from the butte tops on the east to Bent Creek on the west. The location of the trading post buildings, however, is contained within a relatively small 6-acre tract measuring 871 feet north-to-south and 300 feet east-to-west. This area was deeded to the Panhandle-Plains Historical Society in 1923. Except for the privy site, all structures, known graves, and markers lie within this more limited acreage. The trading post site was placed on the National Register of Historic Places and made a Texas State Archeological Landmark in 1978.[1]

A caliche county road crosses the trading post site from northwest to southeast, separating the southwest corner from the remainder of the area. Numerous ranch and tourist footpaths crisscross the immediate area of the post. Through the years significant damage has been caused by the road, trails, grazing livestock, and occasional relic hunters. Before the start of the excavation, the remains of the larger structures were outlined by low rounded ridges forming rectangular patterns with central depressions. Only a conical pit marked the location of the blacksmith shop. The privy was marked by a low, almost imperceptible mound. The buildings were aligned on an approximate north-south line and probably faced east.

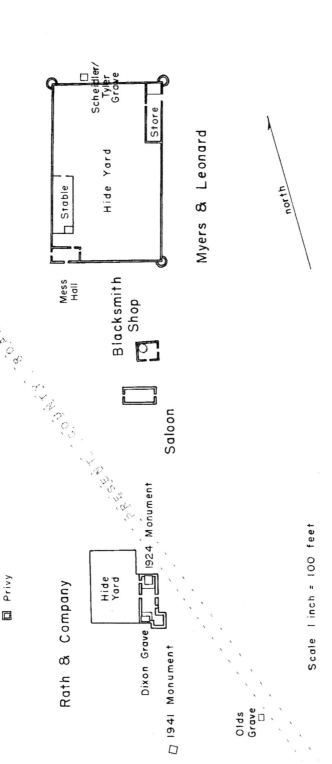

Map 2. General plan of the 1874 Adobe Walls trading post site.

The northernmost structure was the Myers and Leonard compound. This complex was enclosed in a rectangular picket corral, which formed the outer walls of most of its structures. A store building built from pickets smaller than those in the corral fence and daubed with mud stood in the northeast corner of the compound, and a mess hall was built diagonally across in the southwest corner. A stable extended northward from the mess hall along the west corral fence. A shallow water well was dug between the mess hall and the stable almost in line with the east stable wall.

Thomas O'Keefe's blacksmith shop was roughly parallel to and south of the Myers and Leonard complex. The next building to the south was James Hanrahan's saloon. The last major building, the Rath and Company store, stood about two hundred feet south of the saloon and was the southernmost structure. Built for merchants Charles Rath, Robert Marr Wright, and James Langton, this complex consisted of a sod store building and an unfinished sod corral to the west. It is thought that the privy located west of the sod corral formed a part of the Rath and Company compound.[2]

There are three graves at the 1874 Adobe Walls site. All of these are oriented with their 1920s headstones facing east and have iron pipe barriers protecting them. The common grave of Isaac Scheidler, Jacob Scheidler, and Billy Tyler is located a few feet north of and parallel to the north corral fence of the Myers and Leonard complex. The grave of William Olds, however, is located about two hundred feet southeast of the Rath and Company store, almost at the side of the present-day county road. The burial was so close to this roadway, in fact, that it was once threatened by erosion. To prevent any further deterioration at the grave, county maintenance personnel installed a metal culvert between the burial site and the roadway. In 1929 the remains of William Dixon were reinterred in the southwest corner of the Rath and Company store.[3]

Each corner of the Adobe Walls trading post site was marked in the mid-1920s with 1-foot-square concrete blocks with steel rods extending into the ground. All of these markers remain in place except for one on the southwest. The corners of the former buildings were marked with smaller concrete blocks, but most of these have been removed. Two red granite historical monuments stand at the site. One of these, erected in 1924, lists the names of the white participants in the

Fig. 34. Historical marker erected in 1924 on the fiftieth anniversary of the 1874 Battle of Adobe Walls. (Photograph by T. Lindsay Baker.)

Fig. 35. Monument erected in 1941 in memory of Indian warriors killed in the 1874 battle. (Photograph by T. Lindsay Baker.)

1874 Battle of Adobe Walls. It is located in the northwest corner of the Rath and Company store. The second monument bears the names of the Indians known to have fallen in the same battle. It was erected in 1941 some distance south of the Rath and Company store. During the last field season the archeological team placed six Texas State Archeological Landmark markers at the site. A U.S. Geological Survey marker located 30 feet north of the Rath and Company store was used as the primary site datum during the excavation.

One additional feature, located at the extreme southern edge of the trading post site, consists of a circular depression about twenty feet in diameter. Test pits in the bottom of the depression produced a gummy red Permian clay, suggesting that this may have been the source for the daubing used in the picket walls of the Myers and Leonard store building.

Although historical accounts report the burial of several dead horses between the saloon and the Rath and Company store after the 1874 battle, extensive testing in this area failed to locate such a burial. Perhaps this feature was lost to bone collectors during the late 1870s or with the construction of the county road years later.

From the U.S. Geological Survey marker chosen as the site datum, a north-south base line was established at 22°30' east of true north. An east-west base line was then laid out to cross this base line at the center of the brass data plate on the concrete marker. The point of intersection, located north of the Rath and Company complex and west of the county road, was designated NSEW Zero and given a working elevation reference of 100 feet. The field party then established secondary east-west base lines near the presumed locations of each major structure. At the juncture of each secondary base line with the north-south line, a datum was established for each building. From the established base lines a grid of 10-foot-square excavation units was laid over the area where the archeological crew expected to find structural remains.

A single 10-foot square nearest the center of each structure was selected as an excavation starting point, and subsequent units were excavated in a checkerboard pattern. Field party members used shovels to peel back the heavy grass cover. Then both vertical and horizontal techniques and small hand tools were used to remove the remainder of the overburden. After workers located the building floors, they moved toward the walls, which were left untouched as much as possible. When feasible, the crew left artifacts in place for final sketching and photographing, but tourist visitation made this impossible much of the time.

The overburden was similar at all the structures except the saloon, which showed no signs of being burned. In the burned buildings it consisted of a sandy loam mixed with wood ash, charcoal, baked red clay, and, in the Myers and Leonard store, bricklike burned daubing fragments. The overburden ranged in thickness from a few inches to three feet. Except at the Rath and Company complex, little or no backfilling was planned. Consequently, most of the back dirt was spread more or less evenly in some of the tourist footpaths at the periphery of the site. A combination three-screen system employing ¼-, ⅛-, and ¹⁄₃₂-inch mesh was used to sift the overburden. After crews exposed the interior floors of the structures, they excavated the living surface areas immediately outside the buildings. Sketch maps and approximately 2,500 photographs were made before, during, and after the buildings were exposed. Concrete markers were placed on the floor levels at each building corner and wall intersection. In the locations where backfilling was necessary, the exposed wall lines were overlaid with plastic sheeting and then covered with soil. Crew members also placed small amounts of concrete in the bottoms of postholes not associated with building or corral walls. To eliminate seeming discrepancies, the crew spent many evenings surveying and examining the surrounding area for any evidence of other occupations, although none were identified in the immediate trading post area.

Piles of ash, outlines of charcoal, and small uncharred fragments constitute the only remains of recovered artifacts made from wood or other combustible materials. Ferrous objects are only slightly better preserved, as most of them have survived as iron oxide images encased within highly mineralized crusts. Artifacts made from other metallic substances such as lead, brass, and copper are highly oxidized and in varying states of deterioration. Except for heat warpage, patination, and discoloration, however, the artifacts made from stone, glass, earthenware, and other ceramic materials are in remarkably high states of preservation. Bone not damaged by rodents or fire also is exceptionally well preserved.

Artifacts recovered from the Adobe Walls trading post site are classified and described on the following pages according to a modified scheme of object classification presented by Robert G. Chenhall in *Nomenclature for Museum Cataloging*.[4] Some representative artifacts are illustrated and described individually, although most objects are simply enumerated in the tables for each category and are described as groups.

CHAPTER 9

Structures

Evidence from the 1874 Adobe Walls site documents that the builders of the trading post used two different architectural forms, sod and picket construction. Although both sod and picket buildings were commonly used in other parts of the country, neither form was ever used very widely in the Texas Panhandle. This fact adds to the interest of the remains preserved at the trading post site.

Much of the area of the semiarid treeless Texas plains is not especially well suited to either sod or picket architecture. Often the root growth of the bunch grasses is inadequate to hold sod building blocks together. The lack of trees precludes the construction of wooden picket buildings in most areas away from streams. Some limited areas near streams, however, can supply excellent building sod as well as wood for pickets. It is uncertain what role the availability of these materials may have had in the selection of the trading post site in 1874, but sufficient amounts of both definitely were accessible to the builders. High-quality building sod still may be found in the shallow marshes just west of the archeological site. Although not present in commercial quality or quantity, substantial amounts of wood satisfactory for picket production remain from nearby stands of cottonwood, hackberry, and willow trees lining the Canadian and its tributaries.

The builders of Adobe Walls obviously were familiar with both sod and picket architecture. Otherwise, they would not have chosen them. In the 1870s sod was perhaps the principal construction material in western Kansas.[1] Picket structures had been widely used through much of the lower Mississippi valley [2] as well as in the construction of buildings at several Southwestern military outposts.[3] With a small investment of time and money, a man and his family or hired hands could build a substantial sod or picket house in two weeks or less. The origins of both of these architectural forms are obscure, but some elements seem to be almost standard.

"Soddy," "sod house," "adobe," and "'dobe" are all expressions used to identify various types of aboveground earthen structures. There are, however, very basic differences between sod and adobe buildings. A sod structure is one built from blocks of moist sod that have been peeled from the ground with a special plow and then cut to proper length with spades. The blocks are laid into walls and then tamped together while still damp with their vegetation and roots intact. The plant matter serves as a binding agent to hold the blocks together as they dry. For stability, the walls often are thicker at their bases than at their tops. Window and door frames usually are made from vertical timbers held in position by horizontal crossmembers. There may be openings at the tops of door and window frames because of the settling of the sod in drying. These openings often are filled with rags, paper, grass, or left open as transoms until the walls have finished settling. Better sod buildings may have plastered walls and wooden floors, but most have tamped earth floors and walls "shaved" smooth with sharp spades.[4]

Adobe buildings, on the other hand, are built from sun-baked mud bricks that have been molded to uniform sizes and shapes. These bricks are made from a clay mud mixed with straw, grass, or other binding agents. The bricks may be laid with or without mortar, mud mortar being the most commonly used. Adobe walls have the advantage of settling much less than walls made from sod blocks. In addition, the uniformity of the bricks allows an adobe wall to be laid straighter and with a more uniform thickness than one built of sod. Adobe was not used as a building material at the 1874 Adobe Walls trading post, although it was used at the Bent, St. Vrain and Company trading post built in the 1840s about a mile south of the buffalo hunters' post. It was this much earlier site, in ruins by the 1870s, that gave the general area the name "Adobe Walls."[5]

The term "picket" may describe an almost infinite variety of structures built from logs standing on end. This architectural form includes, among other structures, the stockade. Stockades are usually associated in the popular mind with military forts, although they had much wider use. They are constructed from single rows of wooden poles set in the ground and often pointed on their upper ends. These poles are longer, straighter, and more uniform in diameter than those used in constructing picket walls for buildings. They usually are set deeper in the ground because they are freestanding. The stockade may reach a height of ten to fourteen feet, whereas a picket building wall need only be high enough to provide head clearance for the occupants of the structure.

Wall pickets for a building are generally about ten feet long and four to eight inches to diameter. They are set and tamped into a trench two to three feet deep and ten to twelve inches wide. The vertical poles often are alternated on opposite sides of the trench to form two roughly parallel rows. The tops are held together by plates made from cut lumber or hewn timbers. The roof in turn rests on these plates and the tops of the pickets. When waterproofing is desired, the builders fill the open joints between the pickets with mud, rocks, or other materials. Occasionally, the walls may be completely plastered, whitewashed, or otherwise decorated. Door and window frames used in picket houses are similar to those in sod buildings, and the floors likewise may be tamped earth or wooden.[6]

Roofs on sod and picket structures generally represent one of three basic types. In this order of frequency they are gabled, hipped, or shed types. Among these styles, variations occur in the types of building materials, which usually are either cut lumber or combined poles and brush. In either case, the lumber or brush then usually is overlaid with sod, with or without an intervening waterproof barrier material. Some on record have had fabric underliners to prevent soil or vermin in the roofing from sifting down onto the occupants. Some of the better sod and picket buildings in various parts of the country have had roofs covered with boards, tar paper, shingles, or sheet iron, but those at the Adobe Walls trading post had only earthen coverings.[7]

Discrepancies in descriptions of buildings at the Adobe Walls site are almost as numerous as the accounts of its history. These variations stem from differences in personal recollections, the use of colloquial terms in describing buildings, and seeming unfamiliarity with sod and picket architecture. Some of the structures at the site have been de-

TABLE 1

Historical Descriptions of the 1874 Adobe Walls Trading Post Buildings

Date	Source	Description
1874	Henry Joseph Farnsworth[1]	Myers and Leonard store 20 × 30 feet, Myers and Leonard corral 200 × 300 feet, stable providing "stabling for 40 horses," Rath and Company store 20 × 30 feet, saloon 15 × 20 feet
1874	Thomas McFadden[2]	Mentions "pickets of what once was a corral," referring to Myers and Leonard corral
ca. 1890	S. S. Van Sickel[3]	Myers and Leonard corral 300 × 300 feet, Rath and Company store and saloon noted as sod, having bastions, and having portholes for firing weapons, with windows mentioned in the saloon
ca. 1890	Quanah[4]	Described trading post as four or five log buildings
1892	Andrew Johnson[5]	Rath and Company store 24 or 25 feet wide and 50 to 60 feet long, made from sod with lumber roof and protected by two 12 × 12-foot "block houses"
1892	Charles Rath[6]	Rath and Company store built from sod, 25 × 50 feet, with "block houses" 12 or 15 feet square on opposite corners
1892	James H. Cator[7]	Described buildings as being built of "adobe" but mentions wooden pickets in the Myers and Leonard corral
1893	William B. Masterson[8]	Described Rath and Company store as 25 × 100 feet, "constructed principally out of adobe" with a roof built from "cottonwood logs" and sod
1908	Edward Campbell Little[9]	Rath and Company store 30 × 60 feet with "walls of adobe two feet thick," saloon 25 × 80 feet with adobe "walls some two feet thick," Myers and Leonard store 30 × 75 feet with "wooden walls . . . ten inches thick," Myers and Leonard corral 250 × 300 feet made from "poles extending seven feet into the ground and from seven to thirteen feet above," mention of Myers and Leonard "mess house" and an unidentified "sod" outbuilding

1913	Andrew Johnson[10]	Rath and Company store made with sod walls 3 feet thick at the base and 18 inches thick at the top, supporting a roof consisting of "cottonwood logs and poles laid across the walls and covered with sod and dirt"
1914	Olive K. Dixon[11]	Rath and Company store 16 × 20 feet made from sod, saloon 25 × 60 feet made from sod, blacksmith shop 15 feet square made from pickets, Myers and Leonard store a "picket house" 20 × 60 feet, Myers and Leonard corral "made by setting big cottonwood logs in the ground," Myers and Leonard "mess house" mentioned, and lookout posts added to both stores by constructing "a little enclosure with sod walls . . . built on top . . . for lookouts."
1922	Andrew Johnson and Orlando A. "Brick" Bond[12]	Rath and Company store 30 × 60 feet, saloon 20 × 40 feet, blacksmith shop mentioned, Myers and Leonard store 20 × 60 feet, Myers and Leonard kitchen 20 × 60 feet, and Myers and Leonard mess hall 20 × 70 feet
1923	Frederick J. Leonard[13]	Myers and Leonard corral 250 feet square

1. Farnsworth to Field Adjutant, Battalion 8th Cavalry, Sept. 23, 1874, Consolidated File 2815–1874.

2. Thompson McFadden, "Thompson McFadden's Diary of an Indian Campaign, 1874," ed. Robert C. Carriker, *Southwestern Historical Quarterly* 75, no. 2 (Oct., 1971):221.

3. S. S. Van Sickel, *A Story of Real Life on the Plains Written by Capt. S. S. Van Sickel, Born Sept. 6, 1826: A True Narrative of the Author's Experience*, pp. 13–14.

4. Quanah, "Told in English & Signs & Comanche: Quanah Parker's Account of Adobe Walls Fight," MS, [interview with Scott, 1897], ledgerbook vol. 1, p. 16, Hugh Scott Collection.

5. Andrew Johnson, sworn deposition, Oct. 10, 1892, pp. 38, 40–41.

6. Charles Rath, sworn deposition, Oct. 10, 1892, pp. 11¼ to 11½.

7. James H. Cator, sworn deposition, Oct. 10, 1892, p. 24.

8. William B. Masterson, sworn deposition, June 24, 1893, pp. 4, 6.

9. Little, "Battle of Adobe Walls," pp. 76, 79.

10. Johnson, "Andrew Johnson," p. 5.

11. [Dixon], *Life and Adventures*, pp. 176, 178–79, 195–96, 219–20, 222, 224–25, 235.

12. [Untitled plan of 1874 Adobe Walls trading post], ca. Mar. 10, 1923, History—Adobe Walls file.

13. "Texas Frontier Veteran Is Salt Laker: Tells of History-Making Indian Fights: Ridgepole on Saloon Building Credited with Saving Lives of Twenty-Nine," *Salt Lake Tribune*, Feb. 11, 1923, p. 7.

scribed variously as stores, houses, restaurants, saloons, and stockades. Although there was no stockade in the military sense of the word, the picket corral fence at the Myers and Leonard complex may have suggested such a feature. Basic information from major primary sources concerning building sizes, construction materials, and building locations is condensed in table 1.

The northernmost structural remains at the Adobe Walls trading post constituted the Myers and Leonard compound. The entire complex of several buildings enclosed within a rectangular corral was constructed of pickets. After the abandonment of the post, all these picket structures were burned. The outline of the building complex was represented by a continuous picket trench 130 feet on the north and south sides and 210 feet on the east and west sides. This trench was dug to an average depth of 2 feet and a width of 12 inches. The builders used the yellowish-brown sand removed from the trenches to level floors, build up door treadways, and refill the trenches around the wooden pickets once they were put in place. This sand turned almost white and became sandstone-hard after exposure to air and light. As a result of the fire that destroyed the structures, a slight difference in soil and fill sand color provided the only indications of picket diameters, which ranged from 4 to 8 inches.

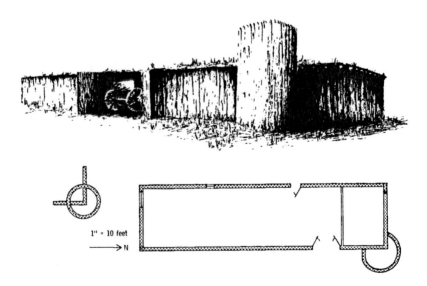

Fig. 36. Plan and reconstructed view of the Myers and Leonard store.

Fig. 37. Balks left for profiles in the excavation of the Myers and Leonard store. Summer, 1976. (Photograph by Billy R. Harrison.)

The wall pickets of the buildings, smaller in diameter than the corral pickets, were set alternately on opposite sides of the trench to form two parallel rows; the space between was filled with mud daubing. As the buildings burned, the daubing was baked to a bricklike hardness, and pieces of this baked material lay all along the wall lines. Most of the daubing had picket impressions, and some examples preserve both picket and cut-lumber impressions on as many as three faces. The corral fence pickets, larger than those used in the buildings, were set in single rows with no daubing, in the style of a stockade. Preserved remains gave no indication of the height of the corral pickets.

The building floors were baked very hard by the collapsed burning roof timbers and other combustible materials. In the instances in which sod or dirt roofs were present, the burned roof supports were overlaid with a thick layer of gummy red clay. The striking contrast between the clay, burned wood, baked floors, and white sand made separation of the layers comparatively easy. Outlines of ash and charcoal on the floors provided the only clues as to the locations of combustible furnishings, fixtures, and supplies within the buildings.

At the northeast corner of the Myers and Leonard complex was the store building. Its site is marked by trenches in which its picket walls stood. The north and east walls of the store served an additional role as outer walls for the rectangular compound. The building measured 17 feet east-to-west and 70 feet north-to-south. A circular trench 10 feet in diameter, dug sometime after the original construction, was discovered at the northeast corner of the store. It supported pickets that formed a defense bastion. Beneath the thin topsoil there was a 1-foot-thick bed of wood ash covering the inside of the circle. Two distinct layers of white sand separated by a thin living surface underlay the ash. The lower sand layer was associated with the store wall construction, and the upper layer, with the bastion. The thick bed of ash suggests that the bastion was built taller and with larger timbers than were the buildings or fences. No bed of red clay, like that in the dirt-roofed store, was present in the bastion area, indicating that it was either unroofed or wooden- or brush-roofed. No means of entry into the bastion could be determined. A "cache" containing approximately thirty-one .50–70 caliber cartridges, some very small glass sherds, a leather shoe, and various scraps of metal were the only artifacts found on the bastion floor.

A row of postholes with corresponding ash and charcoal remains extending southward from the bastion and parallel with the east store wall indicate a shed or porch roof 20 feet long and 5 feet wide along the front of the store building. The 70-foot east wall of the store contained a doorway 7 feet and 7¼ inches wide centered 16 feet and 8½ inches from the northeast corner of the building. Concentrations of fragmented daubing with cut-lumber impressions surrounded each side of the portal. Neither door construction details nor material type could be determined from the debris in and around the entry. No other east opening could be discerned.

The west wall had a 3-foot-wide doorway centered 24 feet and 1 inch from its north end. Charred remnants of a door made from heavy boards were found just inside the entry. An ash outline of a double hung window measuring approximately 24×48 inches consisting of eight 8×10-inch panes in wooden frames was found 24 feet south of the west entry. Outlines of a second double hung window approximately 24×48 inches with 8×10-inch panes in place were found

Fig. 38. Southwest to excavation of the bastion at the northeast corner of the Myers and Leonard store. Spring, 1977. (Photograph by Billy R. Harrison.)

along the south wall line near the southwest corner. The glazing quality and the presence of glazier's points indicate that the windows were commercially manufactured. A badly charred shutter made from 2×10-inch boards with 2×4-inch crosspieces was found inside the building. The imprint of a wagon box complete with hardware fragments was found on the surface immediately south of the building.

Although it cannot be proved by archeological remains, there may have been an east-west partition extending across the store from the north side of the east doorway. The amount of charred burlap, corn, and other unidentified burned material suggests a storage area in this portion of the building. The evidence suggesting such a storage room at the north end of the store is confirmed in the reminiscences of buffalo hunter Seth Hathaway, who noted that the building was divided into two rooms, a larger sales area and a smaller room containing "stacked flour, bacon, corn meal, horse feed, lead, and other things . . . which Meyers [*sic*] traded for hides."[8]

Shelving extended along the east wall from the south side of the

Fig. 39. Charred remains of a shutter found in the Myers and Leonard store. (Photograph by Billy R. Harrison.)

double doorway to the southwest corner and across the south wall of the building. Most of the animal shoes and harness pieces were mixed with charred shelving in the southeast corner. A stout table measuring 3×4½ feet occupied the southwest corner, while a lightweight wooden table 30 inches square was found in the north central part of the floor. Highly oxidized tin cans and pieces of charred denim or other lightweight canvas were on top of the table. Ironstone dishes and oil lamps were found along the west wall between the doorway and window. Two rows of five postholes each were located parallel with and 3 feet, 3½ inches and 5 feet away from the east wall. The rows were 1 foot, 8½ inches apart and extended from 5 feet north of the south wall to 12 feet south of the east entry, a distance of 32½ feet. Ash outlines suggest that these posts were topped with a 2-foot-wide counter top. The floor between the counter and the east wall was covered with 1-inch-thick boards. Seth Hathaway reported "a counter across one side" of the building "behind which was [*sic*] kept the smaller stores."[9] Charred corn and ash outlines at the north end of the counter indicate the location there of a large storage bin. A set of highly oxidized platform scales was found near the center of the building west of the bin.

Apparently, the Indians stacked combustible materials in the center of the building to expedite its burning after the abandonment of the post. Near the scales in the middle of the floor, for example, were

Fig. 40. South to final excavation at the south end of the Myers and Leonard store. Summer, 1976. (Photograph by Billy R. Harrison.)

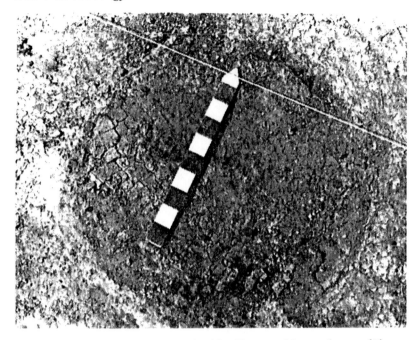

Fig. 41. Charred remains of a barrel in the Myers and Leonard store. (Photograph by Billy R. Harrison.)

the remains of more than a dozen barrels, a table, and a chair. The impression of a wagon box with hardware fragments, coupling pole, tongue, and hitching trees extended across the floor from the east entry. Three or more wooden barrels had been in the box.

The store yielded two highly oxidized rifle barrels, one at the east doorway and the other at the north end of the large table. The latter still retained part of a mineralized fore end with a brass butt plate and trigger guard near enough to be considered parts of the rifle. A small bench grinder complete with a partial stone grinding wheel, as well as a large grinding wheel for a foot-powered grinder, were found at the north end of the building. Ammunition, buttons, clay tobacco pipes, tin cans, bottles, charred cloth fragments, iron scraps, and unidentified charred substances were scattered throughout the building.

The Myers and Leonard compound, as mentioned, was built around the inner edge of its rectangular picket corral fence. This protected area served as both the hide yard and horse corral for the business enterprise. The store stood in the northeast corner of the complex, and connected mess hall and stable structures were built diagonally opposite the store in the southwest corner. The stockade-style picket fence was built 113 feet westward from the store to the northwest corner of the compound. From that point the fence stretched 210 feet to the south. At its south end the corral fence doubled as the outer wall for the west side of the mess hall and stable. On the other side of the compound, the corral fence ran south 140 feet from the store. Connecting the east and west sides of the corral, pickets were set in a trench 130 feet long, completing the barricade between the southeast and southwest corners. At the extreme west end these pickets doubled as the south wall for the mess hall. All these dimensions are based on the measurements of the trenches into which the pickets were placed. The corral pickets themselves averaged 8 to 10 inches in diameter.

Circular picket bastions similar to the one at the store were placed in the southeast and northwest corners of the hide yard. Their date of construction is unknown, but they definitely replaced the original right-angle corners that preceded them. The locations of these bastions are marked by circular trenches 10 feet in diameter; they supported the large stockade-like pickets from which the defense structures were built. A layering of white sand, ash, and living surfaces similar to those in the bastion at the northeast corner of the store was found around the two corral bastions.

Except for complete excavation of the corners, only limited tests were made along the corral fence lines. Excavation of the fence corner areas, around the exterior of the buildings, as well as tests along the fence lines, revealed a thin film of charcoal dust on the 1874 living surface. This presence suggests that a grass fire may have occurred when the buildings burned. The southeast corner of the corral yielded a hatchet, a hame hook, a fragmented stove door, and a broken ladle. Of these objects, only the stove door came from the bastion itself. The northwest corner of the hide yard produced a horseshoe, a singletree hook, scraps of iron objects, thirteen brass buttons and fabric impressions of a military coat, a bottle, and several pieces of lead shot.[10]

A 12-foot north-to-south by 29-foot east-to-west picket building of similar construction as the store stood in the extreme southwest corner of the Myers and Leonard hide yard. Most primary sources

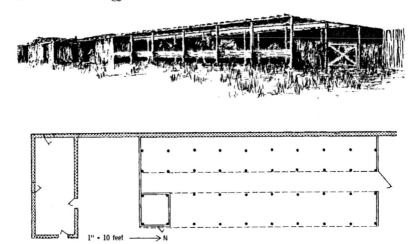

Fig. 42. Plan and reconstructed view of the Myers and Leonard mess hall and stable.

mentioning the structure identify it as a "mess house" or "boarding house" operated as a restaurant serving meals for both transients and Myers and Leonard employees.[11] It is known to have had two and possibly four doors. A 3-foot-wide portal was located in the east wall 2 feet from its north end, and another 3-foot entry was located in the north wall 8 feet from its east end. Possibly, a door was almost centered in the south wall, and yet another was centered 6 feet from the north end of the west wall. A 3-foot-diameter hole 2 feet deep, dug by relic hunters, was found in and to the outside of the identified north doorway. Hinges, a doorknob, and charcoal suggest this door was still in place at the time the building burned. No solid evidence was found to document windows in the building, although it is not inconceivable that openings in the south and west walls may have served the purpose. The roof was either thicker at the center or had some other structure such as a lookout post above it. Additional layers of ash and red clay above the charred roof-support timbers gave the impression of a double roof over this portion of the building.

The north and east walls of the mess hall apparently were lined with shelves holding dishes and other utensils. In these areas the excavators were very surprised to find high-quality ironstone china, as they had expected food service items to be of the military field type. Even though all of the ironstone was broken, restoration of many specimens was possible. Most of the ironstone dishes have impressed makers' marks and/or blue transfer trademarks on their bases. A large cast-iron cookstove probably occupied the area near the south entry. It had been broken and its pieces scattered, many of the fragments being almost beyond recognition. Identifiable parts included round lids, door fragments, lid lifters, and a grate fragment.[12] Sherds from a

Fig. 43. West along the south wall picket trench at the Myers and Leonard mess hall. Summer, 1976. (Photograph by Billy R. Harrison.)

Fig. 44. West to final excavation of the Myers and Leonard mess hall. Summer, 1976. (Photograph by Billy R. Harrison.)

four-gallon crockery container were found near the northwest corner. Rodents had scattered some of these sherds throughout the entire north and west picket trenches. Eight 4-inch-deep rectangular pits were found in the building floor, their bottoms lined with boards 1 inch thick. Except for one pit, which may have held a roof support, no purpose could be assigned to these depressions or for their placement. They were apparently open when the building burned, for only charcoal remained from the bottom wooden linings.

A covered area 25 feet east-to-west by 18 feet north-to-south formed a separation between the mess hall and the stable to the north. All but a narrow strip across the north side of this area was destroyed by an illegal relic hunter's shovel during late winter or early spring, 1978. Although covered with a thin earthen roof, the area had no apparent east wall. Slight evidence suggests that there may have been a 10×18-foot enclosure in the west half of the area. The corral fence formed the west wall of the enclosure. Circumstantial evidence places a water well in the northeast quadrant of the area, but, unfortunately, specific evidence was destroyed.

North of the Myers and Leonard mess hall and along the west corral fence stood an open-air stable. Most people at Adobe Walls must have considered it to be part of the corrals, for only one known visitor to the post felt it worthy of mentioning in describing the buildings. This was Lt. Henry Joseph Farnsworth, who in 1874 noted in an army report that the Myers and Leonard hide yard included "stabling for 40 horses."[13]

From the stable there remained at the site four rows of nine post-holes, each extending 70 feet northward from the mess hall. These rows of holes were dug at 4-, 10-, 17-, and 26-foot intervals eastward from the west corral fence, which served as an exterior wall. Beds of ash averaging 10 feet wide, intermixed with charred pole and cut-lumber fragments, extended along each long side of the 26×70-foot structure. There were no ash, charcoal, or other structural remains, however, along a 6- to 7-foot-wide center aisle the length of the building. These remains suggest that the posts supported two 10-foot-wide brush roofs along each side with no cover over the center aisle. Some of the pole fragments may have formed stall dividers, but this supposition could not be confirmed. The cut-lumber fragments may represent continuous feed troughs along each side. A partially burned bed of grass or hay lay between the presumed trough bottom and the floor.

Fig. 45. North to final excavation of the Myers and Leonard stable. Summer, 1978. (Photograph by Billy R. Harrison.)

This material could have been either indigenous grass or fodder present at the time the building burned.

A partition across the south end separated the stable from the mess hall. At the southeast corner of the stable, the builders constructed a small 8×9-foot room utilizing the partition as a south wall. Remains gave no hints to indicate the purpose for this chamber. Several sandstone slabs and a sand treadway suggest that it had an east entry, but this could not be otherwise verified. Metal hinges as well as a latch indicate some type of movable closure across the north end of the stable. The picket corral fence served as its west wall, and the presumed troughs formed its east side.

Except for a handsaw near the southwest corner and a few scattered wagon hardware parts, few diagnostic artifacts were found in the stable. Incongruous with its use as stabling for animals were fragments of a cast-iron stove found along the west side of the structure near its center. It is doubtful, however, that the stove was used in this location, for a large, heavily burned area and a small bed of compact ash were found nearby.

While construction was progressing on the Myers and Leonard compound during March and April, 1874, other merchants back in Dodge City were planning to build a store to compete with them for the hide men's trade at Adobe Walls. This competition came from the firm of Charles Rath and Company. Its caravan of heavily laden wagons

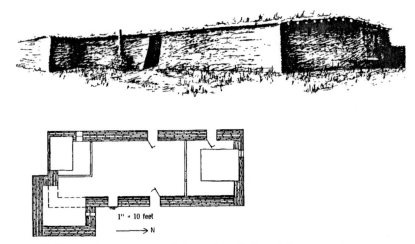

Fig. 46. Plan and reconstructed view of the Rath and Company store.

Fig. 47. North to general view of the final excavation of the Rath and Company store. Summer, 1979. (Photograph by Billy R. Harrison.)

rumbled out of Dodge City in late April, reaching the broad meadow called Adobe Walls on the north side of the Canadian River sometime around the first of May. Upon arrival, the Rath and Company employees started work on their sod store building and its auxiliary structures.[14] The north wall of their building stood 380 feet south of the Myers and Leonard corral.

At the time the Adobe Walls trading post was excavated, the Rath and Company store was the only structural feature with significant remains above the 1874 ground surface. As much as 2 feet of its original sod walls remained intact at this time. These portions of the walls were in all probability preserved by certain factors that destroyed other parts of them.

In 1924 a large red granite marker was set on a concrete base in what had been the northwest corner of the store. Then in 1929 William Dixon's mortal remains were removed from their original burial place at Texline, Texas, and reinterred beneath a stone marker in the southwest corner of the store. Iron pipe barriers were then erected to protect both monuments. Although excavation for the footings for the markers and for the grave destroyed elements of the cultural remains, the monuments as well as a small sandstone-capped hillock near the south end of the store helped to preserve certain parts of the structure. During the severe drought of the 1930s, these features combined to affect wind currents and caused some leeside duning of sand. As a result, parts of the building were covered rather than blown away, the fate of other structures at the site. The height of the wall remnants at the Rath and Company store and their excellent preservation revealed more information about this building than could be learned about any other structures at the site. The burning of the store interior baked part of the walls to almost ceramic hardness, further enhancing their preservation.

The interior of the sod walls at the Rath and Company store measured 16½ feet east-to-west and 52 feet, 9½ inches north-to-south.[15] The wall thickness averaged slightly less than 3 feet at the base, with a

Fig. 48. Southwest to general view of the completely excavated bastion at the southeast corner of the Rath and Company store. Summer, 1979. (Photograph by Billy R. Harrison.)

Fig. 49. North to the north wall of the bastion at the Rath and Company store, showing the preserved tiers of sod blocks. Summer, 1979. (Photograph by Billy R. Harrison.)

definite sloping of the exterior surface. This gives the exterior dimensions of approximately 22½×59 feet. A defense bastion measuring 13 feet north-to-south by 12 feet east-to-west on the inside was added at the southeast corner of the store at some date after the original construction. Its outside dimensions were approximately 18×19 feet. The walls of the bastion abutted the store walls; the sod layers were not interlaced, as they were at all the other sod building corners. Historical accounts record a similar bastion at the northwest corner,[16] but this could not be verified from preserved remains. The building undoubtedly had an earthen roof, as shown by a thick bed of red clay. Ash and charcoal in and beneath the clay suggest more than simple pole supports. The dirt was probably supported on timbers covered with cut-lumber roofing. A thick pile of reddish-gray sandy clay, overlying all building and other cultural debris, was centered about 12 feet north and 6 feet east of the southwest corner of the building. These remains probably represent the lookout post built atop the roof after the June 27, 1874, battle. The ladder from which William Olds fell to his death could have been attached to a partition that crossed the building at this point. Adjoining partitions formed a 10 × 10-foot room in the southwest corner of the building. Wear patterns on the floor indicate entry into the room at the juncture of the partition and the west store wall. This room probably comprised the living quarters for store employees Hannah and William Olds.

Another partition crossed the store east-to-west 14 feet south of the north wall. The 14 × 16½-foot chamber thus created was the location of the restaurant operated by Mrs. Olds. Except for scattered fragments elsewhere, all the ironstone china, crockery, and cooking utensils in the Rath and Company store were found north of this partition. Total excavation of this room was prevented by the granite historical marker. Both east and west walls north of the partition were hard baked from the fire, and they appeared to have had shelving or similar wooden structures attached to them. Some large spikes or nails were still embedded in these walls.

Entry into the restaurant portion of the store from the building interior was through a doorway located 5 feet west of the store front through the partition. A 3-foot exterior entry to the restaurant area was located in the west wall 5 feet from its north end. A second 3-foot-wide portal through the west wall was centered 24 feet south of the north wall. These openings were well defined by the baking of the walls from burning door jambs and the accumulated sand in their treadways; 8½ feet of the east wall and 3½ feet of the south wall were cut away after or at the time that the bastion was added. A buildup of sand at the southeast corner of the store was similar to the accumulations of sand in the other known doorways in the building, but no doorway was found.

Enough evidence was found only to suggest where windows may have been placed in the walls of the Rath and Company store. This situation was further complicated by the fact that the window frames and doors were removed, probably by Indians, and stacked in the center of the building, where in 1874 they burned into a pile of charcoal, ash, and extremely warped window glass. Slightly burned remains from jamb pieces left in place tend to locate one window in the north wall near the northwest corner of the building. Another similar area

Fig. 50. View east into the remnants of the fireplace in the east wall of the Rath and Company store, as excavated in summer, 1979. (Photograph by Billy R. Harrison.)

was located about halfway between the southernmost west door and the southwest corner. Both 10 × 12-inch and 8 × 10-inch windowpanes have been pieced together from sherds recovered from the building center. Glass and wood imprints were found from a small two-pane window located on the exterior surface of the corner formed by the bastion and the east building wall. As the imprints were oriented east-to-west, the window probably was in the bastion wall.

A unique and at first puzzling construction was found in the east wall interior centered 36 feet south of the north wall. Excavation revealed that it was a fireplace that had been constructed by the removal of part of the completed sod wall. The sides of the 3-foot-wide fireplace were then lined with Permian sandstone and a layer of sand placed in front of that. A few of the rocks remained in place, although most were scattered on the surface around the fireplace on the building exterior. The rocks, building walls, and hearth all exhibited alteration from extreme heat, forming a dark orange surface.

The packed earthen floor, which varied less than 2½ inches in elevation through the building, was hardened by heat from falling burning timbers. Accumulations of sand extended through each doorway and fanned out on both the interior and exterior surfaces. Only one pit was found in the floor, a rectangle 3 feet, 2½ inches east-to-west by 2 feet north-to-south and 1 foot deep near the center of the bastion. This depression may have been the well dug inside the store by Andrew Johnson after the 1874 battle.[17] Several circular shallow holes were located in the south end of the building, but excavation failed to determine whether they were rodent dens or shallow postholes. One depression associated with the southwest room partition may have held a roof support within the partition, but no other evidence of such vertical supports was found. Except in the restaurant area, few diagnostic artifacts were found, although several cartridge cases and cartridges were recovered on the bastion floor. One curiosity was the remains of a bisón femur in the northwest restaurant corner. Rodents had mostly destroyed the bone, but it was found in a vertical position and may have served as a marker in the building construction. Four iron spikes also were driven into the floor at the wall juncture in this corner.

Most exterior debris was outside the north and east walls. A few wagon hardware parts, bone scraps, and approximately sixty rusted tin cans lay in a fan-shaped pattern sloping away from the north wall outside the presumed location of the restaurant window. Rocks from the fireplace littered the area along the south half of the exterior east wall. Buttons, ironstone fragments, cartridges and cases, clay tobacco pipe and glass sherds, meat bones, and other debris were scattered on both sides of the east doorway. An unexplained depression surrounded the northwest corner outside the building. Some of the tin cans had slid into it and become covered with what appeared to be collapsed roof or wall material.

Based on archeological evidence, it is doubtful that the sod corral at the Rath and Company complex was ever completed.[18] Probably only two or at most three courses of sod were laid. The excavators found very little direct evidence of the corral wall and no slump of eroded sod. The earthen fence, however, was laid out to extend 56 feet west from the southwest corner of the store, thence 86 feet north, thence 52 feet east, thence 28 feet south, and thence 6 feet east to join the northeast corner of the store. From the scant preserved evidence,

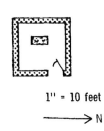

1" = 10 feet

————→ N

Fig. 51. Plan and reconstructed view of the Rath and Company privy.

the wall is believed to have been about 2 feet thick. A shoe last head was found in the northwest corner of the corral, and it may have been used as an alignment string anchor. There was less than scant evidence of sod layers between the north corral fence and the building corner. A line of ash and a few minute wood fragments suggest that some form of movable wooden barrier may have been used to close the gap at this point.

The Rath and Company privy, located 66 feet west of the southwest corral corner, presents an interesting enigma. Judging from the very limited written accounts of the structure,[19] it should be of sod construction. Archeological evidence, however, points to a small structure built similarly to the picket blacksmith shop. The 8×9-foot structure offered no evidence whatever of sod walls, sod roof, or slump from either. On the other hand, the abundance of ash covering the floor area indicates that a considerable amount of wood was used in the building, but no nails of any kind were found. The accumulation of sand on the floor and on the immediate exterior surface created a channeling effect similar to that found at the blacksmith shop. Further complicating the situation is the fact that the structure is much larger than would be expected or needed for a privy. A 2- to 3-foot-thick sod

Fig. 52. West across the final excavation of the Rath and Company privy. Summer, 1979. (Photograph by Billy R. Harrison.)

wall would have reduced the interior space to a more reasonable size. A thin wooden wall, as indicated by the channeling, and the pit location would require the construction of a large bench or seat or, alternately, one set away from the walls. A thicker sod wall would have permitted a seat of reasonable size to be set in the southwest corner and still cover the pit.

Whatever structure type may have existed, it is believed that entry was through the north half of the east wall. The pit was dug 3 feet, 1¼ inches north-to-south by 1½ feet east-to-west by 2 feet, 8½ inches deep. The southwest corner of the depression was 2½ feet east and north of the southwest building corner. Two mushroomed bullets, a clay tobacco pipe stem fragment, and a horse metatarsal were the only objects found in the privy. All but one bullet came from the pit.

After work was completed for the store proper at the Rath and Company complex, Andrew Johnson, who supervised the construction, undertook a second building project at Adobe Walls. His employer, Charles Rath, sometime in April or May had made arrangements with James N. Hanrahan to pool their resources in opening a saloon at the trading post. When Rath returned to Dodge City in May it was "to send material for a saloon." Hanrahan may have accompanied him on the trip, as he also went back to Dodge about this time, returning to the Panhandle sometime in the second week of June. As Rath's chief builder, Johnson[20] constructed the saloon between the two store complexes 204 feet north of the Rath and Company store and 153 feet south of the Myers and Leonard corral.

Built of sod, the interior walls of the saloon building measured 17 feet north-to-south by 36 feet east-to-west. The 3-foot walls of the building gave it outside dimensions of approximately 23×42 feet. At the time of the excavation very little remained of the original building except remnants of the bottommost tiers of sod blocks. One area of the wall near the northeast corner did reveal four distinguishable sod courses, each about 3½ inches thick and 3 feet long. One problem in locating the walls was the damaging presence of rodent tunnels, which had destroyed much of the floor/wall juncture area.

Although the saloon was the only structure that showed no indication of having been destroyed by fire, a possible addition at its west end may have burned. The excavators found no charcoal or ash inside the building, and the only wooden remains discovered were very small fragments of uncharred wood on the building floor. A 10-foot-diameter depression, some artifacts, ash, charcoal, and a fire pit all suggest a small, burned addition at the west end of the saloon, al-

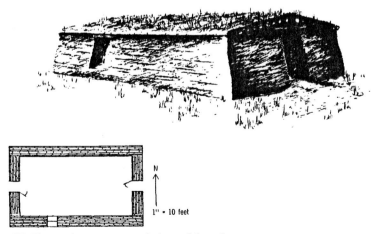

Fig. 53. Plan and reconstructed view of the saloon.

Fig. 54. Northwest to final excavation of the saloon. Summer, 1975. (Photograph by Billy R. Harrison.)

though no evidence of walls or support posts could be found there. If in fact such a frame addition existed, it burned completely and had no supports that penetrated the ground. The fire pit in this area was approximately 1½ feet square and filled with ash and charcoal. The bowled bottom of the 1-foot-deep pit contained slightly more than a pound of lead slag.

Data derived from the cross-sectional areas of the sod wall slump provide the basis for determining the wall height. This is estimated to have been 6 to 7 feet at the eaves. Small windowpane sherds were recorded about midway along the interior of the south wall. These sherds were the only verification for windows mentioned in many historical accounts. Breaks in the sod layers centered in both east and west walls represent two 3-foot doorways. Fan-shaped sand treadways extended through the entries a short distance on both sides of the walls. Postholes 8 inches in diameter were located on each interior side of both doorways. The four holes probably held the base of a wooden structural framework that supported a heavy wooden ridgepole the length of the roof. Shallow depressions crossed the treadways parallel to the exterior sides of the walls. These depressions most likely served as water traps, although the one at the east entry also contained artifacts including tobacco pipe fragments, a flattened pail, and rifle paraphernalia.

The elevation of the hard-packed earthen floor in the saloon varied less than 2½ inches. In addition to the four postholes at the doors, the floor contained two additional holes. One 12-inch-diameter circular pit was centered along the east-west building axis 12 feet from the west wall. This 12-inch-deep depression probably contained the base of a vertical support for the ridgepole. Situated against the south wall 13 feet from the east wall was another 12-inch-deep pit, this one 12 inches square, the function of which is unknown.

The majority of the bottles, footwear fragments, and other artifacts from the saloon were found on the floor along the walls in the west half of the building. Tobacco pipe fragments, ammunition, and other objects were randomly scattered over the entire floor. More than a hundred cartridge primers littered the southeast quadrant of the area. A pit 1 foot deep and 1½ feet square was located at the exterior southwest corner of the building. In the northeast corner of this depression the excavators found a bison femur with its head slightly below the 1874 ground level. This may have served as an alignment stake during the construction of the building. One pair of butt hinges and a door/gate latch were found just outside the west wall north of the west doorway.

Completing the buildings erected at the Adobe Walls trading post was Tom O'Keefe's blacksmith shop. He built his picket building 95 feet south of the Myers and Leonard corral and 35 feet north of the saloon. It was roughly in line with the front of the Myers and Leonard corral.

Although Tom O'Keefe erected a picket building to house his blacksmith shop, it differed from the picket structures that Myers and Leonard had built because it had no trench to support its walls. O'Keefe instead set substantial wooden posts in the ground at each of the corners and on either side of the entries. He then attached split-log type top and bottom plates to the posts and filled the space between the posts with small vertical pickets held in position by the plates. The entire floor and ground surface immediately around the walls of the building was built up with sand. This fill in effect created a shallow

Fig. 55. Bison femur marking the southwest corner of the saloon. Summer, 1975. (Photograph by Billy R. Harrison.)

channel containing the bottom plates and the lower ends of the small vertical pickets. Beneath the overburden at the blacksmith shop, only a thin bed of ash covered the floor. The absence of red gummy clay suggests a thatch or brush roof, certainly not one covered with sod or earth. No evidence was found to indicate that the walls had been daubed or otherwise sealed. A 6-foot doorway was centered in the east or front wall and a 3-foot doorway was centered on the south wall. The only door detail recovered was a brown ceramic doorknob inside the building.

Metal fragments, glass sherds, coal, and forge slag covered the south half of the floor area. Several horseshoes and muleshoes were randomly scattered both inside and outside the west half of the south wall, suggesting that they had been either hanging on the wall or resting on shelves attached to the wall when the building burned. Numerous lumps of coal were found in the southeast corner. The unburned coal and a bed of slag indicate the likelihood that a forge operated at

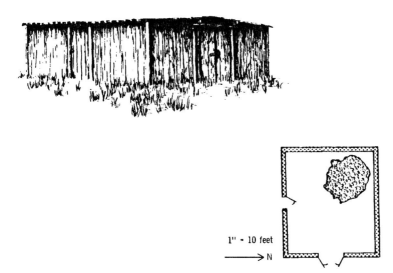

1" = 10 feet

⟶ N

Fig. 56. Plan and reconstructed view of the blacksmith shop.

Fig. 57. West to final excavation of the blacksmith shop. Summer, 1978. (Photograph by Billy R. Harrison.)

the east side of the south entry. The northeast corner of the floor was relatively free of debris. This situation, combined with a highly compacted surface of the earthen floor in this corner, suggests that it was here that the animals were shod. A pit was located in the northwest corner of the building. Excavation showed this depression to be part of the original structure. The approximately 10-foot-diameter and 2-foot-deep conical pit is believed to have served as a water tank for setting wagon tires and for quenching hot metal. The presence of five beer bottles in the blacksmith shop suggests that the water in the depression may also have served as a place where O'Keefe cooled his beer. The surface of the pit, with large distinct shrinkage cracks, has all the appearances of a dry pond or lake bed. Small scraps of metal, mostly horseshoe dubbings, were found all along the sloping sides of the depression.

An interesting aspect of the blacksmith shop is its orientation. It faces more northeastly than do the other east-facing structures that compose the trading post. Tom O'Keefe may have planned this alignment so that he could take advantage of the prevailing southwesterly breezes, which would have blown through the entries across his forge area and improved ventilation.

The buildings at the 1874 Adobe Walls trading post yielded an interesting array of building fragments. As shown in table 2, these include such materials as mud daubing, door hardware, and window glass. Permian clay served as the base substance used for mixing the daubing for the picket buildings in the Myers and Leonard compound. The natural red color of the daubing turned pinkish-gray to black through the actions of heat, smoke, and organic stains, and the gummy consistency changed to an almost bricklike hardness. The daubing appears to have had grass or straw mixed with the clay, but no significant impurities were found. Hundreds of daubing fragments from pea to cobble size were excavated from the Myers and Leonard store and mess hall, but only representative samples were salvaged.

Of the three glazed clay doorknobs found at the trading post site, only one was complete. These knobs are very similar to the roughly contemporary agateware knobs found at Fort Richardson, Texas,[21] and the brown mineral glaze knobs recovered at Fort Bowie, Arizona.[22] All the Adobe Walls examples are made from at least two kinds of clay, creating a cream- to rust-colored internal marbling effect. The glazed

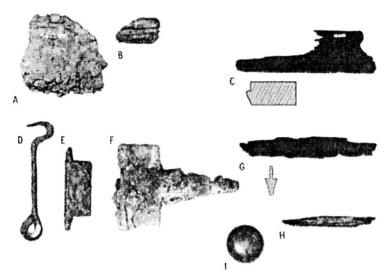

Fig. 58. Building fragments: (*A*) Picket wall daubing 4½ × 4⅞ inches. (*B*) Picket wall daubing 2¼ × 1½ inches. (*C*) Window sash fragment 7 inches long and 2⅛ × 1 inches in cross section. (*D*) Door/gate hook 6¾ inches long. (*E*) Butt hinge 1½ × 4¹¹⁄₁₆ inches. (*F*) T hinge 7⅛ inches long. (*G*) Window sash fragment 7 inches long and ½ × ¼ inch in cross section. (*H*) Window sash fragment 4¹³⁄₁₆ inches long. (*I*) Ceramic doorknob.

surfaces are a translucent yellowish-orange and brown color. The knobs are 2¹⁄₃₂ inches in diameter by 1⁹⁄₆₄ inches thick. The ²¹⁄₃₂-inch mounting holes are threaded, and the one complete knob still has mounting lead in the bottom of its hole.

Seven butt and three T hinges were recovered. The butt hinges all appear to be the loose pin variety. Illustrated is one of a pair having acorn-shaped tips that measure 1½×4¹¹⁄₁₆ inches. All three T hinges are 7⅛ inches long and made from heavy wrought iron. They are similar to Sears, Roebuck and Company No. 13808 hinges, which listed for $0.98 per dozen pairs in 1897.[23] One hinge fragment was unidentifiable.

Two hooks made from heavy wrought iron represent the only door or gate fastenings found at the site. The illustrated 6¾-inch hook came from the west saloon door opening, and the smaller 4-inch hook

TABLE 2
Building Fragments

	M & L Store	Mess Hall	Stable	R & Co. Store	Saloon	Blacksmith Shop
Brick fragment				1		
Daubing salvaged	30	2				
Door hook		1			1	
Doorknob		1		1		1
Door pull		1				
Flashing		3				
Butt hinge			5		2	
T-strap hinge	2		1			
Hinge fragment		1				
Hinge hasp eye		1				
8 × 10-inch partial windowpane	15					
10 × 12-inch partial windowpane				8		
Window putty	83			22		
Unidentified charred wood	5	17			12	
Window sash fragment				6		
White lead				31 lb.		

Fig. 59. Shattered remains of 10 × 12-inch windowpanes in the Rath and Company store. (Photograph by Billy R. Harrison.)

came from the north end of the stable. The hinge hasp eye listed in table 2 may have been used as an eye for this shorter hook.

Remains of glass windowpanes were recovered at both the Myers and Leonard store and the Rath and Company store. During the nineteenth century three production methods were used for making flat window glass: the crown, casting, and cylinder methods. By the late nineteenth century the cylinder process had become the most common, as it produced larger sheets of more uniform thickness at a lower cost per sheet.[24] Breakage, heat warpage, and patination make it difficult to prove, but it seems reasonable to assume that the window glass found at Adobe Walls was made by the cylinder process. All the examples have a bluish-green tint.

From the sherds collected in the Myers and Leonard store, it was possible to piece together fifteen partial 8 × 10-inch panes, and eight 10 × 12-inch panes were assembled from sherds found in the Rath and Company store. Of the panes assembled, only the one illustrated shows any evidence of having been broken by a bullet or other projectile.

Fig. 60. An 8 × 10-inch windowpane showing evidence of breakage by a projectile.

Window sash remains appear to have been similar to Sears, Roebuck and Company No. 14390,[25] with all but one being eight-light sashes with 8×10-inch panes. One twelve-light sash in the Rath and Company store was glazed with 10×12-inch panes. There were no weights or other evidence to suggest anything other than ordinary rail sashes. Only four small charred fragments of sash wood were salvageable, and they originated from three separate sashes. An unburned but shattered window near or in the Rath and Company bastion was apparent, but only enough remained of the sash and panes to determine that it had two lights. Glazing points and glazing compound (putty) found in the ash, charcoal, and other window debris in both stores indicate that the windows were factory-made and brought to the site from Kansas.

A tiny edge fragment of red brick of undetermined origin was located in the Rath and Company store. One incomplete metal artifact found near the north end of the stable probably represents a door or gate pull. Small pieces of sheet metal found under the wall and roof debris of the mess hall had been nailed to wood, suggesting their use as flashing. Thirty-four small scraps of wood, mostly charred, were salvaged for possible identification. One piece is ash or oak; the others are cottonwood, chinaberry, and hackberry.

Some limited remains of paint were discovered. A single lump of mud daubing found in the Myers and Leonard mess hall has what appears to be traces of blue paint on one surface. A circular area of the floor in the Myers and Leonard store was found to be covered with a blue stain about the size of a quart can, blue paint or indigo dye being two of the possible substances that may have created the stain. In the Myers and Leonard store, a very small fragment of hard-baked earth, either daubing or fire-hardened earthen floor, retained an area of red stain. Completing the evidence of paint at Adobe Walls was 31 pounds of white lead discovered on the floor of the Rath and Company store.

CHAPTER 10

Building Furnishings

A̲MONG the remains recovered at the 1874 Adobe Walls trading post site were objects representing two general categories of building furnishings—pieces of furniture and lighting devices. Only fragments of the former were found, telling us comparatively little, but the site yielded surprisingly interesting preserved elements of lighting devices.

The articles of furniture left at the trading post when it burned were completely consumed by fire except for limited charred remnants of two tables and one chair. A tabletop found in the north central part of the open sales room at the Myers and Leonard store measured 30 inches square and had a thin ½-inch-wide metal band around its edge similar to that on some modern card tables. A second table was located in the southwest corner of the same store. Made much more heavily, it measured approximately 3×4½ feet. Only a few small fragments of chair spindle were salvaged, making positive identification of type and style of chair impossible.

The saloon yielded an intriguing homemade candleholder with a candle fragment still in place. The holder base was probably fashioned from one side of a model 1861 U.S. Army canteen, and it consists of a metal bowl 1 inch deep and 6¼ inches in diameter.[1] A small can topped by a brass canteen spout is soldered to this base. Neither the candle nor the holder showed any deterioration beyond that caused by use and age.

The other lighting devices found at Adobe Walls were the remains of three kerosene lamps. These lamps are comparatively difficult to

TABLE 3
Lighting Devices

	M & L Store	R & Co. Store	Saloon	Blacksmith Shop
Candle			1	
Lamp font	2			
Lamp font sherds	11			
Lamp burner	2		1	
Lamp chimney sherd	573	1	1	11
Wall bracket	1			

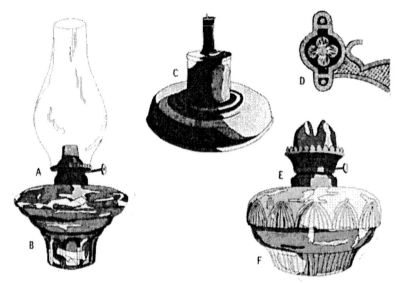

Fig. 61. Artist's reconstruction of lighting devices based on archeological remains: (*A*) Plume and Atwood kerosene lamp burner with 1¾-inch base. (*B*) Glass font associated with the larger Plume and Atwood burner. (*C*) Homemade candleholder with candle fragment. (*D*) Cast-iron lamp support bracket 4⅛ × 4¾ inches. (*E*) Edward Miller and Company kerosene lamp burner with 2¼-inch base. (*F*) Glass font associated with the Edward Miller and Company burner.

date. The first successful kerosene lamp burner was introduced into the United States in 1856. John J. Marcy in 1863 received one of the earliest American patents for these burners, and he assigned his rights to the firm of Edward Miller and Company of Meriden, Connecticut, which in time became one of the largest lamp manufacturers in America.[2] In 1873 another important patent was granted to Lewis J. Atwood of the Plume and Atwood Manufacturing Company, Waterbury, Connecticut, which became one of the major competitors for the Edward Miller firm.[3] These two companies produced the lamps found at Adobe Walls.

Kerosene lamps of the 1860s and 1870s were relatively plain, but certain roughly datable design elements did appear in them through the two decades. During the early 1860s, for example, a slightly elongated glass font typical of earlier whale oil lamps was superseded by a globular font that today is more often associated with kerosene lamps.

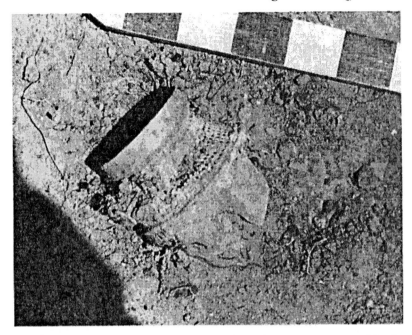

Fig. 62. The Edward Miller and Company lamp burner, as recovered in the Myers and Leonard store. (Photograph by Billy R. Harrison.)

Then toward the middle of the decade the font tended to become somewhat flatter in shape. Also by this time lamps made entirely from pressed glass with brass burners became popular, but they competed for the market with all-metal varieties. Lamps made from the 1880s through 1900s, by contrast, were much more heavily decorated.[4] The examples from Adobe Walls are all quite simple and have globular fonts.

Three brass lamp burners were recovered at the trading post site. The Myers and Leonard store contained both an Edward Miller and a Plume and Atwood burner, and the saloon yielded a smaller Plume and Atwood burner. None of these had sufficient markings to identify their model or type. Interesting markings, however, were found on them. Both of the Plume and Atwood burners bear on their thumb wheels the patent date August 16, 1870, referring to patent number 106,303 by Benjamin Franklin Adams for an improved lamp burner.[5] The Plume and Atwood specimen from the saloon also bears the figures "870" on one fragment and the figure "0" on another. Only small pieces of the

THE PLUME & ATWOOD MANUFACTURING CO.

WATERBURY, CONN.

MANUFACTURERS OF

Sheet Brass & German Silver

BRASS, COPPER AND GERMAN SILVER WIRE,

Copper and Brass Rivets and Burs,

PRINTERS' BRASS SHEETS AND RULE STRIPS,

Kerosene Burners and Lamp Trimmings,

PRINTERS' RULES

AND

Galley Plates, Etc.

STORES:

No. 80 Chambers street, N. Y.,

13 Federal street, Boston.

JOHN C. BOOTH, *President.* D. S. PLUME, *Treasurer.* L. J. ATWOOD, *Secretary.*

Fig. 63. Advertisement for kerosene lamps and other goods produced by the Plume and Atwood Manufacturing Company. (From *Price, Lee & Co.'s Waterbury Directory for 1877* [New Haven, Conn.: Price, Lee & Company, 1877], p. viii of front advertising section.)

EDWARD MILLER & CO.,

MANUFACTURERS OF

Sheet & Cast Brass

BRONZE LAMPS,

Bronze Ornaments,

KEROSENE and FLUID BURNERS,

Lamp and Lantern Trimmings, Brass Kettles,

MACHINE OILERS,

Tinners' Hardware, Cast Brass, Etc.

DIE SINKING AND FORGING DONE TO ORDER.

Meriden, Conn.

Store, No. 4 Warren Street, New York.

EDWARD MILLER, Pres't.
EDWARD MILLER, Jr., Ass't. Treas.

W. H. PERKINS, Sec'y and Treas.
N. P. IVES, Agent, New York.

Fig. 64. An 1870s advertisement for kerosene lamps and other products made by Edward Miller and Company. (From *Price, Lee & Co.'s Meriden Directory for 1876* [New Haven, Conn.: Price, Lee & Company, 1876], p. 188.)

TABLE 4

Dimensions of Lamp Burners and Fonts

| | Saloon | M & L Store | |
	Plume and Atwood (*inches*)	Plume and Atwood (*inches*)	Edward Miller (*inches*)
Burner, maximum diameter	1⅛	1¾	2½ to 3⅛ [1]
Burner, base diameter	⅞	1¾	2¼
Burner, maximum height	1¾	2¼ [1]	3¾
Wick wheel, shaft length	2	2⅝	3 [1]
Thumb wheel, diameter	9/16	9/16	½
Font, maximum diameter	2	6	6 [1]
Font, base diameter	2	6 [1]	4 [1]
Font collar, depth	2	⅜	⅜
Font collar, inside diameter	2	1¾	2⅜

1. Estimated.
2. No glass preserved.

perforated bases were recoverable. Corrosion and age had made all three burners extremely fragile, but careful cleaning freed the wick wheel on the smaller Plume and Atwood example. The wick holder in this burner also had a small piece of uncharred wick intact. The Edward Miller burner is somewhat flattened and has a scalloped gallery holder, but each of the Plume and Atwood burners bears four branch frames known as shade holders. All three specimens have threaded bases, the Edward Miller and the large Plume and Atwood having attached collars. The collar on the former has two incised rings on both its interior and outer surfaces. The dimensions of the burners and their associated fonts are given in table 4.

The smaller Plume and Atwood burner had no glassware associated with it, but partially melted and fragmented fonts and chimney glass were found near the other two burners. No description or other identification was possible for the chimney glass, but more can be ascertained from the remains of the heavier glass fonts. That with the larger Plume and Atwood lamp, as shown in the reconstructed drawing, is approximately 6 inches in maximum diameter, 4 inches tall, and has a base 2½ inches in diameter. Around the base of this font is an embossed scalloped pattern. The font associated with the Edward Miller burner, roughly the same size, has an embossed vertical straight-line pattern around its base with a meridian line pattern around the body center, as illustrated in the reconstructed drawing.

Mixed with the glass sherds and other debris around the Plume and Atwood lamp in the Myers and Leonard store was a cast-iron fragment with a floral design. The fragment had a wood screw through it, and it is assumed that it was part of a wall-type lamp support bracket. A total of 591 lamp chimney sherds, two branches from a shade holder, and 11 glass sherds that probably belong to the two partial fonts complete the inventory of lighting device remains found at the site.

CHAPTER 11

Tools and Equipment

Tools and equipment represent one of the largest classifications of artifacts recovered at Adobe Walls. The category includes such objects as animal shoes, weapons, cooking and eating utensils, metal- and woodworking tools, and weighing devices.

Virtually all the draft and riding animals used by the hide men and merchants in the Panhandle were shod with iron shoes. These shoes prevented the splitting of hooves and protected the animals from lameness. When one considers the importance of these animals at that time, it is not surprising that considerable numbers of shoes were recovered at the site. Horse-, mule-, and oxshoes were found at the trading post, most of them where they might be expected—in the blacksmith shop. The presence of these three types of shoes documents the use of all three types of animals by the hide men and merchants, confirming historical evidence on the subject.[1]

The horseshoe inventory from Adobe Walls consists of seven left front, one right front, one left rear, two right rear, and five unidentifiable fragments, as well as one matched pair of front and one unused rear shoe. The right front shoe from the matched pair is illustrated and is typical of the examples recovered. All the specimens have at least the roots of drawn toe clips and calks and high chisel-pointed heel calks. Nail holes are mostly obscured, but the shoes appear to be the grooved English style with small knobs of encrustation along the grooves that are assumed to be nail head remains. Three of the shoes came from the Myers and Leonard store, five from the Rath and Company store, and the remainder from the blacksmith shop.

TABLE 5
Animal Shoes

	M & L Store	R & Co. Store	Saloon	Blacksmith Shop
Horseshoe	3	5		11
Muleshoe	1	2		6
Oxshoe		1	1	
Horseshoe dubbing				72
Horseshoe fragment				7
Horseshoe nail	1			

Fig. 65. Animal shoes: (*A*) Right front horseshoe 5½ inches long. (*B*) Left front or rear muleshoe 4½ inches long. (*C*) Left half oxshoe 4¾ inches long. (*D*) Right half oxshoe 4⅝ inches long. (*E–I*) Calks.

The muleshoes differ from the horseshoes by being slightly smaller and narrower in relation to their length, as well as being flared at the heel. The Adobe Walls muleshoe inventory includes two left front, two right rear, two left rear, one unused, and two right and one left that could be either front or rear. With the exception of the unused example, all have evidence of heel calks similar to those on the horseshoes, but only one has evidence of a toe calk and none shows any sign of clips. These shoes, like the horseshoes, are in a deteriorated condition, and consequently, little can be ascertained about their nail holes. The right rear shoe shown in the illustration is typical of the muleshoes. One specimen came from the Myers and Leonard store, two from the Rath and Company store, and the remainder from the blacksmith shop.

Oxshoes differ completely from horse- and muleshoes because they are designed in two pieces to fit the cloven hooves of oxen. Each foot requires both right and left halves. Only two such halves, one right and one left, were recovered at the site. No determination could

TABLE 6
Weapons

	M & L Store	Mess Hall	Stable	R & Co. Store	Saloon
Edged					
Metal arrow point	1			1	1
Flint dart point	1				
Unworked Alibates flake	4	1	5	4	1
Firearms					
Rifle barrel	2				
Rifle sight				1	
Butt plate	2			1	
Magazine, Spencer					1
Hammer, Spencer	1				
Trigger guard	1		1		

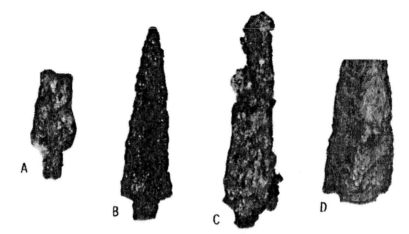

Fig. 66. Arrow and dart points: (*A*) Metal arrow point 1⅜ inches long. (*B*) Metal arrow point with corner notches, 2½ inches total length. (*C*) Metal arrow point with corner notches, 2¾ inches total length. (*D*) Base of Tecovas jasper dart point with shoulders, 1¹³⁄₁₆ inches total length.

be made as to which foot the halves are for or whether they are inside or outside halves. The right half came from the saloon and the left half from the Rath and Company store, although they are illustrated as if they were a pair. It should be noted that these shoes sometimes are referred to as bullshoes rather than oxshoes.

Completing the animal shoe inventory are horseshoe fragments, five toe calks, and seventy-two dubbing-off fragments from the blacksmith shop, and a single horseshoe nail salvaged from the Myers and Leonard store.

Weapons from both Indians and whites were found during the excavations conducted at Adobe Walls. Among these objects were one dart point made from Tecovas jasper and three iron arrow points. All the specimens were found on the 1874 living surfaces within the trading post buildings.

The single flint dart point, recovered inside the Myers and Leonard store, is made from Tecovas jasper. This is a mottled red-yellow-brown-purple stone that occurs in the colorful shale layers of the Tecovas Formation from the Triassic Period. Most of the known outcrops of this stone are located along the eastern escarpment on the southeastern edge of the Panhandle, but there is one known locality on the Canadian River about twenty-five miles west of Adobe Walls where it also occurs.[2] Most likely, the example found at Adobe Walls was picked up by a hide man as a curiosity and brought to the trading post as a souvenir. The actual point is broken, having both its tip and its base missing, and it measures 1¹³/₁₆ inches long. Its shape suggests that it was a corner-notched point with a contracting stem and convex blade edges.

The saloon, the Myers and Leonard store, and the Rath and Company store each yielded one iron arrow point. Such metal points had been used by North American Indians since the 1700s, and through much of the nineteenth century, pieces of iron and files with which to shape them were popular trade goods. In addition, factory-made metal arrow points also were traded in large numbers to native Americans in some areas.[3]

The three iron arrow points found inside buildings at Adobe Walls appear to have been fashioned from either barrel straps or wagon tire material. Although they are heavily encrusted with rust, measurements are possible from all the specimens. One is 2¾ inches long, has a contracting stem with a convex base, and measures ¾ inch wide at its shoulder. Its tip is missing. The second example is identical in shape but smaller in size. It measures 1⅜ inches long, ⅝ inch wide at the shoulder, and ¼ inch wide at its stem. The third example has an asymmetrical base and stem and measures 2½ inches long by ¹¹/₁₆ inch wide at the shoulder. The metal arrow points found at the trading post site are significant indicators that the Plains tribes in 1874 continued to use bows and arrows in their hunting and warfare, although most accounts of the Battle of Adobe Walls mention only their use of firearms and lances.

The Adobe Walls site yielded an additional group of chipped stone artifacts. A total of fifteen man-made flakes of Alibates agate were found in four of the buildings. This flint material originates in Permian deposits in the Alibates dolomite of the Quartermaster Formation. The nearest sources for this stone are approximately ten to fifteen miles upstream on the Canadian. It is a beautiful stone banded in shades of maroon, brown, white, and red.[4] The fact that these remains from flint knapping were found on the 1874 living surface suggests that some of the white hide men may have picked them up elsewhere and brought them to the trading post as attractive curiosities.

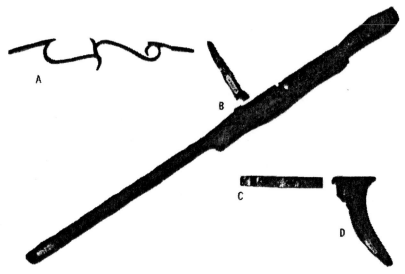

Fig. 67. Firearms: (*A*) Brass rifle trigger guard with front and rear mounting extensions 9½ inches long. (*B*) Round rifle barrel 22 inches long with oxidized wood forearm. (*C*) Brass toe tang plate 4⅛ × ½ × ¹⁄₃₂ inches. (*D*) Brass butt plate 4½ inches high and 2½ inches long at top.

In addition to the presence of Indian weapons, the excavation of the Adobe Walls site revealed the remains of several hide men's weapons and associated accoutrements and ammunition. The inventory of firearms recovered includes only one partial rifle, which was broken and scattered, although additional parts of firearms were discovered.

Near the center of the Myers and Leonard store a round rifle barrel, an ornate brass trigger guard, and a brass butt plate with a separate toe tang plate were found in a localized area. It is assumed that these parts belong to one rifle. The wood along the remaining 22-inch-long barrel was permeated with iron oxide and thus preserved to such an extent that it indicated the gun was a half-stock muzzle-loading rifle. It is certain that the barrel was longer in its original configuration. The cast-brass butt plate measures 4½ inches in overall length, 2½ inches along the heel plate, and has a 4⅛ × ½ × ¹⁄₃₂-inch brass toe plate with three mounting holes. A hole 2 inches above the toe still retains the head of an iron screw, as does the heel plate. The 9½-inch-long ornamental, curved, cast-brass trigger guard has no identifying marks of any kind. The only statement about the gun that can be made with any certainty is that it represents the class of firearms known as the "Plains rifle."[5]

A second rifle barrel found in the Myers and Leonard store measures 26½ inches in length and 1⅛ inches in diameter and appears to be round in cross section. Indications of the bolster, nipple, and upper tang are found at the breech end. X-ray photographs were made of this barrel, but they provided little additional information concerning the structure, identification, or maker of the object. An iron butt plate with a ¾-inch-diameter hole near its center was found in the southeast corner of the Myers and Leonard store. A transverse groove perpendicular to the long axis at the base of the heel was present. Two holes for screw mounting to the stock are perpendicular to the long axis. This butt plate is seemingly identical to those on Spencer rifles in the firearms collection of the Panhandle-Plains Historical Museum.[6] A single 3¼-inch-long rifle hammer that is offset to the outside also found in the Myers and Leonard store may be part of the same gun as the butt plate.

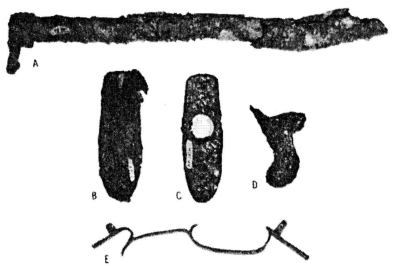

Fig. 68. Additional firearms: (*A*) Spencer rifle magazine. (*B*) Butt plate 4½ inches long. (*C*) Spencer rifle butt plate 4½ inches long. (*D*) Spencer rifle hammer 3¼ inches long. (*E*) Brass trigger guard 7¾ inches long.

A second isolated iron butt plate was found under a pile of burned windows in the Rath and Company store. Its length is 4½ inches and it is shaped like an upside-down L with a partial mounting screw still intact on the upper heel plate. A single ¼-inch-diameter hole for attachment to the butt is located 1¼ inches from the oval toe. The configuration of this piece suggests that it is from a U.S. martial rifled musket or a breech-loading conversion of such a gun.

Within a pit in front of the saloon building, a rifle magazine was found that is identical to Spencer rifle magazines preserved in the Panhandle-Plains Historical Museum firearms collection.[7] A single ornate brass trigger guard was found at the south end of the stable. It is 7¾ inches long, 6 inches between mounting lugs, and has a front lug ⅝×¼×¹⁄₁₆ inch, back lug ⅜×¼×¹⁄₁₆ inch, variable width from ¼ to ¹¹⁄₁₆ inch, and 1-inch depth at finger loop. The numbers "1" and "2" are stamped on the front end of the trigger guard, perhaps indicating the number 12. The guard may be broken at its rear end. Attempts made to identify this specimen met with no success, though it is typical of guards from late Kentucky or lightweight Plains rifles.

The remaining firearms part found at Adobe Walls is a silver blade front sight that is lanceolate and mounted in a rectangular piece of brass. A similar sight is present on an octagon barrel muzzle-loading sporting rifle in the Panhandle-Plains Historical Museum firearms collection.[8]

Several firearms accessories have been identified among the artifacts recovered during the excavation of the trading post site. Among these are two spring-loaded brass chargers of the type used on powder flasks and powder horns of the period 1850−80. These devices were used to measure powder automatically for loading cartridges or muzzle-loading guns. One example is intact but bent and has a brass attachment band that is ⁷⁄₁₆ inch wide and contains three small holes through an incised line at its lower edge. The charger has a spout 1⅜ inches long with a raised rope design ¼ inch below its mouth. The threaded spout is screwed into a 1⅝-inch diameter base. The spout is made from two separate interlocking tubes and has three different adjustments for light, medium, and heavy powder charges. In an identical charger in the Panhandle-Plains Historical Museum,[9] the weight in grains at each of the settings was measured, giving the following results: light charge 59 grains, medium charge 62 grains, and heavy

TABLE 7
Firearms: Accessories

	Stable	R & Co. Store	Saloon
Powder flask charger		2	
Bullet swage			1
Friction primer		1	
Cleaning rod brush	1		1

charge 66 grains. The second powder charger is similar but smaller and lacks the spout and attachment band. Its base is 1 inch in diameter with a 5/16-inch-diameter spout base hole. The springs are missing from both chargers, but both have the thumb release levers and powder stops.

Although badly rusted, a single bullet swage from the saloon was identified. The iron swage is 1¾ inches long, ¾ inch in diameter and has a ½-inch blind hole. A swage is a device used to join two pieces of a bullet, usually of different compositions, that were cast in different molds.

An L-shaped two-piece brass tube with a small hole at the angle has been identified as a friction primer. These primers were used to ignite military cannon.[10] The only known explanation for the presence of this object on the living surface at Adobe Walls is the fact that army troops visited the site following the June 27, 1874, battle both before and after the burning of the trading post buildings by the Indians.

Two brass gun-cleaning brushes were recovered. Both are so badly fragmented that their original overall length cannot be ascertained. Neither brush retains its bristles. The base section or attaching end on both examples measures ⅞ inch in length with ⅜-inch-long threaded ends that bear twenty threads per inch. The bases are 5/16 inch in maximum diameter and have threaded ends 7/32 inch in diameter. These brushes appear to be similar to known Civil War vintage carbine-cleaning brushes.[11]

A total of 465 cartridges, bullets, balls, and cases found at Adobe Walls represents ammunition for at least two dozen different firearms. This figure might be greater, as some rifles, pistols, and revolvers utilized the same caliber cartridges or balls.

Four different muzzle-loading firearms are represented by the

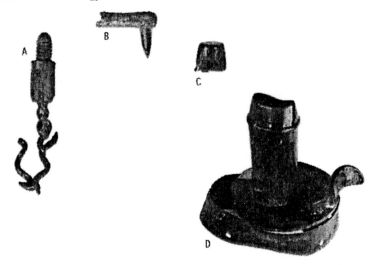

Fig. 69. Firearm accessories: (*A*) Rifle cleaning brush 1¼ inches long. (*B*) Friction primer ¾ inch long. (*C*) Percussion cap 0.18 inch in diameter and 0.21 inch high. (*D*) Powder measure 1⅝ inch high.

twenty-six musket balls found at the site. These include the calibers of .38, .40, .45, and .56.

From the group of 140 lead bullets recovered, twenty-seven are unidentifiable either because of melting, impact, or other alteration. These bullets range in caliber from .38 to .56. Both solid base and hollow base styles are represented, as well as patched and grooved forms. They were found both inside and outside the trading post buildings, making it difficult to determine if they were shot by Indians or dropped by hide men. Many of the examples, however, are mushroomed, a condition that suggests the possibility of their having been fired by Indians at the time of the 1874 battle.

The 244 copper and brass cartridge cases substantially outnumber the other forms of ammunition artifacts from Adobe Walls. They represent at least twenty different types or sizes of cases. It can be assumed that the majority were dropped by white men during the period of occupancy. Most are copper.

A total of at least eleven different firearms are represented by the fifty-five complete metallic cartridges recovered. Thirty of these came from a single cache in the bastion at the Myers and Leonard store.

TABLE 8

Firearms: Ammunition

	M & L Store	Mess Hall	Stable	R & Co. Store	Privy	Saloon	Blacksmith Shop	Surface
Musket balls								
.38 cal.	7			3				
.40 cal.	1							
.45 cal.	4			6		1		
.56 cal.	1			1				
unidentified	2							
Bullets								
.38 cal.	2			2			1	
.40 cal.	1							
.44 cal.	16		2	7		11		
.45 cal.	4			7				
.50 cal.	17	5	4	19	1	10	2	1
.56 cal.	1							
unidentified	15		1	7		3	1	
Shot								
No. 2	15							
No. 4	6			2				
No. 5				4				
No. 0 buck						2		
No. 00 buck						1		
No. 3 buck				3				
BB	1			17				

TABLE 8 *continued*
Firearms: Ammunition

	M & L Store	Mess Hall	Stable	R & Co. Store	Privy	Saloon	Blacksmith Shop	Surface
Cartridges								
.44 Henry R.F.	1			1				
.44 S&W Amer. C.F.						1		
.44–77 C.F.	1			2				
.44–90 C.F.				1				
.45 Colt C.F.			1					
.45 U.S. Gov't. C.F.			2					
.50 Remington pistol C.F.[1]	1							
.50–70 U.S. Gov't. C.F.	2		1	4		1		
.50–90 C.F.				2				
.50–70 or 90 C.F.						1		
.56–56 Spencer carbine R.F.						1		
Cache of .50–70 U.S. Gov't. C.F.	30							
unidentified	1			1				
Cases								
.32 long R.F.	1							
.44 Colt C.F.						7		
.44 Evans short C.F.[2]	1							
.44 Henry R.F.	15		1	3		6		1
.44 long C.F.[3]				1				
.44 S&W Amer. C.F.	3			2		1		
.44–77 C.F.	13	3	3	11		3		

.44–77 or 90 C.F.	6					
.44–90 C.F.	3					
.45 Colt C.F.			9	2		
.45–70 U.S. Gov't. C.F.	4		1			
.45–70 Van Choate C.F.			1			
.50 Remington pistol C.F.[1]	3	3 (3)			2	
.50–70 U.S. Gov't. C.F.	30 (6)[4]	3	27 (2)	5 (3)	2	
.50–70 or 90 C.F.	5	1	3	2	1	
.50–90 C.F.	12	1	2	4		1
.56–50 Spencer R.F.[5]	5	2				
.56–52 Spencer R.F.	1		3			
.56–56 Spencer R.F.			2	2		
unidentified[6]	10	7	2			
Cartridge wad paper						
.50 cal.	1	1				
Primers						
Benét	210	1	38			
Berdan	11	2	9	219	1	
Percussion caps			2	4	1	

1. For Model 1871 Army pistol.
2. Supposedly not introduced until 1875.
3. For Martin Ballard, not introduced until ca. 1875–76.
4. Parentheses indicate the number of rimfire cases within the total, the remainder having Berdan center fire primers.
5. One has "S.A.W." head stamp and was manufactured by the Sage Ammunition Works, Middletown, Conn.
6. Except for the four illustrated, all are fragments.

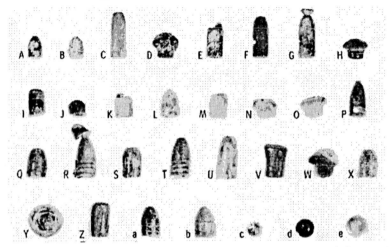

Fig. 70. Bullets and balls: (*A*) .38 caliber 0.375 inch in diameter. (*B*) .38 caliber 0.421 inch in diameter. (*C*) .40 caliber 0.406 inch in diameter. (*D*) .44 caliber 0.453 inch in diameter. (*E*) .44 caliber 0.4375 inch in diameter. (*F*) .44 caliber 0.435 inch in diameter. (*G*) .44 caliber 0.445 inch in diameter. (*H*) .44 caliber, mushroomed. (*I*) .44 caliber 0.4375 inch in diameter. (*J*) .44 caliber 0.445 inch in diameter. (*K*) .44 caliber 0.4219 inch in diameter. (*L*) .45-caliber Colt 0.4667 inch in diameter. (*M*) .45 caliber 0.460 inch in diameter. (*N*) .45-caliber Colt 0.460 inch in diameter. (*O*) .45 caliber 0.4609 inch in diameter. (*P*) .45 caliber 0.437 inch in diameter. (*Q*) .50 caliber 0.525 inch in diameter. (*R*) .50 caliber 0.500 inch in diameter. (*S*) .50 caliber 0.4844 inch in diameter. (*T*) .50 caliber 0.500 inch in diameter. (*U*) .50 caliber 0.5078 inch in diameter. (*V*) .50 caliber 0.500 inch in diameter. (*W*) .50 caliber, mushroomed. (*X*) .50 caliber 0.500 inch in diameter. (*Y*) .50 caliber 0.500 inch in diameter. (*Z*) .50 caliber 0.500 inch in diameter. (*a*) .50 caliber 0.500 inch in diameter. (*b*) .56 caliber 0.539 inch in diameter. (*c*) .38-caliber ball 0.375 inch in diameter. (*d*) .45-caliber ball 0.460 inch in diameter. (*e*) .56-caliber ball 0.531 inch in diameter.

From these examples only two remain unidentified. Judging from the numbers of cartridges, cases, and identifiable bullets, .50-caliber firearms seem to have been preferred by the hide men at Adobe Walls. The only known prices paid for cartridges purchased at Adobe Walls come from a receipt dated May 21, 1874. On that day the Cator brothers purchased from the Myers and Leonard store two hundred .50-caliber cartridges for $8.50, or four and a quarter cents apiece, and one hundred .44-caliber cartridges for $3.50, or three and a half cents each.[12]

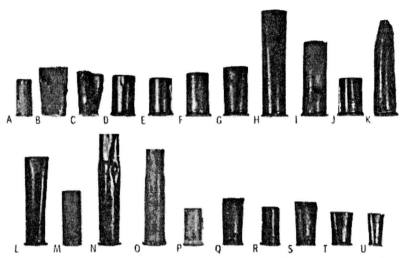

Fig. 71. Ammunition cases: (*A*) Unidentified case with Boxer primer 0.438 inch in diameter at the rim and 0.875 inch long. (*B*) Unidentified rimless 1 3/16 inches long. (*C*) Unidentified C.F. 0.5 inch in diameter at rim and 1.046 inches long. (*D*) Unidentified R.F. 0.64 inch in diameter at rim and 0.984 inch long. (*E*) .56–56 Spencer carbine. (*F*) .56–52 Spencer. (*G*) .56–50 Spencer. (*H*) .50–90 Sharps Straight. (*I*) .50–70 Gov't. (*J*) .50 Remington pistol. (*K*) .45–70 Van Choate. (*L*) .45–70 Gov't. (*M*) .45 Colt. (*N*) .44–90 Sharps Necked. (*O*) .44–77 Sharps or Remington Necked. (*P*) .44 S&W American. (*Q*) .44 long. (*R*) .44 Henry. (*S*) .44 Colt. (*T*) .44 long. (*U*) .32 long.

A total of 469 Berdan center-fire primers were recovered from the buildings. The saloon and the Rath and Company store appear to have been the locations where the bulk of cartridge reloading took place, as 219 of these primers came from the saloon and 210 from the Rath and Company store. A single Benét inside primer was found in the Myers and Leonard mess hall.

Twenty-six percussion caps were recovered at the site. Measurements were possible from all but three of the caps, and five different sizes were identified. With a diameter of 0.18 inch and a height of 0.21 inch, fourteen caps fall into the range of the Eley-Kynoch No. 18 or Remington No. 12. The other sizes of Eley-Kynoch style caps were identified, two being No. EB and five being No. 21. These measure 0.242 inch in diameter and 0.24 inch tall and 0.183 inch in diameter and 0.21 inch tall, respectively. Single specimens of two other types and sizes found were a Remington No. 13 measuring 0.24 inch tall and

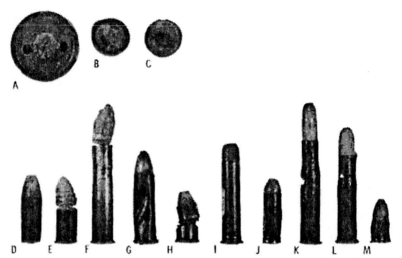

Fig. 72. Firearm cartridges: (*A*) Benét primer ¹⁵⁄₁₆ inch in diameter. (*B*) Berdan primer ¼ inch in diameter. (*C*) Fired Berdan primer. (*D*) Rimless unidentified. (*E*) .56–56 Spencer carbine. (*F*) .50–90 Sharps Straight. (*G*) .50–70 Gov't. (*H*) .50 Remington pistol. (*I*) .45–70 Gov't. (*J*) .45 Colt. (*K*) .44–90 Sharps Necked. (*L*) .44–77 Sharps or Remington Necked. (*M*) .44 Henry.

0.18 inch in diameter and a RSW Sinoxid No. 1075 measuring 0.17 inch tall by 0.17 inch in diameter.[13]

Many of the hide men in the Texas Panhandle cast their own bullets for reloading metallic cartridges. This fact is attested by the lead remains from bullet molding found in most of the buildings at the Adobe Walls trading post. During the excavation both slag and sprues, the waste lead that solidified in the hole at the top of a bullet mold, were found in both stores, the saloon, the blacksmith shop, and in the Myers and Leonard stable, with slag alone being found in the Myers and Leonard mess hall. In all, 9½ pounds of this waste lead were recovered. It is interesting to note that according to receipts kept by James and Robert Cator, in June, 1874, bulk lead sold for fourteen cents a pound at the Rath and Company store and for fifteen cents a pound in the Myers and Leonard store.[14]

Among the tools and equipment found at Adobe Walls are interesting food preparation and food service artifacts, not to mention remains of food items. The latter remains are among the most revealing

Fig. 73. Cache of .50-caliber cartridges as uncovered in the bastion at the Myers and Leonard store. (Photograph by Billy R. Harrison.)

Fig. 74. Cache of .50-caliber cartridges after stabilization in the laboratory.

TABLE 9
Firearms: Expendable Supplies

	M & L Store	Mess Hall	Stable	R & Co. Store	Saloon	Blacksmith Shop	Total Weight
Lead sprue	2.0 oz.		0.96 oz.	2.0 oz.	17.5 oz.	1.0 oz.	1 lb. 7.5 oz.
Lead slag	40.6 oz.	0.96 oz.	14.0 oz.	14.4 oz.	51.0 oz.	8.0 oz.	8 lb. 1 oz.

objects recovered at the trading post, for they shed important light on the diet of the 1870s hide men and merchants in the Texas Panhandle.

Several historic sources note the popularity of wild plums among the men at the trading post,[15] and the consumption of the fruit is substantiated by fifteen plum pits found in the Myers and Leonard store and one in the Myers and Leonard mess hall. Only one peach pit was recovered, being found in the Myers and Leonard stable. Fresh peaches are known to have been freighted to the trading post from Dodge City, and they sold for twenty-five cents per pound according to a receipt dated June 21, 1874.[16] Kernels of corn were found on the living surfaces in the Rath and Company store, the Myers and Leonard store, and the Myers and Leonard stable, but these probably represent feed for livestock rather than humans. In 1874 bulk corn sold for $3.00 to $3.50 per hundredweight at the Myers and Leonard store[17] and for $2.85 a hundredweight at the Rath and Company store.[18]

Remains of more than a hundred badly deteriorated tin cans were uncovered during the excavation, almost half of them outside the north window at the Rath and Company store, where they appear to have been thrown during the period of occupancy. Many of these cans still showed their having been opened with knives or can openers, but only one possessed evidence of its contents. This is an individual can of green peas left behind inside the Myers and Leonard store. When the building burned, the peas inside the can charred to considerable hardness, which allowed their preservation through the next century while the container rusted away. Extant receipts from the two stores written in the spring and summer of 1874 record sales of fruit, soup, and tomatoes in cans.[19]

Historical accounts noting the consumption of coffee by the hide men and merchants during the period of occupancy[20] are confirmed by the recovery of twenty coffee beans from the Myers and Leonard mess hall. Coffee sold for forty to forty-five cents a pound in the trading post stores.[21] Twenty years after the site was abandoned, Andrew Johnson, James H. Cator, and Charles Rath all remembered distinctly that the merchants had left coffee behind when they removed their merchandise from the stores after the battle.[22]

An interesting variety of bones from animals apparently killed for their meat was found at the site. The most numerous bone remains are from bison, suggesting that the buffalo was the favored or most easily

TABLE 10
Food Remains

	M & L Store	Mess Hall	Stable	R & Co. Store	Saloon	Blacksmith Shop
Bison remains						
Mandible				1		
Vertebra	2 (1)			28 (10)	2	
Scapula				5 (2)		
Radius				4 (3)		
Ulna				3 (2)		
Pelvis fragment		1	1	1	1	
Sacrum				1		
Femur	1	1	1	4	1	
Tibia		1	1	2	1	
Rib	1	1	4 (2)	53 (7)	1	
Hyoid				2		
Caudal vertebra				6		
Metatarsal	2			2		
Metacarpal				2		
Astragalus		1		3		
Calcanium		1		4		
Phalange	7	2		16		
Patella	2		3	3		
Teeth	2	3	1	19	11	1
Sternum			(1)	3		
Deer/antelope remains						
Skull	1			2		
Mandible				1		
Vertebra		1		4		

Scapula			1
Humerus	1		2 (1)
Radius			2 (1)
Ulna			1
Pelvis			1
Sacrum			1
Rib			15
Metatarsal			3
Metacarpal			4
Calcanium			2
Phalange		1	20
Teeth	3		3
Antler			3 (1)
Duck remains			
Humerus			1
Ribs			3
Tarsometarus			2
Pelvis			1
Ulna			1
Fish remains			
Unidentified			1
Rabbit remains			
Pelvis			1
Sacrum		1	
Turkey remains			
Skull			2
Mandible			1
Vertebra			7

TABLE 10 *continued*
Food Remains

	M & L Store	Mess Hall	Stable	R & Co. Store	Saloon	Blacksmith Shop
Scapula				2		
Humerus				4		
Radius				2		
Ulna				1		
Pelvis	1			4		
Sacrum				1		
Femur				6		
Tibia		1		7		
Rib				5		
Tarsometatarus	1			15		
Metacarpal	1			12		
Phalange	1			70		
Coracoid				3		
Sternum				4		
Floral remains						
Chinaberry seeds	11					
Coffee beans		20				
Corn kernels	50	32	15			
Green peas	50					
Peach pit			1			
Plum pits	15	1				

NOTE: Numbers in parentheses indicate the numbers of individual bone types showing butchers' marks.

obtained meat at the trading post. Evidence further indicates that wild turkey was preferred over deer and/or antelope. The bone remains of rabbits, ducks, and fish suggest that they, too, were eaten by the men at the post, but less frequently.

Several different food preparation artifacts were found at Adobe Walls. They represent a number of varied cooking and food storage utensils. Evidence from the site suggests that most of the cooking utensils used at the post were made from cast iron, as fragments of such items were found in three buildings. Part of a three-legged 9-inch diameter cast-iron frying pan or Dutch oven bottom were recovered in the Rath and Company store, this being the only artifact in this class for which sufficient remains were found for a positive identification of style. The same building yielded the remains of one brass kettle. The evidence for this cooking vessel takes the form of a brass bail ear attached to a rolled brass rim by two copper rivets.

The only food-cutting implement found was a single butcher or skinning knife located in the Myers and Leonard mess hall. Although the tip of the slightly curved blade is missing, it appears to have had a sheepfoot or beak point. The blade was attached to a wooden handle by six iron rivets. Although no guard is present, the blade has a slight choil.

A single fragment of what appears to have been a colander was also found in the mess hall. In this object a series of three holes occur in the iron fragment, which has one rolled edge.

The Myers and Leonard store yielded a coffee mill with two mounting legs attached to an upper grinding element that is complete except for its wooden mounting box and the outer end of its handle. The bowl portion of the grinder measures 5 inches in diameter and 2 inches deep. The bowl is separated from the upper grinding element as a result of having been bent. Although it bears no maker's mark, the mill is similar to No. 15677 illustrated in the 1897 Sears, Roebuck and Company catalog.[23] Two small fragments of a second food or coffee grinder were found in the Rath and Company store. They show a graduated vertical grinding surface on the interior with a raised half-inch-wide band on the exterior edge.

Fragments of glass and crockery food preparation and/or storage utensils also were found. The most impressive of these are the remains of two earthenware salt-glazed crocks from the Myers and Leonard

TABLE 11
Food Preparation Artifacts

	M & L Store	Mess Hall	Stable	R & Co. Store
Iron utensil fragments	1		2	1
Copper kettle ear				1
Butcher/skinning knife		1		
Colander fragment		1		
Coffee mill	1			
Food grinder fragments				2
¾-gal. crock				1
4-gal. crock		1		
Canning-jar fragments				13
Ash-box door fragments		7	3	
Stovepipe flange			1	
Stove grate fragments		4	2	
Stove lids (covers)		4		
Stove lid divider		1		
Stove lid lifters		2		
Stovepipe wall collar	1			
Stove ornament			1	
Stove knob (?)			1	

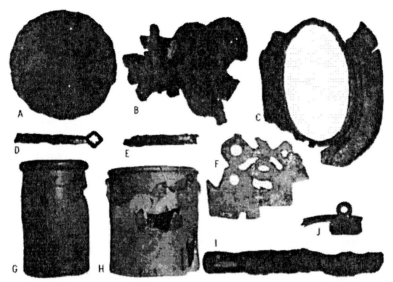

Fig. 75. Food preparation artifacts: (*A*) Stove lid 8½ inches in diameter. (*B*) Coffee grinder 6½ inches high. (*C*) Stovepipe flange with mouth 7 inches at widest point. (*D*) Stove lid lifter 6¾ inches long. (*E*) Stove lid lifter 4 inches long. (*F*) Stove grate fragment 6 × 8 inches. (*G*) ¾-gallon crock 9½ inches high. (*H*) 4-gallon crock 13 inches high. (*I*) Brass kettle bail ear 1½ inches high. (*J*) Butcher knife 8½ inches long.

mess hall and from the Rath and Company store. Both are representative of styles popular during the 1860s and 1870s. The smaller of the two, from the Rath and Company store, has a ¾-gallon capacity, a tan, glazed exterior, and a brown slip interior. Its decoration consists of a simple incised line ⅛ inch wide 2 inches below its upper edge. A round ¾-inch-diameter rim forms the mouth of the vessel. The 9½-inch-tall crock measures 6 inches in diameter both at its base and at its rim. There is a slight narrowing between an incised decorative line and the rolled edge of the rim, where it flares out to its original diameter.

The second crockery vessel, with a capacity of four gallons, bears the decorative motif of a cobalt-blue bird painted on its gray exterior. By the 1860s decorative painting with blue cobalt oxide in patterns of flowers, forest scenes, birds, and human figures had become quite popular in American crockery manufacture. The interior surface of the container is brown, and the crock displays in one area a circular hole with outward radiating cracks, indicating that it may have been struck by a bullet or other sharp object. It is cylindrical, 13 inches tall, and bears two upside-down horseshoe-shaped lugs on opposite sides below its rounded rim.[24]

Although thirteen sherds of clear canning-jar glass were found during the excavation, they are not datable and may have been deposited during any of the several twentieth-century anniversary celebrations at the trading post site. Of the thirteen sherds, only two have threads for screw-on type closures, and none have any embossed identifying marks.[25]

Ten small broken pieces of heavy cast iron from the Myers and Leonard mess hall and stable have been identified as stove ashbox door fragments. A partially complete stovepipe flange also was found in the stable. It is oval, has a flat 1¾-inch attaching base, and has overall measurements of 8¾ inches long, 7¼ inches wide, and 1 inch high. Stove grate fragments are represented by six artifacts, some having

Fig. 76. Broken ironstone dishes and ceramic doorknob found along the north wall of the Myers and Leonard mess hall. (Photograph by Billy R. Harrison.)

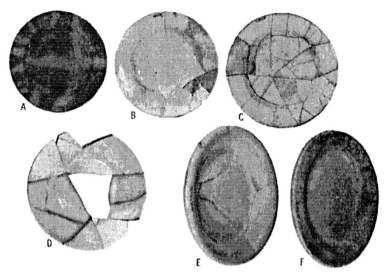

Fig. 77. Food service artifacts: (*A*) Meakin and Company ironstone dinner plate 9 inches in diameter. (*B*) J. and G. Meakin ironstone serving bowl 10 inches in diameter. (*C*) Powell and Bishop ironstone dinner plate 10 inches in diameter. (*D*) Ironstone serving bowl 5¾ inches in diameter. (*E*) Francis C. Eames (importer) ironstone vegetable bowl 4¾ × 6 inches. (*F*) Kerr's China Hall (importer) ironstone platter 5 × 7⅛ inches.

corrugated surfaces and others having holes. The examples with corrugations may be firebox fragments. Concentrated near the south side of the mess hall, four 8½-inch diameter stove lids or covers were exposed, along with a butterfly-shaped divider. Of two cover lifters recovered, one measures 6¾ inches long and has an end missing. The intact end is diamond-shaped and bears a ⁹⁄₁₆-inch-square hole. The second specimen is 4 inches long and has an arched ½-inch-wide tang with a half-round handle. A wall collar for a stovepipe was found in the Myers and Leonard store. Having a 6-inch inside diameter and a 9-inch outside diameter, the 1½-inch-wide ferrous metal ring has a fibrous material bonded between its two thin metal layers, its overall thickness varying from ⅛ to ¼ inch. A cylindrical iron object with a raised ring on one end could possibly be a stove ornament.

Sherds representing at least thirty-five individual ironstone china dishes were recovered during the excavations at Adobe Walls. Most of these artifacts came from either the Rath and Company store or the

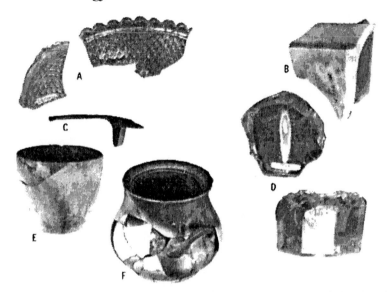

Fig. 78. Additional food service artifacts: (*A*) Decorative pressed-glass bowl sherds, smaller 1⅜ × 2⅜ inches and larger 1¾ × 3⅜ inches. (*B*) Unidentified ironstone bowl sherd 2 × 2½ inches. (*C*) Ironstone bowl lid sherd 5¼ × 6 inches. (*D*) Pressed drinking glass sherd with 2-inch diameter base. (*E*) Ironstone handleless cup with 3¾-inch diameter at rim. (*F*) Johnson and Eames (importer) ironstone sugar bowl (?) with 6-inch overall diameter.

Myers and Leonard mess hall, although smaller numbers were found in the Myers and Leonard store, the Myers and Leonard stable, and the saloon, as shown in table 12. Among the types of dishes represented by the sherds found at the site are cups, saucers, dinner plates, soup plates, serving bowls, oval vegetable bowls, platters, and a sugar bowl.

The specimens recovered appear to represent inexpensively manufactured "export ware." All sherds bearing makers' marks can be traced to specific Staffordshire makers. It is interesting to note, however, that several of the sherds also bear the names and trademarks of their American importers, which were placed on the dishes when they were produced in England. The British producers of ironstone food service artifacts found at Adobe Walls are the following:

Edward Clarke, Tunstall, ca. 1865–77[26]
James Edwards and Son, Burslem, 1851–82[27]
John Edwards, Fenton, ca. 1853–1900[28]

Thomas Hughes, Burslem, 1860–94[29]
Meakin and Company, Cobridge, 1873–76[30]
J. and G. Meakin, Hanley, 1851–present[31]
Powell and Bishop, Hanley, 1867–78[32]

The three American importers whose names were placed on dishes represented by remains found at Adobe Walls are Francis C. Eames of Kansas City, Johnson and Eames of Kansas City,[33] and Kerr's China Hall of Philadelphia.[34]

A lacy, clear glass bowl with a hobnail rim is represented by seven sherds found on the east side of the Rath and Company store. The one large preserved rim sherd has a straight side that slopes inward toward the base of the bowl. By projecting an arc, one can estimate the overall diameter of the rim at 5 inches, the diameter of the flat base being 3¼ inches. The ornamented rim has an average of approximately two and one-half hobnail knurls per inch.

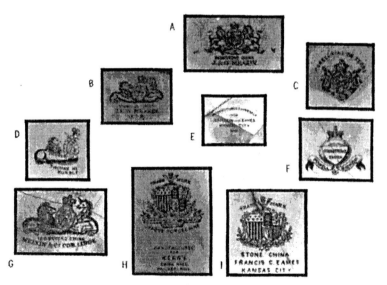

Fig. 79. Ironstone china trademarks: (*A*) "J. & G. Meakin." from serving bowl. (*B*) "J. & G. Meakin. 1869." from plate sherd. (*C*) "Porcelain de Terre" (John Edwards) from dish sherd. (*D*) "Thomas Hughes Burslem" from saucer sherd. (*E*) "Johnson and Eames Kansas City Mo" from sugar bowl. (*F*) "Powell & Bishop" from dinner plate. (*G*) "Meakin & C° Cobridge" from dinner plate. (*H*) "Edward Clarke Tunstall Opaque Porcelaine" from vegetable bowl. (*I*) "Francis C. Eames Kansas City" from vegetable bowl.

TABLE 12
Food Service Artifacts

	M & L Store	Mess Hall	Stable	R & Co. Store	Saloon
Ironstone china					
Vegetable bowls made by Edward Clarke for Francis C. Eames	2	5	1	1	
Vegetable bowl made by Edward Clarke for Kerr's China Hall				1	
Vegetable bowl sherds made by Edward Clarke				6	
Unidentified vegetable bowl sherds				3	
Serving bowl made by J.&G. Meakin		1			
Unidentified serving bowl sherds		11		1	
Unidentified serving bowl				1	
Sugar bowl made for Johnson and Eames		1			
Bowl or chamber pot lid sherds				4	
Cups without handles	2	3		3	
Unidentified U-shaped dish handle				1	
Unidentified bowl rim sherd		1	1		

Unidentified vessel made by James Edwards				1	
Unidentified vessel made by John Edwards		1			
Dinner plates made by Powell & Bishop		2			
Dinner plates made by Edward Clarke for Francis C. Eames		4			
Dinner plate with floral ornamentation made by Meakin & Co.		1			
Unidentified dinner plate with rope ornamentation		1			
Dinner plate base made by J.&G. Meakin				1	
Platters made by Edward Clarke for Kerr's China Hall		1			
Saucer bases made by Thomas Hughes		2			
Unmarked ironstone china sherds					
Vegetable bowl		21	18	13	
Serving bowl		11		1	
Cup without handle	10	3	57	33	9
Unidentified dishes	3	13	466	80	1
Dinner plate		57		48	2
Platter				1	4

TABLE 12 *continued*
Food Service Artifacts

	M & L Store	Mess Hall	Stable	R & Co. Store	Saloon
Pressed glass					
Sherds of lacy bowl with hobnail rim				1	
Drinking glass with fluted base				3	
Drinking glass with plain base				1	
Octagonal drinking glass with concave base				1	
Eating utensils					
Dinner fork					1
Dinner knife	1				1
Teaspoon					1

Remnants of five clear drinking glasses were recovered in the Rath and Company store in the form of their bases. Three of the examples appear to be of the same design, with a base diameter of 2 inches and decorative flutes around and up the outer edges of the bases. A fourth specimen is represented by a single clear glass base fragment that measures 2 inches in diameter but that lacks the decorative flutes. Numerous rim sherds from drinking glasses were also recovered, most of them having a ⅜-inch etched band bordered by two horizontal lines ¹³⁄₃₂ inch below the lip. It is not known to which of the bases these rim fragments belong.

A single, heavy, octagonal clear glass base 2¼ inches in diameter at its widest point also came from the Rath and Company store. This glass is quite different from the others, being made from very thick material and having a rounded concave bottom. The base of the glass is fluted, with half moons at the tops of the flutes. Judging from the thickness of the glass and the size of the object, it is thought that it may represent the remains of either a shot glass or a small cylindrical mug.

Four eating utensils were found at Adobe Walls. One of these, from outside the saloon, was a single dinner fork, which appears to have had three tines. It has a two-piece wooden handle attached with

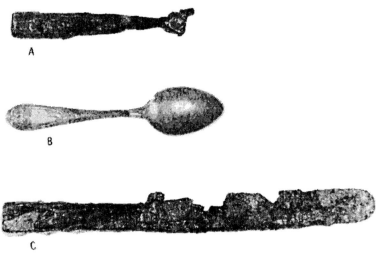

Fig. 80. Eating utensils: (*A*) Dinner fork 5½ inches long. (*B*) Teaspoon 5¾ inches long. (*C*) Dinner knife 9¾ inches long.

TABLE 13
Leatherworking Tools and Supplies

	M & L Store	Stable	R & Co. Store	R & Co. Corral	Saloon	Blacksmith Shop
Belt rivets	23	4	5		3	2
Belt rivet burrs	4		1			
Shoe last				1		
Flint hide scraper			1			

five small brass rivets. The handle is 3 inches long, ¾ inch wide at the back, and ½ inch wide at the tine end.

Two different dinner knives were found at the site, one in the saloon and the other in the Myers and Leonard store. The specimen from the saloon is missing its blade but has a two-piece wooden handle attached with two brass rivets. The wooden handle measures 3¼ inches long and ¾ inch wide. The small remaining portion of the blade suggests that it was widest near the handle, where it measures 1 inch across. A nearly complete dinner knife from the Myers and Leonard store is 9¾ inches long and has a rounded point. A two-piece wooden handle is recognized from the charred remains secured by three brass mounting rivets. The handle measures 3½ inches long by ¾ inch wide. As in the case of the other dinner knife, the blade is widest near the handle, where it measures 1 inch across.

A brass teaspoon with a decorative floral design on its handle came from the saloon building. It measures 5¾ inches long, with the bowl of the spoon being 1¼ inches wide and 2⅛ inches long. The back of the spoon handle bears the partially legible stamped name, ". . . M MFG. CO."

During the excavation at Adobe Walls, a small number of objects best classified as leatherworking tools and supplies were found. The most numerous of these objects are copper rivets and burrs, artifacts used in conjunction with each other to fasten pieces of leather together. Rivets are cut from metal rods and formed by special machines into "mushroom" or flat-top shape; burrs are annular discs of metal with small central holes placed over the stub ends of rivets before swaging.

Three rivets without burrs and two with burrs were found in the Rath and Company store; the saloon yielded three rivets, two of which still had both burrs and remnants of leather pieces attached. Twenty-three additional rivets, thirteen with burrs, were found in the Myers and Leonard store; small numbers of these were recovered in the stable and blacksmith shop.

A broken iron object found on the inside northeast corner of the Rath and Company corral is thought to be part of a shoe last. Its location and orientation suggest that it may have been used as a marker or stake in laying out the sod corral when its construction was begun.

One final leatherworking artifact recovered at Adobe Walls is

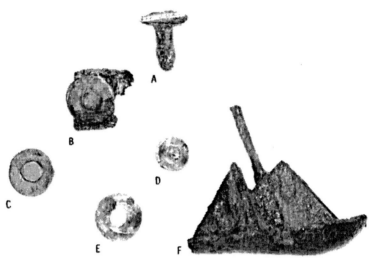

Fig. 81. Leatherworking tools and supplies: (*A*) Belt rivet with $^{15}\!/_{32}$-inch diameter and $^{1}\!/_{8}$ × $^{1}\!/_{2}$-inch shank. (*B*) Belt rivet, including leather fragment around head with $^{15}\!/_{32}$-inch diameter head and $^{1}\!/_{4}$-inch-long shank. (*C*) Belt rivet with $^{7}\!/_{16}$-inch diameter head and $^{1}\!/_{8}$ × $^{1}\!/_{2}$-inch shank. (*D*) Belt rivet with $^{11}\!/_{32}$-inch diameter head and $^{1}\!/_{8}$ × $^{1}\!/_{4}$-inch shank. (*E*) Belt rivet burr $^{1}\!/_{2}$ inch in diameter with $^{1}\!/_{8}$-inch hole. (*F*) Shoe last $5^{1}\!/_{4}$ inches long.

probably far older than the period of white occupancy at the trading post. This object is a flint hide scraper chipped from Alibates agate. It measures $1^{1}\!/_{2}$ by $1^{1}\!/_{4}$ inches and is oval. Perhaps one of the hide men from Kansas picked it up elsewhere on the buffalo range and brought it back to the trading post as a curio or to be used to strike a fire by flint and steel.

Several different types of metalworking tools were found at Adobe Walls, among them files, sharpening stones, ladles, and shims. The blacksmith shop and the Myers and Leonard store both yielded artifacts in this first category. In each building the excavators found square section cotter files, which probably were used for either dressing burrs on metal or trimming hooves on draft animals. The specimen from the blacksmith shop is $8^{3}\!/_{4}$ inches long, and that from the stable is slightly longer, at $9^{3}\!/_{4}$ inches. Because of the deteriorated condition of the two artifacts, it is not possible to determine whether they may have been longer at one time.

TABLE 14
Metalworking Tools and Supplies

	M & L Store	Mess Hall	Stable	M & L Corral	R & Co. Store	Blacksmith Shop
Files			1			1
Bench grinder	1					
Grinder wheel flange					1	
Grindstone, foot-actuated	1					
Grindstone fragments					6	11
Shims	2					
Ladle				1		
Whetstones	2	1			1	

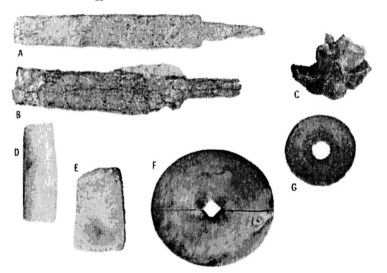

Fig. 82. Metalworking tools: (*A*) Square section cotter file 9¾ inches long. (*B*) Square section cotter file 8¾ inches long. (*C*) Bench-type grindstone 6¼ inches high. (*D*) Cylindrical whetstone 4 inches long. (*E*) Biface whetstone 3¼ inches long. (*F*) Sandstone wheel from hand- or foot-actuated grindstone 19 inches in diameter. (*G*) Metal flange from wheel of grindstone 4 inches in diameter.

Two different types of sharpening stones are known to have been used by the hide men and merchants at Adobe Walls, one being whetstones. The site yielded one complete example and three partial specimens. All appear to be local sandstone and are presumed to have been shaped by individual men for their personal use. The complete specimen is made from gray micaceous sandstone and is rectangular. It measures 2 inches wide at one end, 1¾ inches wide at the opposite end, and ¾ inch thick. It has a deep concave honing surface on one side, but its other face is relatively flat and bears nine or ten incised parallel grooves. The narrow sides flatten toward the edges.

A single small mid-section of another micaceous sandstone whetstone from the Rath and Company store suggests that the original tool was lanceolate; its wide edges were convex in cross section and its smaller edges flat. Another whetstone fragment found in the Myers and Leonard mess hall, also made of gray micaceous sandstone, is elliptical and has both ends broken off. The final fragment of whetstone was shaped less skillfully from brown ferruginous sandstone. It is irregular in shape, and only one convex face shows evidence of having been used for sharpening.

Whetstones are among the simplest of all implements for sharpening metal instruments, whereas grindstones are more complex. They are larger circular stones mounted so that they can rotate in order to sharpen instruments more easily, quickly, and evenly. Remains of at least four different grindstones were found at the trading post. The most complete of these is a small hand-operated bench-mounted grinder with one-third of a 9-inch-diameter, 1-inch-thick sandstone grinding wheel intact. It has the remains of an iron water tray covering the lower half of the stone as well as an intact handle spindle less the actual wooden handle. Its base has four mounting bolts that retain charred fragments of the table or bench on which it was mounted in the Myers and Leonard store. The grinder appears to be similar in de-

Fig. 83. Bench-type grindstone, as it was uncovered inside the Myers and Leonard store. (Photograph by Billy R. Harrison.)

sign to the slightly smaller Sears, Roebuck and Company No. 13144 grinder, which sold for sixty cents in 1897.[35]

The remains of the other three grinding wheels are less well preserved. One is represented by a single wheel flange and several broken pieces of stone averaging about 1 inch thick. Since none of the fragments retain any portion of the spindle hole, little more can be ascertained about this object. Another grinding wheel is represented by pieces of a fine-grained yellow stone wheel found in the blacksmith shop. Because of its relative thinness, only about 1 inch, it is assumed that this stone also represents a bench-mounted grinder. A complete hand- or foot-actuated grinder was found in the Myers and Leonard store. Its gray micaceous sandstone wheel is 19 inches in diameter and 2¼ inches thick, bearing the scratched number "52" on one side. None of the grinders has any makers' marks.

One ladle was located in the northeast corner of the Myers and Leonard corral. Although badly fragmented, it appears to have an 18-

Fig. 84. Wheel from hand- or foot-actuated grindstone, as it was found in the Myers and Leonard store. (Photograph by Billy R. Harrison.)

inch-long handle and a 4- to 5-inch-diameter circular bowl without a pouring lip. Similar to item No. 8506 illustrated in the 1897 Sears, Roebuck and Company catalog, it is thought that hide men used this ladle to pour molten lead into molds used to cast bullets for their own hand-loaded cartridges.[36]

Although they are small, two pieces of laminated lead or foil were recovered in the Myers and Leonard store. These are thought to be the remains of two shims. Such materials are placed between two parts on a variety of hand tools, agricultural implements, and transportation vehicles to make a fit or to take up space where there is too great a void between two parts.

At least one historical account of Adobe Walls mentions the use of a timepiece by a hide man at the post.[37] This reference may be substantiated by an interesting brass and iron artifact found in the Myers and Leonard store. This object consists of a ⅝-inch-diameter brass ring connected to a small brass bell, which also includes the remains of an iron mounting screw. Although not positively identified, it is thought that this object may represent a hand ring from an alarm clock. A number of small brass clocks were found at the roughly contemporary Fort Bowie site in Arizona.[38]

The excavation of the Myers and Leonard store revealed a wheeled platform scale manufactured by the Buffalo Scale Company of Buffalo, New York, a nineteenth-century maker of weighing devices ranging from druggists' scales to equipment designed for weighing entire railway cars. The example from Adobe Walls is their platform scale number 5, serial number 16081, with a 20×28-inch platform and a capacity of 1,200 pounds, as illustrated in the company's 1874 catalog. The brass balance beam is graduated in half-pound increments from 0 to 50 pounds and has the number "11" and the name "BUFFALO SCALE WORKS" stamped on both faces. The beam's iron balance ball for fine adjustments is intact.[39] Considering its large capacity, this scale was probably used for weighing the bulk commodities that were sold in the store by the hundreds of pounds.

The Adobe Walls site yielded a wide range of woodworking tools, equipment, and supplies. These artifacts, listed in table 15, include a hatchet, an adz, a handsaw, a spokeshave, and a variety of staples, nails, tacks, and screws. The one hatchet discovered at the site came from the southeast corner of the Myers and Leonard corral. Remaining from

Fig. 85. Remains of wheeled platform scale inside the Myers and Leonard store. (Photograph by Billy R. Harrison.)

the tool was the highly oxidized head, which retained in its oval eye an amount of iron oxide-impregnated wood from the handle. The butt of the hatchet head is square and slightly flattened from hammering. The head measures 6 inches from butt to blade, the cutting edge is 4 inches wide, and the entire head weighs 1¼ pounds.

The head from a carpenter's adz was found beneath a pile of

TABLE 15

Woodworking Tools and Supplies

	M & L Store	Mess Hall	Stable	R & Co. Store	Saloon	Blacksmith Shop
Hatchet	1					
Adz				1		
Hand saw			1			
Spokeshave						1
Staples					3	
Nails	716	212	444	1181	305	529
Tacks with brass shanks	11			1	1	
Tacks with iron shanks		2			11	
Wood screws	2					

Fig. 86. Adz recovered at the Rath and Company store. (Photograph by Billy R. Harrison.)

burned windows inside the Rath and Company store. The hand-wrought tool has an oval eye and convex poll. Its cutting edge measures 4½ inches wide, the overall length of the head is 10 inches, and it weighs slightly more than 4 pounds.

The stable yielded the only handsaw found at the trading post. This specimen retains most of its blade, which was cut with six points per inch, as well as most of the partially charred handle, which is attached with three brass screws. The center screw is the largest and bears an embossed image of a mounted horseman and the words "WARRANTED SUPERIOR" on its top and bottom margins.

The blacksmith shop contained a specialized wagonmaker's tool known as a radius spokeshave. This is an iron instrument 7½ inches long fitted with "winged" handles and a removable, centrally located cutting blade used in trimming wooden spokes for vehicle wheels.

A variety of fastening devices used in woodworking were found at Adobe Walls. Three definitely identified large staples were found out-

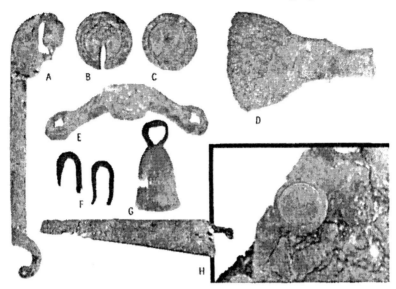

Fig. 87. Weighing devices and woodworking tools and equipment: (*A*) Brass balance beam from the wheeled platform scale 18 inches long. (*B*) Balance weight 4¼ inches in diameter. (*C*) Platen balance weight 4⅜ inches in diameter. (*D*) Hatchet head 6 inches long. (*E*) Spokeshave 7½ inches long. (*F*) Staples 3½ inches long. (*G*) Carpenter's adz head 10 inches long. (*H*) Six-point hand saw 25 inches long, with detail of decorative brass screw in handle.

side the west wall of the saloon building. They measure 3½ inches long and 1½ inches wide at their pointed ends. These artifacts were not attached to any other objects where they were discovered, so it was impossible to learn their specific use at the trading post.

Hundreds of nails were found in all the major buildings at the site. Because of their deteriorated condition, their numbers given in table 15 must be considered approximate. Most of the better preserved specimens appear to have been the 6d size. Tacks were also found at Adobe Walls. Used for fastening together small objects made from a variety of materials, they are listed among woodworking supplies for the purpose of organization in this study. The excavators found two types of brass tacks at the site, all of them having ⅜-inch-diameter flat brass heads. Some of these tacks have square brass shanks, but others have round steel shanks, one authority stating that most other known specimens with the steel shanks were manufactured later than the pe-

TABLE 16
Bolts, Nuts, and Washers

	M & L Store	Mess Hall	Stable	R & Co. Store	Saloon	Blacksmith Shop
Carriage bolt	1		1		5	1
J bolt					1	
Eye bolt						1
Machine bolt	1					
Unidentified bolt	1					11
Square nut with ⅛-inch hole						1
Square nut with ¼- to ⅜-inch hole			1		1	23
Square nut with ¼-inch bolt fragment						1
Square nut with 3⁄16-inch hole						13

Item			
Square nut with 5/16-inch hole	1		
Square nut with 1/2-inch hole	3	1	
Square nut with 1/2-inch bolt fragment	4		1
Square nut with 5/8-inch hole	2		
Square nut with 3/4-inch hole			1
Square nut with 3/4-inch bolt fragment		1	
Flat washer, 7/8-inch diameter	2		
Flat washer, 1 1/4-inch diameter	4		
Flat washer, 1 1/2-inch diameter	1		

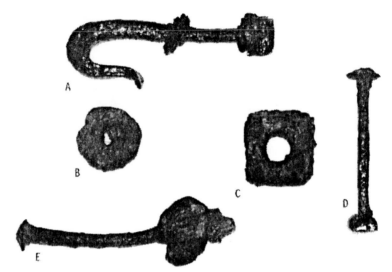

Fig. 88. Fastening devices used in woodworking: (*A*) J bolt with nut and two washers, 5 inches total length. (*B*) Flat washer 1½ inches in diameter. (*C*) Nut 1½ inches square and 1¼ inches thick with ½-inch hole. (*D*) Carriage bolt with square nut 5½ inches total length. (*E*) Carriage bolt with flat washer and nut, 4 inches total length.

riod of occupation at the site.[40] Completing the inventory of wood-fastening implements are two loose wood screws found in the Myers and Leonard store.

The Adobe Walls site yielded a number of nuts, bolts, and washers, most of them coming from the area of the blacksmith shop. These artifacts are listed in table 16. Thirteen individual bolts were recovered, eight of them having been identified as carriage bolts. With round heads that are half oval in cross section, their lengths vary from 2½ to 7 inches. One ¼-inch specimen with a square shank just below its head still retains a 1¾-inch flat washer and a ⅝-inch square nut. A single J bolt or hook bolt came from the saloon. It is 5 inches long and has attached two 1-inch flat washers and one ¾-inch square nut. Such bolts in the nineteenth and early twentieth centuries frequently were attached to wagon sideboards as anchors for ropes to hold the vehicle contents securely during travel.

A large variety of nuts was found at Adobe Walls, most of the specimens being located in the blacksmith shop. All the identifiable examples are square, were tapped with threads to receive threaded bolts, and range from ³⁄₁₆ to 1½ inches across. Several of the specimens have portions of bolts still in place and exhibit evidence of having been cut off with cold chisels.

Several washers were recovered at the site, but they were not numerous. Fragments of seven loose washers were discovered in the blacksmith shop, but only one was complete enough to provide accurate measurements. It has an overall diameter of 1½ inches, is ¹⁄₁₆ inch thick, and has a ⁵⁄₁₆-inch-diameter central bolt hole.

Coal cinders were found in only two buildings at Adobe Walls, the blacksmith shop and the stable. Approximately 20 pounds of slag and cinders located along the south wall of the blacksmith shop strongly indicate that this was the area where Tom O'Keefe's forge stood inside the picket building. The cinders at the south end of the stable, an area that was disturbed by an illegal relic hunter, probably represent refuse from the mess hall cookstove and may even suggest this as its location in 1874.

One preserved fragment of rope was found in the excavation at Adobe Walls. A single piece of charred ¼-inch three-strand natural fiber rope tied into an overhand knot was recovered inside the Myers and Leonard store.

Only one positively identified communication artifact was recovered at the trading post site. This is a clear, flint glass blown inkwell and stopper found on the floor of the Myers and Leonard store. The well is both badly fragmented and heat warped, probably because of the fire that destroyed the store building. The base of the inkwell body is concave, measures 3¾ inches in diameter, and is very heavy, to prevent its tipping over. The body measures 1⅞ inches high, but the mouth for its stopper is badly heat warped. The glass stopper is double spherical in shape and is 1¾ inches long. The lower bubble (sphere) of the stopper shows considerable wear as a result of use and bears a glassblower's break mark on its lower side. No maker's mark is present.

CHAPTER 12

Transportation

T HE excavation conducted at Adobe Walls yielded interesting remains from a number of animal-drawn vehicles. The locations where several of these artifacts were found suggest that some of the vehicles may have been moved to these places just before or at the time that the Indians burned the trading post in order to facilitate the combustion of the wagons, buildings, or both. The transportation artifacts are listed in table 17.

Wagon box rod collars represent at least three different wagons from the site. One of these from the saloon appears to be machine-made and has chamfered mounting holes in each end and a 5/16-inch threaded center rod hole. The other examples, from the Myers and Leonard stable and from the Rath and Company store, seem to be handmade. A semicircular fragment of what is thought to be a fifth wheel from a wagon was found inside the Rath and Company store. It measures 13½ inches long, 1¼ inches wide, and 1/16 inch thick, with both ends showing evidence of having been cut off with a cold chisel.

Near the gate area at the northwest end of the Rath and Company store, a single wagon bolster brace was found. Further excavation here might have revealed more wagon parts, but financial constraints prevented additional work in this area. The brace is U-shaped and has flat attachment rings or lugs on both sides. A ½-inch-diameter hole is located at the center of the U for attachment, and the lugs have ⅝-inch-diameter holes for fastening to the fifth wheel mechanism.

The interior of the Myers and Leonard store yielded two carriage

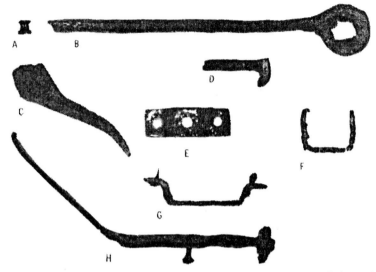

Fig. 89. Transportation vehicle parts: (*A*) Carriage knob ⁹⁄₁₆ inch long. (*B*) Wagon box rod 9¾ inches long. (*C*) Wagon box rod nut 1½ inches long. (*D*) Coupling pin fragment 3¾ inches long. (*E*) Wagon box rod collar ¾ × 2½ inches. (*F*) Wagon box bow/stake staple 2 × 2½ inches. (*G*) Wagon box stake iron 6 inches long. (*H*) Wagon box strap 14½ inches long.

top knobs. Made from wood, they are covered with drawn brass jackets. The fact that the shanks are missing from both examples makes it impossible to determine whether the knobs are the driven or screw type. No other specific evidence of a carriage was found at the site, so it is possible that these knobs represent merchandise left behind in the store. This building also yielded the only wagon wheel nut recovered in the excavation. It measures 4 inches in diameter, has a 1½-inch-diameter central hole, and has a 2½-inch-square outward projection with tapered edges designed to receive a wagon wrench for tightening and loosening.

Two wagon tailgate parts were found, both of them apparently handmade box rod nuts. The example from the Myers and Leonard store has a diamond-shaped head that tapers outward to provide room for a user's fingers; the specimen from the blacksmith shop has only a slight outward curve and a round head.

One coupling pin was found. This item was hand-forged, is J-

TABLE 17
Transportation Artifacts

	M & L Store	Mess Hall	Stable	R & Co. Store	Saloon	Blacksmith Shop
Wagon box rod collar			1	1	1	
Wagon bolster brace				1	1	
Carriage top knob	2					
Wagon axle nut	1					
Wagon box rod nut	1					1
Coupling pin						1
Wagon box stake iron			1			
Wagon box bow/stake staple	2		1			
Double-leaf seat spring	1					
Wagon stay chain ring	1					
Wagon fifth wheel				1		
Wagon box rod	1		1			
Wagon skein fragment			1	1		1
Wagon box strap			2			
Wagon wheel tire fragment						1
Jointed bridle bit	1					
Harness buckle (?)	2	1	1			
Harness leather fragment		1		1		2
Harness leather fragment with conchas and pad screw	1					

Item						
Pad screw	1					
Singletree ferrule hook	1					
Hame terret		1				1
Doubletree clevis			2			
Singletree hook	1					
Singletree strap						1
Neck yoke ring						1
Buggy wrench	2					
Trace chain fragment			1			
Chain link				1		
Chain repair link					2	
Chain ring					2	
Hame fragment			1			
Hame hook	1					
Harness ring	2				2	
Hame line ring		1				
Singletree center clip			1			

shaped, made from ½-inch iron rod, and has been cut to only 3¾ inches long. Two wagon box rods were found, both of them retaining their "eye" heads but seeming to have been shortened by cutting. The "eye" heads are 1¾ inches in diameter, with lengths of 9¾ inches and 41 inches. Fragments of three artifacts have been identified as the remains of wagon skeins, but they are represented only by the wheel-bearing surfaces.

A single wagon box stake iron was recovered. Apparently made from tire iron, it retains nail heads intact and on one edge has a ¼-inch hole. The purpose of this hole may have been to provide an opening for a nail driven to hold the stake in its proper place. The stake width appears to have been 3½ inches. Three wagon box bow/stake staples similar to those illustrated in the 1897 Sears, Roebuck and Company

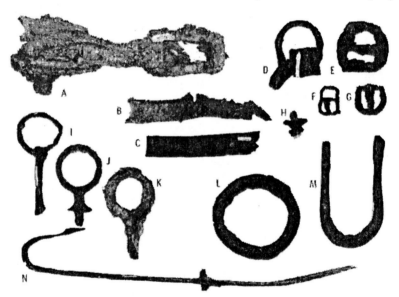

Fig. 90. Transportation accessories: (*A*) Buggy wrench 8¾ inches long. (*B*) Harness leather fragment 6½ inches long. (*C*) Harness leather fragment 5⁵⁄₁₆ inches long. (*D*) Singletree ferrule hook 1 inch wide at small end, 1¼ inches wide at large end, and bearing ⅜-inch hook. (*E*) Harness buckle 2 inches long and 2 inches wide. (*F*) Harness buckle 1 inch long and ½ inch wide. (*G*) Harness buckle 1½ inches long and 1¼ inches wide. (*H*) Pad screw ½ inch long. (*I*) Jointed bridle bit 4½ inches long. (*J*) Hame terret 3½ inches long. (*K*) Singletree hook 5 inches long. (*L*) Neck yoke ring 3⅜ × ⅝ inches. (*M*) Doubletree clevis 4½ inches long. (*N*) Singletree strap 16½ inches long.

catalog were collected.[1] All are the same size, with 2½-inch-wide openings and 2-inch-long tangs, which are clinched. Two wagon box straps are represented. One appears to be factory made and is similar to the example illustrated in the 1897 Sears, Roebuck and Company catalog.[2] Only one rivet is present near the threaded end; its opposite end has been cut off. The second specimen may have been added to the wagon later, as it is not so wide as the former and it appears to be hand forged.

A set of double-leaf regular riveted head seat springs also was found. The set measured 28 inches long and 1¾ inches wide, but they were in such deteriorated condition that they could not be salvaged. Except for their width, they are similar to the springs illustrated in figure 10557 of the 1909 George Worthington Company catalog.[3]

Along with parts of vehicles, remains of a number of transportation accessories also were found at Adobe Walls. These artifacts, also presented in table 17, are mostly parts of equipment used to control draft animals. Two of these items, however, should receive more than passing notice. They are two buggy wrenches located in the Myers and Leonard store. Measuring 8¾ inches long, each tool bears tapered rectangular slots from ¾ to 1 inch wide in both ends, which would permit them to fit nuts of varying sizes.

CHAPTER 13

Containers

FOR the purposes of this study, containers have been divided into two categories: product packages and unclassified containers. The former group consists of articles created to serve as containers for known substances that were to be sold. Most of these artifacts from Adobe Walls are represented by embossed glass bottles. The second category, unclassified containers, are objects that were produced to hold materials that cannot be identified from an examination of the container.[1] The majority of these artifacts from the site also are glass bottles or sherds therefrom. All the product packages and unclassified containers are listed in table 18.

A total of at least thirty-seven glass bottles from Adobe Walls fall into two groups of product packages as containers for either alcoholic beverages or proprietary medicines. At least fourteen different product manufacturers are known from their trade names embossed in the glass of these artifacts. Many of the specimens are incomplete but sufficiently intact to be identified. Four actual glassworks have been identified as producers of some of the bottles recovered.

Based on known contents of bottles recovered, it appears that bitters and beer were the favorite alcoholic beverages at Adobe Walls. Although little known today, bitters were popular drinks through the eighteenth, nineteenth, and early twentieth centuries. Their name comes from the characteristic infusion of herbs that gave them an acrid taste and purportedly medicinal and laxative qualities. In reality, however, many customers purchased bitters for their alcohol con-

Fig. 91. Product packages: (*A*) Brandon and Kirmeyer beer bottles and base 9 inches tall and 3½ inches in diameter. (*B*) J. Walker's Vinegar Bitters bottle and base 8⁷⁄₁₆ inches tall and 3 inches in diameter. (*C*) Hostetter's Stomach Bitters bottle and base 9 inches tall and 2½ inches square. (*D*) S. McKee and Company beer bottle and base 11¾ inches tall and 3 inches in diameter. (*E*) H. T. Helmbold's Genuine Fluid Extracts bottle 6 inches tall. (*F*) F. Brown's Essence of Jamaica Ginger bottle 5½ inches tall with base 1½ × 2¼ inches. (*G*) J. A. Hamlin and Brother Wizard Oil bottle 5½ inches tall. (*H*) Mexican Mustang Liniment bottle 4 inches tall. (*I*) Cunningham and Ihmsen beer bottle base 3 inches in diameter.

tent. The beverage increased in popularity as the Prohibition movement grew, many men and women accepting the healing bitters with gratitude.[2]

Among the bitters bottles found at Adobe Walls, where the drinks sold for $1.50 a bottle,[3] were four specimens that held Dr. Joseph Walker's Vinegar Bitters. Embossed "J. WALKER'S V B," the specimens measure 8½ inches in height and 3 inches in diameter at their bases. The maker, Joseph Walker, entered the bitters business in California in 1866 and within two decades it made him a millionaire. Although advertised as a nonalcoholic bitters, his product during at least some of the years of its production contained 7½ percent alcohol.[4]

Another bitters represented by bottles found at Adobe Walls is

TABLE 18
Containers

	M & L Store	Mess Hall	Stable	R & Co. Store	Saloon	Blacksmith Shop
J. Walker's Vinegar Bitters bottle	2				1	
Hostetter's Stomach Bitters bottle	3	1		1	2	
John W. Steele's Niagara Star Bitters bottle					1	
Brandon & Kirmeyer Beer bottle						8
Beer bottle made by S. McKee & Company with 5 dots on base				1		
Beer bottle made by Cunningham & Ihmsen				2		
London Royal Nectar Gin bottle					1	
Mercer Agnew & Company London Swan Gin bottle					1	
Merchant's Gargling Oil bottle	1			1		
Davis Vegetable Pain Killer bottle	1	1				
H. T. Helmbold Genuine Fluid Extract bottle	1					

Item		
Ayer's Compound Extract of Sarsaparilla bottle	2	
Frederick Brown's Essence of Jamaica Ginger bottle	1	1
Hamlin's Wizard Oil bottle	3	
Mexican Mustang Liniment bottle	1	
Centaur Liniment bottle	1	
Keg lid	1	
Primer can	1	
Unidentified clear, coffin-type, flask bottle		1
Unidentified clear, ball neck-type medicine bottle	4	1
Unidentified clear, oval bottle, possibly for strychnine	3	
Unidentified clear, rectangular bottle, possibly for strychnine	1	
Unidentified clear, partial bottle with embossed letters	1	
Unidentified clear, round, prescription-type bottle with 2¼-inch diameter	1	
Unidentified clear, round, prescription-type bottle with 2-inch diameter 5¼ inches tall	1	1

TABLE 18 continued
Containers

	M & L Store	Mess Hall	Stable	R & Co. Store	Saloon	Blacksmith Shop
Unidentified clear, ball-neck panel bottle approx. 6⅛ inches tall	1					
Unidentified clear neck sherd from bottle		1				
Unidentified fragment from bottle		2		2	1	
Unidentified fragment from flask-shaped bottle bearing an embossed eagle	1					
Unidentified molten mass from clear glass bottle		1				
Bucket bail ear			2			
Tin can with lid				1		
Tin can with hole in center				2		
Unidentified round lid from tin can			1			
Unidentified rectangular lid from tin can	1			1		
Unidentified tin can cap				1		
Zinc or pewter can spout			1			
Crockery partial lid			1			
Clear glass stopper				1		
Tub handle			2			
Round tin cans	25	2	7	57	20	
Rectangular tin cans	3		1	1		2
Gunpowder can lid	1					

Fig. 92. Additional product packages: (*A*) Davis Vegetable Pain Killer bottle 5½ inches tall. (*B*) John W. Steele Niagara Star Bitters bottle 10¼ inches tall. (*C*) Lid from powder keg 5¼ inches in diameter. (*D*) Mercer, Agnew and Company London Swan Gin bottle 9⅞ inches tall. (*E*) London Royal Nectar Gin bottle 9½ inches tall. (*F*) Merchant's Gargling Oil bottle 5½ inches tall. (*G*) Ayer's Compound Extract of Sarsaparilla bottle 8½ inches tall. (*H*) Centaur Liniment bottle shoulder and neck 2¹⁵⁄₁₆ inches long.

the once-popular Hostetter's Stomach Bitters. This beverage/medicine was developed by Dr. Jacob Hostetter, a Pennsylvania physician, who prescribed the drink as a tonic for many of his patients. Beginning in 1853 his son, David, began marketing the formula under the name of Hostetter and Smith, the firm becoming Hostetter and Company in December, 1884. Hostetter's was advertised as a cure for flatulence and dyspepsia and as a preventive for fever and ague. Twenty-five percent alcohol by volume, the product also contained nux vomica seed, from which strychnine is extracted; cinchona bark, from which quinine is made; and anise flavoring. By 1902 the Hostetter family reputedly had made more than $18 million from the sales of the bottled formula. The beginning of national prohibition of alcohol in 1919, however, spelled the end for the product, and its manufacture ceased.

Six amber glass Hostetter's bottles were recovered from three of the buildings. Only one of these specimens is complete enough for measurement, but the others appear to be approximately the same size and shape. The most complete example is rectangular, 9 inches tall, has a 2½-inch square base and a capacity of 18 fluid ounces. The examples bear, in conical concavities in their bases, the bottle maker's mark, which is the embossed letters "W. MC C & CO," indicating that they were blown at the works of William McCulley and Company, a firm manufacturing bottles in Pittsburgh from the 1840s to 1880s. In addition to the bottle maker's mark, the bottoms of the four best preserved specimens also bear the additional embossed marks "H," "D," "F," and "8." The example found in the Myers and Leonard mess hall was so shattered and melted that no data could be read on its base, and the sixth specimen consists of only parts from its top and base.[5]

One more type of bitters used at Adobe Walls is represented by a single John W. Steele's Niagara Star Bitters bottle, which was found in the saloon. Steele, in partnership with others, began producing this bitters at Lockport, New York, in the 1860s, continuing its manufacture at least into the 1870s. His bottles are identified as having been blown by the Lockport Glass Works, a major New York State bottle maker from the 1840s to the 1880s. This factory produced other bottles recovered at Adobe Walls. Both the glass works and Steele's enterprise are listed in the New York State and Lockport city directories from 1874. The example of this bottle from the trading post is dark olive amber in color, rectangular with rounded corners, and has a domed base measuring 2⅞ inches square; it stands 10¼ inches tall. The words "JOHN W. STEELE'S/NIAGARA STAR BITTERS" are marked on two lines on one indented panel; the opposite indented panel bears the lettering "JOHN W. STEELE/NIAGARA ★ BITTERS" on two lines. In one dome-topped indented panel there is a flying eagle facing right with three arrows in its talons. A five-pointed star is present on three sides of the roofed shoulders, and the date "1864" is embossed on the fourth side above the one plain indented panel.[6]

The bottles recovered indicate that beer was almost as popular as bitters among the hide men and merchants at Adobe Walls. Eight bottles found in the blacksmith shop held beer or ale produced by the Brandon and Kirmeyer Brewery in Leavenworth, Kansas. This partnership of John Brandon and Michael Kirmeyer is known to have been producing ale and soda water at a plant on the southeast corner of Second and Kiowa streets in Leavenworth as early as the 1860s, continu-

ing production at least into the late 1870s. By 1870 they were advertising the production and sale of "soda water, cream and stock ale,
[and] porter and lager beer."

Two varieties of Brandon and Kirmeyer bottles are represented
by remains found at the trading post. All the examples are amber and
cylindrical, are molded with broad sloping collar necks, measure 9
inches tall, and have dish-shaped bases 3½ inches in diameter. The differences occur in their embossed lettering. The first style bears front
embossing with "BRANDON" forming an arc at the top of the shoulder
with "KIRRMEYER" and "LEAVENWORTH" forming two straight lines
horizontally across the center of the bottle. The second style has the
words "BRANDON & KIRMEYER" forming an arc near the shoulder,
beneath which the words "LEAVENWORTH" and "KANSAS" also are
embossed horizontally on separate lines across the front. One specimen of the latter pattern also has the letters "B & K" at the center of its
dish-shaped base, but none of the other bases bear any inscription. The
name "Kirmeyer" is spelled two ways, both on the bottles and in
nineteenth-century business directories.[7]

Three additional amber glass bottle fragments have been classified as parts of beer bottles. One of these specimens is nearly complete
and on its base the name "S. MC KEE AND CO" is embossed together
with a series of dots arranged in a star pattern. This bottle was the
product of S. McKee and Company of Birmingham, Pennsylvania,
which made glassware from the 1830s to the 1880s. The other two
specimens consist of bases only, but both examples bear the clearly
embossed lettering "C & I." They are products made by the firm of
Cunningham and Ihmsen of Pittsburgh, Pennsylvania, a manufacturer
that produced bottles from 1865 to 1879. The McKee bottle measures
11¾ inches tall, has a 3-inch-diameter base, and holds 18 fluid ounces.
The two bases marked "C & I" both measure 3 inches in diameter.[8]

The only archeological evidence for the presence of hard liquor
at Adobe Walls comes from two gin bottles recovered from the saloon
building. From preserved receipts, however, it is known that gin sold
over the counter at the Myers and Leonard store for $1.50 a bottle.[9]
One of the two clear glass gin bottles from the saloon is marked on
three of its four sides with the words "LONDON/ROYAL/NECTAR
GIN." Its unmarked panel at one time may have had a paper label. The
bottle measures 9½ inches high, has an unmarked 2¾-inch-square

base, and will hold 23 fluid ounces. The other specimen is of similar general shape and bears embossed lettering on three of its four sides that reads "LONDON ENG./MERCER AGNEW & CO./LONDON SWAN GIN." Also holding 23 fluid ounces, the bottle is 9⅞ inches tall and has a 2½-inch-square unmarked base. No further information could be found on either product.

A variety of interesting proprietary medicine bottles recovered at Adobe Walls visibly illustrate the concern that the hide men and merchants had for their health. This is not surprising for men who found themselves in potentially hostile country more than a hundred miles from the nearest physician. Among the several patent medicines represented is Merchant's Gargling Oil, for which fragmentary remains of two bottles were found. The product was developed by Dr. George W. Merchant in 1833 and within three decades had become a standard "cure-all" sold in virtually all parts of the country. In 1866 alone Merchant used one million glass bottles for the distribution of his products. During the 1860s and 1870s almost all these containers were manufactured under contract by the Lockport Glass Works of Lockport, New York, the firm that also made the Niagara Star Bitters bottles. Gargling Oil contained 44 percent alcohol by volume as well as one grain of opium per fluid ounce; it must have been a successful pain killer. The bottle specimens from the trading post are emerald green in color, represent the 2-ounce size that cost twenty-five cents in 1874, and are 5½ inches high. They are rectangular, and embossed on their front panels are the words "GARGLING OIL/LOCKPORT, N. Y."[10]

Another widely sold patent medicine used at Adobe Walls was the Davis Vegetable Pain Killer, a product developed in the 1830s by Perry Davis. While practicing his trade as a shoemaker at Dartmouth, Massachusetts, Davis's health deteriorated from the effects of a severe chest cold. After trying a number of available medicines with no relief, he devised his own cure with the purported aid of Providence and began using it both externally and internally with favorable results. Prompted by his wife, he called the substance a "pain killer" because it killed his pains. Within two decades the product became popular throughout the country and even remained available into the mid-twentieth century. The one complete Davis Vegetable Pain Killer bottler from the trading post, which was extremely heat warped, was found inside the Myers and Leonard store. The panel-style bottle stands 4½ inches tall and has a rectangular base ¾ × 1¼ inches. One front panel has a recessed area near its arched top where it bears the embossed name "DAVIS." One side panel has the embossed lettering "VEGETABLE," and the opposite side panel reads "PAIN KILLER." Additional fragments with embossed letters from another specimen were found in the Myers and Leonard mess hall.[11]

The trading post site produced one bottle that originally contained a medicine known as Helmbold's Fluid Extracts of Buchu. The developer of this product was Henry T. Helmbold, a Philadelphia chemist, who created the formula in 1850. He soon placed it on the market, but it did not start reaching a national market until he became a partner with Demas Barnes and John D. Park, who distributed the medicine in New York and Cincinnati, respectively. Henry T. Helmbold continued manufacturing his extracts into the 1880s, when his son assumed management of the business, which existed into the twentieth century. Buchu was advertised as a remedy for rheumatism, constipation, epilepsy, nervousness, deafness, and other afflictions. The Adobe Walls specimen of this bottle came from the Myers and Leonard store. Made from aqua-colored glass, it is rectangular, measures 6 inches tall, and has a base measuring 1¼×2 inches. Its front indented panel bears the words "GENUINE/FLUID EXTRACTS," in two lines, and the side panels read "H. T. HELMBOLD" and "PHILADELPHIA."[12]

Two bottles that held Ayer's Compound Extract of Sarsaparilla were recovered in the excavations at the trading post site. The manufacturer of this medicinal product, the J. C. Ayer Company of Lowell, Massachusetts, had its origin in the activities of James Cook Ayer. He received a degree in medicine in 1841 and soon thereafter purchased a drugstore in Lowell. There he developed his first commercial medicine, Ayer's Cherry Pectoral. Devoting most of his profits to advertising, soon he marketed an entire line of family remedies, one of which was his extract of sarsaparilla. It is noted as having been produced at least between 1858 and 1894.

Both of the Ayer's bottles from Adobe Walls are the same size and design. They measure 8½ inches in height and have 1½×2¾-inch rectangular bases. They are the panel type, aqua, and have front panels bearing the word "AYER'S" embossed at the center. The back panels read "LOWELL, MASS. U. S. A.," and "COMPOUND EXT" and "SARSAPARILLA" are spelled out on the two side panels. Shallow depressions are found in the centers of the bases.[13]

Another bottle that contained an internal patent medicine is one for Frederick Brown's Essence of Jamaica Ginger. This product was made by Frederick Brown, an importer and manufacturer of medicinal goods from the 1850s to the 1890s. He is listed in the 1873 and 1874 Philadelphia business directories as operating both retail and wholesale outlets at the corner of Chestnut and South Fifth streets in the city. The single example of this bottle, the 6-ounce size, is aqua and was found in front of the Rath and Company store. It stands 5½ inches tall and has an oval base measuring 1½×2¼ inches. The following embossed lettering is placed vertically in four lines on one face: "F. BROWN'S/ESS OF/JAMAICA GINGER/PHILADᴬ."[14]

An additional medicine represented by bottles found at the site is Hamlin's Wizard Oil. This product was developed by John A. Hamlin of Cincinnati sometime before the Civil War. During the conflict he moved to Chicago, where he and his successors continued to manufacture Wizard Oil and other patent medicines into the twentieth century. Wizard Oil was advertised as a cure for ailments ranging from cancer to hydrophobia. Although a number of variants in bottle design were used in these containers, the three specimens from Adobe Walls, only one of which is complete, all appear to be the 3-ounce style in a rectangular paneled aqua bottle. The front panel bears the lettering "J. A. HAMLIN & BRO/CHICAGO," and the back reads "WIZARD OIL." The one complete specimen stands 5½ inches tall, measures 1×1¾ inches at the base, and has a shallow ⅝-inch concave depression in the center of its base.[15]

Two liniment bottles were found at Adobe Walls. These are Mexican Mustang Liniment and Centaur Liniment. One clear round prescription-type bottle for Mexican Mustang Liniment was found inside the Myers and Leonard store. This external medicine was produced by the Lyon Manufacturing Company of New York at least from the 1860s to the 1890s. The 3-ounce size bottle from the trading post measures 4 inches tall and 1½ inches in diameter. It bears five rows of vertical embossed lettering that spell out the following words: "MEXICAN/MUSTANG/LINIMENT/LYON MFG CO/NEW YORK." Four different sizes and varieties of Mexican Mustang Liniment bottles were found in excavations at Fort Laramie, Wyoming, and Fort Union, New Mexico.[16]

Centaur Liniment is the second external medicine represented by a product package found at the trading post. Also coming from the Myers and Leonard store, the specimen consists only of the lip, neck, and upper portion of a round clear prescription type bottle. The bottle diameter is estimated to have been 1⅝ inches; the bottle's rounded shoulder bears the words "CENTAUR LINIMENT." This product was known in the 1870s and 1880s as a universal liniment. It was advertised as a cure for such diverse maladies as opium dizziness and saber wounds.[17]

The remaining product package artifacts recovered at Adobe Walls consist of a keg lid, a gunpowder can lid, and two specialized tin cans. One uncharred keg lid was located outside the Myers and Leonard store, and it is thought to have come from a keg of black powder. It measures 5¼ inches in diameter and ¼ inch thick. One unmarked pewter gunpowder can lid was found in the Myers and Leonard store. It measures 1 inch in diameter and ⅜ inch thick, including ¼ inch of remaining threads. The lid bears a simple line decoration around its rim as well as two narrow rectangular cut slots through opposite sides of the rim perpendicular to the long axis of the lid. Two tin cans that were salvaged from the site have been classified product packages, as

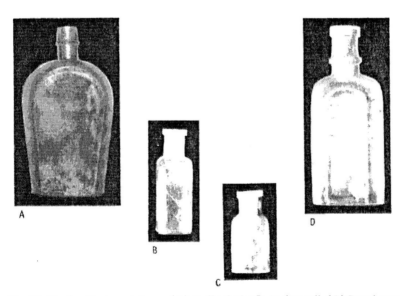

Fig. 93. Unclassified containers: (*A*) Coffin flask 8⅞ inches tall. (*B*) Panel-type rectangular bottle 2¾ inches tall. (*C*) Oval bottle (possibly for strychnine) 2⅛ inches tall. (*D*) Ball neck panel bottle 4¾ inches tall.

they appear to be primer cans. Both are 1½ inches in diameter, 1 inch high, and have ¼-inch-wide overlapping lids.

A number of unclassified containers were found at Adobe Walls. All of these objects are listed in table 18. Further comments are appropriate for several of these objects.

A single clear, coffin-type flask bottle was found in the saloon. It is a type commonly used for whiskey. A decorative band is present at the center of the neck; the specimen measures 8⅞ inches tall, 5×2¼ inches maximum width, and 4×2⅛ inches at its base. Its capacity is 24 fluid ounces.[18]

Ball-neck panel bottles were fairly common at the site. Six clear examples with oval panels near their tops were recovered. They probably contained some type of proprietary patent medicine, but none of the specimens bear any markings. Five are identical in style and measure 4¾ inches in height with rectangular bases ¹⁵⁄₁₆×1¹⁵⁄₁₆ inch. The sixth example measures 6⅛ inches high, though its base is missing.

The site yielded three very small clear oval bottles with no markings; they may have contained strychnine. This substance was commonly used as a poison for carnivorous animals that followed the hide men of the 1870s. The specimens measure 2⅛ inches tall with bodies 1 inch wide and ¾ inch thick. Each has a capacity of ⅛ fluid ounce. An additional small, clear, panel-type rectangular bottle with a ⅛-ounce capacity was found in the northwest corner of the Myers and Leonard corral. It also may have contained strychnine. The bottle measures 2¾ inches tall and has a base 1 inch square with beveled corners.

Fourteen clear glass sherds of undeterminable bottle shape were found in the Myers and Leonard store. One sherd has the following embossed letters: "———N'S/———NCER/DA." Positive identification of the maker or substance contained was not possible.

Two different isolated bucket bails ears were found in the stable, and both retain two iron rivets. One is 1¾ inches long, and part of the bucket is still attached. The other appears to have been attached to a larger bucket, as it is 2⅛ inches long and has a slightly larger base.

Tin cans were impossible to expose because of their deterioration and the grass roots growing through them. The majority appear to have been 3 inches in diameter by 4 to 5 inches long and bear solder seals in the centers of one end.

Personal Artifacts

PERSONAL artifacts are those objects created to serve the personal needs of individuals. They include clothing, body protection, adornment, grooming aids, and symbols of beliefs and achievements.[1] A wide variety of these objects were recovered in the excavation at the Adobe Walls trading post, as shown in table 19. Interestingly, they represent the belongings not only of the white merchants and hide men, but also of the Indians who occupied the area both before the establishment of the post and after its abandonment.

Among the articles of adornment discovered at the site were a variety of glass, copper, bone, and shell beads. It is not known whether these artifacts were lost by the Indians before or after the white men came or were taken from the bodies of dead warriors by the hunters after the battle and subsequently lost. Some of the beads may have been used by the whites for their personal adornment.

The range of names given to various types of beads is almost as endless as their modes and materials of production. The name "trade bead" might be given to virtually any bead, but the term generally refers to the small glass beads manufactured in the factories of Venice, Italy, for more than five centuries. Many of these European-made beads found in American historical archeological sites are tiny and usually called "seed beads." For the purposes of this study, only two classifications are used; the small, round, glass varieties are termed "seed beads," and "tubular bead" denotes all elongated forms, whether made from copper, bone, or shell. All of the bead types recovered at Adobe Walls are illustrated.

TABLE 19
Personal Artifacts

	M & L Store	Mess Hall	Stable	R & Co. Store	Privy	Saloon	Blacksmith Shop	Surface
Beads	9	1		9		1		
Gemstone	1							
Footwear								
Screw sole			1					
Sewn and screw sole	1			4				
Sewn sole	1			3		3		
Nondiagnostic sole			2	3		3	15	
Glass buttons								
Clear glass with brass wire shank	4		3					
Black glass	2			1				
Milk glass, two-hole			4					
Milk glass, four-hole	37	9	7	12		7		
Milk glass with shank	11	1		4		5	1	
Milk glass fragments	1					1		
Rubber buttons				1		1		
Bone buttons								
Two-hole	1							
Four-hole, shirt		1		2				
Four-hole, coat	13							
Fragment	1							
Shell buttons								
Two-hole	6	1		2				
Four-hole	6	1						
Shank type	1					2		

	1	2	3	4	5	6	7	8
Iron buttons								
Four-hole	6			16		1		
Shank type with brass rivets	2			5		3	1	
Fragments	2			1				1
Brass buttons								
Eagle device, coat	4		6	2				
Eagle device, cuff or vest			8					
Fabric covered	2			1		4		
Two-piece four-hole	5	2		3		1		
Three-piece with brass rivets	3			11		3	1	
Suspender	3			3				
Spherical with ferrous wire shank	1		4	3				
Two-piece with ferrous wire shank	2			3				
Two-piece, four-hole with mark								
Self-shank with mark							1	
Cone with shank				1				
Fragments of compound type	1			1				
Iron buckle				1				
Brass buckle	2							
Clay tobacco pipes								
Bird bowl sherd	21			16		18		
Bird stem sherd	9			10		8		
Basket bowl sherd				11		7		
Basket stem sherd				1		2		
Acorn bowl sherd	1		2			2		
Acorn stem sherd	2		2		1		1	
Bearded-man bowl sherd	29			5		1		
Bearded-man stem sherd	7			2		1		

TABLE 19 *continued*
Personal Artifacts

	M & L Store	Mess Hall	Stable	R & Co. Store	Privy	Saloon	Blacksmith Shop	Surface
Smooth with raised ring bowl sherd				2				
Unidentified bowl sherd	21			1		12		
Unidentified stem sherd	14	2		4		4		
Unidentified sherds	33		1	1		99		
Tobacco plug labels				4				
Conchas	3			3				
Combs	2	1		4				
Hand looking glass	1							
Mirror (?) glass sherds						152		
Marbles				1			1	
Coins	2			2				
Eyeglasses lens				1				

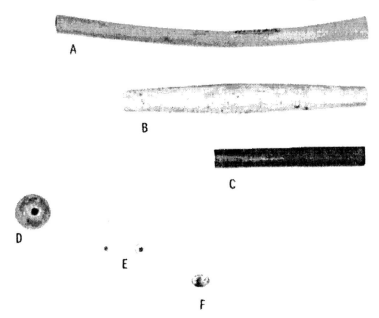

Fig. 94. Beads: (*A*) Tubular bone bead 3⁷⁄₃₂ inches long. (*B*) Shell "hair pipe" bead 2½ inches long. (*C*) Copper tubular bead 1⅝ inches long. (*D*) "Pony" or "pound" bead ⅜ inch in diameter. (*E*) White seed beads ¹⁄₁₆ inch thick and ³⁄₃₂ inch in diameter. (*F*) Artificial gemstone with hexagonal mixed cut ¼-inch square.

Ten white and six blue seed beads were recovered at the site. One of the blue beads is of a larger size often designated as "pony" or "pound" beads. The smaller beads averaged about ¹⁄₃₂ inch wide and ³⁄₃₂ inch in diameter. They are typical of thousands of beads found in historic sites throughout North America and most likely are of European origin. Such beads have been traded, bought, and given as gifts in the New World since the arrival of the first European explorers. They were imported in great quantities by such trading firms as the American Fur Company and Hudson's Bay Company.[2]

One copper, one bone, and two shell examples represent the four tubular beads found at Adobe Walls. The copper bead is made from a small single-thickness copper sheet that was rolled to form a tube. It is similar to other tubular copper beads that have been found in the eastern United States, although it has no apparent overlapping of its edges, as in the cases of other known examples.[3] It measures 1⅝ inches long by ³⁄₁₆ inch in diameter, and its ends are rounded smooth.

The one tubular bone bead is the type commonly identified as a "hair.pipe" bead, a name taken from the practice by some Indians of using them as hair ornaments. It is 3¹⁄₃₂ inches long, with both ends cut and polished. As it is made from a turkey radius, its diameter measurements vary considerably, but they average about ¼ inch.

Though the name "hair pipe" may be applied to virtually any tubular bone or shell bead, the most common material type in demand by the Plains Indians in the 1870s was made from West Indian conch shells by a firm known as the Campbell Brothers' Wampum Mill at Pasacack (now Park Ridge), New Jersey. They were one of the most popular of all the trade items in the period.[4] Two of these shell beads were found at Adobe Walls. One is 2½ inches long by ¹⁵⁄₁₆ inch in diameter; the other is 2 inches long and ¼ inch in diameter. Both taper toward their ends and are highly polished. The shorter example is broken near its midpoint.

One artificial gemstone is the only jewel found at the site. It is made from a brilliant glass material usually called paste or strass. The girdle of the gem is ¼ inch square with rounded corners. The table facet is hexagonal and measures approximately ³⁄₆₄ inch across the flats. The crown is faceted with a scissors cut and the pavilion is faceted with a step cut, creating a combination of cuts known as a hexagonal mixed cut.[5] The gem measures approximately ³⁄₁₆ inch from the table facet to the tip of the conical pavilion. No remains exist to suggest the type of article on which the gem was mounted, but the rounded edges of the facets indicate considerable wear.

The Adobe Walls site yielded thirty-six footwear artifacts. From these thirteen were diagnostic, meaning that there were sufficient remains preserved to date them, to identify them, and to understand their use. The artifacts from the site consist primarily of soles, heel and counter fragments, brass eyelets attached to small upper leather fragments, and brass screws. Some of the fragments are badly charred and all are friable. From the collection only two examples retain enough of their uppers to be identified positively as shoe remnants. The others could be either shoes or boots. All but three of the soles have a distinctively squared toe typical of military footwear of the period.[6]

The soles were fastened to the uppers by thread, screws, or a

Fig. 95. Detail of shoe as found in the excavation of the Myers and Leonard store in 1977. (Photograph by Billy R. Harrison.)

combination of both. No thread was found, but the sewn soles are characterized by elongated holes, thread indentations between the holes, and often the absence of metal fastenings. Most metal fastenings found were brass screws ranging from ⁷⁄₁₆ to ⁹⁄₁₆ inch long and averaging 0.093 inch in diameter. All have threads shaped similarly to the Whitworth Standard.[7]

A single footware sole has only brass screw fastenings and shows no evidence of sewing. It has two thick outsole layers, with the top one made from two pieces that overlap at the back of the ball. A thin layer representing the burned upper separates the outsoles from a relatively thick insole. The sole is shaped for the right foot and measures 9½ inches long by 3⅛ inches wide at the heel and 2 inches across the shank. A row of fifty brass screws spaced about ¼ inch apart follows the outline of the sole ¼ inch from its outside edge. One other screw is centered ⅝ inch behind the toe and another at the back of the ball. The screws average ¹⁷⁄₃₂ inch long.

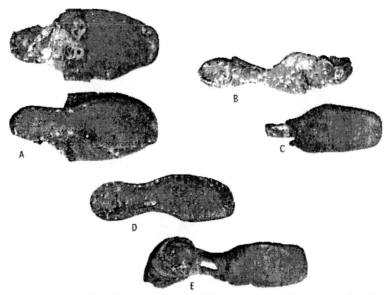

Fig. 96. Footwear: (*A*) Top and bottom of low-cut shoe with sewn and nailed sole 9½ inches long. (*B*) Goodyear welt sole 10 inches long. (*C*) Sewn sole 9½ inches long. (*D*) Sole, with brass screw fastenings only, 9½ inches long. (*E*) Sewn sole 9 inches long.

Five examples of combination sewn and screwed soles were recovered. Based primarily on the proximity of the location of these examples, probably two represent matched pairs. One pair appears to be a ladies' oxford style. A fragment of the left half of the upper for one from this pair has six brass eyelets intact and a hole for a seventh. A line of stitch holes borders the eyelet row. One small counter fragment is fire-reddened or made from a reddish colored nonleather fiber. Because the soles have almost identical sides, it is impossible to distinguish right from left. The heels appear to be smaller than those on any of the other examples. The soles measure 9 inches long by 2½ inches wide at the ball, 1⅜ inches across the shank, and 1⅞ inches across the heel. Fragments of brass screws are visible around the heel and toe. The soles are double stitched from heel breast to the ball and single stitched to within 1 inch of the toe.

The other pair of soles in this group is severely charred, with only the shank and heel parts remaining. The shank area of one is double stitched, and the heel area is secured with brass screws. The heel is represented by an almost solid bar of iron oxide that has replaced the original heel fastenings. The shank stitching is reinforced on one side by two brass screws 1¼ inches apart. The heel of the sole is 2¾ inches wide, and the shank is 1¾ inches wide. Neither length nor right/left distinction can be determined. A small charred fragment of counter and a narrow strip of upper between the soles complete the examples.

Another example of the combined stitched and screwed group is a left low shoe top similar to a modern man's oxford. It is almost complete, with only the heel, counter, and partially disintegrated quarter missing. The vamp has a 1 × 1½-inch, two-eyelet lace tab stitched to either side of the instep. The wearer may have suffered from corns or bunions, as one hole was cut at the point of the big toe and another at the ball behind the little toe. Both of these openings were patched over with thin, soft leather, but both patches disintegrated during transfer from the site to the laboratory. The sole measures 9½ inches long by 3⅜ inches wide at the ball, 1¾ inches at the shank, and 2¼ inches at the heel. A double row of stitch holes extends from the heel breast to within 1¼ inches of the toe. Three brass screws 1 inch apart reinforce the stitching on either side of the shank. Thirteen brass screws secure the toe edges, and six more form a triangle in the toe center. The heel was secured by iron fastenings, but the sole is secured by brass screws in the heel area.

All but one of the seven other footwear artifacts possessing diagnostic features have elongated stitch holes and have only minor evidence of metal fastenings. From this group, two represent a matched pair. This pair has triple-layer soles composed of two outsole layers and one insole, with narrow strips of upper leather between the outsoles and insoles. A double row of stitch holes is visible around both outsoles and insoles. Both examples have most of the counter with fragments of quarter around them, and one has a fragment of upper in its toe area. The heels may have been as high as 2 inches and were 2½ inches square. The soles measure 9 inches long by 2¾ inches wide at the ball and 1⅞ inches wide at the shank.

Another example from this group is represented by a left sole that has the toe cap and most of the counter intact as well as a fragment of the upper with three brass lace eyelets. It is doubtful that the eyelet row is complete. This sole has a sewn-on half sole that may first have been tacked in place with two nails, but only holes remain as evidence. The example originally was stitched all around, as stitch holes are visible on both soles. It measures 9 inches long by 2¾ inches across the ball and 1¼ inches across the shank. The heel is about 1½ inches high and 2 inches square.

A single sole about 11 inches long by 3¾ inches wide at the ball and 2 inches wide at the shank was found. With a row of stitch holes along its edges, it represents yet another such example from the site.

Only two items of footwear with iron shanks were found at Adobe Walls. Both shanks were held in place by small nails or rivets. One of these artifacts is represented by only two sole fragments, a heel fragment, and the iron shank. The two sole fragments, one from the toe and the other from the heel, have four to five elongated stitch holes per inch. The iron shank is 4¾ inches long by ¾ inch wide and is broken into two pieces. Fabric weave impressions and six small nails or rivets are visible on one side of the shank. The heel is about 1 inch high by 1½ inches wide and 1⅞ inches from front to back.

The other iron shank measures 10¼ inches long by 3 inches wide at the ball and 2⅛ inches across the squared toe. Two rows of round holes are visible around the entire sole. One row is ⅛ inch from the edge, and the other row is ⁵⁄₁₆ inch from the edge. The round holes indicate some type of peg or screw fastening, but definite indentations between the holes also indicate stitching. The outer row of ¹⁄₆₄-inch-diameter holes has eleven per inch, and the inner row of ¹⁄₃₂-inch-diameter holes contains five per inch. One hole is located in the center of the toe point and others are found on each side, 1⅛ inches behind the toe. Rust stains indicate iron fastenings that were probably reinforcements added at some time after the article was originally manufactured. The heel on this example is 1⅛ inches high by 1⅛ inches wide and 2 inches from front to back.

Among the most interesting of the fully sewn footwear items is a sole that appears to be of Goodyear welt manufacture.[8] There is no evidence of stitching or other fastening on the top side of the insole, but a definite rib showing stitching is indicated on the bottom of the insole. Stitching also is indicated by holes around the edge of the outsole, with a double row around the heel section and a single row around the remainder of the sole. A disconnected counter fragment has the same stitch pattern as that found around the heel of the sole.

The sole is shaped for the left foot, has a heavy leather shank, and is much less squared at the toe than are the other footwear artifacts. The heel measures 1¾ inches high by 2⅛ inches wide and 2 inches from front to back. There is very little likelihood that this object could have been introduced to the site after its abandonment and burning in 1874.

Buttons constituted the most numerous of all the personal artifacts found at Adobe Walls. In all, 266 buttons were recovered during the excavation of the site. They represent a great variety of materials, among them glass, rubber, bone, shell, iron, and brass. From the wide range of buttons, only those made from hard rubber and those manufactured for use on military uniforms offer any possibility of accurate dating other than the fact that they were found on a site that was occupied only in 1874.[9]

Seven clear glass buttons with brass wire loop shanks and one black glass button of undetermined shank type were found at the site. The clear examples appear to have been molded with the shanks embedded in the glass, but from the evidence it is not possible to ascertain how the shank was attached to the black glass example. The latter measures 2.22 cm in diameter[10] and has a slightly convex back, a cog- or gear-shaped edge, and four elliptical depressions on a flat front. All of the clear glass buttons have flat backs and convex fronts with decorative patterns molded on both sides. One of these has a 1.16-cm diameter and a pattern of six hearts radiating around a tiny peak in the front center. The back has a ring of small circles near its outer edge. Another two clear glass examples have 1.1-cm diameters, a ring of small dots around the back, and a twelve-petal pattern around a small crater-shaped center on the front. The remaining clear glass buttons have diameters of 1.34, 1.37, and 1.38 cm. Each has a ring of small dots on the back with a radiating line and dot pattern around a crater-shaped center on the front as well as traces of blue paint on the back.

Brown glass buttons with four holes are represented by three specimens. All three have convex backs with crater-shaped fronts. They range in diameter from 1.0 to 1.11 cm and in thickness from 0.29 to 0.41 cm.

A considerable number of the buttons from Adobe Walls are made from milk glass.[11] Perhaps the simplest among these are those having only two holes. Six specimens represent the two styles of two-hole milk glass buttons recovered. All of these are convex on both sides,

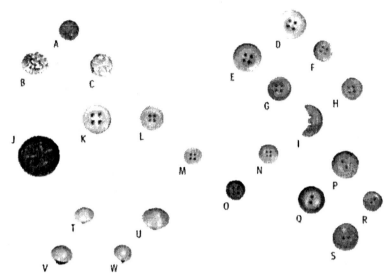

Fig. 97. Glass buttons: (*A–C*) Clear glass from 1.11 cm to 1.34 cm in diameter. (*D–I*) Four-hole milk glass 1.08 cm to 1.57 cm. (*J*) Black glass 2.22 cm. (*K–L*) Four-hole milk glass 1.28 cm to 1.49 cm. (*M*) Four-hole milk glass 0.99 cm. (*N*) Four-hole milk glass 1.05 cm. (*O*) Four-hole brown glass 1.05 cm. (*P–S*) Two-hole milk glass 1.07 to 1.44 cm. (*T–U*) Conical molded milk glass 1.03 to 1.45 cm. (*V–W*) Domed milk glass 1.01 to 1.12 cm.

but one of the styles represented by three buttons has a flattened border on the front. On two of these the flattened border is blue. All three examples have 1.44-cm diameters and are 0.45 cm thick at the center. The second style is plain white. Two examples are 1.07 cm in diameter and 0.34 cm thick; the third has a 1.44-cm diameter and is 0.45 cm thick at the center. All six of these two-hole milk glass buttons have a linear depression connecting the holes.

Five styles of four-hole milk glass buttons recovered at Adobe Walls are represented by seventy-two specimens. Two single examples represent two of these styles. Both have convex backs and centrally dished fronts. One has a 1.28-cm diameter, is 0.39 cm thick, and has radiating linear indentations between the dish and the rim. The other is 1.49 cm in diameter, 0.32 cm thick, and is beveled from the dish to the rim.

Eight specimens represent a third style of four-hole milk glass button, all of them having convex backs and indented fronts surrounded by doughnut-shaped rims. They range in diameter from 0.9 to 1.0 cm, with most of the examples being the larger variety. Thicknesses range from 0.3 to 0.32 cm.

A fourth style of four-hole milk glass button is represented by forty-one specimens. They vary from 0.99 to 1.7 cm in diameter and from 0.31 to 0.44 cm thick, with most of the examples being smaller. All are convex on both sides with dish-shaped depressions around the four thread holes on the front.

The fifth four-hole milk glass style is represented by fourteen white milk glass buttons.Two styles of milk glass, shank-type buttons are represented by twenty-two specimens. All have flat backs with iron shank loops fastened into small grooved or threaded holes. Most of the shanks are partly or completely corroded away. The buttons range in diameter from 1.01 to 1.45 cm; most are smaller varieties. Thirteen of these specimens have dome-shaped fronts, and the other seven have conical fronts.

Two small milk glass edge fragments from buttons of unidentified style complete the inventory of glass buttons from the site.

Only two hard rubber buttons were found in the excavations at Adobe Walls. The examples have two holes, are black, and have very nearly flat backs. Both were made by the Novelty Rubber Company of New Brunswick, New Jersey, from a rubber material that was patented by Nelson Goodyear in 1851. The two specimens on their backs, in fact, have the words, "GOODYEAR'S P=T. 1851." The date numerals are larger than the letters on the smaller of the two examples. In addition, the smaller button has three larger letters and one smaller letter spelling out "N. R. C°.," and the larger button has four uniformly sized letters reading "N. R. CO."[12] The smaller hard rubber button measures 2.45 cm in diameter and has a thicker outer edge 0.42 cm thick encircling a thinner recessed center. The larger example is 2.48 cm in diameter and 0.55 cm thick, with a concave border around a convex center. A linear depression connects the two holes on this example.

Three styles of bone buttons from Adobe Walls are represented by eighteen individual specimens. All the examples but one are four-hole, sew-through buttons. Three brown bone buttons of the four-hole sewn-on variety have 1.68-cm diameters and average 0.21 cm thick. They are flat on both sides and have recessed centers around the holes on the front.

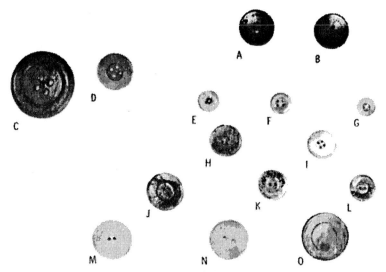

Fig. 98. Rubber, bone, and shell buttons: (*A*) Two-hole Goodyear rubber button 2.45 cm diameter. (*B*) Two-hole Goodyear rubber button 2.48 cm. (*C*) Four-hole bone 3.0 cm. (*D*) Four-hole bone 1.68 cm. (*E*) Four-hole shell 0.96 cm. (*F*) Four-hole shell 0.92 cm. (*G–H*) Four-hole shell 0.82 cm. (*I*) Four-hole shell 1.29 cm. (*J–N*) Two-hole shell 1.15 to 1.78 cm. (*O*) Shell with unidentified shank 2.13 cm.

Thirteen four-hole bone buttons found in a row on the floor of the Myers and Leonard store came from the same garment, but no identification of the clothing type was possible. Most of these buttons are extremely charred, broken, and/or heat warped. Because of their fire damage, only an approximate diameter of 3 cm can be estimated. These buttons have slightly convex backs with doughnut-shaped rims around otherwise flat fronts. Because of the effects of heat, the original brown color of the bone was altered to a chalk white.

The one two-hole bone button from the site is 1.4 cm in diameter, has a flat front with the center recessed around the holes, and has a flat back with small convex depressions around the holes. The specimen is blackened from the effects of fire. The remaining bone button is an unidentifiable fragment.

The Adobe Walls site yielded nineteen shell buttons, some of which are fragmented. Deterioration of these specimens is second only to that of ferrous metal objects from the site. Some of these buttons have undergone delamination in a manner similar to the deterioration of Muscovite (isinglass). All of the examples appear to be made from white shell or mother-of-pearl, although heat damage to the specimens increases the difficulties of identifying particular shell types.

All of the nine identifiable two-hole shell buttons are of a similar style. They have virtually flat backs and slightly convex fronts with small raised areas around the holes. Plano-convex indentations connect the holes. The examples range in diameter from 1.15 to 1.78 cm and in thickness from paper-thin to 0.33 cm.

Of the nine four-hole shell specimens, three are only half-button fragments. Six are of a similar style with flat backs and fronts with small recessed areas around the holes on the front. They range in diameter from 0.82 to 1.46 cm and in thickness from 0.22 to 0.25 cm. One of the four-hole specimens has a convex back, a very narrow, flat front ring that is double beveled toward a recessed center and the rim, and measures 0.92 cm in diameter. Another four-hole example 0.96 cm in diameter has a flat back and a front with an eight-point star pattern around a center indentation.

One shell button is of the shank variety, but no shank type identification was possible because of the deterioration of the example. The reddish-purple to green specimen is 2.13 cm in diameter, has a flat back with a slight taper near its rim, and a 0.35-cm diameter recessed center for shank attachment. It is 0.32 cm thick. The front has an incised ring near the rim and tapers toward a slightly embossed moon-shaped center.

Thirty-seven iron buttons were found at Adobe Walls. Nine of these examples appear to be various types of four-hole sew-through fly or suspender buttons. Because of the degree of deterioration, no meaningful dimensions can be estimated for these specimens, but they appear to have been 1.52 cm in diameter. In the few unencrusted spots on these objects, plain fronts, which appear to have been black japanned, were visible. These could have been either civilian or military in origin. Similar buttons were recovered in excavations at Fort Bowie, Arizona.[13]

Eleven iron buttons of an unidentified type have brass rivets driven into hollow shanks similar to twenty three-piece brass buttons found at the site and described later in this discussion. They have fronts similar to the iron fly or suspender buttons except that they ap-

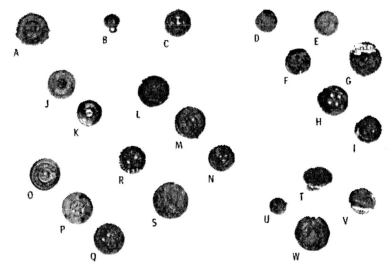

Fig. 99. Brass and iron buttons: (*A*) Four-hole two-piece brass 1.7 cm in diameter. (*B*) Two-piece spherical brass 0.9 cm. (*C*) Four-hole two-piece brass 1.42 cm. (*D–E*) Iron button front 1.2 cm. (*F–G*) Iron with brass rivet shank 1.6 and 1.8 cm. (*H*) Four-hole iron black japanned 1.6 cm. (*I*) Four-hole iron black japanned 1.45 cm. (*J–K*) Two-hole two-piece brass, formerly fabric covered, 1.34 and 1.5 cm. (*L–N*) Three-piece brass with rivet shank 1.4 to 1.7 cm. (*O*) Two-piece self-shank brass marked "Depose" 1.69 cm. (*P*) Four-hole two-piece brass 1.69 cm. (*Q*) Four-hole brass by Dixon Nasser & Co. 1.67 cm. (*R*) Black japanned brass button back 1.5 cm. (*S*) Brass button back with unidentified shank 1.93 cm. (*T*) Two-piece brass with ferrous wire shank 1.6 cm. (*U*) Spherical brass with loop shank 0.9 cm. (*V*) Two-piece brass with ferrous wire shank 1.47 cm. (*W*) Two-piece brass with ferrous wire shank 1.95 cm.

pear to have hollow centers rather than holes. The backs appear to be flat recessed surfaces between doughnut-shaped rims and hollow shanks. All but two of these buttons still have brass rivets intact. The rivet heads have small indentations in their centers, but no identifiable shape. As with the four-hole iron buttons, no meaningful measurements are possible other than an estimated average diameter of 1.88 cm. The remaining iron button specimens appear to be small button fronts, although they may represent the socket parts of ball-and-socket-type snaps.

A total of sixty-six brass buttons were recovered in the excavation of the 1874 Adobe Walls site. From this collection, twenty-one are clearly of military origin and bear various eagle devices as ornamentation. From the remaining forty-five brass buttons, some may have been of military origin, but others are clearly types worn by civilians.

All of the twenty-one brass army uniform buttons with eagle devices were made from three separate pieces that at the factory were pressed together to form the individual buttons. The three parts are a convex ornamented front, a back plate, and a bent wire shank. Twelve of the examples are coat size; nine are vest or cuff size. All but two of the specimens have been identified as general service buttons of the type used ca. 1855–75.

Four of the twelve coat buttons, all of which measure 2 cm in diameter and 1.28 cm in thickness (with shank), were made by the Waterbury Button Company of Waterbury, Connecticut, and they bear the back mark of that firm. Two of these four bear a single star, one a double star, and the other is crushed so that only the company name is legible. Six non-Waterbury Button Company coat buttons are part of a set from an unidentified garment found in the northwest bastion of the Myers and Leonard corral. They all bear the "SCOVILL MFG/WATERBURY" back mark, indicating that they were made by the Scovill Manufacturing Company, also of Waterbury, Connecticut. One of the two

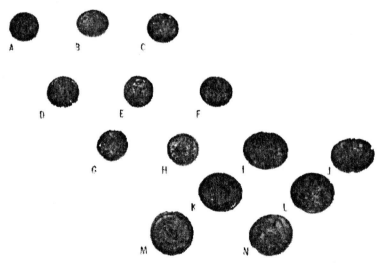

Fig. 100. Brass military buttons: (*A–H*) Cuff and vest buttons. (*I–N*) Coat buttons.

WATERBURY BUTTON COMPANY,

MANUFACTURERS OF

Army, Navy, Railroad, Police, State, Livery and Fancy Dress

BUTTONS

Ladies' Belt Buckles and Clasps,

DOOR KNOB TRIMMINGS.

Special attention given to orders for goods made from Brass or other Metals.

Factory, South Main Street   -   Waterbury, Conn.

DEPOT, 27 READE ST.. NEW YORK.

Fig. 101. An 1870s advertisement for the Waterbury Button Company, the maker of several buttons recovered in the excavation of the 1874 Adobe Walls trading post. (From *Price, Lee & Co.'s Waterbury Directory for 1877*, p. xiv of front advertising section.)

unidentified coat buttons has no back mark. Its shank is missing, leaving a small hole in the back plate. In its ornamentation the shield is somewhat smaller than on the other examples and the eagle is thinner bodied. Corrosion has obliterated the mark on the back of the other unidentified coat button, and its front has a large hole where the shield should be.

Eight of the nine vest or cuff buttons are apparently from the same garment that bore the six coat buttons found in the northwest bastion of the Myers and Leonard corral. Their back marks read "SCOVILLS & C°/EXTRA," and the ninth vest button, found outside the saloon, though badly crushed has the inscription "&C°/—XT," suggesting that it is the same type as the others. These buttons measure 1.49 cm in diameter and 0.92 cm thick with shank.[14]

Forty-five brass buttons from Adobe Walls are probably of civilian origin, although some of them may have been worn by army personnel who visited the site in the summer and fall of 1874. Seven of these brass buttons were originally fabric covered and are of two-piece construction, with the front element folded over the back. Six of these have semicircular pieces cut from their back plates to leave small bars across their centers and full circles cut from their fronts. A two-hole button is formed when these two pieces are fastened together. Four of the two-part brass buttons measure 1.43 cm in diameter, and the others measure 1.19, 1.34, and 1.5 cm.

Nine two-piece, four-hole brass buttons with approximately 1.4-cm diameters were found. These appear to be the same style as fly buttons excavated at the 1862−94 Fort Bowie site in Arizona. All these have cross-hatched fronts around center depressions, and one has evidence of possible black japanning. Iron oxide residue indicates that the backs were made of a ferrous metal. Mineralized thread fragments are present in some of the holes. Six other brass buttons identical in construction and pattern to these possible fly buttons are similar to suspender buttons recovered at Fort Bowie. All six of the latter measure 1.7 cm in diameter.[15]

Twenty three-piece buttons consisting of front, back, and brass rivet were recovered; they have cross-hatched fronts similar to those on the presumed fly and suspender buttons. Instead of having holes through their fronts, they have ring indentations around their convex centers. The ferrous metal backs do not have holes, but rather have hollow shank extensions into which brass rivets are driven. The backs from the shanks to the rims are convex. All but three have diameters of approximately 1.7 cm, the others measuring approximately 1.4 cm.

Seven spherical two-piece brass buttons were found. They are probably the best preserved metal buttons recovered at the site. The spherical fronts are wrapped around convex backs with brazed-on brass shanks. The backs complete the spherical shape, making the buttons almost round 0.9 cm balls. The brass wire shanks form 0.43-cm diameter circles.

Four two-piece brass buttons appear to be identical to roughly contemporary examples found in excavations at Fort Sill.[16] They have plain convex fronts with back plates cone-shaped out to the shanks. No measurements could be made for one example because of its deteriorated condition, but the other three have diameters of 1.47, 1.6, and 1.95 cm. The iron shanks have corroded to form shapeless, encrusted masses.

Three two-piece brass buttons, two four-hole specimens from the

Myers and Leonard store, and one self-shank example from the black-smith shop are the only buttons other than the military specimens that have any makers' marks. One of the four-hole specimens has a 1.67-cm diameter and a flat front with a conical depression at its center. It bears a dot pattern ring around the depression and its front reads "DIXON NASSER & CO./BRADFORD." The back is flat with the hole area coned outward. The other four-hole example has a similar front, except that the indentation is sharp and it bears two dot rings. The second ring is around the rim and includes the words "FINE/QUALITE." The back presents a mirror image of the front except that it has a radiating line pattern around the edge. The 1.69-cm diameter self-shank button is of the same construction as the fabric-covered brass buttons already described. The front has two circular indentations bordered by dot pattern rings. Between the indentations is an impressed convoluted ring with five-point stars at each convolution. The back is flat with the shank bar depressed to form a V similar to a cutout shank. The word "DEPOSE" is embossed above a stylized crown on the back.

One 0.9-cm diameter shanked button is made from sheet brass formed into a small cone. Its edges are rolled inward to create a bead edge at the back of this cone. The shank, separated from the button, appears to have been a pigtail type made of small-gauge brass wire with one end soldered inside the peak of the cone.

Two specimens appear to be the backs of compound buttons. One is a flat, 1.93-cm diameter rounded piece of brass with a solder ring where a shank may have been attached. The other has a conical self-shank surrounded by six small holes and is probably the back of a two-piece button. It has a 1.5-cm diameter and may have been black japanned.

One iron buckle from the Rath and Company store and two brass buckles from the Myers and Leonard store have been identified as apparel buckles. Mineralized fabric fragments are adhered to the encrustation on the iron specimen. It appears to be the same type of buckle as that used on ladies' shoulder braces and button clasp hose supporters illustrated in the 1897 Sears, Roebuck and Company catalog.[17] It measures 1¼ inches long by ⅞ inch wide.

One of the two brass apparel buckles was stamped from a single piece of sheet brass and bears no identifying marks. It has two cross-bars connecting two sides of a 1¾-inch-wide frame. One of the cross-

B

A

Fig. 102. Buckles: (*A*) Brass suspenders buckle 1¾ inches wide. (*B*) Brass apparel buckle 1¾ inches wide.

bars is truncated to accommodate a ¹³⁄₁₆-inch-long roller. The other brass buckle is made from a 1¾-inch-wide strap and may have been used on suspenders. It has a thirteen-tooth pressure bar connected to two small ears turned up at the ends of a single crossbar. The pressure bar has a petal-like pattern stamped into it. The top bar of the frame bears the embossed word "NATIONAL," and the bottom bar has the embossed letters "SUSP CO" and includes an ornamental extension. A rectangular tab with a round end has been cut in the extension and formed into a clip.

The excavation yielded a total of 347 sherds representing the remains of at least thirty-four clay tobacco pipes. This count includes no unbroken stems and only four unbroken bowls. All of the specimens except for two sherds are from unglazed, unmarked, short-stem, one-piece pipes of the general type very common in nineteenth-century America. They were imported or manufactured in the United States in vast numbers. The most common material used in the manufacture of nineteenth-century clay tobacco pipes was kaolin, a mineral consisting of hydrous silicate of aluminum $Al_2Si_2O_5(OH)_4$. It is an important constituent of many soils and also is used in the production of such diverse products as paper, china, brick, tile, and crockery. A few of the Adobe Walls examples exhibit small pieces of brick-red impurities, but otherwise with only two exceptions they are made from this white clay material.[18] Such pipes in the mid-1870s sold wholesale for between fifty cents and $1.20 per gross.[19]

From the pipe sherds recovered at the archeological site, it has been possible to piece together several nearly complete specimens.

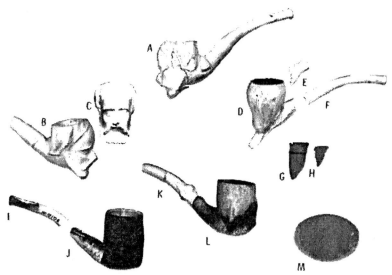

Fig. 103. Clay tobacco pipes and eyeglasses lens: (*A*) Bearded man pipe 4½ inches long. (*B*) Bearded man pipe. (*C*) Bearded man pipe with ¹³⁄₁₆-inch-diameter bowl. (*D*) Acorn pipe with ¹³⁄₁₆-inch-diameter bowl. (*E*) Acorn pipe stem fragment ⅞ inch long. (*F*) Acorn pipe stem 2½ inches long. (*G–H*) Sherds of reddish-brown pipe bowl ⅝ and 1 inch long, possibly of Pamplin origin. (*I*) Basket pipe stem 2¾ inches long from tip to bowl. (*J*) Basket pipe bowl ¹³⁄₁₆ inch in diameter. (*K*) Bird pipe stem 1¹¹⁄₁₆ inches long. (*L*) Bird pipe stem and bowl with ¹³⁄₁₆-inch diameter. (*M*) Oval eyeglasses lens 1⅜ inches long.

They average 4⅜ inches in overall length, 1¾ inches from top to bottom of the bowl with an inside bowl depth of 1¹⁵⁄₁₆ inches, and 1¼ inches outside diameter at the rim of the bowl with a ¾-inch inside diameter of the bowls. All of the pipes represent one of five distinct decorative styles, which arbitrarily have been designated for the purposes of this study as bird, basket, acorn, bearded man, and smooth with raised ring. Four of these five designs have been associated with similar examples found in other locations.

Bird pipes similar to those from Adobe Walls have been found at two roughly contemporary military posts. A stem fragment from Fort Union, New Mexico, matches the stem from the Adobe Walls bird pipes,[20] and a bowl of the same style was recovered at Fort Sully, South Dakota.[21] The head and body of the bird have ornamentation that represents either feathers or limb scales. The head of the bird is about midway on the stem with the beak pointing toward the mouthpiece. Three long talons extend upward and along the sides and front of the bottom three-quarters of the otherwise smooth bowl. The centerline bore of the stem is set at approximately a 60-degree angle to the centerline bore of the bowl, and it has a slight downward curve from the bird head toward the mouthpiece. All of the Adobe Walls pipe stems are set at approximately the same angle and have the same downward curve.

A so-called Dublin-style Victorian clay pipe excavated from the banks of the River Thames in London, England, now in the collections of the Panhandle-Plains Historical Museum, has a bowl pattern very similar to the basket pipes from Adobe Walls. Both bowls have a warp-and-woof decorative motif resembling a basket weave. The British example has a whorl pattern extending from the basketlike decoration at the base of the bowl and along its stem, whereas the specimen from Texas has a bird-foot ornamentation on the base of its bowl that is almost identical to that on the bird pipe already described. On the latter example a vertical line pattern fills the space between the talons.[22]

The acorn pipe recovered at Adobe Walls is similar to a pipe excavated at the 1868–1900 Mero Site in Door County, Wisconsin. Its bowl is shaped like an acorn, which is attached to a twig with oak leaves that extend about one-third of the length of the pipe stem. The remainder of the stem and bowl are smooth. The twig extends past the bowl to form a ½-inch spur that protrudes downward and forward from the base of the bowl.[23]

A fourth style of white clay tobacco pipe from Adobe Walls has not yet been correlated with any other known examples. Its bowl is formed like the head of a man with a sharply squared beard and prominent mustache. The face shows high cheekbones and pronounced eyebrows. The figure is represented wearing an ornamental headdress with a large tassel extending down from the back over the left side of the stem. Except for a ½-inch raised band around the stem at the back of the bowl, the stem is undecorated.

The fifth pipe style is represented by only two small sherds from a reddish-brown glazed bowl. One of the sherds has a raised ring below a smooth rim. This sherd is similar to several styles of pipes that were made in the Pamplin area of Virginia, but the preserved remains are too limited to allow documentation of their place of manufacture.[24]

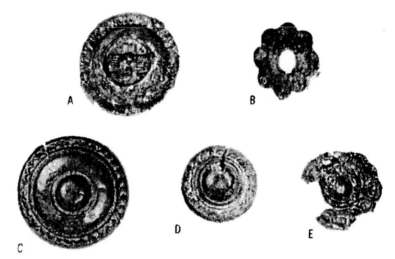

Fig. 104. Conchas: (*A*) Concha 1⅛ inches in diameter. (*B*) Concha ¹³⁄₁₆ inch in diameter. (*C*) Concha 1⅜ inches in diameter. (*D*) Concha ¹³⁄₁₆ inch in diameter. (*E*) Concha ¹³⁄₁₆ inch in diameter.

Along with the clay pipes comes one more category of tobacco-related artifacts recovered at Adobe Walls. Four presumed tobacco plug labels were found in the Rath and Company store. All of them are ⅝-inch-diameter paper-thin metal discs, each having a pair of pointed tabs.

Six Adobe Walls artifacts have been classified as conchas. These are shell-shaped metal discs used as decoration on clothing and harness that in other studies have been termed "rosettes" and "button faces."[25] Five of the six conchas are stamped from thin sheet brass and have back-side cavities filled with lead; the sixth example differs considerably from the others.

Two thin brass conchas found in the Myers and Leonard store have reversed plate or shallow bowl cross-sectional shapes. They have ⁷⁄₁₆-inch-diameter lead-filled hemispheric cups with ³⁄₃₂-inch flared flat rims sweated over deep concavities on their backs. It is uncertain how these pieces were mounted. One of the two, 1⅛ inch in diameter, has a ½-inch-diameter recessed center containing a raised ³⁄₁₆-inch-diameter hemisphere with four radiating crossarms that measure ⅛ inch wide and consist of six lines each. The central depression is surrounded by a ⁷⁄₃₂-inch-wide smooth surface sharply tapering toward the back. The outer ³⁄₃₂-inch-wide ring is made up of a rounded bird-track design radiating outward; the outer edge is rolled sharply toward the back. The second concha from the Myers and Leonard store, ¹³⁄₁₆ inch in diameter, is too deteriorated to allow determination of a pattern beyond what appears to be a hemispheric center with a chain pattern near its outer scalloped edge.

All of the three thin brass conchas from the Rath and Company store still have remnants of small-gauge wire fastenings embedded in the lead on their backs. Two of these specimens are identical and have maximum diameters of 1⅜ inches; the fronts are formed by a series of concentric rings. The ⁵⁄₁₆-inch-diameter center is hemispherical, and is surrounded by a ³⁄₆₄-inch-wide recessed ring with radiating lines. The next ring is a ³⁄₁₆-inch-wide slightly convex smooth surface tapering slightly outward to a very narrow raised rope-pattern ring. The outer ³⁄₆₄-inch-wide ring is formed by a series of connecting crescent shapes arching to the outer edge of the concha. The arches of the crescents have small radiating lines within them, and the very narrow outer edge of the concha is rolled slightly toward the back.

The third concha from the Rath and Company store also is made from thin brass. It has a ¹³⁄₁₆-inch maximum diameter and a pattern of concentric rings similar to the two other examples from the store. The hemispheric center has a ⅜-inch diameter surrounded by a ¹⁄₁₆-inch-wide ring of radiating lines sharply tapering toward the back. The radiating line ring is surrounded in turn by rope and crescent rings, as on the other two similar specimens. The crescents are further ornamented by raised dots rather than by lines, and the narrow outer edge is decorated with radiating lines.

The sixth concha from Adobe Walls is made from much heavier material than are the other five examples. Recovered in the Myers and Leonard store, it was cut from ³⁄₃₂-inch-thick sheet brass and has three square-shank, chisel-pointed, ¼-inch-long tack fastenings soldered to one face. The eight-point scalloped rim has a ¹³⁄₁₆-inch maximum diameter, and a ⁷⁄₃₂-inch-diameter hole has been punched in its center. The outer edges of the scalloped rim are beveled toward the rear.

Fragments or pieces of seven combs were recovered in the excavation at Adobe Walls, four of them in the Rath and Company store. The specimens are all machine-made from either hard rubber or celluloid. The hard rubber combs began appearing on the marketplace in

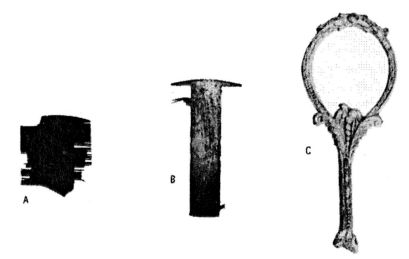

Fig. 105. Combs and looking glass handle: (*A*) Hard rubber comb fragment 1¾ inches long. (*B*) Hard rubber comb with broken-off teeth 3 inches total length. (*C*) Pewter looking glass handle 5⅛ inches long.

the 1850s; the latter entered production after the invention of celluloid in 1869.[26]

Two fragments of hard rubber, fine-toothed, double-edged combs appear to be similar to examples recovered at Fort Bowie, Arizona. One of these has "I. R. COMB CO. GOODYEAR 1851" stamped on its face. This refers to the India Rubber Comb Company, which is known to have existed at least as early as the 1880s, and to the 1851 invention of the hard rubber material from which the comb is made.[27] The presence of the comb at the 1874 Adobe Walls site suggests that the company produced its combs at an earlier date than the 1880s. The other fragment has no discernible markings. It is assumed that the two combs were the same size, as all of the obtainable measurements for both are the same: overall length, 3 inches (India Rubber Company example only); overall width, 1⁹⁄₁₆ inches; width of back, ²³⁄₃₂ inch; thickness of back, ³⁄₃₂ inch; and thirty teeth per inch.

The third hard rubber comb differs from the others in that it has a thick back and a single row of coarse teeth, which number twelve to the inch. Two single teeth from similar combs also were found in the excavation, one in the Myers and Leonard store and the other in the Myers and Leonard mess hall.

A fourth comb from the site also is sufficiently intact to permit some description. It is represented by six connected teeth from an assumed celluloid back or side comb. The back has a discernible arch, and its teeth, which number twelve to the inch, taper toward a slightly smaller diameter round point and are dark blue at the base, fading to colorless at the tip.

An ornamental pewter handle from the Myers and Leonard store is assumed to be from a hand looking glass from which the mirror is missing. A floral and beaded design ornaments the entire handle, and it appears to have been gold plated, although this has not been verified. The attaching end is badly fragmented, but it appears to have contained a cup-shaped depression with internal threads. The overall length of the intact portion of the handle is 5⅛ inches, with an average diameter of about ¼ inch.[28] The hand loop at the base of the handle is 2⅜ inches long by 2 inches wide. No measurement can be obtained from the fragments of the attaching end.

In the saloon building 152 tiny sherds of very thin glass were found. They are assumed to be mirror sherds, but they could also be

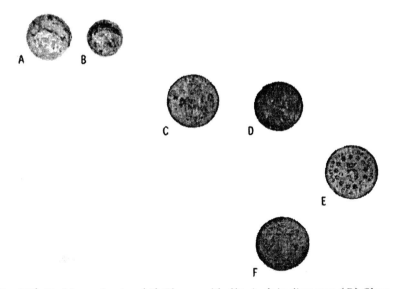

Fig. 106. Marbles and coins: (*A*) Glass marble ¹¹⁄₁₆ inch in diameter. (*B*) Glass marble ⁹⁄₁₆ inch in diameter. (*C*) 1869 shield nickel. (*D*) 1919 Lincoln penny. (*E*) 1874 shield nickel. (*F*) 1868 shield nickel.

picture frame glass or glass from some other object. Many of the sherds have flecks of gold, black, and/or white paint on one surface; some have what appears to be silvering material adhering to them. A few of the sherds have beveled round edges.

The area near the fireplace in the Rath and Company store yielded a single clear eyeglasses lens. It is oval with a plano-convex cross section, and its edges are ground to fit into a wire frame. The lens is 1 inch wide at the center and 1⅜ inches long. Because of patination, no attempt was made to determine the vision correction it afforded its user.

Only two recreational artifacts were recovered at the trading post site, both of them glass marbles. Although they are heavily patinated, the specimens are of the swirl variety containing uneven bands of color. They measure ¹¹⁄₁₆ and ⁹⁄₁₆ inch in diameter. The smaller example contains bands of yellow, red, and several shades of blue; the larger has white, green, blue, and peppermint shades of red.

Hard cash often was scarce on the frontier, and buffalo hides were the principal means of exchange at Adobe Walls, so it is not surprising that only three coins contemporary with the trading post were found. All the specimens are the shield-type nickels made from 1866 to 1883 minted under the authority of an act of Congress dated May 16, 1866. Their specific dates are 1868, 1869, and 1874. One additional coin recovered at Adobe Walls, a single 1919 Lincoln cent, was found near the granite monument at the north end of the Rath and Company store. It most likely was lost at the site during one of the celebrations held there during the twentieth century.[29]

CHAPTER 15

Unclassifiable, Geologic, and Zoological Artifacts

AN artifact remnant is a segment or incomplete part of an object originally created to fulfill some human function that cannot be determined or inferred from the fragment. In this study such remnants are considered unclassifiable artifacts, and as such they are listed in table 20. More than two hundred unidentified artifacts were collected at the Adobe Walls site. They are made from eleven different types of material. Often it was impossible to apply names to these objects, so the material name always appears first in the table. The second term in the name is a descriptor such as rod, bar, and the like. Illustrations show a few of the best preserved unclassifiable artifacts.

A 3¾-inch-long rectangular, split brass tube with one end closed and the other slightly flared was found inside the Myers and Leonard store. It may be a percussion cap holder.

Many pieces of what appears to be a charred granular substance were found in two of the buildings. Numerous samples have fiber impressions on one side, indicating that the substance was held in cloth sacks. Sugar and salt are granular commodities that were sold in sacks in both stores, and the charred remnants may be one or the other or both of these substances.

Some hunter, skinner, or merchant seemingly spent some time carving a small clay dowel. The dowel measures 1⁵⁄₃₂ inches long and is ³⁄₁₆ inch in diameter. Both ends have been rounded by a cutting im-

TABLE 20
Unclassifiable Artifacts

	M & L Store	Mess Hall	Stable	R & Co. Store	Saloon	Blacksmith Shop
Brass split tube	1					
Charred granular substance	1 lot	1 lot	1 lot			
Argilaceous clay dowel				1		
Iron coupling			1			
Glass container	2					
Iron bracket			1			
Iron buckle (?)			1			
Iron bar in shape of hobbles			1			
Iron brace eyed at both ends				1		
Iron bracket/brace				1		
Iron cap				1		
Iron clamp	1					
Iron cube, 1-inch square					1	
Iron handle/pull				1		
Brass J hook				1		
Brass bolt				1		
Iron loop			1			
Iron plate	2					
Iron ring	1					
Lead disc						1
Iron guide	1					
Iron clip/pin	1					
Iron object, unidentified			1	1		

Item					
Brass sheet stamped with floral design					1
Brass strap with bend in each end					
Brass trim with nail	1				
Brass trim (from pocket knife?)	1				
Brass tube flattened (cartridge case?)			1		
Brass/copper D ring	1				
Copper bar, parallelogram-shaped	1				
Copper disc, crescent-shaped		1			
Copper trim, fingernail-shaped				1	
Copper wire (fiber-covered?)					
Glass sherd, clear (from bottle/window?)	43	3	30		
Glass sherd, aqua (from bottle?)	3	2	69		
Glass sherd, pressed			6		
Iron bar forked with rivets	1				1
Iron bar with hole (butt plate?)					1
Iron bar, concave, convex in cross section with holes					1
Iron bar with one end rounded and one ½-inch hole in end					3
Iron bar, same as above but with ends missing					1
Iron handle(?)					1
Iron lug (stove?)	1				
Iron object, unidentified	1		3		
Iron pipe(?)					1
Iron point	1				
Iron rod					2
Iron sheet					1

Table 20 *continued*
Unclassifiable Artifacts

	M & L Store	Mess Hall	Stable	R & Co. Store	Saloon	Blacksmith Shop
Iron snap(?)				1		
Iron strap 2¼ × 1⅝ × ¼ inch			1			
Iron wire with 2⅝-inch loop	1					
Iron/glass unidentified object				1		
Leather strap fragment	1					
Paper fragment white with black dots	1					
Pewter spool or spout						1
Hard black rubber fragment	4					
Textile fragment (burlap bag?)	40	1	1	4		
Textile fragment (canvas?)	2					
Textile fragment (denim?)	3			3		
Textile fragment (silk?)	1					

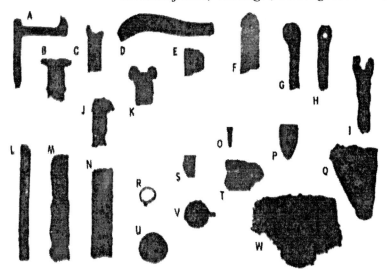

Fig. 107. Unclassifiable artifacts: (*A*) Iron handle 5 inches long. (*B*) Pewter spool 1½ inches long. (*C*) Flat iron bar 4 inches long. (*D*) Iron rod 5⅝ inches long. (*E*) Iron lug 1⅛ × 1⅜ inches. (*F*) Iron bar 5¼ inches long. (*G*) Iron bar 5½ inches long. (*H*) Iron brace 5½ inches long. (*I*) Iron rod 3½ inches long. (*J*) Iron tube 2¾ inches long. (*K*) Iron clamp 1⅝ inches long. (*L*) Iron bar 9½ inches long. (*M*) Iron pipe 7¼ inches long. (*N*) Iron bar 7½ inches long. (*O*) Copper bar ¼ × ¾ inch. (*P*) Copper trim 1⁵⁄₁₆ inches long. (*Q*) Iron bracket 7½ inches long. (*R*) Brass ring with ½-inch inside diameter. (*S*) Brass trim fragment ⁷⁄₁₆ × ¹³⁄₁₆ inch. (*T*) Stamped brass sheet ⅞ × ¹¹⁄₁₆ inch. (*U*) Unidentified iron and glass object 2 inches in diameter. (*V*) Unidentified iron object 1⅛ inches in diameter. (*W*) Burlaplike textile fragment 6 × 8 inches.

plement, as indicated by whittle marks. Made from an argilaceous clay material that is not present in the immediate area, the dowel could possibly be Indian in origin.

An iron coupling found in the stable may have been a wagon part. Examinations of both contemporary vehicles and wagon trade literature, however, failed to yield an identification of the object.

Two small, severely melted clear glass containers found in the Myers and Leonard store could represent salt and pepper shakers, but it is doubtful that they will ever be identified because of their altered condition.

An 8-inch-long by 1¼-inch-wide bracketlike iron bar was found with its two ends bent at a 45-degree angle toward the center of the

Fig. 108. More unclassifiable artifacts: (*A*) Iron clip 5½ × 9¼ inches. (*B*) Iron bracket 6 inches long. (*C*) Front and side views of iron guide 1⅞ × 3⅛ inches. (*D*) Front and side views of iron wedge-shaped object 4½ inches long. (*E*) Front and side views of lead plug ⅞ inch in diameter. (*F*) Hobble-shaped iron bar 13½ inches long. (*G*) Brass object, termed a "bolt," 1 inch long. (*H*) Possible coupling 5½ inches long. (*I*) "Dogbone"-shaped iron object 8 inches long. (*J*) J-shaped brass hook 2⅜ inches long. (*K*) Half-round iron bar 11½ inches long.

bar. Two ¼-inch holes are present 1 and 3½ inches toward the center from one end.

An iron object 5 inches long by 2 inches wide has two rounded ends and is no thicker than heavy-gauge steel. It bears a raised lug on one face 1 inch from one rounded end and a small oval slot at its opposite end. It appears to be some type of buckle or cinching implement.

Bent into shape like an ox yoke, one iron artifact has an open loop at each end. Similar to hobbles, the ¾-inch-wide by ¼-inch-thick iron bar would be too heavy to bend to encircle the fetlocks or shanks of horses' feet. The object is 13½ inches long; one oval loop measures 6 inches by 3¼ inches at its widest point, and the opposite loop measures 4¼ inches by 2¼ inches at its widest point.

A possible iron brace with a countersunk hole in both rounded ends is 9 inches long and has one end bent back double. It appears to have originally been S shaped.

Two 9-inch-long flat iron bars ⅞ inch wide have been riveted together at pointed ends to form a scissorslike hinge. The rounded ends opposite the hinge have small holes in them for attachment. This object may have been used as a bracket or brace for a wagon or buggy.

An iron cap almost identical to a simple modern gasoline tank cap was found in the Rath and Company store. Its overall diameter is 2¼ inches with a 1¾-inch-diameter stop that would fit into a tank, can, or other container. Its thickness is ⅝ inch.

A single iron clamp found in the Myers and Leonard store is very similar to the electrical wire or antenna clamps used in the 1980s. Instead of having a square or hexagonal nut to put pressure on the two parts for binding, the specimen from the Walls has a wing nut. Its purpose is not known.

A 1-inch-square solid iron cube was found in the saloon building. Its purpose is also unknown.

A single handle or pull, which may have come from a trunk or lightweight clothes closet, was found in the Rath and Company store. It has a flat base 3¾ inches long and 1¾ inches wide with three ³⁄₁₆-inch-diameter holes for mounting. The bail or pull is 3½ inches outside diameter by 1¼ inches wide and is attached to two hand-forged half-rings that are riveted on the opposite side. The running ends of the bail are turned outward to keep them from coming loose.

One J-shaped brass hook was found in the Rath and Company store. It measures 2⅜ inches in length and ⁵⁄₃₂ inch in diameter and has twenty-six threads per inch.

Similar in shape to a violin or guitar key, a small unidentified brass object termed a bolt was also found in the Rath and Company store. It is 1 inch long with a total of eight threads and has a round head fitted with a ³⁄₁₆-inch hole.

Noted on the table as an iron loop, a bar 4 inches long by ½ inch wide has an oval-eyed end formed by doubling the bar over. The end opposite the eye has two rivets forming a ½-inch-wide space for mounting. It may have been a type of pole cap.

Two sizes of identically made iron objects may have served as wagon bed protectors. These implements prevent the front wheels of a wagon from rubbing against the bed when the vehicle makes sharp

TABLE 21
Geologic Artifacts

	M & L Store	Mess Hall	Stable	R & Co. Store	Blacksmith Shop
Chalcedony nodule					
Alabaster gypsum pebble	2			1	
Limestone pebble		1			
Quartzite flake				1	
Quartzite pebble					1
Sandstone pebble			1		
Sandstone slab		1			

Table 22
Zoological Artifacts

	M & L Store	Mess Hall	Stable	R & Co. Store	Privy
Bison hair			1		
Horse cannonbone			1		1
Horse metatarsal with cuproid and splint	1			1	
Horse third phalanx, left front				1	
Human left fibula, adult				1	
Human skull fragments			8	1	
Human molar			1		
Oyster shell	1				

turns. Shaped like bow-ties, they bear three mounting bolts or screw fragments still intact, one in each end and the third in the center. The artifacts appear to be cast iron.

A thin lead disc ¾ inch in diameter was found with cut marks on its edges.

An unusual iron object with a convex ½-inch groove below a ¾-inch countersunk hole reminiscent of a guide was found at the northwest corner of the Myers and Leonard corral. A single bullet-shaped lug is offset from the center on its reverse side.

Also recovered was one iron object similar in design to a picket pin but which is made too heavily to serve that function. Its prongs are 1 inch square and too blunt to be pushed into hard ground. Because of its shape, it has been termed an iron clip/pin.

Another unclassifiable iron object is similar in shape to a modern beer bottle opener but is considerably larger.

A wedge-shaped object that had been attached to a round wooden handle or brace was identified by a telephone company employee as a pole jack. Its condition suggests that it may have been deposited at the site after the 1874 period of occupancy.

Completing the inventory of artifacts recovered at the Adobe Walls site are those classified as geologic and zoological. The geologic artifacts, shown in table 21, are unaltered geologic specimens found at the site but of rocks and minerals that do not outcrop locally. The zoological artifacts in table 22 are animal remains not thought to have been left from foods consumed by the inhabitants of the trading post.

CHAPTER 16

Conclusion

T HE 1874 Adobe Walls site is the only known merchants' and buffalo hunters' trading post on the southern Great Plains to be excavated systematically. Because the location was unoccupied before the establishment of the post and remained deserted for the century after its abandonment, the site in essence "freezes" a six-month period in 1874 frontier history. The artifacts recovered at Adobe Walls not only shed light on the individuals who inhabited and visited the site, but also, and more importantly, they document important aspects of the lifestyles of the buffalo hunters and skinners and of the merchants who supplied their needs. Because of the relevance of the Adobe Walls artifacts to Western history in general, their significance extends far beyond the borders of the Texas Panhandle.

Specifically, the artifacts found at Adobe Walls illustrate the material culture of the western Kansas frontier in the mid-1870s and Western trade patterns in general. All the artifacts, with the exception of a handful of objects of Indian origin, were brought from Kansas to Texas by white men. The merchandise sold at the post was the same as that sold by the same trading companies in Dodge City. The sources of many of the manufactured articles, however, were far more distant than Kansas. Because of the railroad connections at Dodge City with other parts of the United States and thus contact with the world beyond, teamsters from the Kansas town were able to haul to Adobe Walls substantial numbers of items that were produced in faraway areas. These include bitters bottled in New York State, patent medicines produced in Chicago, or kerosene lamps manufactured in Connecticut.

It should be understood that the objects found at Adobe Walls do not represent all the artifacts that were used by the hide men on the plains. The articles found were those left behind when the post was abandoned. For the most part, these things were the least valuable, they were the heaviest and consequently the most expensive to freight back to the settlements, or they had been used up and discarded. Since only those items of merchandise, furniture, or supplies that would fit on the Kansas-bound wagons could be taken, the company employees left behind the things that the merchants considered the least worth hauling back. Consequently, for instance, at least four grindstones were abandoned at the post, most likely because of their weight. Similarly, a number of old shoes and boots were left behind. When the last white men left the site in August, 1874, they undoubtedly "made the rounds" to pick up anything they thought they might be able to carry away and use. The things left behind were those not considered worth the bother of taking away.

After the white men departed, Indians visited the site in October, 1874, and attempted to destroy the post by fire, leaving only the saloon building unburned. Archeological evidence shows that they placed wagons and other combustible materials in and around the buildings in their efforts to destroy the vestiges of the white men's presence. This determined effort at demolition destroyed or damaged many of the objects the white men had abandoned.

Geography and climate combined to rob us of many artifacts at Adobe Walls. The high water table in the meadow where the post was built caused the severe deterioration of ferrous metal and shell objects. Severe wind erosion during the Dust Bowl years of the 1930s further destroyed remains of buildings, leaving artifacts exposed at the surface, where they were collected by visitors through the subsequent years.

Despite removal by the original inhabitants, intentional destruction by the Indians, deterioration through weathering, and removal by surface collectors, much was left at Adobe Walls. These remains permit one of the most important aspects of the archeological investigations—the positive and negative corroboration of historical sources and individual reminiscences concerning the trading post. For the first time, for instance, we know accurately the configuration, sizes, construction materials, and relative positions of the buildings at Adobe Walls.

When the merchants came to the Texas Panhandle in 1874, they obviously were planning a permanent trading post. They came to stay. The permanence of their buildings may be seen not only in their size and materials, but also in the factory-made windows and doors with which they were fitted. All of the major buildings except the blacksmith shop included commercially manufactured wooden windows with 8×10-inch or 10×12-inch glass panes; at least some of the doors came with attractive ceramic doorknobs. The traders obviously had comfort, convenience, a bit of luxury, and—above all—permanence in mind when they outfitted their buildings.

Excavation of the trading post structures documented for the first time the layout and organization of their interiors. From the remains we know, for instance, the location and approximate size of the counters and shelves along the south and east walls of the Myers and Leonard store, the position of the grain bin and scales, and the size of the stock storage room behind a partition at its north end. Similarly, the excavations revealed that a stable area was constructed north of the Myers and Leonard mess hall and that it was divided into rows of stalls on either side of a central alley. No known secondary accounts even mention the existence of a stable. Other unexpected details of buildings were found, such as documentation of the use of red and blue paint in some structures.

Occasionally the archeological evidence failed to confirm historical information presented in reliable accounts. This occurred in the case of the Rath and Company store, where numerous original manuscript sources uniformly record that bastions were built on both the southeast and northwest corners of the building. Remains of a bastion were found on the southeast, but not on the northwest. The preserved remains of the southeast bastion, however, did have in their center an otherwise unexplained depression, which is presumed to have been the well excavated into the floor of the store by Andrew Johnson after the June 27 battle. Interestingly, the Rath and Company store was the only structure at the post with a fireplace, and it had evidence of more windows than any other structure. A considerable amount of instructive 1874 refuse was found on its north and east sides. Archeological evidence confirms the documentary sources stating that a sod corral behind the store was started but never finished.

Wagons were an integral part of the operations at the Adobe Walls trading post, being the chief means of transportation for men, merchandise, and hides. Thus the numbers of wagon parts are not surprising. The animal shoes that were found document conclusively the use of horses, mules, and oxen as draft animals.

Excavation of the blacksmith shop showed that it was both oriented and constructed to take advantage of the cooling breezes of the prevailing southwesterly winds. The structure, as might be expected, contained the majority of the animal shoes, nuts, bolts, and iron bars, rods, and fragments at the post. It also yielded all six of the Brandon and Kirmeyer beer bottles, suggesting that blacksmith Tom O'Keefe enjoyed the beverage. Since they were found in the same structure as the water-filled pit where O'Keefe shrank wagon tires and quenched hot metal, it is likely that he used the reservoir to cool the bottles before he drank their contents.

Gun parts and ammunition document a great variety of firearms as having been used at the trading post. At least two dozen types and/or sizes of firearms are represented by the evidence. The most popular gun, as indicated by the artifacts, was the .50-caliber size, followed closely by .44 caliber. The fact that only two firearms were left behind when the post was destroyed shows their value and importance to both hide men and Indians, for only these unusable examples were abandoned. Much evidence in the form of sprues, lead slag, incomplete bullets, swages, and large numbers of primers document bullet casting and cartridge reloading. The location of most of the primers inside the saloon and the Myers and Leonard store indicate these as the favored places for reloading at the post. Surprisingly few mushroomed bullets were found during the excavation. Rather than suggesting that the 1874 battle was less violent than reported by participants, this more likely shows the activity of surface collectors through the years. The metal arrow points confirm the continued use of bows and arrows by Plains Indians as late as 1874. Indian presence in the Adobe Walls area also is demonstrated by the beads found on the 1874 living surface.

Artifacts found at the Adobe Walls trading post tell us much about the daily lives of the hide men and merchants in the Panhandle. Personal grooming for at least some individuals is evidenced by such objects as combs, presumed mirror glass, and a hand looking glass. Six conchas show their use in ornamenting saddles, harness, and/or belts. The one gemstone indicates the presence of jewelry. As only one was left behind, skinning and butcher knives must have been highly valued by the men at the post. The importance of knife sharpening is illustrated by the presence of not only four hand whetstones but also four rotary grindstones. The variety of medical problems and concerns for personal health of the hide men and merchants are indicated by the number and range of patent medicines represented by bottles. Considerable numbers of boots, shoes, and articles of clothing were left behind at the post, the latter represented by the more than two hundred buttons recovered. The white men in the Panhandle seemingly enjoyed collecting novelties. This inclination toward gathering relics, noted in historical narratives, is confirmed by the presence on the 1874 living surface of an Archaic dart point, man-made flakes of Alibates agate, and a presumably Indian-made flint hide scraper. The recovery of a mere three coins at the post that date from before its period of occupancy illustrates the slight need for cash money on the buffalo range, where hides were the chief means of exchange and where the only place to spend money at a store or saloon was Adobe Walls.

Food remains and related artifacts instruct us about the diet of the hide men and merchants in the Panhandle. The Myers and Leonard mess hall yielded the majority of the dishes, crockery, and stove parts. Bone evidence documents the consumpton of bison, deer/antelope, duck, fish, turkey, and rabbit. Canned foods obviously were popular, for several dozen heavily rusted tin cans were found near the buildings. Beer and bitters, as evidenced by numerous bottles, seem to have been about equally popular as beverages. As might be expected, the widest variety of bottles came from the saloon. Interestingly, no ceramic beer or ale bottles nor sherds from them were found, although they are common at other contemporary Great Plains sites. Preserved remains suggest that cast iron was the most popular material for cooking vessels; ironstone china was used for meals at the post. All china bearing makers' marks can be traced to specific English makers in Staffordshire.

Artifacts discovered at the 1874 Adobe Walls site give us a new perspective on the lives of the hide men and the merchants who supplied them on the southern Great Plains. Through these objects used by the hunters and traders in 1874, we find a partial reinterpretation of their lifestyles. We now know conclusively that all was not primitive

on the buffalo range, that the people of 1874 also enjoyed their pleasures and a few finer things in daily life. They took pleasure in eating
from English china, preferred looking through windows of factory-
made glass, and looked forward to sitting down for a smoke with a clay
pipe. Many of the discoveries made at Adobe Walls also can be applied
to the buffalo hunt in general, for many of the particulars from this site
are confirmed by written records from areas elsewhere on the plains
where the hunt was conducted.

Most importantly, the artifacts brought to Adobe Walls by the
Kansas hide men and merchants today give us tangible links with the
human beings who once owned and used them. From written sources
we have only two-dimensional understandings of such men as Andrew
Johnson, Frederick J. Leonard, and James N. Hanrahan. However, when
we look through window glass that Andy Johnson installed, examine
the brass balance beam from the scale Fred Leonard used to weight
the lead that he sold to the hunters, and see sunlight reflected by an
amber bottle of Niagara Star Bitters that Jim Hanrahan sold in his
saloon to a hide man with a bellyache, these people come to life in
our minds.

Notes

NOTES TO PART 1
Notes to Chapter 1

1. Josiah Wright Mooar to John Wesley Mooar, Feb. 22, 1872, John Wesley Mooar Papers.

2. For general accounts of the buffalo hunt, see among others E. Douglas Branch, *The Hunting of the Buffalo;* John R. Cook, *The Border and the Buffalo: An Untold Story of the Southwest Plains;* Wayne Gard, *The Great Buffalo Hunt;* Mari Sandoz, *The Buffalo Hunters: The Story of the Hide Men.*

3. Although no general biography of William Christian Lobenstine is available, elements of his life story and records of his activities may be found in the following: J. H. Ballenger and W. C. Howe, *Ballenger & Howe, Fourth Annual City Directory of . . . the City of Leavenworth for 1875,* p. 128; *Barclay's Business Directory of Leavenworth for 1859,* p. 42; Charles Collins, comp., *Collins' City Directory of Leavenworth,* p. 139; *Daily Conservative* (Leavenworth, Kans.), Sept. 16, 1864, p. 1; Willis Skelton Glenn, "Shelton [*sic*] Glenn Buffalo Hunt Manuscript," ca. 1910, pp. 10, 14; *Kansas State Gazetteer . . . 1878,* p. 494; William Christian Lobenstine, Diaries 1851–58; William Christian Lobenstine, *Extracts from the Diary of William C. Lobenstine December 31, 1851–1858; Biographical Sketch by Belle W. Lobenstine;* *Merwin's Leavenworth City Directory for 1870–71,* p. 89; J. Wright Mooar to J. Evetts Haley, interviews, Nov. 25, 1927, and Jan. 4, 1928, pp. 9–11, J. Evetts Haley Papers; *Mooney & Morrison's General Directory of the City of San Antonio, for 1877–78,* p. 216; Henry Tanner, comp., *Directory & Shippers' Guide of Kansas & Nebraska . . . ,* p. 230; *Texas Business Directory, for 1878–79,* pp. 157, 158. Most writers and indeed some of Lobenstine's own advertisements misspell his surname as Lobenstein.

4. Combs to Josiah Wright Mooar, Jan. 24, 1872, John Wesley Mooar Papers; J. Wright Mooar to F. P. Hill, J. B. Slaughter, Jr., and Jim Weatherford, interview, May 15, 1936, pp. 1–3, Frank P. Hill Papers; J. Wright Mooar, "Buffalo Days," ed. James Winford Hunt, *Holland's, The Magazine of the South* 52, no. 1 (Jan., 1933): 13.

5. For biographical data on the two Cator brothers, see Ernest Cable, Jr., "A Sketch of the Life of James Hamilton Cator," *Panhandle-Plains Historical Review* 6 (1933): 12–23; "Cator First Judge Hansford County," *Amarillo Daily News,* Feb. 20, 1921, sec.

6, p. 6; [Olive K. Dixon], *Life and Adventures of "Billy" Dixon of Adobe Walls, Texas Panhandle,* ed. Frederick S. Barde, pp. 159, 161.

6. J. Bertie Cator to Robert H. Cator and James H. Cator, July 27, 1874, Robert H. Cator Papers.

7. Louie Cator to James Cator, Sept. 23, 1874, and Oct. 17, 1874 [one letter of two dates], Robert H. Cator Papers.

8. For accounts of J. Wright Mooar's life, see Charles G. Anderson, *In Search of the Buffalo: The Story of J. Wright Mooar*; Fred Frank Blalock, "J. Wright Mooar and the Decade of Destruction," *Real West* 17, no. 123 (Jan. 1974): 50–57; Wayne Gard, "The Mooar Brothers, Buffalo Hunters," *Southwestern Historical Quarterly* 63, no. 1 (July, 1959): 31–45; J. Wright Mooar, "The First Buffalo Hunting in the Panhandle," *West Texas Historical Association Year Book* 6 (1930): 109–11; Lydia Louise Mooar, "The Mooar Brothers and Adobe Walls," n.d., Mooar Family Papers; B. B. Paddock, ed., *A Twentieth Century History and Biographical Record of North and West Texas* I, 247–52, also available as "J. Wright Mooar," *Frontier Times* 5, no. 12 (Sept., 1928): 449–53.

9. J. Wright Mooar to Haley, interviews, Nov. 25, 1927, and Jan. 4, 1928, pp. 16–17.

10. J. Wright Mooar to Earl Vandale, J. Evetts Haley, and Hervey Chesley, interview, Mar. 2, 3, and 4, 1939, Earl Vandale Collection. Portions of this interview appear in Hervey E. Chesley, *Adventuring with the Old Timers: Trails Travelled—Tales Told,* ed. B. Byron Price, pp. 39–55.

11. For biographical data on Orlando A. "Brick" Bond, among others see: "'Brick' Bond First Meat Salesman," *Dodge City Daily Globe,* Mar. 29, 1939, B-5; "Buffalo Hunters Resent Slight to Prowess," *Dodge City Daily Globe,* Nov. 8, 1933, p. 4; "Death Comes to O. A. Bond, Noted Dodge Pioneer," *Dodge City Daily Globe,* May 9, 1927, p. 1; "Funeral Service for 'Brick' Bond to Be on Friday," *Dodge City Daily Globe,* May 11, 1927, p. 1; F. A. Hobble, "Dodge City Pioneers and Buffalo Hunters," TS, n.d., p. 1; *Kansas State Gazetteer. . . . 1882–3,* p. 324; *Kansas State Gazetteer . . . 1884–5,* p. 396; J. Wright Mooar to Haley, interviews Nov. 25, 1927, and Jan. 4, 1928, pp. 16–17; Ida Ellen Rath, *Early Ford County,* pp. 125–28; Heinie Schmidt, "It's Worth Repeating: O. A. (Brick) Bond, Buffalo Hunter," *Dodge City Journal,* Feb. 5, 1948, p. 2.

12. J. Wright Mooar to Vandale, Haley, and Chesley, interview Mar. 2, 3, and 4, 1939.

13. For information on Henry Born's life and activities on the Plains, see Henry Born to Charles A. Siringo, July 6, 1920, Charles Siringo Papers; Carl W. Breihan, "Horse Thief Deluxe," *Real West* 18, no. 137 (Apr., 1975): 28–33; "Dutch Henry. (Henry Borne.)," TS, n.d.; J. Evetts Haley, *Charles Goodnight: Cowman & Plainsman,* pp. 287–88, 335–36; Nyle H. Miller and Joseph W. Snell, "Some Notes on Kansas Cowtown Police Officers and Gun Fighters," *Kansas Historical Quarterly* 27, no. 3 (Autumn, 1961): 383–87, 446; W. E. Payne, "Dutch Henry's Raid near Fort Elliott," *Frontier Times* 1, no. 4 (Jan., 1924): 24–27, also available as W. E. Payne, "Tells of Dutch Henry Raid," *Frontier Times* 23, no. 6 (Mar., 1946): 95–98; *Rocky Mountain News,* Jan. 3, 1879, p. 1; Mar. 1, 1879, p. 4; Mar. 2, 1879, p. 4; Zoe A. Tilghman, *Marshal of the Last Frontier: Life and Services of William Matthew (Bill) Tilghman for 50 Years One of the Greatest Peace Officers of the West,* pp. 79–81, 102, 110–12, 119–20, 330; Zoe A. Tilghman, "The Story of 'Dutch Henry' Borne," TS [1941]. Born's surname is sometimes misspelled Borne or Bourne.

14. "'Dutch Henry,' the Chief of the Outlaws of the Western Plains Overtaken at Trinidad; Some of the Exploits of the Greatest Horse Thief in the West; the Man with a Secret," *Daily Denver Tribune,* Mar. 1, 1879, p. 4.

15. *Dodge City Times,* June 1, 1878, p. 1.

16. "Indian Fighter Dead," *Pagosa Journal* (Pagosa Springs, Colo.), Jan. 13, 1921, p. 1.

17. J. Wright Mooar to Haley, interviews, Nov. 25, 1927, and Jan. 4, 1928, pp. 16–17.

18. J. E. McAllister to J. Evetts Haley, interview, July 1, 1926, p. 1, J. E. McAllister Papers.

19. Seth Hathaway, "The Adventures of a Buffalo Hunter," *Frontier Times* 9, no. 3 (Dec., 1931): 130; Andrew Johnson, sworn deposition prepared at Wichita, Kans., Oct. 10, 1892, in the case of Charles Rath and Company v. the United States and the Cheyenne, Kiowa, and Comanche Indians, U.S. Court of Claims, Indian Depredation Case Files, Case 4593, Charles Rath and Company Claimants, MS, p. 49, RG 123, National Archives, hereafter cited as Andrew Johnson, sworn deposition, Oct. 10, 1892.

20. For account of Dixon's life, see E. A. Brininstool, "Billy Dixon, a Frontier Hero," *Hunter-Trapper-Trader* 50, no. 3 (Mar., 1925): 11–13; 50, no. 4 (Apr., 1925): 15–17; [Dixon], *Life and Adventures,* pp. 1–314; Mrs. Sam Isaacs, "Billy Dixon: Pioneer Plainsman," *Frontier Times* 16, no. 8 (June, 1939): 372–74; John L. McCarty, *Adobe Walls Bride: The Story of Billy and Olive K. Dixon,* pp. 1–281; Paul I. Wellman, "Some Famous Kansas Frontier Scouts," *Kansas Historical Quarterly* 1, no. 4 (Aug., 1932): 354–56.

21. J. Wright Mooar to Vandale, Haley, and Chesley, interview Mar. 2, 3, and 4, 1939.

22. [Dixon], *Life and Adventures,* pp. 109–10; Gard, *Great Buffalo Hunt,* pp. 129–31.

23. [Dixon], *Life and Adventures,* pp. 109–44; Gard, *Great Buffalo Hunt,* pp. 129–36; J. Wright Mooar, "Buffalo Days," *Holland's* 52, no. 2 (Feb., 1933): 44; J. Wright Mooar, "First Buffalo Hunting," pp. 109–10.

24. Charles J. Kappler, comp., *Indian Affairs: Laws and Treaties* II, 977–89; Rupert N. Richardson, "The Comanche Indians and the Fight at Adobe Walls," *Panhandle-Plains Historical Review* 4 (1931): 32–33. For accounts of the negotiations of the 1867 Treaties of Medicine Lodge, see E. S. Godfrey, "Medicine Lodge Treaty Sixty Years Ago," *Frontier Times* 5, no. 3 (Dec., 1927): 102–103; Douglas C. Jones, *The Treaty of Medicine Lodge: The Story of the Great Treaty Council Told by Eyewitnesses,* p. 1–237.

25. J. Wright Mooar to Hill, Slaughter, and Weatherford, interview May 15, 1936, pp. 3–4; J. Wright Mooar, "Buffalo Days," 52, no. 2 (Feb., 1933): 44; J. Wright Mooar, "First Buffalo Hunting," pp. 109–10.

26. Cable, "Sketch of James Hamilton Cator," pp. 17–18; James H. Cator, sworn deposition prepared at Wichita, Kans., Oct. 10, 1892, in the case of Charles Rath and Company v. the United States and the Cheyenne, Kiowa, and Comanche Indians, U.S. Court of Claims, Indian Depredation Case Files, Case 4593, Charles Rath and Company Claimants, MS, pp. 25–27, RG 123, National Archives, hereafter cited as James H. Cator, sworn deposition, Oct. 10, 1892; [Dixon], *Life and Adventures,* pp. 129–31.

27. J. Wright Mooar to Hill, Slaughter, and Weatherford, interview May 15, 1936, p. 4; J. Wright Mooar, "Buffalo Days," 52, no. 2 (Feb., 1933): 44; J. Wright Mooar, "First Buffalo Hunting," p. 110. Col. Dodge apparently changed his mind, for in 1882 he wrote: "This slaughter was all in violation of law, and in contravention of solemn treaties made with the Indians, but . . . these parties spread all over the country, slaughtering the buffalo under the very noses of the Indians." Richard Irving Dodge, *Our Wild Indians: Thirty-three Years' Personal Experience among the Red Men of the Great West,* p. 296.

For scattered data on Steele Frazier, sometimes spelled Steel Frasure, who accompanied Mooar in his interview with Col. Dodge in 1873, see W. C. Cox to Ethel McConnell, interview, n.d., p. 4, Ethel McConnell Papers; J. Wright Mooar to Haley, interviews Nov. 25, 1927, and Jan. 4, 1928, pp. 16, 17; J. Wright Mooar, "Buffalo Days," 52, no. 2 (Feb., 1933): 44 and 52, no. 4 (Apr., 1933): 5.

28. [Dixon], *Life and Adventures*, pp. 144–46; Gard, *Great Buffalo Hunt*, p. 137; Sandoz, *Buffalo Hunters*, pp. 177–78.

29. Data on Alexander Charles Myers are at best sketchy. For some of the fragments, see [Dixon], *Life and Adventures*, pp. 145–46; *Dodge City Messenger*, June 25, 1874, p. 3; Fred A. Hunt, "The Adobe Walls Argument," *Overland Monthly* 53, no. 6 (May, 1909): 384; J. Wright Mooar to Haley, interviews Nov. 25, 1927, and Jan. 4, 1928, pp. 5–7; Rath, *Early Ford County*, p. 49.

30. Far more information is available on Myers's partner, Frederick J. Leonard. See: "Fred J. Leonard," *Salt Lake Tribune*, Aug. 8, 1928, p. 6; "Last Survivor of Indian Fight in Texas Dies: Manager of Cullen Hotel for Past Eighteen Years Victim of Arthritis," *Salt Lake Tribune*, Aug. 5, 1928, p. 20; "Texas Frontier Veteran Is Salt Laker: Tells of History-Making Indian Fights: Ridgepole on Saloon Building Credited with Saving Lives of Twenty-Nine," *The Salt Lake Tribune*, Feb. 11, 1923, p. 7. Fred Leonard credited his partner, Myers, with having been the first person to suggest that a trading post be established for the hunters in the Panhandle. [Frederick J. Leonard], "Memorandum on the Adobe Walls Trading Post and the Battle of Adobe Walls," TS and MS, n.d., p. 1.

31. [Dixon], *Life and Adventures*, pp. 144–46; [Leonard], "Memorandum," p. 1; J. Wright Mooar, "Buffalo Days," 52, no. 2 (Feb., 1933): 44; J. Wright Mooar, "First Buffalo Hunting," p. 111; J. Wright Mooar, "Frontier Experiences of J. Wright Mooar," *West Texas Historical Association Year Book* 4 (1928), reprinted as J. Wright Mooar, "Frontier Experiences of J. Wright Mooar," *Frontier Times* 28, no. 12 (Sept., 1951): 358; "Texas Frontier Veteran," p. 7.

32. [Dixon], *Life and Adventures*, pp. 145–72; Emanuel Dubbs, "Personal Reminiscences," in *Pioneer Days in the Southwest from 1850 to 1879: Thrilling Descriptions of Buffalo Hunting, Indian Fighting and Massacres, Cowboy Life and Home Building*, 2nd ed., pp. 45–46; J. Wright Mooar to Haley, interviews Nov. 25, 1927, and Jan. 4, 1928, pp. 6–7; J. Wright Mooar, "Buffalo Days," 52, no. 2 (Feb., 1933): p. 44; J. Wright Mooar, "Frontier Experiences," p. 89. Leonard estimated his goods at Adobe Walls to be worth about $40,000. "Texas Frontier Veteran," p. 7.

33. Ernest R. Archambeau to T. Lindsay Baker, interview, Sept. 6, 1978, p. 1, Adobe Walls—Geography file, Adobe Walls research files; [Dixon], *Life and Adventures*, p. 176; Edward Campbell Little, "The Battle of Adobe Walls," *Pearson's Magazine* 19, no. 1 (Jan., 1908): 76; Nelson A. Miles to Assistant Adjutant General, Department of the Missouri, Mar. 4, 1875, U.S. Department of War, Army, Office of the Adjutant General, Letters Received Relating to "Campaign against Hostile Indians in the Indian Territory," Consolidated File 2815–1874, RG 94, National Archives, hereafter cited as Consolidated File 2815–1874; this letter also available in U.S. Department of War, Secretary, *Report of the Secretary of War*, 44th Cong., 1st sess., H. Exec. Doc. 1, Pt. 2, I, 78–85, and in Joe F. Taylor, comp. and ed., "The Indian Campaign on the Staked Plains, 1874–1875: Military Correspondence from War Department Adjutant General's Office, File 2815–1874," *Panhandle-Plains Historical Review* 34 (1961): 197–216.

34. Andrew W. Evans to Acting Assistant Adjutant General, Headquarters Company, District of New Mexico, Jan. 23, 1869, U.S. Department of War, Army, Office of the Adjutant General, Letters Received, File M 1560/6 (1869), Report of Maj. Andrew W. Evans on Canadian River Expedition, RG 94, National Archives; Henry Joseph Farnsworth to

Field Adjutant, Battalion 8th Cavalry, Sept. 23, 1874, Consolidated File 2815–1874, also reprinted in Joe F. Taylor, "Indian Campaign on the Staked Plains," pp. 58–61.

35. Edgar Rye, *The Quirt and the Spur: Vanishing Shadows of the Texas Frontier*, p. 319.

36. Dubbs, "Personal Reminiscences," p. 46.

37. Andrew Johnson, "The Fight at 'Dobe Walls," *Kansas City Star*, Aug. 6, 1911, A-5.

38. Frank D. Baldwin, Diary Transcript for Aug. 19–20, 1874, ca. Feb. 20, 1890, lf. 2, also available on microfilm in Maj. George W. Baird Papers.

39. [Dixon], *Life and Adventures*, p. 142; George Bird Grinnell, "Bent's Old Fort and Its Builders," *Collections of the Kansas State Historical Society* 15 (1919–21): 42; George Bird Grinnell, *The Fighting Cheyennes*, pp. 308–10; George Bird Grinnell, *Pawnee, Blackfoot and Cheyenne*, pp. 260–61.

40. Lowell H. Harrison, "The Two Battles of Adobe Walls," *Texas Military History* 5, no. 1 (Spring, 1965): 1–11; Iseeo, "Kit Carson's Fight," MS [interview with Hugh Scott ca. 1897], Ledgerbook, II, 79–80, Hugh Scott Collection; C. B. McClure, ed., "The Battle of Adobe Walls 1864 [*sic*]," *Panhandle-Plains Historical Review* 21 (1948): 18–65; George H. Pettis, "Kit Carson's Fight with the Comanche and Kiowa Indians," *Weekly New Mexican*, Mar. 22, 1879, p. 1; Mar. 29, 1879, p. 1; Apr. 5, 1879, p. 1; George H. Pettis, *Personal Narratives of the Battles of the Rebellion: Kit Carson's Fight with the Comanche and Kiowa Indians*, Historical Society of New Mexico [pamphlet] No. 12, pp. 1–35; Rupert Norval Richardson, *The Comanche Barrier to South Plains Settlement*, pp. 285–87; Robert M. Utley, "Kit Carson and the Adobe Walls Campaign," *American West*, 2, no. 1 (Winter, 1965): 4–11, 73–75.

41. [Dixon], *Life and Adventures*, pp. 176–77; Dubbs, "Personal Reminiscences," pp. 46–47.

42. For scattered data on Charles Edward Jones, see Olive K. Dixon, *Life of "Billy" Dixon: Plainsman, Scout and Pioneer*, rev. ed., ed. Joseph B. Thorburn, p. 80; *Dodge City Times*, June 29, 1878, p. 2; "'Farmer Jones,' First White Settler in Oklahoma Panhandle, Buffalo Hunter Dies," Charles Edward Jones Papers; J. H. Hopkins to L. F. Sheffy, interview Dec. 31, 1929, pp. 3–4, J. H. Hopkins Papers; [Bill Jones], "James H. Jones & Esther T. Clarke Family List," Charles Edward Jones Papers; Henry Hubert Raymond, "Diary of a Dodge City Buffalo Hunter, 1872–1873," ed. Joseph W. Snell, *Kansas Historical Quarterly* 31, no. 4 (Winter, 1965): 375, 389–91, 393; Rath, *Early Ford County*, p. 263; Coila Sieber, "Trail Maker," pp. 1–2, Charles Edward Jones Papers.

43. Information on Joe Plummer is even more fragmentary than that on his partner, Charles E. Jones. See: [Dixon], *Life and Adventures*, pp. 189–90; *Dodge City Times*, June 29, 1878, p. 2; July 7, 1878, p. 2; *Leavenworth Daily Commercial*, July 26, 1874, p. 2; Raymond, "Diary of a Dodge City Buffalo Hunter," p. 387.

44. C. E. (Ed) Jones to L. F. Sheffy, interview, Dec. 31, 1929, p. 2, C. E. Jones Papers; Jones to Sheffy, Jan. 27, 1930, Charles Edward Jones Papers; [Leonard], "Memorandum," p. 1. Much of this route was part of what was later known as the Jones and Plummer Trail.

45. Jones to Sheffy, interview, Dec. 31, 1929, p. 2; J. Wright Mooar to Johnson, Jan. 20, 1923, Andrew Johnson Papers; J. Wright Mooar, "Buffalo Days," 52, no. 2 (Feb., 1933): 44.

46. James H. Cator, sworn deposition, Oct. 10, 1892, p. 24; [Dixon], *Life and Adventures*, pp. 178–79; Dubbs, "Personal Reminiscences," p. 47; Johnson, "The Fight at 'Dobe Walls," A-5; [Leonard], "Memorandum," p. 1; H. B. Leonard, "In the Fight at 'Dobe

Walls," *Kansas City Star*, July 21, 1911, p. 7; Rye, *Quirt and Spur*, p. 320; "Texas Frontier Veteran," p. 7. For a description of the remains from the Myers and Leonard corral, see Part 2 of this study.

47. Frank D. Baldwin, Diary Transcript for Aug. 19–20, 1874, lf. 2; William E. Connelley, "In Relation to the Visit of Tom Stauth of Dodge City, Kansas, to the Site of the Battle of Adobe Walls, on the Canadian in the Panhandle of Texas," TS, ca. Mar. 10, 1923, pp. 2–3; Little, "Battle of Adobe Walls," p. 76; [Untitled drawing of corral gate at 1874 Adobe Walls Trading Post], MS, ca. Mar. 10, 1923; S. S. Van Sickel, *A Story of Real Life on the Plains Written by Capt. S. S. Van Sickel, Born Sept. 6, 1826: A True Narrative of the Author's Experience*, p. 14.

48. [Dixon], *Life and Adventures*, pp. 176, 195–96; Dubbs, "Personal Reminiscences," pp. 46–47; Hathaway, "Adventures of Buffalo Hunter," p. 130; Little, "Battle of Adobe Walls," p. 76; McAllister to Haley, interview July 1, 1926, p. 1, J. E. McAllister Papers; Rye, *Quirt and Spur*, p. 320; Van Sickel, *A Story of Real Life*, p. 14. For a description of the remains of the Myers and Leonard store, see Part 2 of this study.

49. Hathaway, "Adventures of Buffalo Hunter," p. 130. Portions of this description are drawn from archeological evidence.

50. [Dixon], *Life and Adventures*, pp. 195–96; Little, "Battle of Adobe Walls," p. 76; Rye, *Quirt and Spur*, p. 320; Van Sickel, *A Story of Real Life*, p. 14. For a description of the mess hall and of artifacts recovered there, see Part 2 of this study.

51. Farnsworth to Field Adjutant, Sept. 23, 1874, Consolidated File 2815–1874; Rye, *Quirt and Spur*, p. 320; Van Sickel, *A Story of Real Life*, p. 14. Much of this description is based on archeological remains. For a complete report on this structure, see Part 2 of this study.

52. Connelley, "In Relation to the Visit," pp. 3–4; Little, "Battle of Adobe Walls," p. 79; "Texas Frontier Veteran," p. 7. For a description of the remains of the bastions and the artifacts recovered there, see Part 2 of this study. Accounts of trading post history that indicate the bastions were added only after the battle on June 27 appear to be untrue. In his letter to Myers on July 1, 1874, reporting the battle, Fred Leonard stated that "the bastions . . . were useless to us" and "we had to do our fighting from the store." *Atchison Daily Champion*, July 10, 1874, p. 2.

53. Sources of information on Charles Rath, a most important figure in the mercantile history of southwestern Kansas and the Texas Panhandle during the 1870s and 1880s, include: "Charles Rath, an Early Merchant of Dodge City, Did Business in Partnership with Robert M. Wright, under the Name of Charles Rath & Co.," TS and MS, n.d.; "Chas. Rath and Company," TS, n.d.; *Dodge City Times*, Nov. 24, 1877, p. 4; Dec. 8, 1877, p. 4; Rath, *Early Ford County*, pp. 5–9; Ida Ellen Rath, *The Rath Trail*; Robert M. Rath to Seymour V. Connor, interview, June 26, 1953, Robert M. Rath Papers.

54. Data on Robert Marr Wright, prominent in the early history of Dodge City, may be found in the following: *Dodge City Times*, Dec. 22, 1877, p. 1; Rath, *Early Ford County*, pp. 123–24; "Robert M. Wright Dead," *Dodge City Kansas Journal*, Jan. 8, 1915, p. 1; "Robert M. Wright, Dodge Pioneer Merchant, Died This Morning," *Dodge City Globe*, Jan. 5, 1915, p. 1; "Robt. M. Wright Noted Pioneer Passes Away," *Amarillo Daily News*, Jan. 8, 1915, p. 8; Robert M. Wright, *Dodge City: The Cowboy Capital and the Great Southwest in the Days of the Wild Indian, the Buffalo, the Cowboy, Dance Halls, Gambling Halls and Bad Men*; Robert M. Wright, "Early Days in Dodge City," *Frontier Times* 26, no. 12 (Sept., 1949): 317–22; Robert M. Wright, "Personal Reminiscences of Frontier Life in Southwest Kansas," *Transactions of the Kansas State Historical Society* 7 (1901–1902): 47–83.

55. R. M. Wright, sworn deposition prepared at Wichita, Kans., Oct. 10, 1892, in the case of Charles Rath and Company v. the United States and the Cheyenne, Kiowa, and Comanche Indians, U.S. Court of Claims, Indian Depredation Case Files, Case 4395, Charles Rath and Company Claimants, MS, p. 14, RG 123, National Archives, hereafter cited as R. M. Wright, sworn deposition, Oct. 10, 1892; R. M. Wright, sworn deposition prepared at Wichita, Kans., Oct. 11, 1892, in the case of James H. Cator and Arthur J. L. Cator v. the United States and the Cheyenne, Kiowa, and Comanche Indians, U.S. Court of Claims, Indian Depredation Case Files, Case 4601, James H. Cator and Arthur J. L. Cator Claimants, MS, p. 26, RG 123, National Archives, hereafter cited as R. M. Wright, sworn deposition, Oct. 11, 1892.

56. For data on James Langton, one-third owner and on-site manager of the Rath and Company store at Adobe Walls, see Susannah W. Breaden to T. Lindsay Baker, Mar. 26, 1980, Langton—James file, Adobe Walls research files; George Curry, *George Curry, 1861–1947: An Autobiography*, ed. H. B. Hening, p. 5; "James Langton Hurled to Death," *Deseret Evening News*, July 21, 1913, p. 3; "James Langton Meets Death in Auto Accident," *Salt Lake Tribune*, July 21, 1913, pp. 1, 12; *Kansas State Gazetteer . . . 1882–3*, p. 326; *Kansas State Gazetteer . . . 1884–5*, pp. 398, 399; *Kansas State Gazetteer . . . 1888–9*, p. 303; "Members of the Western Stock Growers' Association," *Globe Live Stock Journal*, July 15, 1884, p. 6; "Texas Frontier Veteran," p. 7.

57. Charles Rath, sworn deposition prepared at Wichita, Kans., Oct. 10, 1892, in the case of Charles Rath and Company v. the United States and the Cheyenne, Kiowa, and Comanche Indians, U.S. Court of Claims, Indian Depredation Case Files, Case 4593, Charles Rath and Company Claimants, MS, pp. 2, 11–11¾, 12½, RG 123, National Archives, hereafter cited as Charles Rath, sworn deposition, Oct. 10, 1892; Charles Rath, sworn deposition prepared at Wichita, Kans., Oct. 11, 1892, in the case of James H. Cator and Arthur J. L. Cator v. the United States and the Cheyenne, Kiowa, and Comanche Indians, U.S. Court of Claims, Indian Depredation Case Files, Case 4601, James H. Cator and Arthur J. L. Cator Claimants, MS, p. 27, RG 123, National Archives, hereafter cited as Charles Rath, sworn deposition, Oct. 11, 1892; R. M. Wright, sworn deposition, Oct. 10, 1892, p. 17.

58. [Andrew Johnson], "Adobe Walls Survivor Tells about Fight: Andrew Johnson Relates Details of Indian Battle," *Amarillo Daily News*, June 29, 1924, p. 10; Andrew Johnson, "Andrew Johnson," Mar. 19, 1913, p. 5, Andrew Johnson Papers; "Andy" Johnson, "The Battle of Adobe Walls," June 27, 1924, p. 1, Adobe Walls manuscript file; Johnson, "Fight at 'Dobe Walls," A-5; Andrew Johnson, sworn deposition prepared at Wichita, Kans., Oct. 10, 1892, in the case of Charles Rath and Company v. the United States and the Cheyenne, Kiowa, and Comanche Indians, U.S. Court of Claims, Indian Depredation Case Files, Case 4593, Charles Rath and Company Claimants, MS, pp. 40–41½, hereafter cited as Andrew Johnson, sworn deposition, Oct. 10, 1892; Charles Rath, sworn deposition, Oct. 10, 1892, pp. 1, 11¾–12, 27.

59. Data on Johnson may be found in the following: "Andy Johnson, Survivor of Famous Adobe Walls Battle, Passes away in Dodge City," *Amarillo Globe*, June 21, 1925, sec. 2, p. 4; "Came to Dodge from Sweden," unidentified newspaper clipping, Scrapbook no. 1782, p. 23; "Dodge Man Is Survivor of 'Dobe Walls Battle," *Topeka Daily Capital*, June 28, 1914, B-10; Hobble, "Dodge City Pioneers," pp. 1, 2; Johnson, "Andrew Johnson," pp. 1–7; *Kansas State Gazetteer . . . 1878*, p. 220; *Kansas State Gazetteer . . . 1882–3*, p. 324; *Kansas State Gazetteer . . . 1888–9*, p. 303; *Polk's Kansas State Gazetteer . . . 1904*, p. 270; Raymond, "Diary of a Dodge City Buffalo Hunter," p. 367; Rath, *Early Ford County*, pp. 47, 83–86, 222; Heinie Schmidt, "It's Worth Remembering: The

Last Survivor of Adobe Walls," *High Plains Journal*, Aug. 3, 1950, sec. 1, pp. 11, 15; "Survivor of Famous Indian Fight at Dobe Walls Has Lived in the Community for More Than 50 Years," *Dodge City Daily Globe*, June 28, 1921, p. 1; Wright, *Dodge City*, pp. 305–306.

60. The description of the plow is based on the plow itself, which in 1921 was donated to the Kansas State Historical Society. "Kansas Gets Historical Plow That Turned the Sod at Adobe Walls," *Topeka Capital*, Oct. 28, 1921, p. 16; A. B. McDonald, "The Recent Re-Burial in Texas of 'Billy' Dixon Recalls the Indian Fight at 'Dobe Walls," *Kansas City Star*, July 7, 1929, C-1; "Plow," MS, ca. Oct. 17, 1921, pp. 1–3, Artifact Documentation File 21.45; Stauth to Connelley, Oct. 17, 1921, Artifact Documentation File 21.45. For accounts of sod house architecture on the central Great Plains, see Barbara Oringderff, *True Sod: Sod Houses of Kansas*, and Roger L. Welsch, *Sod Walls: The Story of the Nebraska Sod House*.

61. [Johnson], "Adobe Walls Survivor," p. 10.

62. For a description of the remains of the Rath and Company store, see Part 2 of this study.

63. Curry, *Autobiography*, p. 5; [Dixon], *Life and Adventures*, pp. 200, 207, 217; Johnson, "Fight at 'Dobe Walls," A-5; Raymond, "Diary of a Dodge City Buffalo Hunter," p. 393. From hundreds of accounts of the trading post, only one gives Mrs. Olds's first name of Hannah, and this comes from one of her fellow employees of Rath and Company, George Curry, who visited the post from Dodge City and undoubtedly knew her better than did the hunters and other transients. The description of the kitchen interior is based on archeological evidence.

64. This additional description of the store interior is based on archeological evidence; for a technical description, see Part 2 of this study. Andrew Johnson twice commented on the doors of the Rath and Company store. In 1924 he noted that the doors were made from pine wood, suggesting that at least the lumber from which they were made had to have been hauled from Dodge City. In 1911 he described one of the doors, most likely the east front door, as being "made of 2-inch plank" with "a crossbar inside." Johnson, "Battle of Adobe Walls," p. 2; Johnson, "Fight at 'Dobe Walls," A-5.

65. Connelley, "In Relation to the Visit," pp. 3–4; Andrew Johnson, sworn deposition, Oct. 10, 1892, pp. 38, 40; [Johnson], "Adobe Walls Survivor," p. 10; Johnson, "Battle of Adobe Walls," pp. 1, 5–6; W. Thornton Parker, *Personal Experiences among Our North American Indians from 1867 to 1885*, p. 59; Charles Rath, sworn deposition, Oct. 10, 1892, pp. 11¼–11½. Significantly, virtually all descriptions of the bastions at the Rath and Company store state that there were two, one at the southeast corner and one at the northwest corner of the store. Excavation, however, failed to document the existence of a northwest bastion. For a description of the documented bastion, see Part 2 of this study.

66. [Johnson], "Adobe Walls Survivor," p. 10; Johnson, "Fight at 'Dobe Walls," A-5; Charles Rath, sworn deposition, Oct. 10, 1892, pp. 11¼, 12½.

67. Andrew Johnson, sworn deposition, Oct. 10, 1892, p. 41½; Charles Rath, sworn deposition, Oct. 10, 1892, pp. 11¾–12; Charles Rath, sworn deposition, Oct. 11, 1892, p. 27. George Eddy's surname is spelled many ways in the historical sources, including Ebey, Ebs, and Enby, but in most it became standardized as Eddy. John Coulter, "The Adobe Walls Fight," *Leavenworth Daily Times*, Nov. 17, 1877, p. 2; [Dixon], *Life and Adventures*, p. 207; Andrew Johnson, sworn deposition, Oct. 10, 1892, p. 41½; Little, "Battle of Adobe Walls," pp. 77, 81.

68. Curry, *Autobiography*, p. 5. Johnson suggested that Langton may have been on

the site by the time Charles Rath departed for Dodge City. Andrew Johnson, sworn deposition, Oct. 10, 1892, p. 41½.

69. Andrew Johnson, sworn deposition, Oct. 10, 1892, p. 35; Johnson, "Battle of Adobe Walls," p. 1; Johnson "Fight at 'Dobe Walls," A-5; Charles Rath, sworn deposition, Oct. 10, 1892, p. 11½. For a description of the remains of the sod-walled corral at the Rath and Company store, see Part 2 of this study.

70. For a cryptic description of what must have been the privy at the Rath and Company store complex, see [Dixon], *Life and Adventures*, p. 222. The description here is based on archeological evidence.

71. Johnson, "The Battle of Adobe Walls," p. 1; Coulter, "Adobe Walls Fight," p. 2; J. Wright Mooar to Haley, interviews Nov. 25, 1927, and Jan. 4, 1928, p. 7. For data on James N. Hanrahan, see Robert E. Eagan, "James Hanrahan: Early Day Character of Dodge City," TS, n.d., pp. 1–6; Rath, *Early Ford County*, pp. 48–50.

72. "Bat Masterson's Career. He Is a Square Sport and a Renowned 'Shooter,'" unidentified newspaper clipping, ca. 1888; Dubbs, "Personal Reminiscences," p. 57; [Johnson], "Adobe Walls Survivor," p. 10; Johnson, "Fight at 'Dobe Walls," A-5; Little, "Battle of Adobe Walls," p. 76; Edith B. McGinnis, *The Promised Land*, p. 55; [Untitled plan of Adobe Walls trading post], MS, ca. Mar. 10, 1923; Van Sickel, *A Story of Real Life*, p. 13. For a description of the saloon, see Part 2 of this study.

73. [Dixon], *Life and Adventures*, pp. 176, 196–97; Little, "Battle of Adobe Walls," p. 76; [Leonard], "Memorandum," p. 1; J. Wright Mooar, "Buffalo Days," 52, no. 2 (Feb., 1933): 44. Much of this description is based on archeological evidence.

74. [Dixon], *Life and Adventures*, pp. 176–77, 179–86; Johnson, "The Battle of Adobe Walls," p. 1; Charles Rath, sworn deposition, Oct. 11, 1892, p. 27.

75. *Dodge City Messenger*, June 25, 1874, p. 3; [Leonard], "Memorandum," p. 1.

76. Johnson, "Andrew Johnson," p. 5; Johnson, "Fight at 'Dobe Walls," A-5; "Texas Frontier Veteran," p. 7. For data on the well-known William Barclay "Bat" Masterson, see, e.g.: Robert K. DeArment, *Bat Masterson: The Man and the Legend*; "A Kansas Killer. 'Bat' Masterson, the Noted Frontiersman, Interviewed," *Topeka Daily Capital*, June 26, 1886, p. 5; "Masterson's Death Brings Recollections: Famous Sports Writer in Battle of Adobe Walls," *Amarillo Daily News*, Nov. 5, 1921, sec. 1, p. 6; Richard O'Connor, *Bat Masterson*; Robert M. Wright, *Dodge City*, pp. 299–303.

77. William B. Masterson, sworn deposition prepared at Denver, Colo., June 24, 1893, in the case of Charles Rath and Company v. the United States and the Cheyenne, Kiowa, and Comanche Indians, U.S. Court of Claims, Indian Depredation Case Files, Case 4593, Charles Rath and Company Claimants, MS, p. 3, RG 123, National Archives, hereafter cited as William B. Masterson, sworn deposition, June 24, 1893.

78. Johnson, "Battle of Adobe Walls," p. 1; McAllister to Haley, interview July 1, 1926, p. 1.

79. Hathaway, "Adventures of Buffalo Hunter," p. 129.

80. James H. Cator, sworn deposition prepared at Wichita, Kans., Oct. 11, 1892, in the case of James H. Cator and Arthur J. L. Cator v. the United States and the Cheyenne, Kiowa, and Comanche Indians, U.S. Court of Claims, Indian Depredation Case Files, Case 4601, James H. Cator and Arthur J. L. Cator Claimants, MS, p. 13, RG 123, National Archives, hereafter cited as James H. Cator, sworn deposition, Oct. 11, 1892.

81. Cator brothers' receipts, 1874, Robert H. Cator Papers, hereafter cited as Cator receipts.

82. James H. Cator, sworn deposition, Oct. 10, 1892, pp. 28–29; James H. Cator,

sworn deposition, Oct. 11, 1892, pp. 5–6, 13; Andrew Johnson, sworn deposition, Oct. 10, 1892, p. 50; Charles Rath, sworn deposition, Oct. 11, 1892, p. 28; R. M. Wright, sworn deposition, Oct. 11, 1892, p. 25.

83. Cator receipts. Of the weather in summer, 1874, Gen. Miles wrote: "The season was . . . one of intense heat, the whole western portion being parched, blistered and burnt up in a universal drought." Nelson A. Miles, *Personal Recollections and Observations . . .* , p. 163.

84. Cator receipts.

85. [Dixon], *Life and Adventures*, p. 177; "Texas Frontier Veteran," p. 7.

86. James H. Cator, sworn deposition, Oct. 10, 1892, pp. 22, 27–28; James H. Cator, sworn deposition, Oct. 11, 1892, p. 16; Cator receipts; Hathaway, "Adventures of Buffalo Hunter," p. 130; Johnson, "Battle of Adobe Walls," p. 4; Johnson, "Fight at 'Dobe Walls," A-5; Andrew Johnson, sworn deposition, Oct. 10, 1892, pp. 36, 37, 46; William B. Masterson, sworn deposition, June 24, 1893, p. 2; Charles Rath, sworn deposition, Oct. 10, 1892, p. 8; R. M. Wright, sworn deposition, Oct. 10, 1892, p. 16.

87. Robert H. Cator, sworn deposition, Oct. 10, 1892, pp. 22, 27, 29; James H. Cator, sworn deposition, Oct. 11, 1892, p. 16; Cator receipts; Curry, *Autobiography*, p. 6; [Dixon], *Life and Adventures*, pp. 208, 218; Hathaway, "Adventures of Buffalo Hunter," pp. 130, 131; Andrew Johnson, sworn deposition, Oct. 10, 1892, pp. 36, 37, 46; James Langton, sworn deposition prepared at Salt Lake City, Jan. 28, 1896, in the case of Charles Rath and Company v. the United States and the Cheyenne, Kiowa, and Comanche Indians, U.S. Court of Claims, Indian Depredation Case Files, Case 4593, Charles Rath and Company Claimants, MS, p. 5, hereafter cited as James Langton, sworn deposition, Jan. 28, 1896; Little, "Battle of Adobe Walls," p. 79; William B. Masterson, sworn deposition, June 24, 1893, p. 2; Parker, *Personal Experiences*, p. 61; Charles Rath, sworn deposition, Oct. 10, 1892, p. 8; Van Sickel, *A Story of Real Life*, p. 16; R. M. Wright, sworn deposition, Oct. 10, 1892, p. 16; Wright, *Dodge City*, p. 199.

88. Cator receipts; "From the Front," *Commonwealth*, Aug. 8, 1874, p. 2; James H. Cator, sworn deposition, Oct. 11, 1892, p. 16; Fred A. Hunt, "Adobe Walls Argument," p. 387; Johnson, "Battle of Adobe Walls," p. 4; Johnson, "Fight at 'Dobe Walls," A-5; J. Wright Mooar to Vandale, Haley, and Chesley, interview Mar. 2, 3, and 4, 1939.

89. [Dixon], *Life and Adventures*, p. 183; "Texas Frontier Veteran," p. 7.

90. Cator receipts.

91. Ibid.; Dennis Collins, *The Indians' Last Fight or the Dull Knife Raid*, p. 223; Hathaway, "Adventures of Buffalo Hunter," p. 132; Johnson, "Battle of Adobe Walls," p. 3; Johnson, sworn deposition, Oct. 10, 1892, p. 46; Little, "Battle of Adobe Walls," p. 81.

92. James H. Cator, sworn deposition, Oct. 11, 1892, p. 16; Cator receipts; John R. Cook, "Incidents of the Buffalo Range," *Frontier Times*, 20, no. 9 (June, 1943): 162; [Dixon], *Life and Adventures*, p. 248; C. E. (Ed) Jones to Sheffy, interview Dec. 31, 1929, p. 3; McAllister to Haley, interview July 1, 1926, p. 2.

93. James H. Cator, sworn deposition, Oct. 11, 1892, p. 16.

94. [Dixon], *Life and Adventures*, p. 180.

95. Cator receipts.

96. Ibid.; Hathaway, "Adventures of Buffalo Hunter," p. 123.

97. Cator receipts.

98. James Langton, sworn deposition, Jan. 28, 1896, p. 8.

99. James H. Cator, sworn deposition, Oct. 10, 1892, p. 23; James H. Cator, sworn deposition, Oct. 11, 1892, p. 16; Cator receipts; [Dixon], *Life and Adventures*, pp. 183, 212; Andrew Johnson, sworn deposition, Oct. 10, 1892, pp. 37, 46; Johnson, "Battle of

Adobe Walls," p. 4; Johnson, "Fight at 'Dobe Walls," A-5; Masterson to Barde, Oct. 13, 1913, photostatic copies in W. S. Campbell Papers and in William Barclay Masterson Collection; William B. Masterson, sworn deposition, June 24, 1893, p. 2; Charles Rath, sworn deposition, Oct. 10, 1892, p. 8; "Texas Frontier Veteran," p. 7.

100. Cator receipts. The Cator brothers, born and reared in England, bought tea almost every time they purchased supplies; accustomed to tea from childhood, they may have used more than most hide men.

101. James H. Cator, sworn deposition, Oct. 10, 1892, p. 23; Cator receipts; [Dixon], *Life and Adventures*, p. 212; Andrew Johnson, sworn deposition, Oct. 10, 1892, pp. 37, 46; Johnson, "Battle of Adobe Walls," p. 4; Johnson, "Fight at 'Dobe Walls," A-5; Masterson to Barde, Oct. 13, 1913.

102. [Dixon], *Life and Adventures*, pp. 108, 181–82; McGinnis, *The Promised Land*, p. 54; James A. Watson, "The Battle of Adobe Walls: A Survivor of One of the West's Last Great Indian Battles Tells Some Previously Unwritten American History," ed. Edwin V. Burkholder, *True* 16, no. 93 (Feb., 1945): 37.

103. Remains of bottles from this Leavenworth brewery were recovered at the site. For a description, see Part 2 of this study. For data on the brewery see: Ballenger and Howe, *Fourth Annual City Directory*, p. 66; Collins, comp., *Collins' City Directory*, p. 75; *Kansas State Gazetteer . . . 1878*, p. 476; *Merwin's Leavenworth*, p. 34.

104. Cator receipts; William C. Ketchum, Jr., *A Treasury of American Bottles*, pp. 93–102; Richard Watson, *Bitters Bottles*, pp. 13–16. For a description of bitters bottles recovered at the site, see Part 2 of this study.

105. Cator receipts. For a description of gin bottles recovered at the Myers and Leonard store, see Part 2 of this study.

106. Cator receipts; Johnson, "Battle of Adobe Walls," p. 3; Little, "Battle of Adobe Walls," p. 81. For descriptions of the clay pipes, see Part 2 of this study.

107. Raymond, "Diary of a Dodge City Buffalo Hunter," pp. 379–90.

108. J. Bertie Cator, to Robert H. Cator and James H. Cator, Oct. 18, 1874, Robert H. Cator Papers.

109. Joseph K. Baldwin, *A Collector's Guide to Patent and Proprietary Medicine Bottles of the Nineteenth Century*, pp. 85, 222, 338–39; Doreen Beck, *The Book of Bottle Collecting*, p. 63; Kay Denver, *Patent Medicine Picture*, pp. 41–42; Larry Freeman, *Grand Old American Bottles*, p. 428; Hellen McKearin and Kenneth M. Wilson, *American Bottles & Flasks and Their Ancestry*, pp. 137–42; Bill Wilson and Betty Wilson, *19th Century Medicine in Glass*, pp. 24, 42, 108, 119. For descriptions of medicine bottles recovered, see Part 2 of this study.

110. J. Wright Mooar to Haley, interviews Nov. 25, 1927, and Jan. 4, 1928, pp. 8–9.

111. Ibid.; Cator receipts; Gard, *Great Buffalo Hunt*, pp. 125–27; Johnson, "Battle of Adobe Walls," p. 4; Johnson, "Fight at 'Dobe Walls," A-5; Raymond, "Diary of a Dodge City Buffalo Hunter," p. 386.

112. Cator receipts; William B. Masterson, sworn deposition, June 24, 1893, pp. 2–3; J. Wright Mooar to Vandale, Haley, and Chesley, interviews Mar. 2, 3, and 4, 1939.

113. [Dixon], *Life and Adventures*, pp. 189, 247; J. Wright Mooar to Vandale, Haley, and Chesley, interview Mar. 2, 3, and 4, 1939.

114. Cator receipts; [Dixon], *Life and Adventures*, pp. 185, 207; William B. Masterson, sworn deposition, June 24, 1893, pp. 2–3; "Texas Frontier Veteran," p. 7. Remains from numerous articles of clothing were recovered, and some of these comments are based on archeological evidence. For a discussion of the artifacts, see Part 2 of this study.

115. *Dodge City Times*, Sept. 22, 1877, p. 1; James A. Watson, "Battle of Adobe Walls," p. 37. For the original photograph of Billy Dixon, see item RH, MS, 153:3.1a, Carl Julius Adolph Hunnius Collection, Spencer Research Library, University of Kansas, Lawrence, Kansas.

116. [Dixon], *Life and Adventures*, pp. 181–82; *Dodge City Times*, July 6, 1878, p. 2; [Leonard], "Memorandum," p. 1.

117. [Dixon], *Life and Adventures*, pp. 181–82; Hathaway, "Adventures of Buffalo Hunter," pp. 129–30.

118. Dubbs, "Personal Reminiscences," pp. 62–63.

119. [Dixon], *Life and Adventures*, pp. 150–52, 199; Hathaway, "Adventures of Buffalo Hunter," p. 130; James A. Watson, "Battle of Adobe Walls," p. 37.

120. [Dixon], *Life and Adventures*, pp. 108, 181; Olive K. Dixon, *Life of "Billy" Dixon*, p. 80; Hathaway, "Adventures of Buffalo Hunter," p. 130; Fred A. Hunt, "Adobe Walls Argument," p. 384. There are several accounts of purported gunplay in Hanrahan's saloon involving Masterson and stemming from gambling, but as all are fictional or semi-fictional, they must be discounted. For examples see "Bat Masterson Was in Adobe Walls Fight," *Randall Country News*, Nov. 17, 1921, p. 7; "Bat Masterson's Career."

121. [Dixon], *Life and Adventures*, pp. 91, 108, 150–52.

122. For typical examples of the hunters' knowing Hannah Olds as "Mrs. Olds," see [Dixon], *Life and Adventures*, p. 217; Johnson, "Fight at 'Dobe Walls," A-5; McGinnis, *The Promised Land*, pp. 54–56; J. W. McKinley, "J. W. McKinley's Narrative (by Himself)," p. 3, J. W. McKinley Papers, also available as "J. W. McKinley's Narrative," *Panhandle-Plains Historical Review* 26 (1963): 61–69; J. Wright Mooar, "Buffalo Days," 52, no. 3 (Mar., 1933): 24.

123. Johnson, "Battle of Adobe Walls," p. 6; Johnson, "Fight at 'Dobe Walls," A-5. For fictional accounts of the colt, Inez, see Alfred Henry Lewis, "Inez of the 'Dobe Walls," *Kansas City Times*, July 19, 1911, p. 6; Alfred Henry Lewis, *The Sunset Trail*, pp. 59–80. The story of Inez is further confused by a 1928 article asserting that the animal was A. C. Myers's pet mule, which clearly was incorrect. C. J. Phillips, "The Battle of Adobe Walls," *Hunter-Trader-Trapper*, 57, no. 6 (Dec., 1928): 19.

124. Curry, *Autobiography*, p. 6; [Dixon], *Life and Adventures*, pp. 209, 224, 229, 252–53; [Johnson], "Adobe Walls Survivor," p. 10; Johnson, "The Battle of Adobe Walls," p. 4; Alfred Henry Lewis, "William Barclay Masterson: An Adventure Story with a Live Hero," *Colorado Springs Gazette*, Dec. 22, 1912, p. 10; Little, "Battle of Adobe Walls," pp. 77–78, 82; Van Sickel, *A Story of Real Life*, p. 17.

125. "Billy" Dixon, "A Story of Adobe Walls When Indians and Buffaloes Roamed in Texas," *Denver Times*, June 9, 1902, p. 4; [Dixon], *Life and Adventures*, pp. 200, 203, 208; Glenn, "Shelton [sic] Manuscript," p. 7; Hathaway, "Adventures of Buffalo Hunter," p. 130; Andrew Johnson, sworn deposition, Oct. 10, 1892, p. 39, 42, 48–49; Johnson, "Fight at 'Dobe Walls," A-5; Parker, *Personal Experiences*, p. 59; James A. Watson, "Battle of Adobe Walls," pp. 37, 72; Wright, *Dodge City*, p. 198.

126. Dave Dudley was a Dodge City hunter who knew and had hunted with such other Kansas hide men as Bat Masterson, Jim Barbour, Tom Nixon, and H. H. Raymond. Raymond, "Diary of a Dodge City Buffalo Hunter," pp. 362, 368, 379–82, 384–87, 390, 392.

127. Tommy Wallace, killed in 1874, should not be confused with another buffalo hunter of a similar name, Thomas B. Wallace, who died a natural death at Denver in 1935. "Funeral of Pioneer Buffalo Hunter to Be Conducted Friday," *Denver Post*, Aug. 29, 1935, p. 19.

128. [Dixon], *Life and Adventures*, pp. 189–91; Andrew Johnson, sworn deposition, Oct. 10, 1892, pp. 39, 42; J. Wright Mooar to Haley, interviews Nov. 25, 1927, and Jan. 4, 1928, p. 18; J. Wright Mooar, "Buffalo Days," 52, no. 3 (Mar., 1933): 24; Richard Henry Pratt to Spencer F. Baird, Feb. 9, 1878, in Richard Henry Pratt, *Battlefield and Classroom: Four Decades with the American Indian, 1867–1904*, ed. Robert M. Utley, pp. 141–43; Van Sickel, *A Story of Real Life*, p. 13.

129. [Dixon], *Life and Adventures*, pp. 190–91; W. S. Mabry, "Early West Texas and Panhandle Surveys," *Panhandle-Plains Historical Review* 2 (1929): 35–36. The Maddox party was conducting one of the first surveys performed in the Texas Panhandle.

130. For data on William Benjamin Munson, the first graduate of the University of Kentucky, see Ada D. Refbord, ed., *Distinguished Alumni, University of Kentucky*, p. 18; University of Kentucky, *University of Kentucky Centennial Founders Day Convocation*, unpaged.

131. William Benjamin Munson to Laura V. Hamner, June 29, 1921, p. 2, W. B. Munson Papers.

132. McAllister to Haley, interview July 1, 1926, p. 1.

133. E. C. Lefebre to John D. Miles, June 14, 1874, Microfilm Roll CAA 24 (Cheyenne and Arapahoe Agency—Depredations 1868–1927), "Cheyenne and Arapahoe Agency: Military Relations and Affairs 1869–1932," Indian Archives; Munson to Hamner, June 29, 1921, p. 2, W. B. Munson Papers.

134. Coulter, "Adobe Walls Fight," p. 2; *Dodge City Messenger*, June 25, 1874, p. 2; Van Sickel, *A Story of Real Life*, p. 12.

135. John Thomson Jones, a twenty-year-old Englishman who hunted out of Dodge City, was known variously as "Antelope Jack" and "Cheyenne Jack." After his death his family in England tried unsuccessfully to have his remains located. [Dixon], *Life and Adventures*, pp. 191–92; Robert Jones to T. Lindsay Baker, Jan. 10, 1982, "John Thomson Jones" file, Adobe Walls research files; Robert Jones, comp., "The Family and Forbears [*sic*] of Philip Jones & Robina Agnes Thomson," genealogical chart, 1980, in the possession of Robert Jones; [Philip Jones and James Jones], genealogical record of the family of James Jones (1778–1822), in end papers of the family Bible of the James Jones family of Chester, England, in the possession of Robert Jones.

136. W. Muhler is identified in almost every account of this incident as "Blue Billy." Only the report in the *Dodge City Messenger*, June 25, 1874, p. 2, gives his true name.

137. [Dixon], *Life and Adventures*, pp. 191–92; *Dodge City Messenger*, June 25, 1874, p. 2; J. Wright Mooar to Haley, interviews Nov. 25, 1927, and Jan. 4, 1928, p. 18; J. Wright Mooar, "Buffalo Days," 52, no. 2 (Mar., 1933): 24.

138. Mart Galloway, also noted as Mart Gallway and Martin Gallaway, was a Kansas and Texas hide man who at times worked with J. Wright Mooar and on other occasions was a partner with Phillip Sisk on the buffalo range. He was in a party that left Adobe Walls for Dodge City in July, 1874. *Leavenworth Daily Commercial*, July 26, 1874, p. 2; J. Wright Mooar to Johnson, Jan. 20, 1923, Andrew Johnson Papers; J. Wright Mooar to Haley, interviews Nov. 25, 1927, and Jan. 4, 1928, p. 16; J. Wright Mooar, "Buffalo Days," 52, no. 2 (Feb., 1933): 44.

139. Phillip Sisk, also noted as Philip Sisk and Phillip Cisk, was another hide man who worked sometimes for J. Wright Mooar and at other times as a partner of Mart Galloway. He also was in the party of men who departed the trading post for Dodge City in July, 1874. See note 138.

140. Lem Wilson, whose complete name was Lemnot T. Wilson, was a hide man who worked for J. Wright Mooar at least during the first half of 1874 and who in August

of that year became a scout for the U.S. Army in its campaign against hostile Indians on the Texas plains. Frank D. Baldwin, Diary Transcript for Aug. 19–20, 1874, pp. 4, 5; Fred A. Hunt, "Adobe Walls Argument," p. 384; J. Wright Mooar to Johnson, Jan. 20, 1923, Andrew Johnson Papers; J. Wright Mooar, "Buffalo Days," 52, no. 2 (Feb., 1933): 44, 52, no. 3 (Mar., 1933): 28. The activities of Lem Wilson are sometimes confused with those of another Kansas hide man, Sam Wilson. The latter was hunting from Dodge City as early as 1873 and knew Bat Masterson, Jim Barbour, and H. H. Raymond. In 1874 he worked for the Cator brothers in the Texas Panhandle, but by the 1880s he had disappeared. In 1892 James H. Cator recollected that "I have not seen him, but must be six years ago when he went for the mountains." James J. Cator, sworn deposition, Oct. 11, 1892, p. 11; Rath, *Early Ford County*, p. 262; Raymond, "Diary of a Dodge City Buffalo Hunter," pp. 370–73.

141. Little is known about Dave Campbell. He was a member of the Mooar outfit in 1874 and returned to Dodge City from Adobe Walls in July that year. *Leavenworth Daily Commercial*, July 26, 1874, p. 2; J. Wright Mooar to Johnson, Jan. 20, 1923, Andrew Johnson Papers; J. Wright Mooar, "Buffalo Days," 52, no. 2 (Feb., 1933): 44.

142. John Hughes, whom J. Wright Mooar also remembered as John Huze, was a member of the Mooar outfit in the Texas Panhandle in spring and summer, 1874. J. Wright Mooar to Johnson, Jan. 20, 1923, Andrew Johnson Papers; J. Wright Mooar, "Buffalo Days," 52, no. 2 (Feb., 1933): 44.

143. Isaac Scheidler, with his brother Jacob ("Shorty"), was a professional teamster on the buffalo range. In most later accounts their surname is misspelled Shadler. *Atchison Daily Champion*, July 7, 1874, p. 2; "From the Front," p. 2; H. B. Leonard, "Fight at 'Dobe Walls," p. 7.

144. For accounts of the Mooar outfit and its encounters with Indians in summer, 1874, see J. Wright Mooar to Vandale, Haley, and Chesley, Mar. 2, 3, and 4, 1939; J. Wright Mooar, "Buffalo Days," 52, no. 2 (Feb., 1933): 44, 52, no. 3 (Mar., 1933): 8, 24.

145. *Dodge City Messenger*, June 25, 1874, p. 2; Lefebre to Miles, June 27, 1874, Microfilm Roll CAA 24 (Cheyenne and Arapahoe Agency—Depredations 1868–1927), "Cheyenne and Arapahoe Agency: Military Relations and Affairs 1869–1932," Indian Archives; P. H. Sheridan to Wm. D. Whipple, Oct. 1, 1874, in U.S. Department of War, Secretary, *Report of the Secretary of War*, 43rd Cong., 2nd sess., H. Exec. Doc. 1, Pt. 2, p. 26.

146. James H. Cator, sworn deposition, Oct. 11, 1892, p. 3 ½.

147. McGinnis, *The Promised Land*, pp. 45–48.

148. Dubbs, "Personal Reminiscences," pp. 51–57.

149. McKinley, "J. W. McKinley's Narrative," pp. 1–2.

150. Hathaway, "Adventures of Buffalo Hunter," p. 130.

Notes to Chapter 2

1. Iseeo, "Iseeo Account" [of 1874 Battle of Adobe Walls], [interview with Scott ca. 1897], "H. L. Scott Material" notebook, p. 59, "Bad Medicine and Good" Research Notes, W. S. Nye Collection.

2. Miles to Assistant Adjutant General, Mar. 4, 1875, Consolidated File 2815–1874.

3. Donald J. Berthrong, *The Southern Cheyennes*, p. 381; Grinnell, *Fighting Cheyennes*, p. 310; George Hyde, *Life of George Bent Written from His Letters*, ed. Savoie Lottinville, pp. 353–55; *New York Times*, July 21, 1874, p. 4; Richardson, "Comanche Indians," pp. 31–32; Donald Frank Schofield, "W. M. D. Lee, Indian Trader," M.A. thesis, 1980, pp. 54–55, also available as Donald F. Schofield, *W. M. D. Lee, Indian Trader*, Pan-

handle-Plains Historical Review, 54. Although as early as 1931 Richardson pointed out that the 1867 Treaties of Medicine Lodge placed no restrictions on hunters who desired to operate either south of the Arkansas River in Kansas or in the Texas Panhandle, the myth of the Arkansas River "deadline" beyond which no white hunters should go has been perpetuated. T. R. Fehrenbach, *Comanches: The Destruction of a People*, p. 522; Richardson, "Comanche Indians," pp. 32–33.

4. Miles to Assistant Adjutant General, Mar. 4, 1875, Consolidated File 2815–1874.

5. [John Wesley Mooar] to Dear Sister, July 7, 1874, John Wesley Mooar Papers.

6. Dubbs, "Personal Reminiscences," p. 48.

7. Berthrong, *The Southern Cheyennes*, pp. 382–84; Charles E. Campbell, "Down among the Red Men," *Collections of the Kansas State Historical Society* 17 (1926–28): 633; Grinnell, *Fighting Cheyennes*, pp. 310–11; Hyde, *Life of George Bent*, p. 355; *Leavenworth Daily Commercial*, July 11, 1874, p. 1; Miles to Hoag, Sept. 1, 1873, in U.S. Department of the Interior, Secretary, *Report of the Secretary of the Interior*, 43rd Cong., 1st sess., H. Exec. Doc. 1, Pt. 5, I, 591; Miles to Smith, Sept. 30, 1874, in U.S. Department of the Interior, Secretary, *Report of the Secretary of the Interior*, 43rd Cong., 2nd sess., H. Exec. Doc. 1, Pt. 5, I, 541–42, 544; *New York Times*, July 21, 1874, p. 4; Schofield, "W. M. D. Lee," pp. 55–61.

8. Berthrong, *The Southern Cheyennes*, pp. 381–82, 384; Miles to Hoag, Sept. 1, 1873, *Report of the Secretary of the Interior* (1873), p. 591; Miles to Smith, Sept. 30, 1874, *Report of the Secretary of the Interior* (1874), p. 544; Richardson, "Comanche Indians," p. 30.

9. Berthrong, *The Southern Cheyennes*, p. 382; Miles to Hoag, Sept. 1, 1873, *Report of the Secretary of the Interior*, pp. 589, 591; Miles to Assistant Adjutant General, Mar. 4, 1875, Consolidated File 2815–1874; Richardson, "Comanche Indians," p. 26.

10. Berthrong, *The Southern Cheyennes*, p. 380; Frank D. Baldwin, Diary Transcript for Aug. 19–20, 1874, pp. 3–4; James M. Haworth to E. P. Smith, May 15, 1874, U.S. Department of the Interior, Office of Indian Affairs, Letters Received from Kiowa Agency, RG 75, National Archives, cited in Schofield, "W. M. D. Lee," pp. 62–64; Aubrey L. Steele, "Lawrie Tatum's Indian Policy," *Chronicles of Oklahoma* 22, no. 1 (Spring, 1944): 92. As early as 1867, Charles Rath, a merchant with a branch at Adobe Walls in 1874, was accused of selling illegal firearms to the Kiowas. Douglas to Commanding General of the Division [of the Missouri], Jan. 13, 1867, in U.S. President, *Difficulties with Indian Tribes, . . .* , 41st Cong., 2nd sess., H. Exec. Doc. 240, p. 46.

11. For arguments supporting the "traders' war" theory of causes for Indian unrest in 1873–74, see Schofield, "W. M. D. Lee," pp. 64–67, 77–79. Schofield's position is strengthened by an independent report from Charles Goodnight, pioneer Panhandle rancher and a friend of Quanah, who in 1928 told historian J. Evetts Haley that Lee and Reynolds were indeed behind at least some of the Indian problems. Goodnight declared: "Lee had been an army officer and would do anything to keep down competition. So when Charlie Rath moved his trading post down to Adobe Walls, Lee wired Quanah Parker and Tipped Deer, a big fat Kiowa, to come down and run them out. They came. The battle of Adobe Walls took place and they got the dickens licked out of them." Goodnight to Haley, interview, Sept. 17, 1928, pp. 1–2, Interview File, Charles Goodnight Collection.

12. Isatai's name has been translated in many ways, most of them annoyingly euphemistic because of Victorian delicacy. James L. Haley is probably the most direct with his translation of "Wolf Shit"; other versions include "Coyote Droppings," "Rear End of a Wolf," "Little Wolf," and "White Eagle." Gard, *Great Buffalo Hunt*, p. 156; James L.

Haley, *The Buffalo War: The History of the Red River Indian Uprising of 1874*, p. 232; Wilbur Sturtevant Nye, *Carbine & Lance: The Story of Old Fort Sill*, 2nd ed., p. 190; Ernest Wallace and E. Adamson Hoebel, *The Comanches: Lords of the South Plains*, p. 319. Isatai is confused in several accounts of the buffalo range in 1874 with the Cheyenne chief Minimic, later imprisoned at Ford Marion, Fla., for his depredations. Collins, *Indians' Last Fight*, p. 212; Phillips, "Battle of Adobe Walls," pp. 19, 32; Pratt to Baird, Feb. 9, 1878; Pratt, *Battlefield and Classroom*, p. 138; Wright, *Dodge City*, pp. 198–99.

13. Nye, *Carbine & Lance*, pp. 182–84.

14. Campbell, "Down among the Red Men," p. 633; "Billy" Dixon, "Story of Adobe Walls," p. 4; Haworth to Smith, Sept. 1, 1874, *Report of the Secretary of the Interior* (1874), p. 528; *New York Times*, Aug. 8, 1874, p. 4; Nye, *Carbine & Lance*, pp. 189–90; Parker, *Personal Experiences*, p. 62; Poafebitty, Frank Yellow Fish, Felix Cowens, and Several Old Women to Wilbur Sturtevant Ney, interview, n.d., notes in note pad no. 9, p. 19, *Carbine and Lance* research materials, W. S. Nye Collection; Quanah, "Told in English & Signs & Comanche: Quanah Parker's Account of Adobe Walls Fight," [interview with Scott 1897], ledgerbook vol. I, 15, Hugh Scott Collection; Van Sickel, *A Story of Real Life*, pp. 17–18.

15. Numerous articles and books have been written about Quanah, e.g.: Clarence C. Coyle, "Stories of Quanah Parker," *Texas Magazine* 4, no. 4 (Aug., 1911): 30–32, 4, no. 5 (Sept., 1911): 64–66; Charles Goodnight, "True Sketch of Quanah Parker's Life," *Southwest Plainsman*, Aug. 7, 1926, p. 1, also reprinted as Charles Goodnight, "True Sketch of Quanah Parker's Life," *Frontier Times* 4, no. 2 (Nov., 1926): 5–7; William T. Hagan, "Quanah Parker," in *American Indian Leaders: Studies in Diversity*, ed. R. David Edmunds, pp. 175–91; Zoe A. Tilghman, *Quanah, the Eagle of the Comanches*.

16. Much confusion surrounds the death of Quanah's relative on the Double Mountain Fork of the Brazos. Many sources say that it was indeed his nephew; some, his uncle. The confusion arises because, as George Hunt pointed out in 1940, the Comanche word for nephew and uncle is the same; only context shows the greater likelihood of its having been nephew. Quanah himself clouded the issue by sometimes calling the dead man a "friend." The circumstances surrounding the death are equally confusing, as many sources say that he was killed by the Tonkawa Indians rather than by white men. In the notes of Quanah's 1897 interview with Hugh Scott, the text first says the man was "killed by the white people," then "white people" is scratched out and "Tonkaways" added in the same handwriting. Regardless, Quanah's desire for vengeance clearly had its impact on the history of the region. Hunt to Nye, May 6, 1940, "Bad Medicine and Good" correspondence file, "Bad Medicine and Good" research notes, W. S. Nye Collection; Iseeo, "Iseeo Account," p. 59; Quanah, "Told in English & Signs," p. 14; Roy Riddle, "Indian Survivors of Adobe Walls Visit Site 65 Years after Fight," *Amarillo Daily News*, Apr. 26, 1939, p. 13; Joe Sargent, "War-Paint Off, Comanches Return to Scene of Second Battle of Adobe Walls," *Hutchinson County Herald*, Apr. 29, 1939, p. 3.

17. Quanah, "Told in English & Signs," p. 14.

18. Fehrenbach, *Comanches*, pp. 533–35; Ralph Linton, "The Comanche Sun Dance," *American Anthropologist* 37, no. 3 (July–Sept., 1935): 420–28; Nye, *Carbine & Lance*, p. 190; Richardson, "Comanche Indians," pp. 26–30; Steele, "Lawrie Tatum's Indian Policy," pp. 92–93; Wallace and Hoebel, *The Comanches*, pp. 319–24.

19. Poafebitty et al. to Nye, interview, p. 19.

20. Quanah, "Told in English & Signs," pp. 14–15.

21. Botalye to Wilbur Sturtevant Nye, interview, Mar. 6, 1935, note pad no. 16, p. 19, *Carbine and Lance* research materials, W. S. Nye Collection; Iseeo, "Iseeo Ac-

count," p. 58–60; Nye, *Carbine & Lance*, pp. 188–91; Nye to Archambeau, Mar. 2, 1961, Ernest R. Archambeau Papers; Quanah, "Told in English & Signs," p. 14.

22. Grinnell, *Fighting Cheyennes*, p. 312; Hyde, *Life of George Bent*, p. 357; Iseeo, "Iseeo Account," p. 60; Quanah, "Told in English & Signs," p. 14; Richardson, "Comanche Indians," p. 35; Schofield, "W. M. D. Lee," pp. 67–70.

23. Campbell, "Down among the Red Men," p. 645; Dennis Collins, *Indians' Last Fight*, pp. 212–13, 221; Hyde, *Life of George Bent*, pp. 358, 360; "Indian Fighter Dead," p. 1; Stuart N. Lake to W. S. Campbell, Apr. 16, 1951, W. S. Campbell Papers.

24. Grinnell, *Fighting Cheyennes*, pp. 312–13; Hyde, *Life of George Bent*, pp. 358–59; Quanah, "Told in English & Signs," pp. 15–16; Riddle, "Indian Survivors," pp. 1, 13; Sargent, "War-Paint Off," pp. 1, 3; Harry Stroud to Ophelia D. Vestal, interview, Jan. 5, 1938, Interview no. 9606, pp. 11–14, Indian Pioneer Papers, vol. 87, Indian Archives. The Indian attack on the trading post came very near to the true astronomical full moon. R. W. Bligh, comp., *The New York Herald Almanac and Financial, Commercial and Political Register for 1874*, unpaged astronomical calendar section.

Notes in Chapter 3

1. [Dixon], *Life and Adventures*, pp. 194–95, 199–201; Hathaway, "Adventures of Buffalo Hunter," p. 130; Andrew Johnson, sworn deposition, Oct. 10, 1892, pp. 39, 42; James A. Watson, "Battle of Adobe Walls," pp. 37, 72. For the best two syntheses of the battle, see J'Nell Pate, "The Battles of Adobe Walls," *Great Plains Journal* 16, no. 1 (Fall, 1976): 2–44, and G. Derek West, "The Battle of Adobe Walls (1874)", *Panhandle-Plains Historical Review* 36 (1963): 1–36.

2. Virtually everyone recounting the battle commented on the breaking ridgepole. The versions from Masterson and Dixon, who were in or near the saloon, may be found in "The 'Adobe Walls': Graphic Account of a Bloody Battle with Comanches and Kiowas," *Dallas Morning News*, Mar. 13, 1888, p. 6; "Bat Masterson's Career," n.p.; "Billy" Dixon, "A Story of Adobe Walls," p. 4; [Dixon], *Life and Adventures*, pp. 201–203, 240–41; Lewis, "William Barclay Masterson," pp. 10–11; Parker, *Personal Experiences*, pp. 59, 62; Phillips, "Battle of Adobe Walls," p. 19; Champ Traylor, "Attack on 'Adobe Walls': Distastrous Results of Advice Given Panhandle Indians by a Comanche 'Medicine Man,'" *Dallas Morning News*, Feb. 7, 1904, p. 14. Johnson and Leonard heard and observed the proceedings at the saloon from the two stores. See Johnson, "The Battle of Adobe Walls," p. 1; [Johnson], "Adobe Walls Survivor," p. 10; Johnson, "Andrew Johnson," p. 6; Johnson, "Fight at 'Dobe Walls," A-5; [Leonard], "Memorandum," p. 1; "Texas Frontier Veteran," p. 7. For further accounts of this significant element in the history of the fight from men who were there or from people who knew them, see Coulter, "Adobe Walls Fight," p. 2; Curry, *Autobiography*, pp. 6–7; Glenn, "Shelton [sic] Manuscript," p. 7; Hathaway, "Adventures of Buffalo Hunter," pp. 130–31; Fred A. Hunt, "Adobe Walls Argument," pp. 386, 388; McKinley, "J. W. McKinley's Narrative," p. 2; Little, "Battle of Adobe Walls," p. 77; McGinnis, *The Promised Land*, pp. 44–45; Rye, *Quirt and Spur*, p. 321; James A. Watson, "Battle of Adobe Walls," pp. 37, 72, 76; Wright, *Dodge City*, pp. 201–202. Comments on the time of the moon's setting are based on the calendar for June, 1874, available in Bligh, *New York Herald Almanac*, unpaged astronomical calendar section.

3. Grinnell, *Fighting Cheyennes*, pp. 312–13; Quanah, "Told in English & Signs," pp. 16–17; Riddle, "Indian Survivors," pp. 1, 13; Sargent, "War-Paint Off," pp. 1, 3; Stroud to Vestal, interview, Jan. 5, 1938, pp. 13–14.

4. "The 'Adobe Walls': Graphic Account," p. 6; "Billy" Dixon, "A Story of Adobe Walls," p. 4; [Dixon], *Life and Adventures*, pp. 203–206; William Dixon, sworn deposi-

tion prepared at Panhandle, Texas, July 25, 1898, in the case of Frederick J. Leonard and A. C. Myers, trading as Myers and Leonard, v. the United States and the Kiowa, Comanche, and Cheyenne Indians, U.S. Court of Claims, Indian Depredation Case Files, Case 10102, Frederick J. Leonard and A. C. Myers Claimants, MS, [lvs. 2–3], RG 123, National Archives, cited hereafter as William Dixon, sworn deposition, July 25, 1898; Dubbs, "Personal Reminiscences," p. 58; Fred A. Hunt, "Adobe Walls Argument," p. 386; Little, "Battle of Adobe Walls," p. 77; William B. Masterson, sworn deposition, June 24, 1893, pp. 1–2; Parker, *Personal Experiences*, pp. 59–60; Phillips, "Battle of Adobe Walls," p. 19; Sargent, "War-Paint Off," p. 3. The times for the moon's setting and the sun's rising in this and the preceding paragraph are from the calendar for June, 1874, in Bligh, *New York Herald Almanac*, unpaged astronomical calendar section.

5. "The 'Adobe Walls': Graphic Account," p. 6; "Billy" Dixon, "A Story of Adobe Walls," p. 4; William Dixon, sworn deposition, July 25, 1898, [lvs. 2–3]; Little, "Battle of Adobe Walls," p. 77; Parker, *Personal Experiences*, pp. 59–60; Quanah, "Told in English & Signs," p. 17.

6. [Dixon], *Life and Adventures*, pp. 206–208; Dubbs, "Personal Reminiscences", pp. 58–59; Hathaway, "Adventures of Buffalo Hunter," p. 131; Little, "Battle of Adobe Walls," pp. 77–79; Parker, *Personal Experiences*, p. 60.

7. "Billy" Dixon, "A Story of Adobe Walls," p. 4; [Dixon], *Life and Adventures*, pp. 206–209; William Dixon, sworn deposition, July 25, 1898, [lvs. 2–3]; Hathaway, "Adventures of Buffalo Hunter," pp. 131–32; Little, "Battle of Adobe Walls," pp. 77–79; Van Sickel, *A Story of Real Life*, pp. 15–16.

8. Collins, *Indians' Last Fight*, pp. 213–20; Hyde, *Life of George Bent*, p. 360; J. L. Puckett to James R. Carselowey, interview ca. 1937, interview no. 7120, pp. 382–83, Indian-Pioneer Papers, vol. 70, Indian Archives; Quanah, "Told in English & Signs," p. 17; Riddle, "Indian Survivors," pp. 1, 13; Stroud to Vestal, interview, Jan. 5, 1938, pp. 14–15.

9. Collins, *Indians' Last Fight*, pp. 213–20; "Dodge Men Find the Long Lost Grave of an Adobe Walls Victim . . . ," *Dodge City Daily Globe*, Jan. 2, 1923, p. 1; [Johnson], "Adobe Walls Survivor," p. 10; Johnson, "The Battle of Adobe Walls," pp. 1–2; Johnson, "Fight at 'Dobe Walls," A-5; Little, "Battle of Adobe Walls," pp. 77–78; "Survivor of Famous Indian Fight," p. 1.

10. [Dixon], *Life and Adventures*, p. 234; [Johnson], "Adobe Walls Survivor," p. 10; Johnson, "The Battle of Adobe Walls," p. 2; Little, "Battle of Adobe Walls," p. 84; McKinley, "J. W. McKinley's Narrative," p. 3; J. Wright Mooar, "Buffalo Days," 52, no. 3 (Mar., 1933): 24; Van Sickel, *A Story of Real Life*, p. 16.

11. Collins, *Indians' Last Fight*, pp. 217–18.

12. *Atchison Daily Champion*, July 10, 1874, p. 2; "From the Front," p. 8; [Leonard], "Memorandum," p. 1; H. B. Leonard, "Fight at 'Dobe Walls," p. 7; Little, "Battle of Adobe Walls," pp. 78–79; J. Wright Mooar, "Buffalo Days," 52, no. 3 (Mar., 1933): 28; Phillips, "Battle of Adobe Walls," p. 19; "Texas Frontier Veteran," p. 7.

13. *Atchison Daily Champion*, July 10, 1874, p. 2; [Dixon], *Life and Adventures*, pp. 224–25; [Johnson], "Adobe Walls Survivor," p. 10; Johnson, "The Battle of Adobe Walls," p. 3; "Texas Frontier Veteran," p. 7.

14. Little, "Battle of Adobe Walls," p. 79.

15. [Dixon], *Life and Adventures*, p. 212; Fred A. Hunt, "Adobe Walls Argument," p. 387. Johnson agreed that Tyler was killed "in the door of Myers & Leonard's store while attempting to get a shot at the Indians." Johnson, "Fight at 'Dobe Walls," A-5.

16. H. B. Leonard, "Fight at 'Dobe Walls," p. 7.

17. Coulter, "Adobe Walls Fight," p. 2.

18. Phillips, "Battle of Adobe Walls," p. 32; Wright, *Dodge City*, p. 202.

19. Curry, *Autobiography*, p. 6; Hathaway, "Adventures of Buffalo Hunter," p. 131; James A. Watson, "Battle of Adobe Walls," p. 74.

20. J. Wright Mooar, "Buffalo Days," 52, no. 3 (Mar., 1933): 24.

21. Cox to McConnell, interview, n.d., p. 3; [Dixon], *Life and Adventures*, p. 208; William Dixon, sworn deposition, July 25, 1898, [If. 3]; Dubbs, "Personal Reminiscences," p. 59; Little, "Battle of Adobe Walls," pp. 78–80.

22. Hyde, *Life of George Bent*, p. 360; Puckett to Carselowey, interview ca. 1937, pp. 382–83; Riddle, "Indian Survivors," p. 1; Stroud to Vestal, interview, Jan. 5, 1938, pp. 14–15.

23. *Atchison Daily Champion*, July 10, 1874, p. 2. In this quotation "40" refers to a .40-caliber firearm.

24. Hathaway, "Adventures of Buffalo Hunter," pp. 131–32.

25. J. Wright Mooar to Haley, interviews, Nov. 25, 1927, and Jan. 4, 1928, p. 9.

26. J. Wright Mooar to Vandale, Haley, and Chesley, interview, Mar. 2, 3, and 4, 1939; J. Wright Mooar, "Buffalo Days," 52, no. 3 (Mar., 1933): 8, 24, 28.

27. For data on Amos Chapman, who became famous as a participant in the Sept. 12, 1874, Battle of Buffalo Wallow, see, e.g.: "Amos Chapman" [published notice of cattle brands and markings], *Globe Live Stock Journal*, Sept. 29, 1885, p. 8; "Buffalo Wallow Battle Survivor Has Passed Away," *Amarillo Daily News*, July 26, 1925, p. 9; Wayne Montgomery, "Amos Chapman: An Early Journey of the Hero of the Buffalo Wallow Fight," *Frontier Times* 46, no. 3 (Apr.–May, 1972): 26–28, 44, 46–47; Heinie Schmidt, "Chapman's Life Is History of Frontier Scout," *High Plains Journal*, Mar. 15, 1956, pp. 2–3; Glen Shirley, *Buckskin and Spurs: A Gallery of Frontier Rogues and Heroes*, pp. 145–52; U.S. Department of War, Army, 5th Infantry, General Orders No. 28, Camp near Fort Sill, Indian Territory, Jan. 24, 1875, William Dixon Papers. Chapman was in a position to know about the impending attack on the trading post, for his Cheyenne father-in-law participated in the fight. Peter T. Lieneman to Linnaeus B. Ranck, interview, Nov. 30, 1937, Interview no. 9401, p. 217, Indian-Pioneer Papers, vol. 109, Indian Archives.

28. The best sources for Mooar's propositions concerning the "secret warning" and the ridgepole breaking may be found in J. Wright Mooar to Vandale, Haley, and Chesley, interview, Mar. 2, 3, and 4, 1939, and in J. Wright Mooar, "Buffalo Days," 52, no. 3 (Mar., 1933): 8, 24, 28.

29. For data on Jordan Edgar McAllister, see Dulcie Sullivan, "The McAllisters: Panhandle Pioneers," pp. 1–5, Dulcie Sullivan Papers; May McAllister Weills to Curtis C. Cadenhead, interview, June 12, 1971, and May McAllister Weills to Larry Bobbitt, interview, June 29, 1974, pp. 3–15, both in May McAllister Weills Papers.

30. McAllister to Haley, interview, July 1, 1926, p. 1.

31. *Dodge City Messenger*, June 25, 1874, p. 2; J. Wright Mooar, "Buffalo Days," 52, no. 3 (Mar., 1933): 24; Charles Rath, sworn deposition, Oct. 10, 1892, p. 12; Charles Rath, sworn deposition, Oct. 11, 1892, pp. 27, 29.

32. *Dodge City Messenger*, June 25, 1874, p. 2.

33. [Olive K. Dixon], "Life and Adventures of William ("Billy") Dixon of Adobe Walls, Texas Panhandle," 1913, TS, p. 165, "Battle of Adobe Walls" file, Frederick S. Barde Collection; J. Wright Mooar to Vandale, Haley, and Chesley, interview, Mar. 2, 3, and 4, 1939. The *Life and Adventures of "Billy" Dixon* does say that the hunters were unable to find the break in the ridgepole. [Dixon], *Life and Adventures*, pp. 240–41.

34. *Atchison Daily Champion*, July 7, 1874, p. 2; Coulter, "Adobe Walls Fight,"

[p. 2]; "Dodge Citizens Find Grave at Adobe Walls: History of Old Plains Battle Recalled by Comrades after Finding Bones," *Miami Chief*, Jan. 18, 1923, p. 8; "Dodge Men Find the Long Lost Grave," p. 7; Dubbs, "Personal Reminiscences," p. 59; "From the Front," p. 2; H. B. Leonard, "Fight at 'Dobe Walls," p. 7; Little, "Battle of Adobe Walls," p. 78; Phillips, "Battle of Adobe Walls," pp. 19, 32; Van Sickel, *A Story of Real Life*, p. 17.

Subsequent accounts present a perplexing variety of spellings for the Scheidler brothers' surname, but that used here appears in most initial accounts of their deaths and is standard spelling for the surname in German. The variant spellings include Sheidler, Shidler, Sheider, Shyler, Shindler, Shidley, Shadler, Schadler, Schaddler, Shadley, Shalder, and Saddler. *Atchison Daily Champion*, July 7, 1874, p. 2, July 10, 1874, p. 2; "Bat Masterson's Career," n.p.; Collins, *Indians' Last Fight*, p. 213; Coulter, "Adobe Walls Fight," p. 2; "Billy" Dixon, "A Story of Adobe Walls," p. 4; [Dixon], *Life and Adventures*, pp. 208–209, 220, 227; "From the Front," p. 2; Johnson, "The Battle of Adobe Walls," p. 3; Johnson, "Fight at 'Dobe Walls," A-5; [Leonard], "Memorandum," p. 1; H. B. Leonard, "Fight at 'Dobe Walls," p. 7; William B. Masterson, sworn deposition, June 24, 1893, p. 2; J. Wright Mooar to Johnson, Jan. 21, 1923, Andrew Johnson Papers; Raymond, "Diary of a Dodge City Buffalo Hunter," p. 392; Rye, *Quirt and Spur*, p. 322; "Texas Frontier Veteran," p. 7; Van Sickel, *A Story of Real Life*, p. 17; James A. Watson, "Battle of Adobe Walls," pp. 72–74; Wright, *Dodge City*, p. 202.

35. Curry, *Autobiography*, p. 6; "Dodge Citizens Find Grave," p. 8; "Dodge Men Find the Long Lost Grave," p. 7; Hathaway, "Adventures of Buffalo Hunter," pp. 131–32; Little, "Battle of Adobe Walls," p. 78.

36. Coulter, "Adobe Walls Fight," p. 2; "Billy" Dixon, "A Story of Adobe Walls," p. 4; [Dixon], *Life and Adventures*, pp. 208–209, 220; Fred A. Hunt, "Adobe Walls Argument," p. 387; Johnson, "Fight at 'Dobe Walls," A-5; J. Wright Mooar, "Buffalo Days," 52, no. 3 (Mar., 1933): 28; Parker, *Personal Experiences*, p. 60; Phillips, p. 32; Rye, *Quirt and Spur*, p. 322; Van Sickel, *A Story of Real Life*, p. 17; James A. Watson, "Battle of Adobe Walls," pp. 73–74; Wright, *Dodge City*, p. 202.

37. Quanah, "Told in English & Signs," p. 17; Riddle, "Indian Survivors," p. 13; Sargent, "War-Paint Off," p. 3.

38. [Dixon], *Life and Adventures*, p. 220.

39. Ibid., p. 209; Fred A. Hunt, "Adobe Walls Argument," p. 387; Little, "Battle of Adobe Walls," p. 78; Phillips, "Battle of Adobe Walls," p. 32; Van Sickel, *A Story of Real Life*, p. 17.

40. Collins, *Indians' Last Fight*, p. 213; Glenn, "Shelton [*sic*] Manuscript," p. 7; Johnson, "Fight at 'Dobe Walls," A-5; Phillips, "Battle of Adobe Walls," p. 32; Wright, *Dodge City*, p. 202.

41. [Dixon], *Life and Adventures*, p. 208; William Dixon, sworn deposition, July 25, 1898, [lf. 3]; H. B. Leonard, "Fight at 'Dobe Walls," p. 7; Little, "Battle of Adobe Walls," p. 80.

42. Andrew Johnson, sworn deposition, Oct. 10, 1892, p. 34; James Langton, sworn deposition, Jan. 28, 1896, p. 3; Little, "Battle of Adobe Walls," p. 81; Phillips, "Battle of Adobe Walls," pp. 19, 34; Van Sickel, *A Story of Real Life*, p. 18; Wright, "Personal reminiscences," p. 83; Wright, *Dodge City*, p. 200. The warrior in this incident has been identified, perhaps correctly, as the Cheyenne brave Stone Calf's Son. James L. Haley, *The Buffalo War*, p. 72; Phillips, "Battle of Adobe Walls," pp. 19, 34.

43. Connelley, "In Relation to the Visit," p. 3.

44. Parker, *Personal Experiences*, p. 61.

45. "Billy" Dixon, "A Story of Adobe Walls," p. 4; [Dixon], *Life and Adventures*, pp. 213–14; Olive Dixon to Barde, Apr. 12, [1913], W. S. Campbell Papers, TS copy also in Frederick S. Barde Collection.
46. Collins, *Indians' Last Fight*, pp. 221–22; [Dixon], *Life and Adventures*, pp. 209–10, 213; Little, "Battle of Adobe Walls," p. 80.
47. [Dixon], *Life and Adventures*, pp. 239–40; Tilghman, *Quanah*, pp. 90–91.
48. Glenn, "Shelton [*sic*] Manuscript," p. 8; Little, "Battle of Adobe Walls," p. 78; Rye, *Quirt and Spur*, p. 322.
49. Goodnight to Haley, interview, Sept. 17, 1928, p. 2; Goodnight to Mrs. Olive Dixon, Apr. 9, 1913, W. S. Campbell Papers, TS copy also in Frederick S. Barde Collection.
50. Quanah, "Told in English & Signs," p. 17.
51. Dubbs, "Personal Reminiscences," pp. 62–63; Gard, *Great Buffalo Hunt*, pp. 123–25; Hathaway, "Adventures of Buffalo Hunter," pp. 129–30; Ned H. Roberts and Kenneth L. Waters, *The Breech-Loading Single-Shot Match Rifle*, pp. 6–16, 202–52.
52. "The 'Adobe Walls': Graphic Account," p. 6; Coyle, "Stories of Quanah Parker," 4, no. 5 (Sept., 1911): 65; Little, "Battle of Adobe Walls," p. 81; Phillips, "Battle of Adobe Walls," p. 32; Rye, *Quirt and Spur*, p. 324; Steele, "Lawrie Tatum's Indian Policy," p. 93; Tilghman, *Quanah*, pp. 91–92; Wright, *Dodge City*, pp. 200–201.
53. "Billy" Dixon, "A Story of Adobe Walls," p. 4; [Dixon], *Life and Adventures*, pp. 216–17; Little, "Battle of Adobe Walls," p. 82; Parker, *Personal Experiences*, pp. 61–62. To estimate the time the men took to dash from the saloon to the two stores, the author, at age thirty-two and in good physical condition, ran the same distances between the entrances of the buildings at the site, requiring seventeen seconds to run from the saloon to the Rath store and twenty to the Myers and Leonard store. T. Lindsay Baker, "Notes on Time Required to Run and Walk between Buildings at the Adobe Walls Archaeological Site," Aug. 28, 1979, Adobe Walls—Description—General file, Adobe Walls research files.
54. "Billy" Dixon, "A Story of Adobe Walls," p. 4; [Dixon], *Life and Adventures*, pp. 218–19, 223–24; Johnson, "The Battle of Adobe Walls," p. 3; Little, "Battle of Adobe Walls," p. 82; Parker, *Personal Experiences*, pp. 61–62.
55. Co-hay-yah to Wilbur Sturtevant Nye, interview, Mar. 18, 1935, note pad no. 16, "Carbine and Lance" research materials, W. S. Nye Collection (portions, very freely edited, available in Nye, *Carbine & Lance*, p. 191); Puckett to Carselowey, interview, ca. 1937, p. 7.
56. Goodnight to Haley, interview, Sept. 17, 1928, p. 2; Riddle, "Indian Survivors," pp. 1, 13.
57. For typical examples of recent stories perpetuating the story of Dixon's "long shot," see Nan Keck and Katherine Albers, "Mile-Long Shot Ends Indian Siege," *Amarillo Daily News*, Aug. 18, 1980, C-1; Ed Syers, "Adobe Walls Site of Historic Single Long Range Shot," *San Antonio Express*, Dec. 2, 1971, B-8; Ed Syers, "History's Greatest Shot by Indian Fighter Dixon," *San Antonio Evening Sun*, Nov. 8, 1963, B-7.
58. [Dixon], *Life and Adventures*, pp. 232–33.
59. Glenn, "Shelton [*sic*] Manuscript," p. 8.
60. J. Wright Mooar to Haley, interviews, Nov. 25, 1927, and Jan. 4, 1928, p. 9.
61. W. S. Carter to Margaret Haley, interview, Dec. 28, 1945, pp. 3–4, Margaret Haley Papers.
62. "Adobe Walls Celebration Plans Advancing Rapidly as June 27 Approaches," *Amarillo Daily News*, June 8, 1924, Western Weekly Supplement, p. 10; [Dixon], *Life*

and Adventures, p. 232; Olive K. Dixon, *Life of "Billy" Dixon*, unpaged illustration of "High Bluff East of Adobe Walls"; Glenn, "Shelton [*sic*] Manuscript," p. 8; Dubbs, "Personal Reminiscences," pp. 62–63; Phillips, "Battle of Adobe Walls," p. 32.

63. Jean M. Burroughs, "Chief Satanta and His Bugle," *Southwest Heritage* 4, no. 4 (Summer, 1974): 21–28; *Emporia News*, Aug. 21, 1874, p. 2; Nye to Archambeau, Feb. 21, 1962, Ernest R. Archambeau Papers; Quanah, "Told in English & Signs," p. 17; D. Harper Simms, "Battle of the Bugles at the Adobe Walls," *Corral Dust, Potomac Corral of the Westerners* 2, no. 3 (Sept. 1957): 19.

64. "Bat Masterson's Career," n.p.; Collinson to Bugbee, Jan. 17, 1935, Harold Bugbee Papers; Collinson to Gerdes, Dec. 16, 1937, Bruce Gerdes Papers; Coulter, "Adobe Walls Fight," p. 2; "From the Front," p. 2; Fred A. Hunt, p. 387; Lewis, "William Barclay Masterson," pp. 10–11; Little, "Battle of Adobe Walls," pp. 79–80; McKinley, "J. W. McKinley's Narrative," p. 3; Masterson to Barde, Oct. 10, 1913, W. S. Campbell Papers, portions of this letter reprinted in [Dixon], *Life and Adventures*, pp. 211–12; William B. Masterson, sworn deposition, June 24, 1893, p. 2; J. Wright Mooar, "Buffalo Days," 52, no. 3 (Mar., 1933): 28; Phillips, "Battle of Adobe Walls," p. 19; Riddle, "Indian Survivors," p. 13. The black bugler killed at Adobe Walls may have been the one who accompanied a war party that attacked J. Wright Mooar's outfit prior to the fight. J. Wright Mooar to Haley, Vandale, and Chesley, interview, Mar. 2, 3, and 4, 1939. For an apparently fanciful account of the bugler's death at the hands of Armitage, see James A. Watson, "Battle of Adobe Walls," pp. 74–75.

65. Hathaway, "Adventures of Buffalo Hunter," p. 133.

66. R. C. Crane, "Old Man Keeler," *West Texas Historical Association Year Book* 4 (1928): 100–104; R. C. Crane, "The Unsung Hero of Adobe Walls," *Frontier Times* 5, no. 12 (Sept., 1928): 458–59; Lowell H. Harrison, "Indians vs Buffalo Hunters at Adobe Walls," *American History Illustrated* 2, no. 1 (Apr., 1967): 25; Little, "Battle of Adobe Walls," p. 82; Dolores Stark, "Terror at Adobe Walls!" *Gasser* 20, no. 10 (Oct. 1963): 8–9.

67. Lewis, *Sunset Trail*, pp. 75–77.

68. The smallest estimated number of defenders reported by a participant is fifteen, a figure undoubtedly too low. In 1893 Masterson reported that "there was about 20 men at Adobe Walls," and several participants or hide men who came in just after the fight remembered twenty-one. Johnson, one of the most reliable sources, for years maintained there were twenty-one, but in 1924, during ceremonies at the site, he raised his number to twenty-eight men plus Mrs. Olds. Perhaps he altered his figure so as not to conflict with Mrs. Dixon, who reported a higher number and who was in attendance at the celebration. A 1928 account based on participants' reminiscences noted twenty-four hide men in the fight, and Born remembered fewer than twenty-five. Dixon's first published reminiscences in 1888 reported twenty-five men. An 1887 article on Masterson, purportedly drawn from his information, noted twenty-six men in the fight; James W. McKinley, another participant, noted twenty-seven, also reported by Leonard, the manager of the Myers and Leonard store. The number reported most often was twenty-eight men plus Hannah Olds. This figure appears in Billy Dixon's 1902 article in the *Denver Times*, Olive K. Dixon's biography of her husband, the reminiscences of participant Sam Smith, and the memoirs of J. Wright Mooar, who knew most of the men who were there. The first narrative of the fight as a historical event, an 1877 article by John Coulter of the *Leavenworth Daily Times*, reports twenty-nine defenders; perhaps the highest estimate, thirty, appeared in a report published in the Topeka *Commonwealth* only eleven days after the battle. "The 'Adobe Walls': Graphic Account," p. 6; Collins, *Indians' Last Fight*, p. 211; Coulter, "Adobe Walls Fight," p. 2; "Billy" Dixon, "A Story of Adobe Walls," p. 4;

[Dixon], *Life and Adventures*, p. 207; "From the Front," p. 2; "Indian Fighter Dead," p. 1; [Johnson], "Adobe Walls Survivor," p. 10; Johnson, "Andrew Johnson," p. 6; "A Kansas Killer," p. 5; McKinley, "J. W. McKinley's Narrative," p. 2; William B. Masterson, sworn deposition, June 24, 1893, p. 2; J. Wright Mooar, "Buffalo Days," 52, no. 3 (Mar., 1933): 24; Phillips, "Battle of Adobe Walls," p. 19; Rye, *Quirt and Spur*, p. 325; "Texas Frontier Veteran," p. 7; Van Sickel, *A Story of Real Life*, p. 16. In 1892 Johnson remembered there being twenty-two participants: Johnson, sworn deposition, Oct. 10, 1892, p. 34.

69. *Atchison Daily Champion*, July 10, 1874, p. 2; Frank D. Baldwin, Diary Transcript for Aug. 19–20, 1874, p. 2; Davidson to Assistant Adjutant General, Department of Texas, July 7, 1874, U.S. Department of War, Army, Department of Texas, Letters Received 2723 D Texas 1874 "Indian File," RG 393, National Archives, hereafter cited as Department of Texas, Letters Received 2723; Hathaway, "Adventures of Buffalo Hunter," p. 131; Miles, *Personal Recollections*, p. 160; Van Sickel, *A Story of Real Life*, p. 15.

70. "The 'Adobe Walls': Garphic Account," p. 6; "Billy" Dixon, "A Story of Adobe Walls," p. 4; William Dixon, sworn deposition, July 25, 1898, [lf. 3]; Parker, *Personal Experiences*, p. 60.

71. [Dixon], *Life and Adventures*, p. 208; [Olive King Dixon], "Life and Adventures of William ("Billy") Dixon," p. 170.

72. Dubbs, "Personal Reminiscences," p. 58; Andrew Johnson, sworn deposition, Oct. 10, 1892, p. 37; James Langton, sworn deposition, Jan. 28, 1896, pp. 3, 8, 9.

73. Informants estimating five hundred to seven hundred attackers include Hanrahan, Wright, Coulter, James H. Cator, Johnson, Masterson, Indian Territory trader Robert B. Thomas, and two Comanche participants in the fight, Timbo and Yellowfish. "Bat Masterson's Career," n.p.; Robert Goldthwaite Carter, *On the Border with Mackenzie: or, Winning West Texas From the Comanches*, p. 213; James H. Cator, sworn deposition, Oct. 10, 1892, p. 20; Collins, *Indians' Last Fight*, p. 217; Collinson to Gerdes, Dec. 16, 1937, Bruce Gerdes Papers; Coulter, "Adobe Walls Fight," p. 2; [Johnson], "Adobe Walls Survivor," p. 10; Johnson, "Fight at 'Dobe Walls," A-5; Johnson, "Battle of Adobe Walls," p. 3; C. E. Jones to Sheffy, interview, Dec. 31, 1929, p. 2; Harlan B. Kauffman, "Hunting the Buffalo," *Overland Monthly* 66, no. 2 (Aug., 1915): 165; Lewis, "William Barclay Masterson," p. 10; Phillips, "Battle of Adobe Walls," p. 19; Sargent, "War-Paint Off," p. 1; "Survivor of Famous Indian Fight," p. 1; "Texas Frontier Veteran," p. 7; Robert B. Thomas to J. S. Clark, interview, Oct. 1, 1937, interview no. 8768, pp. 369–70, Indian-Pioneer Papers, vol. 46, Indian Archives; Wright, *Dodge City*, pp. 200, 201.

74. J. Wright Mooar to Haley, Vandale, and Chesley, interview, Mar. 2, 3, and 4, 1939; J. Wright Mooar, "Buffalo Days," 52, no. 4 (Apr., 1933): 22.

75. Rye, *Quirt and Spur*, p. 320.

76. Curry, *Autobiography*, p. 5.

77. McGinnis, *The Promised Land*, p. 44.

78. Glenn, "Shelton [*sic*] Manuscript," p. 7.

79. Stark, "Terror," p. 7. If indeed this many warriors had attacked Adobe Walls, the odds would have been more than 200 to 1 in favor of the Indians.

80. Hathaway, "Adventures of Buffalo Hunter," p. 133.

81. *Atchison Daily Champion*, July 7, 1874, p. 2; James H. Cator, sworn deposition, Oct. 10, 1892, p. 21; *Fort Scott Daily Monitor*, July 9, 1874, p. 4; Parker, *Personal Experience*, p. 61; Quanah, "Told in English & Signs," p. 15.

82. Frank D. Baldwin, Diary Transcript for Aug. 19–20, 1874, p. 2; Davidson to Assistant Adjutant General, July 8, 1874, Department of Texas Letters Received 2723;

Charles Rath and Co. and Myers and Leonard to Gov. Osborn, [July] 8, 1874, telegram, T. A. Osborn Papers.

83. Cox to McConnell, interview, n.d., p. 4; "Billy" Dixon, "A Story of Adobe Walls," p. 4; [Dixon], *Life and Adventures*, pp. 227–28; Traylor, "Attack on Adobe Walls," p. 14; Van Sickel, *A Story of Real Life*, p. 18.

84. Dubbs, "Personal Reminiscences," p. 59; Fred A. Hunt, "Adobe Walls Argument," p. 387; Andrew Johnson, sworn deposition, Oct. 10, 1892, pp. 39–40, 48; Andrew Johnson, sworn deposition, Oct. 11, 1892, p. 19; Johnson, "The Fight at 'Dobe Walls," A-5; Thompson McFadden, "Thompson McFadden's Diary of an Indian Campaign, 1874," ed. Robert C. Carriker, *Southwestern Historical Quarterly* 75, no. 2 (Oct., 1971): 201; Phillips, "Battle of Adobe Walls," p. 19; Wright, *Dodge City*, p. 200.

85. Quanah, "Told in English & Signs," p. 17.

86. Haworth to Smith, Sept. 1, 1874, *Report of the Secretary of the Interior* (1874), p. 528; Hyde, *Life of George Bent*, p. 360.

87. Poafebitty et al. to Nye, interview, n.d., p. 19.

88. Nye, *Carbine & Lance*, p. 191.

89. *Atchison Daily Champion*, July 10, 1874, p. 2.

90. "From the Front," p. 2; Miles, *Personal Recollections*, p. 160; Quanah, "Told in English & Signs," p. 15.

91. C. E. Jones to Sheffy, interview, Dec. 31, 1929, p. 2.

92. Collinson to Bugbee, Jan. 17, 1935, Harold Bugbee Papers.

93. Johnson, "Andrew Johnson," p. 6; Johnson, "The Fight at 'Dobe Walls," A-5.

94. Hathaway, "Adventures of Buffalo Hunter," p. 135.

95. Coulter, "Adobe Walls Fight," p. 2.

96. "The 'Adobe Walls': Graphic Account," p. 6.

97. Lewis, "William Barclay Masterson," p. 11.

98. [Leonard], "Memorandum," p. 1; "Texas Frontier Veteran," p. 7.

99. H. B. Leonard, "Fight at 'Dobe Walls," p. 7.

100. Curry, *Autobiography*, p. 6; "A Kansas Killer," *Topeka Daily Capital*, June 26, 1888, p. 5.

101. J. Wright Mooar to Haley, Vandale, and Chesley, interview, Mar. 2, 3, and 4, 1939; J. Wright Mooar, "Buffalo Days," 52, no. 4 (Apr., 1933): 22.

102. "Billy" Dixon, "A Story of Adobe Walls," p. 4; Andrew Johnson, sworn deposition, Oct. 10, 1892, pp. 39–40; McGinnis, *The Promised Land*, p. 53; Parker, *Personal Experiences*, p. 62.

103. Grinnell, *Fighting Cheyennes*, p. 313; Hathaway, "Adventures of Buffalo Hunter," p. 135; Hunt to Nye, May 6, 1940, W. S. Nye Collection; J. Wright Mooar, "Buffalo Days," 52, no. 4 (Apr., 1933): 22; Nye, "H. L. Scott Material" spiral notebook, pp. 57–58, "Bad Medicine and Good" research notes, W. S. Nye Collection; Nye, *Carbine & Lance*, p. 191; Quanah, "Told in English & Signs," p. 17; Riddle, "Indian Survivors," p. 1.

104. James H. Cator, sworn deposition, Oct. 10, 1892, pp. 26, 31; [Dixon], *Life and Adventures*, pp. 221–24, 236; *Leavenworth Daily Commercial*, July 26, 1874, p. 2; Johnson, "The Battle of Adobe Walls," p. 4; Andrew Johnson, sworn deposition, Oct. 10, 1892, pp. 47, 48.

105. Field Museum of Natural History, Chicago, Accession Card No. A 15335 Acc. 870; Johnson, "The Battle of Adobe Walls," p. 4; Mooney to Davis, May 28, 1904, Department of Anthropology, Field Museum of Natural History; Mooney to Johnson, July 3, 1904, Andrew Johnson Papers; Mooney to Johnson, Aug. 29, 1903, Andrew Johnson Papers; Mooney to Johnson, Feb. 9, 1904, Andrew Johnson Papers; Mooney to Johnson,

Feb. 22, 1904, Andrew Johnson Papers; Rabineau to Baker, Jan. 12, 1981, Adobe Walls—Material Culture—Indian Artifacts on Battlefield file, Adobe Walls research files.

106. Olive K. Dixon to Anderson, Dec. 26, 1922, Olive K. Dixon Papers; Olive K. Dixon to Johnson, Jan. 15, 1923, Andrew Johnson Papers; Olive K. Dixon to Johnson, Dec. 6, 1923, Andrew Johnson Papers; Panhandle-Plains Historical Museum, Accession Record Cards Nos. 43/6, 43/7, 43/8, and 43/9.

107. Henry B. Bass, "Quanah Parker's Bonnet," *The War Chief of the Indian Territory Posse of Oklahoma Westerners* 4, no. 3 (Dec., 1970): 3–6; Lowie Museum of Anthropology, Berkeley, Cal., Accession Record Card No. 2–4899; "Scott Collection," ca. 1901, p. 3, Lowie Museum of Anthropology, Berkeley, California; Norrick to Baker, Jan. 28, 1981, Quanah file, Adobe Walls research files.

108. James Eschiti, document transferring title to certain Indian artifacts to the Panhandle-Plains Historical Museum, June 22, 1963; Hampton to McClure, Sept. 10, 1961; Hampton to McClure, Feb. 4, 1964; "Items Purchased 6/22/63 by Mr. & Mrs. Howard Hampton from James Eschiti, Comanche, of Walters, Okla.," TS, 1963; McClure to Mr. and Mrs. Hampton, Feb. 7, 1964, all in Mr. and Mrs. Howard Hampton donor file, Panhandle-Plains Historical Museum; Panhandle-Plains Historical Museum, Accession Record Cards Nos. 1510/165, 1510/166, and 1510/171.

109. Connelley, "In Relation to the Visit," pp. 1, 2, 5; [Dixon], *Life and Adventures*, p. 227; Little, "Battle of Adobe Walls," p. 84; "Texas Frontier Veteran," p. 7; James A. Watson, "Battle of Adobe Walls," p. 76.

Notes to Chapter 4

1. J. Wright Mooar to Johnson, Jan. 20, 1923, Andrew Johnson Papers.

2. Hathaway, "Adventures of Buffalo Hunter," p. 135; McGinnis, *The Promised Land*, pp. 45–53; West, "Battle of Adobe Walls (1874)," p. 34.

3. J. Bertie Cator to Robert H. Cator and James H. Cator, July 27, 1874, Robert H. Cator Papers; J. Bertie Cator to Robert H. Cator and James H. Cator, Dec. 6, 1874, Robert H. Cator Papers; Collinson to Gerdes, Dec. 16, 1937, Bruce Gerdes Papers; Coulter, "Adobe Walls Fight," p. 2; Curry, *Autobiography*, p. 5; [Dixon], *Life and Adventures*, pp. 182–84, 207, 212; [Leonard], "Memorandum," p. 2; Little, "Battle of Adobe Walls," p. 78; Masterson to Barde, Oct. 13, 1913, W. S. Campbell Papers; James A. Watson, "Battle of Adobe Walls," pp. 37, 74–76; West, "Battle of Adobe Walls (1874)," p. 34.

4. Mabel Bennett to Baker, Nov. 28, 1978, Henry Born Papers; Bennett to Baker, Apr. 18, 1980, Henry Born Papers; Born to Siringo, July 6, 1920, Charles Siringo Papers; Mrs. Henry Born to Siringo, Dec. 20, 1923, Charles Siringo Papers; Breihan, "Horse Thief," pp. 28–33; Curry, *Autobiography*, p. 5; [Dixon], *Life and Adventures*, p. 207; *Dodge City Times*, Apr. 7, 1877, p. 8, Apr. 28, 1877, p. 4, Oct. 6, 1877, p. 8, Oct. 13, 1877, p. 4, Oct. 27, 1877, p. 4, June 1, 1878, p. 1, June 29, 1878, p. 2, Dec. 14, 1878, p. 4, Jan. 4, 1879, p. 4; "'Dutch Henry' and James Watts Were Treed by a Bear near Rose's Cabin in the San Juan," unidentified clipping, Will C. Ferrill Scrapbooks, 1890–93, III, 71; "'Dutch Henry' Born 1849–1921," TS, ca. 1921, in possession of Mrs. Mabel Bennett; "Dutch Henry. (Henry Borne.)," pp. 1–4; "'Dutch Henry,' Chief of Outlaws," p. 4; "Frontier Sketches," *Field and Farm* 27, no. 1403 (Dec. 21, 1912): 8; "Frontier Tales," *Field and Farm* 8, no. 417 (Dec. 30, 1893): 6; "Glenwood Sketches. The Man Called Dutch Henry Gives a Page of His Life," Dawson Scrapbooks, 77: 3; Haley, *Charles Goodnight*, pp. 287–88, 335–36; Hathaway, "Adventures of Buffalo Hunter," pp. 133–34; "Indian Fighter Dead," p. 1; Lake to Campbell, Mar. 20, 1951, W. S. Campbell Papers; [Leonard],

"Memorandum," p. 2; Little, "Battle of Adobe Walls," pp. 78–79; "Memories," TS, ca. Jan., 1921, in possession of Mrs. Mabel Bennett; "Obituary," unidentified newspaper clipping, n.d., in possession of Mrs. Mabel Bennett; Peters to Stanley Vestlel [*sic*] [W. S. Campbell], Feb. 2, 1952, W. S. Campbell Papers; "Pioneer Passes Away," *Creede Candle*, Jan. 22, 1921, p. 1; "At Rest," unidentified newspaper clipping, 1894, in possession of Mrs. Mabel Bennett; *Rocky Mountain News*, Jan. 3, 1879, p. 1, Mar. 1, 1879, p. 4, Mar. 2, 1879, p. 4; Tilghman to Baxter, Nov. 24, 1955, in possession of Mrs. Mabel Bennett; Tilghman to Beeson, Sept. 25, 1941, Bill Tilghman vertical file; Tilghman to Campbell, Mar. 23, 1952, W. S. Campbell Papers; Tilghman, *Marshal*, pp. 79–81, 102, 110–12, 119–20, 330; Tilghman, "Story of 'Dutch Henry'"; James A. Watson, "Battle of Adobe Walls," p. 37; West, "Battle of Adobe Walls (1874)," pp. 19, 25, 34.

5. Curry, *Autobiography*, p. 5; [Dixon], *Life and Adventures*, p. 207; [Leonard], "Memorandum," p. 2; Little, "Battle of Adobe Walls," p. 78; "Texas Frontier Veteran," p. 7; West, "Battle of Adobe Walls (1874)," p. 34.

6. Coulter, p. 2; Curry, *Autobiography*, p. 5; [Dixon], *Life and Adventures*, pp. 207, 221; *Leavenworth Daily Commercial*, July 26, 1874, p. 2; James A. Watson, pp. 74–76; West, "Battle of Adobe Walls (1874)," pp. 18, 34; Wright, *Dodge City*, p. 203.

7. Frank Collinson, "Jim Greathouse or Whiskey Jim," TS, n.d., n.p., Frank Collinson Papers; Maurice Garland Fulton, *History of the Lincoln County War*, ed. Robert N. Mullin, p. 381; William A. Keleher, *Violence in Lincoln County 1869–1881*, pp. 283–86, 288–89, 332; West, "Battle of Adobe Walls (1874)," p. 19.

8. Olive King Dixon, "Early Days in Hutchinson County," *Frontier Times* 5, no. 7 (Apr., 1928): 316–17; [Dixon], *Life and Adventures*, pp. 5–9, 310–14; Olive K. Dixon, *Life of "Billy" Dixon*, pp. v–xviii, 248–51; Isaacs, "Billy Dixon," pp. 372–74; McCarty, *Adobe Walls Bride*; Harry Montgomery, "Billy Dixon's Medal to Museum; Story of Battle Is Recalled," *Amarillo Sunday News-Globe*, Mar. 19, 1933, p. 10; Panhandle-Plains Historical Museum, Accession Record Card No. 43/3; Quinn to Barde, Jan. 6, 1911, "Dixon, Billy" vertical file; U.S. Department of War, Army, 5th Infantry, General Orders No. 28, Jan. 25, 1875, William Dixon Papers; Woodall to Dixon, Jan. 4, 1889, William Dixon Papers.

9. Coulter, "Adobe Walls Fight," p. 2; [Dixon], *Life and Adventures*, p. 207; Johnson, "The Battle of Adobe Walls," p. 2; Johnson, "Fight at 'Dobe Walls," A-5; Andrew Johnson, sworn deposition, Oct. 10, 1892, p. 41 1/2; Little, "Battle of Adobe Walls," pp. 77, 81; James A. Watson, "Battle of Adobe Walls," p. 74; West, "Battle at Adobe Walls (1874)," p. 34.

10. Curry, *Autobiography*, p. 5; John P. Dickinson, "On a Government Survey in the Early '70s," *Trail*, 10, no. 7 (Dec., 1917): 19; [Dixon], *Life and Adventures*, pp. 177, 182–84, 207; *Dodge City Times*, Oct. 27, 1877, p. 1, Jan. 26, 1878, p. 4, Mar. 16, 1878, p. 5, Apr. 6, 1878, p. 4, May 18, 1878, p. 2; *Leavenworth Daily Commercial*, July 7, 1874, p. 1; [Leonard], "Memorandum," p. 2; Raymond, "Diary of a Dodge City Buffalo Hunter," pp. 389–90; Schofield, "W. M. D. Lee," p. 58; West, "Battle of Adobe Walls, (1874)" p. 34.

11. Coulter, "Adobe Walls Fight," p. 2; [Dixon], *Life and Adventures*, pp. 147, 194–95, 199, 203, 207, 215, 216–17, 241–43; Eagan, "James Hanrahan," pp. 1–6; [Leonard], "Memorandum," p. 1; Little, "Battle of Adobe Walls," pp. 76–79, 82, 84; William B. Masterson, sworn deposition, June 24, 1893, pp. 2, 5; J. Wright Mooar to Haley, interviews, Nov. 25, 1927, and Jan. 4, 1928, p. 7; J. Wright Mooar to Vandale, Haley, and Chesley, interview, Mar. 2, 3, and 4, 1939; Rath, *Early Ford County*, pp. 48–50; Wright, *Dodge City*, p. 201.

12. *Dodge City Times*, Sept. 1, 1877, p. 4, Oct. 13, 1877, p. 1; Hinsdale County, Colo., County Commissioners' Court, Proceedings, MS, unnumbered vol., p. 220, vol. I, p. 22; *Leavenworth Daily Commercial*, July 26, 1874, p. 2; R. R. Maiden, "Marshal Maiden Compiles Succession of Sheriffs for Colorado Counties," *Colorado Sheriff and Peace Officer* 2, no. 11 (Nov., 1962): 7; [Robert R. Maiden], untitled reference list on Colorado sheriffs, TS, ca. 1967, n.p.

13. Ford to Baker, Jan. 30, 1979, Hanrahan—James file, Adobe Walls research files; I. W. Garrett, comp., *Official Manual of the State of Idaho for the Years 1895–1896*, p. 8; Idaho, Legislature, Senate, *Journal of the Senate of Idaho Third Session . . .* , p. 4; Kauffman, "Hunting the Buffalo," p. 165; "Texas Frontier Veteran," p. 7; Wood to Baker, telephone interview, June 20, 1980, TS notes in Adobe Walls—Battle—Fighting file, Adobe Walls research files.

14. Hathaway, "Adventures of Buffalo Hunter," pp. 129–35; Pate, "Battles of Adobe Walls," p. 42.

15. "Dodge Citian Recounts Battle of Adobe Walls," unidentified newspaper clipping, ca. June, 1923, scrapbook no. 1768, p. 36; [Johnson], "Adobe Walls Survivor," p. 10; Johnson, "Andrew Johnson," pp. 1–7; Johnson, "Battle of Adobe Walls," pp. 1–7; Johnson, "Fight at 'Dobe Walls," A-5; Andrew Johnson, sworn deposition, Oct. 10, 1892; Andrew Johnson, sworn deposition, Oct. 11, 1892; Andrew Johnson, "Tells of Battle," *Topeka Daily State Journal*, Aug. 19, 1911, p. 3; Andrew Johnson, "What Really Happened at the Famous Frontier Fight Which Is Known in History as the Battle of 'Dobe Wall," *Dodge City Globe*, Aug. 8, 1911, p. 4.

16. In the 1890s Charles Rath and his two former partners, Robert M. Wright and James Langton, filed suit in the U.S. Court of Claims for the recovery of losses they suffered in the Indian attack on Adobe Walls. Rath and Wright gathered witnesses to support their case; these men gave depositions at Wichita on Oct. 10, 1892. The witnesses, among them Rath, Wright, James H. Cator, and Andrew Johnson, met two days earlier, as Wright expressed it, to "get together and talk over the matter & refresh our memory." After they got their stories "straight," the men were questioned individually by attorneys, their sworn testimony being recorded. Rath, Wright, and Cator testified that many buffalo hides were left behind at the Rath and Company store because they had been ruined by rain after the Indians had destroyed the stacks. Only Johnson disagreed, reporting that the merchants hauled away all but the heaviest skins when they carried merchandise back to Dodge City in July, 1874. James H. Cator, sworn deposition, Oct. 10, 1892, pp. 22, 24, 28–29; Andrew Johnson, sworn deposition, Oct. 10, 1892, pp. 35, 42½, 43, 46, 49–50; Charles Rath, sworn deposition, Oct. 10, 1892, pp. 3, 8; Wright to Cator Brothers, Sept. 23, 1892, Robert H. Cator Papers; R. M. Wright, sworn deposition, Oct. 10, 1892, p. 18.

17. "Andy Johnson, Survivor," sec. 2, p. 4; "Came to Dodge," p. 23; Collins, *Indians' Last Fight*, pp. 212, 224–25; Connelley, "In Relation to the Visit," pp. 1–4; Coulter, "Adobe Walls Fight," p. 2; Olive K. Dixon to Johnson, Aug. 10, 1924, Andrew Johnson Papers; [Dixon], *Life and Adventures*, p. 207; "Dodge Citizens Find Grave," p. 8; *Dodge City Times*, Mar. 31, 1877, p. 4, Apr. 7, 1877, p. 5, Oct. 13, 1877, p. 4, Oct. 20, 1877, p. 4; "Dodge Man Is Survivor," B-10; "Dodge Men Find Long Lost Grave," pp. 1, 7; Hobble, "Dodge City Pioneers," pp. 1, 2; Andy Johnson, "Andy Johnson, Blacksmith, Wagonmaker and Repairer" [advertisement], *Globe Live Stock Journal*, Sept. 29, 1885, p. 6; *Kansas State Gazetteer . . . 1878*, p. 220; *Kansas State Gazetteer . . . 1882–3*, p. 324; *Kansas State Gazetteer . . . 1888–9*, p. 303; Little, "Battle of Adobe Walls," p. 78; William B. Masterson, sworn deposition, June 24, 1893, p. 5; *Polk's Kansas State Gazetteer . . .*

1904, p. 270; Rath, *Early Ford County,* pp. 47, 83–86, 222; Raymond, "Diary of a Dodge City Buffalo Hunter," p. 367; Schmidt, "It's Worth Remembering: Last Survivor," sec. 1, pp. 11, 15; "Survivor of Famous Indian Fight," p. 1; U.S. Department of the Treasury, Internal Revenue Service, "United States Stamp for Internal Revenue Special Tax, Act of October 1, 1890. Received from Andy Johnson . . . , MS, Dec. 31, 1901, Andrew Johnson Papers; Wright, *Dodge City,* pp. 203, 305–306.

18. Coulter, "Adobe Walls Fight," p. 2; Curry, *Autobiography,* p. 5; [Dixon], *Life and Adventures,* p. 207; Johnson, "Fight at 'Dobe Walls," A-5; Lake to Campbell, Mar. 20, 1951, W. S. Campbell Papers; Little, "Battle of Adobe Walls," pp. 78, 82; [Leonard], "Memorandum," pp. 1–2; "Texas Frontier Veteran," p. 7; West, "Battle of Adobe Walls (1874)," p. 34.

19. Breaden to Baker, Mar. 26, 1980, Langton—James file, Adobe Walls research files; James H. Cator, sworn deposition, Oct. 10, 1892, p. 21; Collins, *Indians' Last Fight,* pp. 211–12, 215–17, 230; Coulter, "Adobe Walls Fight," p. 2; Curry, *Autobiography,* p. 5; [Dixon], *Life and Adventures,* pp. 178, 197–98, 207; *Dodge City Times,* July 21, 1877, pp. 1, 5, July 28, 1877, p. 3, Sept. 29, 1877, p. 4, Oct. 8, 1877, p. 4, Oct. 13, 1877, p. 4, Dec. 15, 1877, p. 4, Dec. 22, 1877, p. 1, Dec. 29, 1877, p. 4, Jan. 19, 1878, p. 4, Mar. 30, 1878, p. 5, Dec. 7, 1878, p. 4; "James Langton Hurled to Death," *Deseret Evening News,* July 21, 1913, p. 3; "James Langton Meets Death in Auto Accident," *Salt Lake Tribune,* July 21, 1913, pp. 1, 12; Johnson, "Fight at 'Dobe Walls," A-5; Andrew Johnson, sworn deposition, Oct. 10, 1892, p. 41½; *Kansas State Gazetteer . . . 1882–3,* p. 326; *Kansas State Gazetteer . . . 1884–5,* p. 398; *Kansas State Gazetteer . . . 1888–9,* p. 303; "Langton & Walker" [notice of cattle brands and markings], *Globe Live Stock Journal,* July 15, 1884, p. 8; James Langton, sworn deposition, Jan. 28, 1896, pp. 1–10; William B. Masterson, sworn deposition, June 24, 1893, p. 5; "Members of the Western Stock Growers'," p. 6; [Leonard], "Memorandum," p. 1; Little, "Battle of Adobe Walls," pp. 76–81; Charles Rath, sworn deposition, Oct. 10, 1892, pp. 2, 11–11¾, 12½; Rath, *Early Ford County,* p. 263; Rath, *The Rath Trail,* pp. 101, 106, 108, 111, 114–15, 119; "Sitler & Langton" [notices of cattle brands and markings], *Globe Live Stock Journal,* July 15, 1884, p. 8, Oct. 6, 1885, p. 8; "Texas Frontier Veteran," p. 7; R. M. Wright, sworn deposition, Oct. 10, 1892, p. 17.

20. Curry, *Autobiography,* p. 5; [Dixon], *Life and Adventures,* pp. 207, 231–33, 243; [Leonard], "Memorandum," p. 2; J. Wright Mooar, "Buffalo Days," 52, no. 3 (Mar., 1933), p. 28; Pate, "Battles of Adobe Walls," pp. 27, 32–33; James A. Watson, "Battle of Adobe Walls," p. 76; West, "Battle of Adobe Walls (1874)," pp. 19, 28, 30, 34.

21. *Atchison Daily Champion,* July 10, 1874, p. 2; Coulter, "Adobe Walls Fight," p. 2; Curry, *Autobiography,* p. 5; [Dixon], *Life and Adventures,* pp. 176, 207, 212; *Dodge City Times,* May 26, 1877, p. 5, Oct. 6, 1877, pp. 4, 5, Oct. 20, 1877, p. 4, Nov. 17, 1877, p. 1, Dec. 1, 1877, p. 4, Dec. 8, 1877, p. 4, Dec. 15, 1877, p. 4, Dec. 22, 1877, p. 4, Dec. 29, 1877, p. 4, Jan. 12, 1878, p. 5, Mar. 16, 1878, p. 4, Apr. 13, 1878, p. 4, June 22, 1878, p. 5, Sept. 7, 1878, p. 3, Nov. 9, 1878, p. 1, Nov. 16, 1878, p. 1; "Fred J. Leonard," p. 6; Johnson, "Fight at 'Dobe Walls," A-5; *Kansas State Gazetteer . . . 1878,* p. 220; "Last Survivor of Indian Fight," p. 20; "Last Man Who Took Part in Adobe Walls Indian Fight Is Dead at Salt Lake City," *Dodge City Daily Globe,* Aug. 9, 1928, p. 7; [Leonard], "Memorandum," pp. 1–2; H. B. Leonard, "Fight at 'Dobe Walls," p. 7; Little, "Battle of Adobe Walls," pp. 78–79, 80; William B. Masterson, sworn deposition, June 24, 1893, p. 5; "Quantrill Hero Dead: Fred Leonard also Took Part in Indian Fight," *Topeka Daily Capital,* Aug. 10, 1928, p. 5; *R. L. Polk & Co.'s Salt Lake City Directory 1891–92,* p. 445; *R. L. Polk . . . 1893,* p. 493; *R. L. Polk . . . 1894–95,* p. 464; *R. L. Polk . . . 1896,* p. 440; *R. L.*

Polk . . . *1899*, p. 509; *R. L. Polk* . . . *1902*, p. 512; *R. L. Polk* . . . *1903*, p. 560; *R. L. Polk* . . . *1906*, p. 553; *R. L. Polk* . . . *1907*, p. 647; *R. L. Polk* . . . *1910*, p. 652; *R. L. Polk* . . . *1911*, p. 621; *R. L. Polk* . . . *1912*, p. 533; *R. L. Polk* . . . *1915*, p. 597; *R. L. Polk* . . . *1920*, p. 544; *R. L. Polk* . . . *1927*, p. 710; Rye, *Quirt and Spur*, p. 323; *Salt Lake City Directory for 1890*, pp. 404, 620; "Texas Frontier Veteran," p. 7; U.S. Court of Claims, Indian Depredation Case Files, Case 10102, Frederick J. Leonard and A. C. Myers, trading as Myers and Leonard, Claimants, RG 123, National Archives.

22. Cator receipts; Coulter, "Adobe Walls Fight," p. 2; Curry, *Autobiography*, p. 5; [Dixon], *Life and Adventures*, pp. 90−92, 110−17, 207; [Leonard], "Memorandum," p. 2; Little, "Battle of Adobe Walls," p. 78; J. Wright Mooar, "Buffalo Days," 52, no. 2 (Feb., 1933): 10, and 52, no. 4 (Apr., 1933): 5; James A. Watson, "Battle of Adobe Walls," p. 37.

23. McKinley, "J. W. McKinley's Narrative," pp. 1−4, also available as "J. W. McKinley's Narrative," *Panhandle-Plains Historical Review* 36 (1963): 61−69.

24. R. T. Alexander to C. Boone McClure, interview, May 10, 1958, R. T. Alexander Papers; Alexander to Hill, July 1, 1954, R. T. Alexander Papers; Coulter, "Adobe Walls Fight," p. 2; Curry, *Autobiography*, p. 5; [Dixon], *Life and Adventures*, p. 207; Little, "Battle of Adobe Walls," p. 78; *Leavenworth Daily Commercial*, July 26, 1874, p. 2; McKinley, "J. W. McKinley's Narrative," pp. 7−9; James A. Watson, "Battle of Adobe Walls," p. 74. The hide men at Adobe Walls must not have known James W. McKinley very well, for his name in various accounts was recalled also as McHenry, McKinstry, and McKinney.

25. Frank D. Baldwin, Diary Transcript for Aug. 19−20, 1874, p. 5; "Bat Masterson," TS, n.d., pp. 1−3; William Barclay Masterson vertical file (B-M393-wb); "Bat Masterson's Career," n.p.; Collins, *Indians' Last Fight*, p. 212; Coulter, "Adobe Walls Fight," p. 2; Curry, *Autobiography*, p. 5; DeArment, *Bat Masterson*; [Dixon], *Life and Adventures*, pp. 150, 207, 229, 241−43, 247; *Dodge City Times*, Nov. 3, 1877, p. 5, Oct. 13, 1877, p. 4, Oct. 20, 1877, p. 4, Oct. 27, 1877, p. 4, Nov. 10, 1877, p. 5, Jan. 12, 1878, p. 4, Jan. 19, 1878, p. 5, Feb. 2, 1878, p. 4, Feb. 9, 1878, p. 1, Feb. 16, 1878, p. 4, Mar. 30, 1878, p. 4, Apr. 13, 1878, p. 4, May 18, 1878, p. 2, June 15, 1878, p. 2, Aug. 3, 1878, p. 3, Aug. 17, 1878, p. 2, Oct. 12, 1878, p. 2, Nov. 30, 1878, p. 1; Johnson, "Fight at 'Dobe Walls," A-5; "A Kansas Killer," p. 5; *Leavenworth Daily Commercial*, July 26, 1874, p. 2; [Leonard], "Memorandum," p. 1; Lewis, "William Barclay Masterson," pp. 10−11; Little, "Battle of Adobe Walls," pp. 78−82, 84−85; William B. Masterson, sworn deposition, June 24, 1893, pp. 1−7; "Masterson's Death Brings Recollections: Famous Sports Writer in Battle of Adobe Walls," *Amarillo Daily News*, Nov. 5, 1921, sec. 1, p. 6; J. Wright Mooar to Johnson, Jan. 20, 1923, Andrew Johnson Papers; O'Connor, *Bat Masterson*; Phillips, "Battle of Adobe Walls," pp. 19, 32, 34; Rye, *Quirt and Spur*, p. 324; "Texas Frontier Veteran," p. 7; James A. Watson, "Battle of Adobe Walls," pp. 37, 72−75; Wright, *Dodge City*, pp. 201, 203, 299−303.

26. *Atchison Daily Champion*, July 10, 1874, p. 2; [Leonard], "Memorandum," pp. 1−2; Little, "Battle of Adobe Walls," p. 78; J. Wright Mooar to Johnson, Jan. 20, 1923, Andrew Johnson Papers; West, "Battle of Adobe Walls (1874)," pp. 19, 34.

27. Coulter, "Adobe Walls Fight," p. 2; Curry, *Autobiography*, pp. 5−6; "Billy" Dixon, "A Story of Adobe Walls," p. 4; [Dixon], *Life and Adventures*, pp. 203, 206, 207; William Dixon, sworn deposition, July 25, 1898, [lf. 3]; *Leavenworth Daily Commercial*, July 26, 1874, p. 2; [Leonard], "Memorandum," p. 1; Little, "Battle of Adobe Walls," pp. 77−78; McKinley, "J. W. McKinley's Narrative," p. 2; J. Wright Mooar, "Buffalo Days," 52, no. 3 (Mar., 1933): 28; Parker, *Personal Experiences*, p. 59; Phillips, "Battle of Adobe Walls," p. 19; Rye, *Quirt and Spur*, pp. 321−22; "Texas Frontier Veteran," p. 7; Van

Sickel, *A Story of Real Life*, p. 15; James A. Watson, "Battle of Adobe Walls," pp. 73–75; Wright, *Dodge City*, p. 202.

28. Coulter, "Adobe Walls Fight," p. 2; Curry, *Autobiography*, p. 5; [Dixon], *Life and Adventures*, pp. 176, 197, 207; Fred A. Hunt, "Adobe Walls Argument," p. 384; Johnson, "The Battle of Adobe Walls," p. 1; Johnson, "Fight at 'Dobe Walls," A-5; *Leavenworth Daily Commercial*, July 26, 1874, p. 2; [Leonard], "Memorandum," p. 1; Little, p. 77; William B. Masterson, sworn deposition, June 24, 1893, p. 2; J. Wright Mooar, "Buffalo Days," 52, no. 2 (Feb., 1933): 44; Rye, *Quirt and Spur*, p. 321; James A. Watson, "Battle of Adobe Walls," p. 74. The blacksmith's name has been spelled O'Keefe, O'Keef, Keef and Keif, the first being most common.

29. Collins, *Indians' Last Fight*, pp. 212, 217–18, 224; Curry, *Autobiography*, pp. 5, 7; [Dixon], *Life and Adventures*, pp. 200, 207, 217, 226–27, 234, 235–36, 241–43, 247; [Johnson], "Adobe Walls Survivor," p. 10; Johnson, "The Battle of Adobe Walls," pp. 2, 5–6; Johnson, "Fight at 'Dobe Walls," A-5; Little, "Battle of Adobe Walls," pp. 77, 84; McKinley, "J. W. McKinley's Narrative," p. 3; J. Wright Mooar, "Buffalo Days," 52, no. 3 (Mar., 1933): 24; Rath, *Early Ford County*, pp. 78, 83; Raymond, "Diary of a Dodge City Buffalo Hunter," p. 393; Van Sickel, *A Story of Real Life*, pp. 16–17; James A. Watson, "Battle of Adobe Walls," pp. 73–74.

30. *Atchison Daily Champion*, July 7, 1874, p. 2, July 10, 1874, p. 2; Coulter, "Adobe Walls Fight," p. 2; Curry, *Autobiography*, p. 6; "Billy" Dixon, "A Story of Adobe Walls," p. 4; [Dixon], *Life and Adventures*, pp. 208–209, 220, 227; Dubbs, "Personal Reminiscences," p. 59; "From the Front," p. 2; Hathaway, "Adventures of Buffalo Hunter," pp. 131, 133; Fred A. Hunt, "Adobe Walls Argument," p. 387; Johnson, "Fight at 'Dobe Walls," A-5; [Leonard], "Memorandum," p. 1; H. B. Leonard, "Fight at 'Dobe Walls," p. 7; Little, "Battle of Adobe Walls," pp. 78, 84; William B. Masterson, sworn deposition, June 24, 1893, p. 2; J. Wright Mooar, "Buffalo Days," 52, no. 3 (Mar., 1933): 24, 28; Parker, *Personal Experiences*, pp. 60–61; Riddle, "Indian Survivors," p. 13; Rye, *Quirt and Spur*, p. 322; Sargent, "War-Paint Off," pp. 1, 3; "Texas Frontier Veteran," p. 7; "Thousands Participate in Fiftieth Anniversary of the Famous Adobe Walls Fight," *Amarillo Daily News*, June 29, 1924, p. 10; Van Sickel, *A Story of Real Life*, p. 17; Wright, *Dodge City*, p. 202.

31. Coulter, "Adobe Walls Fight," p. 2; Curry, *Autobiography*, p. 5; [Dixon], *Life and Adventures*, pp. 201, 207, 215; Lake to Campbell, Mar. 20, 1951, W. S. Campbell Papers; *Leavenworth Daily Commercial*, July 26, 1874, p. 2; Little, "Battle of Adobe Walls," pp. 77–78, 81; William B. Masterson, sworn deposition, June 24, 1893, p. 5; James A. Watson, "Battle of Adobe Walls," p. 74; West, "Battle of Adobe Walls (1874)," p. 34. Variant spellings for Oscar Shepherd include Shepard and Sheppard, and other first names given include Thomas and Fred, although Oscar seems the correct choice and appears in nineteenth-century sources.

32. Coulter, "Adobe Walls Fight," p. 2; [Leonard], "Memorandum," pp. 1–2; "Tomorrow Is Anniversary of Battle of Adobe Walls," *Amarillo Globe*, June 26, 1935, p. 1.

33. Coulter, "Adobe Walls Fight," p. 2; Curry, *Autobiography*, p. 5; [Dixon], *Life and Adventures*, p. 207; Larry Freeman, "Fate Brought Battle of Adobe Walls Instead of Massacre by Indians," *Hutchison Herald*, Nov. 17, 1929, p. 17; Johnson, "The Battle of Adobe Walls," p. 2; Johnson, "Fight at 'Dobe Walls," A-5; *Leavenworth Daily Commercial*, July 26, 1874, p. 2; Little, "Battle of Adobe Walls," pp. 78, 81; Rye, *Quirt and Spur*, pp. 319–26; James A. Watson, "Battle of Adobe Walls," p. 74; West, "Battle of Adobe Walls (1874)," pp. 19, 34.

34. Curry, *Autobiography*, p. 5; [Dixon], *Life and Adventures*, p. 207; [Leonard], "Memorandum," p. 2; Little, "Battle of Adobe Walls," p. 78; "Texas Frontier Veteran," p. 7.

35. *Atchison Daily Champion*, July 7, 1874, p. 2, July 10, 1874, p. 2; George W. Brown, "Life and Adventures of George W. Brown: Soldier, Pioneer, Scout, Plainsman, and Buffalo Hunter," ed. William E. Connelley, *Collections of the Kansas State Historical Society* 17 (1926–28): 115; Connelley, "In Relation to the Visit," pp. 1–2, 5; Coulter, "Adobe Walls Fight," p. 2; Curry, *Autobiography*, pp. 5–6; [Dixon], *Life and Adventures*, pp. 207, 212, 221, 227; "From the Front," p. 2; Hathaway, "Adventures of Buffalo Hunter," p. 131; Johnson, "The Fight at 'Dobe Walls," A-5; [Leonard], "Memorandum," pp. 1–2; H. B. Leonard, "Fight at 'Dobe Walls," p. 7; Little, "Battle of Adobe Walls," pp. 78–79, 84; William B. Masterson, sworn deposition, June 24, 1893, p. 2; J. Wright Mooar, "Buffalo Days," 52, no. 3 (Mar., 1933): 24, 28; Raymond, "Diary of a Dodge City Buffalo Hunter," p. 384; "Texas Frontier Veteran," p. 7; "Thousands Participate," p. 10; James A. Watson, "Battle of Adobe Walls," pp. 74, 76; Wright, *Dodge City*, p. 202.

36. Coulter, "Adobe Walls Fight," p. 2; Curry, *Autobiography*, p. 5; [Dixon], *Life and Adventures*, p. 207; *Leavenworth Daily Commerical*, July 26, 1874, p. 2; Little, "Battle of Adobe Walls," p. 77; Quanah, "Told in Signs & English," p. 15; Rye, *Quirt and Spur*, pp. 321–22; James A. Watson, "Battle of Adobe Walls," pp. 36–37, 72–76.

37. Coulter, "Adobe Walls Fight," p. 2; Curry, *Autobiography*, p. 5; [Dixon], *Life and Adventures*, pp. 201, 207; Johnson, "Fight at 'Dobe Walls," A-5; *Leavenworth Daily Commercial*, July 26, 1874, p. 2; [Leonard], "Memorandum," p. 1; Little, "Battle of Adobe Walls," pp. 77–78; "Texas Frontier Veteran," p. 7; James A. Watson, "Battle of Adobe Walls," pp. 74–75. Johnson, who spoke English as his second language, remembered Welsh as "Tom Wells."

38. Dr. Branham to Richardson, Feb. 16, 1937, "Buffalo, the Frontier, the Indians" notebook, pp. 288–90, Carl Coke Rister Papers.

39. "Battle of 'Dobe Walls, Five-Day Fight with Comanche Band, Thrilling Remembrance of John Clinton, Abilene's Pioneer Police Chief," *Fort Worth Star-Telegram*, Sept. 24, 1916, n.p.; George W. Conover, *Sixty Years in Southwest Oklahoma or the Autobiography of George W. Conover . . .* , p. 82; "Desperate Fighting at Adobe Walls," *Frontier Times* 1, no. 12 (Sept., 1924): 1–4; J. Marvin Hunter, Sr., "The Battle of Adobe Walls," *Frontier Times* 24, no. 7 (Apr., 1947): 380–83; J. Wright Mooar to Johnson, Jan. 20, 1923, Andrew Johnson Papers; Traylor, "Attack on 'Adobe Walls'," p. 14.

40. John Lee, "California Man Says He Was Trapped with 27 at Adobe Walls by Indians," *Amarillo Daily News*, Aug. 27, 1925, p. 7.

41. R. T. Alexander to McClure, interview May 10, 1958, [lf. 3]; Mrs. Clyde Attebury, "The Birth of the Panhandle," TS n.d., pp. 1–5, Mrs. Clyde Attebury Papers; Collinson to Bugbee, Nov. 15, 1936, Harold Bugbee Papers; *Dodge City Times*, Apr. 28. 1877, p. 4, May 19, 1877, p. 4, May 26, 1877, p. 4, June 9, 1877, p. 4, June 23, 1877, p. 8, Sept. 15, 1877, p. 4, Sept. 22, 1877, p. 2, Jan. 12, 1878, p. 5, June 29, 1878, p. 2; Dubbs, "Personal Reminiscences," pp. 29–99; Emanuel Dubbs, "Pioneer Days in the Panhandle," *Frontier Times* 2, no. 4 (Jan., 1925): 4–7; Emanuel Dubbs, "Trials and Tribulations of a Buffalo Hunter," *Frontier Times* 28, no. 11 (Aug., 1951): 324–27; "First Wheeler Judge," *Frontier Times* 9, no. 10 (July, 1932): 448; Haley, *Charles Goodnight*, p. 359; Johnson, "The Battle of Adobe Walls," p. 7; Nita Kountz, "The First Judge in the Panhandle," *Frontier Times* 4, no. 7 (Apr., 1927): 5–8; Paddock, ed., *Twentieth Century History* II, 381–82; "Panhandle Pioneer Will Lecture Here," *Amarillo Daily News*, June 8, 1912, p. 8; Raymond, "Diary of a Dodge City Buffalo Hunter," pp. 376, 379; West, "Battle of Adobe Walls (1874)," p. 13.

42. Collins, *Indians' Last Fight*, p. 213; Johnson, "Fight at 'Dobe Walls," A-5; Phillips, "Battle of Adobe Walls," p. 32; "Texas Frontier Veteran," p. 7; Wright, *Dodge City*, p. 202.

43. Coulter, "Adobe Walls Fight," p. 2.

44. "Adobe Walls. Beeson Museum. April 15, 1935," TS, Apr. 15, 1935, Adobe Walls vertical file; "Adobe Wells [*sic*] Battle Veteran Tells Story," *Sunday Topeka Daily Capital*, June 17, 1934, B-6; Olive K. Dixon to Masters, Feb. 20, 1935, Joseph Masters Collection.

45. John Otterby (Chief Lean Elk), "Early Recollections of the Panhandle," 1940, pp. 1–3, John Otterby (Chief Lean Elk) Papers.

46. "Cator Bros. Account," [Feb., 1878], 3 lvs., Robert H. Cator Papers; Collins, *Indians' Last Fight*, pp. 212, 214, 217, 219, 226, 230; J. Evetts Haley, "Jim East—Trail Hand and Cowboy," *Panhandle-Plains Historical Review* 4 (1931): 47; Otterby, "Early Recollections," p. 1.

47. Coulter, "Adobe Walls Fight," p. 2; *Leavenworth Daily Commercial*, July 26, 1874, p. 2.

48. Fred A. Hunt, "Adobe Walls Argument," p. 384.

49. Collins, *Indians' Last Fight*, pp. 212, 230.

50. Little, "Battle of Adobe Walls," p. 78; West, "Battle of Adobe Walls (1874)," p. 19.

51. Hathaway, "Adventures of Buffalo Hunter," pp. 130, 131.

52. Fred A. Hunt, "Adobe Walls Argument," p. 384.

53. Curry, *Autobiography*, p. 5.

54. Fred A. Hunt, "Adobe Walls Argument," p. 384.

55. M. K. Wyatt is identified as a battle participant in George W. Conover's 1927 book, *Sixty Years in Southwest Oklahoma*, but his own account shows that he was merely a journalist recounting the story. Conover, *Sixty Years*, p. 80; M. K. Wyatt, "Battle of Adobe Walls: Twenty-Eight White Men and One Woman against 800 Indians," *Drummond Times*, June 18, 1926, magazine section, p. 2.

Notes to Chapter 5

1. *Atchison Daily Champion*, July 10, 1874, p. 2.

2. Collins, *Indians' Last Fight*, p. 222; [Dixon], *Life and Adventures*, p. 228; [Leonard], "Memorandum," p. 1; McKinley, "J. W. McKinley's Narrative," p. 3; Rye, *Quirt and Spur*, p. 324; "Texas Frontier Veteran," p. 7.

3. "Texas Frontier Veteran," p. 7.

4. James H. Cator, sworn deposition, Oct. 10, 1892, pp. 21, 25–26, 30; Collins, *Indians' Last Fight*, p. 223; [Dixon], *Life and Adventures*, pp. 230–31; Van Sickel, *A Story of Real Life*, p. 15; V. H. Whitlock (Ol' Waddy), *Cowboy Life on the Llano Estacado*, p. 5.

5. Collins, *Indians' Last Fight*, p. 223; [Dixon], *Life and Adventures*, pp. 230–31; "Texas Frontier Veteran," p. 7.

6. *Atchison Daily Champion*, July 10, 1874, p. 2; Collins, *Indians' Last Fight*, pp. 223–24; Coulter, "Adobe Walls Fight," p. 2; Curry, *Autobiography*, p. 7; [Dixon], *Life and Adventures*, pp. 235–36; "Dodge Citizens Find Grave," p. 8; "Dodge Men Find Long Lost Grave," pp. 1, 7; [Johnson], "Adobe Walls Survivor," p. 10; Johnson, "The Battle of Adobe Walls," p. 5; Andrew Johnson, sworn deposition, Oct. 10, 1892, p. 41½; "A Kansas Killer," p. 5; Little, "Battle of Adobe Walls," p. 84; McKinley, "J. W. McKinley's Narrative," p. 3; William B. Masterson, sworn deposition, June 24, 1893, p. 2; Rye, *Quirt and Spur*, p. 324; "Texas Frontier Veteran," p. 7; Van Sickel, *A Story of Real Life*, pp. 16–17; Wright, *Dodge City*, p. 202.

7. James H. Cator, sworn deposition, Oct. 10, 1892, pp. 21, 25–26.

8. Ibid., pp. 21, 25–26, 30; [Dixon], *Life and Adventures*, p. 229–30; Johnson,

"Battle of Adobe Walls," p. 5; Andrew Johnson, sworn deposition, Oct. 10, 1892, p. 35.

9. McGinnis, *The Promised Land*, p. 48; Whitlock, *Cowboy Life*, p. 5.

10. "Adobe Walls Survivor Says Fight More Important than San Jacinto," *Amarillo Daily News*, July 13, 1936, p. 1; *Atchison Daily Champion*, July 10, 1874, p. 2; James H. Cator, sworn deposition, Oct. 10, 1892, p. 20; John R. Cook, "Incidents of the Buffalo Range," *Frontier Times* 20, no. 9 (June, 1943): 162–63; Cox to McConnell, interview, n.d., pp. 3–4; Curry, *Autobiography*, p. 7; [Dixon], *Life and Adventures*, p. 231; "Dodge Citizens Find Grave," p. 8; [Johnson], "Adobe Walls Survivor," p. 10; Johnson, "The Battle of Adobe Walls," p. 5; Johnson "Fight at 'Dobe Walls," A-5; Andrew Johnson, sworn deposition, Oct. 10, 1892, pp. 35, 44; James Langton, sworn deposition, Oct. 10, 1892, p.4; [Leonard], "Memorandum," p. 1; Little, "Battle of Adobe Walls," p. 84; McKinley, "J. W. McKinley's Narrative," p. 4; J. Wright Mooar, "Buffalo Days," 52, no. 3 (Mar., 1933): 28; Rye, *Quirt and Spur*, p. 324; "Texas Frontier Veteran," p. 7; Tilghman to Campbell, Mar. 23, 1952, W. S. Campbell Papers; Van Sickel, *A Story of Real Life*, pp. 14–15, 18–19; James A. Watson, "Battle of Adobe Walls," p. 76; Whitlock, *Cowboy Life*, p. 5.

11. James H. Cator, sworn deposition, Oct. 11, 1892, pp. 3½–4, 13.

12. McGinnis, *The Promised Land*, pp. 49–51.

13. Dick Bussell, "Hunting Buffalo in the Panhandle," TS, [ca. 1925], p. 1, Dick Bussell Papers; Collins, *Indians' Last Fight*, pp. 228–29; Hathaway, "Adventures of Buffalo Hunter," pp. 133–34.

14. Connelley, "In Relation to the Visit," pp. 2–3; Cox to McConnell, interview, n.d., p. 4; [Dixon], *Life and Adventures*, p. 248; "Dodge Citizens Find Grave," p. 8; "Dodge City Residents Find Grave at Adobe Walls; Old Plains Battle Is Recalled," *Amarillo Daily News*, Jan. 28, 1923, sec. 4, p. 1; Hyde, *Life of George Bent*, p. 360; J. J. Long, "My Indian Expeditions," TS, n.d., [lf. 1], J. J. Long Papers; McAllister to Haley, interview, July 1, 1926, p. 1; McFadden, "Thompson McFadden's Diary," p. 221; Miles, *Personal Recollections*, p. 163; [Untitled drawing of corral gate], 1 lf; J. Phelps White to J. Evetts Haley, interview, Jan. 15, 1927, J. Phelps White Papers. Probably the first published account of the decapitation appeared in "From the Front," Topeka *Commonwealth*, Aug. 8, 1874, p. 2. It reads: "Twelve Indian heads, minus hair, feathers and other *thum nim*, now adorn the gateposts of the corral. The collection is diversified by the *caput* of a negro, who was killed among the Indians with a can of yeast powders in his hand. He didn't 'raise' worth a cent after that."

15. *Atchison Daily Champion*, July 10, 1874, p. 2; James H. Cator, sworn deposition, Oct. 10, 1892, p. 22; James H. Cator, sworn deposition, Oct. 11, 1892, p. 13; Cox to McConnell, interview, n.d., p. 5; [Dixon], *Life and Adventures*, pp. 233–34; Andrew Johnson, sworn deposition, Oct. 10, 1892, pp. 36, 42; Andrew Johnson, sworn deposition, Oct. 11, 1892, p. 20; James Langton, sworn deposition, Jan. 28, 1896, p. 3; [Leonard], "Memorandum," p. 1; H. B. Leonard, "Fight at 'Dobe Walls," p. 7; Little, "Battle of Adobe Walls," p. 84; McKinley, "J. W. McKinley's Narrative," pp. 3–4; Rye, *Quirt and Spur*, pp. 324–25; "Texas Frontier Veteran," p. 7; Van Sickel, *A Story of Real Life*, pp. 18–19.

16. *Atchison Daily Champion*, July 10, 1874, p. 2; *Leavenworth Daily Times*, July 10, 1874, p. 4; *New York Times*, July 14, 1874, p. 5.

17. *Atchison Daily Champion*, July 7, 1874, p. 2, July 10, 1874, p. 2; [Dixon], *Life and Adventures*, pp. 231–33; Glenn, "Shelton [*sic*] Manuscript," p. 9; Johnson, "Andrew Johnson," p. 6; Andrew Johnson, sworn deposition, Oct. 10, 1892, p. 35; McGinnis, *The Promised Land*, p.57; McKinley, "J. W. McKinley's Narrative," p. 4; William B. Masterson, sworn deposition, June 24, 1893, p. 3; J. Wright Mooar, "Buffalo Days," 52, no. 3 (Mar.,

1933): 28; Charles Rath, sworn deposition, Oct. 10, 1892, pp. 5, 12; Charles Rath and Co. and Myers and Leonard to Osborn, July 8, 1874, T. A. Osborn Papers; Rye, *Quirt and Spur*, pp. 324–25; Whitlock, *Cowboy Life*, p. 5.

18. Cox to McConnell, interview, n.d., p. 3; [Johnson], "Adobe Walls Survivor," p. 10; Johnson, "Fight at 'Dobe Walls," A-5; James Langton, sworn deposition, Jan. 28, 1896, p. 4; H. B. Leonard, "Fight at 'Dobe Walls," p. 7; R. M. Wright, sworn deposition, Oct. 10, 1892, p. 15.

19. [Dixon], *Life and Adventures*, p. 235; Dubbs, "Personal Reminiscences," p. 47; [Johnson], "Adobe Walls Survivor," p. 10; Little, "Battle of Adobe Walls," p. 84; McGinnis, *The Promised Land*, p. 50; Van Sickel, *A Story of Real Life*, pp. 13–14.

20. Hathaway, "Adventures of Buffalo Hunter," p. 132; [Johnson], "Adobe Walls Survivor," p. 10; Johnson, "The Battle of Adobe Walls," p. 2.

21. Cox to McConnell, interview, n.d., pp. 3–4; Curry, *Autobiography*, p. 7; [Johnson], "Adobe Walls Survivor," p. 10; Johnson, "The Battle of Adobe Walls," p. 5; Johnson, "Fight at 'Dobe Walls," A-5; Andrew Johnson, sworn deposition, Oct. 10, 1892, pp. 35, 44; James Langton, sworn deposition, Jan. 28, 1896, p. 4; [Leonard], "Memorandum," p. 1; Little, "Battle of Adobe Walls," p. 84; Rye, *Quirt and Spur*, p. 324; Van Sickel, *A Story of Real Life*, p. 19.

22. [Johnson], "Adobe Walls Survivor," p. 10; Johnson, "The Battle of Adobe Walls," pp. 5–6.

23. Johnson, "The Battle of Adobe Walls," p. 6.

24. James Langton, sworn deposition, Jan. 28, 1896, pp. 3–5; "Petition," Nov. 13, 1893, [lf. 1], U.S. Court of Claims, Indian Depredation Case Files, Case 10102, RG 123, National Archives; Charles Rath, sworn deposition, Oct. 10, 1892, pp. 3, 8.

25. [Dixon], *Life and Adventures*, p. 231; [Johnson], "Adobe Walls Survivor," p. 10; Johnson, "The Battle of Adobe Walls," p. 5.

26. [Dixon], *Life and Adventures*, pp. 243–45; *Leavenworth Daily Commercial*, July 26, 1874, p. 2; McGinnis, *The Promised Land*, p. 57; Van Sickel, *A Story of Real Life*, p. 19. For another account of Charlie Sharp's death and burial, see Hathaway, "Adventures of Buffalo Hunter," p. 134. Because the list of Hanrahan party members is the only contemporary source about any large number of hide men at Adobe Walls at one time, it is especially significant. Their names, as spelled in the original newspaper report, are: James Hanrahan, M. Welsh, Wm. Dixon, Arth Abercrombie, Frank Brown, Wm. Ogge, Wm. Thornhill, O. Sheppard, M. Coffee, Bat Masterson, John Clark, Martin Gallaway, George Aiken, Sam Smith, Joe Plummer, Jack Williams, James Carlyle, Henry Wertz, Joshua Fredericks, J. W. McKinley, Joseph Craig, W. W. Murphy, George Wilkes, Chas. Wright, John McCabe, Phillip Cisk, Sylvester Lilly, Tom. O. Keefe, Chas. O'Brien. Rankin Moore, Dave Campbell, Clarke Teneyke, Jim Saunders, Wm. H. Johnston, and Hiram Watson. *Leavenworth Daily Commercial*, July 26, 1874, p. 2.

27. [Johnson], "Adobe Walls Survivor," p. 10; Johnson, "The Battle of Adobe Walls," pp. 5–6; Andrew Johnson, sworn deposition, Oct. 10, 1892, pp. 36, 44; McGinnis, *The Promised Land*, p. 57; James Langton, sworn deposition, Jan. 28, 1896, pp. 4–6, 8–9; Charles Rath, sworn deposition, Oct. 10, 1892, p. 7; Van Sickel, *A Story of Real Life*, p. 19.

28. [Dixon], *Life and Adventures*, pp. 241–43. For a slightly different interpretation from Billy Dixon, see Olive K. Dixon, *Life of "Billy" Dixon*, pp. 187–89.

29. McGinnis, *The Promised Land*, pp. 54–56.

30. DeArment, *Bat Masterson*, pp. 46–48; *Leavenworth Daily Commercial*, July 26, 1874, p. 2; O'Connor, *Bat Masterson*, pp. 60–61.

31. Charles Rath, sworn deposition, Oct. 10, 1892, pp. 5–7, 12–12¼; R. M. Wright, sworn deposition, Oct. 10, 1892, pp. 15–18.

32. Charles Rath and Co. and Myers and Leonard to Osborn, July 8, 1874, T. A. Osborn Papers; Charles Rath and Co. and Myers and Leonard to Gov. Osborn, July 9, 1874, telegram, T. A. Osborn Papers.

33. Pope to Gov. Osborn, July 8, 1874, telegram, T. A. Osborn Papers. For further examples of Gen. Pope's critical attitude toward the traders and hunters at Adobe Walls, see Richard N. Ellis, *General Pope and U.S. Indian Policy*, pp. 181–84; *Emporia News*, July 17, 1874, p. 2; *New York Times*, July 15, 1874, p. 5.

34. Sheridan to Gen. Pope, Aug. 21, 1874, Philip Henry Sheridan Papers.

35. Osborn to Rail Road Agent, July 9, 1874, telegram, T. A. Osborn Papers.

36. [Dixon], *Life and Adventures*, p. 244; Johnson, "Andrew Johnson," p. 6; James Langton, sworn deposition, Jan. 28, 1896, pp. 4–5; Charles Rath, sworn deposition, Oct. 10, 1892, pp. 5–7, 12–12¼; R. M. Wright, sworn deposition, Oct. 10, 1892, pp. 15–18.

37. [Dixon], *Life and Adventures*, pp. 243–44; *Leavenworth Daily Times*, July 19, 1874, p. 6; John Wesley Mooar to Dear Sister, July 7, 1874, John Wesley Mooar Papers. S. S. Van Sickel reported an unusual occurrence not noted by others who waited at Adobe Walls for the relief party. Before it came into the post, "a party arrived from Dodge City with a supply of guns and ammunition, bringing with them a very fine looking woman." Van Sickel, *A Story of Real Life*, pp. 19–20.

38. James H. Cator, sworn deposition, Oct. 10, 1892, p. 22; James H. Cator, sworn deposition, Oct. 11, 1892, p. 14; "From the Front," p. 2; [Johnson], "Adobe Walls Survivor," p. 10; Johnson, "Andrew Johnson," p. 6; Johnson, "The Battle of Adobe Walls," p. 6; Johnson, "Fight at 'Dobe Walls," A-5; Andrew Johnson, sworn deposition, Oct. 10, 1892, pp. 36, 38, 44–45, 49; Little, "Battle of Adobe Walls," p. 84; Charles Rath, sworn deposition, Oct. 10, 1892, pp. 5–7, 12–12¼; "Texas Frontier Veteran," p. 7; R. M. Wright, sworn deposition, Oct. 10, 1892, pp. 15–18. Not all the wagons in the caravan back to Dodge City were loaded with hides or merchandise. Others carried only hunters' supplies and hides. Those of the S. S. Van Sickel outfit, for example, hunted "along the way to get loads of hides to take with us" and tarried along the Cimarron River before finally returning to Dodge. Van Sickel, *A Story of Real Life*, p. 20.

39. [Dixon], *Life and Adventures*, p. 247; "From the Front," p. 2; [Johnson], "Adobe Walls Survivor," p. 10; C. E. Jones to Sheffy, interview, Dec. 31, 1929, p. 2; McAllister to Haley, interview, July 1, 1926, p. 2; [Leonard], "Memorandum," p. 2; William Dixon, sworn deposition, July 25, 1898, [lvs. 5–6].

40. Among the accounts of the Buffalo War are: R. C. Crane, "The Settlement in 1874–5 of Indian Troubles in West Texas," *West Texas Historical Association Year Book* 1 (1925): 3–14; M. L. Crimmins, "General Nelson A. Miles in Texas," *West Texas Historical Association Year Book* 23 (1947): 36–45; James L. Haley, *The Buffalo War*; William H. Leckie, *The Military Conquest of the Southern Plains*; William H. Leckie, "The Red River War 1874–1875," *Panhandle-Plains Historical Review* 29 (1956): 78–100.

41. For data on Lt. Frank Dwight Baldwin, later major general and holder of two Congressional Medals of Honor, see, e.g.: Frank D. Baldwin to Thomas F. Dawson, interview, Mar. 28, 1922, Frank Dwight Baldwin Papers; Frank D. Baldwin, *Memoirs of the Late Frank D. Baldwin, Major General, U.S.A.*, ed. Alice Blackwood Baldwin; "General Frank D. Baldwin, 81, Famed Warrior of Old Indian Fighting Days in West, Dies," *Rocky Mountain News*, Apr. 23, 1923, pp. 1–2; Francis B. Heitman, comp., *Historical Register and Dictionary of the United States Army, from Its Organization, September 29, 1789, to March 2, 1903* I, 185–86; Daniel D. Holt, "Lieutenant Frank D. Baldwin and the Indian Territory Expedition of 1874," *Trail Guide* 10, no. 3 (Sept., 1965): 1–20; "Memo-

randum of Military Services of Brigadier General Frank D. Baldwin, U.S. Army," TS, n.d., Frank D. Baldwin Papers.

42. [Dixon], *Life and Adventures*, pp. 246–48.

43. Frank D. Baldwin, Diary Transcript for Aug. 19–20, 1874, [lvs. 1–2]; [Dixon], *Life and Adventures*, pp. 246–50; Holt, "Lieutenant Frank D. Baldwin," p. 6; Miles to Assistant Adjutant General, Mar. 4, 1875, Consolidated File 2815–1874; Miles, *Personal Reminiscences*, p. 166. The story of the attack on Tobe Robinson and George Huffman (also spelled Hoffman) has been retold often. For some of the versions see McAllister to Haley, interview, July 1, 1926, p. 2; Dubbs, "Personal Reminiscences," pp. 63–64; Little, "Battle of Adobe Walls," p. 84; McGinnis, *The Promised Land*, p. 56; Rye, *Quirt and Spur*, pp. 324–25. For data on Tobe Robinson, whom Fred Leonard had left in charge of the men remaining at the post after the relief party departed, see [Leonard], "Memorandum," p. 2; J. Wright Mooar to Haley, interviews, Nov. 25, 1927, and Jan. 4, 1928, p. 17; J. Wright Mooar to Vandale, Haley, and Chesley, interview, Mar. 2, 3, and 4, 1939; Millie Jones Porter, ed., *Memory Cups of Panhandle Pioneers*, p. 121.

44. Frank D. Baldwin, Diary Transcript for Aug. 19–20, 1874, [lf. 4].

45. Farnsworth to Field Adjutant, Sept. 23, 1874, Consolidated File 2815–1874.

46. [Dixon], *Life and Adventures*, p. 251; William Dixon, sworn deposition, July 25, 1898, [lf. 5]; J. Wright Mooar to Vandale, Haley, and Chesley, interview, Mar. 2, 3, and 4, 1939; J. Wright Mooar, "Buffalo Days," 52, no. 3 (Mar., 1933): 28; Charles Rath, sworn deposition, Oct. 10, 1892, p. 7; Rye, *Quirt and Spur*, p. 325; "Texas Frontier Veteran," p. 7. Portions of this description are based on archeological evidence.

47. [Dixon], *Life and Adventures*, pp. 251–52; Miles to Assistant Adjutant General, Mar. 4, 1875, Consolidated File 2815–1874. The desecration of Indian remains and theft of blankets from the burial sites is confirmed in Scott's marginal notes added to the transcript of his 1897 interview with Quanah. Quanah, "Told in English & Signs," p. 15.

48. [Dixon], *Life and Adventures*, pp. 252–53.

49. This J. Frederick may have been the former hide man Joshua Fredericks, a member of the Hanrahan party, which departed the post before the relief party arrived. *Leavenworth Daily Commercial*, July 26, 1874, p. 2.

50. McFadden, "Thompson McFadden's Diary," pp. 220–21.

51. James H. Cator, sworn deposition, Oct. 10, 1892, pp. 23–24, 29. After about twenty years, James H. Cator remembered being at Adobe Walls in Sept., 1874, but evidence indicates that he and his brother must have been there at a slightly later date.

52. William B. Masterson, sworn deposition, June 24, 1893, p. 4.

53. J. J. Long, "My Indian Expeditions," J. J. Long Papers, [lf. 1].

54. Farnsworth to Field Adjutant, Wingate Battalion, 8th Cavalry, Nov. 7, 1874, Consolidated File 2815–1874.

55. John R. Cook, *The Border and the Buffalo: An Untold Story of the Southwest Plains*, pp. 76–80.

56. Miles to Assistant Adjutant General, Department of the Missouri, Dec. 5, 1874, Consolidated File 2815–1874; Miles to Assistant Adjutant General, Mar. 4, 1874, Consolidated File 2815–1874.

Notes to Chapter 6

1. Quinn to Barde, Jan. 6, 1911, Dixon, Billy vertical file.

2. George A. Simpson to Pearl Spaugh, interview, July 27, 1936, pp. 1–3, Pearl Spaugh Papers.

3. Brown, *Life and Adventures*, pp. 124–25.

4. Edith Shields, "James E. May," TS, p. 3, Edith Shields Papers.

5. Hull to Johnson, Sept. 2, 1924, Andrew Johnson Papers. For sheepherding in the Panhandle in the 1870s and 1880s, see Paul H. Carlson, "Panhandle Pastores: Early Sheepherding in the Texas Panhandle," *Panhandle-Plains Historical Review* 53 (1980): 1–15.

6. Coffee to McClure, Feb. 5, 1949, H. C. Coffee Papers; Cynthia Lumpkin, "The Turkey Track Ranch," TS, n.d., n.p., Cynthia Lumpkin Papers; Orville Howell Nelson to J. Evetts Haley, interview, Feb. 26, 1927, pp. 1–2, Judge O. H. Nelson Papers; "Panhandle Postal History," *Panhandle-Plains Historical Review* 33 (1960): 125; Jim P. Wilson to J. Evetts Haley, interview, Jan. 1, 1928, pp. 4–5, Jim B. Wilson Papers. Although an 1877 article appeared in the *Dodge City Times* describing Adobe Walls as "a fine settlement" with "some twenty families," this seems to have been a bit of promotional writing designed to encourage settlers to move into the area. *Dodge City Times*, Sept. 29, 1877, p. 5.

7. "Dodge to Adobe Walls Once a 9-Day Trip," *Dodge City Daily Globe*, May 10, 1933, p. 5.

8. W. S. Carter to Haley, interview, Dec. 28, 1945, p. 5; Arthur Hecht, comp., *Postal History in the Texas Panhandle*, p. 32; Isaacs, "Billy Dixon," p. 373.

9. Alexander Schneider to J. Evetts Haley, interview, July 15, 1926, p. 1, Alexander Schneider Papers.

10. "Adobe Walls, Site of Famous Indian Battle, Will Be Preserved," *Amarillo Daily News*, July 24, 1930, p. 13; *Constructive Action Taken on "Adobe Walls Field" June 27th, 1924* (n.p., [1924]), handbill; Joseph A. Hill, *The Panhandle-Plains Historical Society and Its Museum*, p. 17; Pollyanna B. Hughes, "Adobe Walls May Rise Again," *Texas Parade* 15, no.5 (Oct., 1954): 34–36; "Mrs. Dixon Lauds Move to Restore Old Adobe Walls," *Amarillo Daily News*, June 28, 1935, p. 1; "Panhandle Photoplay Is Being Considered," *Amarillo Daily News*, Oct. 9, 1914, p. 8.

11. Connelley, "In Relation to the Visit," pp. 1–5; "Adobe Walls Fighters Here," *Miami Chief*, Dec. 7, 1922, p. 1; Olive K. Dixon to Anderson, Dec. 26, 1922, Olive K. Dixon Papers; "Dodge Citizens Find Grave," p. 8; "Dodge City Residents Find Grave," sec. 4, p. 1; "Dodge Men Find the Long Lost Grave," pp. 1, 7; Rath, *Early Ford County*, p. 83. For data on Tom Stauth, the prime figure in arranging the trip of Johnson and Bond to Texas in 1922, see "Death Takes Tom Stauth," *Dodge City Daily Globe*, May 24, 1960, p. 1.

12. "Association Is Formed at Adobe Walls Celebration," *Amarillo Daily News*, July 7, 1923, p. 5; "Adobe Walls Celebration Plans Continue; Hope to Get Funds for Monument," *Amarillo Daily News*, May 20, 1923, sec. 2, p. 6; "Adobe Walls Monument and Fiftieth Anniversary Picnic Plans Discussed at Pampa," *Amarillo Daily News*, Jan. 27, 1924, sec. 1, p. 1; Hill, *Panhandle-Plains Historical Society*, p. 23; T. E. Johnson, "Many Visit Adobe Walls: 2-Day Event Opens with Picnic and Barbecue," *Amarillo Daily News*, June 15, 1923, pp. 1, 5; "Many Speakers to Be Features at Adobe Walls," *Amarillo Daily News*, June 10, 1923, p. 1; "Picnic and Barbecue at Adobe Walls on June 14 and 15," *Randall County News*, May 24, 1923, p. 3.

13. "Adobe Walls Fund Has Been Half Pledged," *Amarillo Daily News*, Apr. 27, 1924, sec. 1, p. 10; "Adobe Walls Monument," sec. 1, p. 1; Olive K. Dixon to Johnson, May 25, 1924, Andrew Johnson Papers; "Monument to Heroes of Adobe Walls Battle," *Topeka Daily Capital*, June 22, 1924, B-6; "Unveiling Adobe Walls Monument Planned June 27," *Amarillo Daily News*, May 20, 1924, p. 8. In April, 1924, the cost of a new

Ford touring car was $295.00 FOB Detroit, Mich. Ford Motor Company advertisement, *Randall County News*, Apr. 10, 1924, p. 6.

14. "Thousands Participate," p. 10.

15. Olive K. Dixon to Johnson, Jan. 15, 1923; Olive K. Dixon to Johnson, May 8, 1923; Olive K. Dixon to Johnson, May 15, 1923; Olive K. Dixon to Johnson, Dec. 6, 1923; Olive K. Dixon to Johnson, May 25, 1924; Olive K. Dixon to Johnson, Aug. 19, 1924, all in Andrew Johnson Papers.

16. Olive K. Dixon to Johnson, May 25, 1924, Andrew Johnson Papers; [Panhandle-Plains Historical Society], *Don't Miss the Big Celebration June 27–28* . . . , handbill; "Thousands Participate," p. 10.

17. "Brothers Meet for First Time in Many Years," *Amarillo Daily News*, June 29, 1924, p. 10; Lloyd M. Brown to T. Lindsay Baker, telephone interview, June 6, 1979, TS notes in Brown—Arthur file, Adobe Walls research files; Olive K. Dixon, "The Celebration at Adobe Walls," [ca. June, 1924], pp. 1–3, Adobe Walls manuscript file; F. L. Dunn, Mayor of the City of Wichita, Kansas, to All to Whom These Presents Come, June 20, 1924, Wichita, Kansas, manuscript file; "Indian Dances Are Portrayed by Boy Scouts," *Amarillo Daily News*, June 29, 1924, p. 10; "Semi-Centennial of the Battle of Adobe Walls," *Chronicles of Oklahoma* 2, no. 4 (Dec., 1924): 402–404; John Sneed, "Monument at Adobe Walls Battleground, One of Two Survivors of Historic Fight and Officer Slain after Picture Taken," *Dallas Morning News*, Apr. 26, 1925, IV-10; "Thousands Participate," pp. 1, 10; "Twenty Beeves Are Barbecued to Feed Crowd," *Amarillo Daily News*, June 29, 1924, p. 10.

18. Olive K. Dixon, "The Celebration of Adobe Walls," p. 2; "Jim Barbour, Oldtimer Visits in Miami," *Miami Chief*, Sept. 11, 1924, p. 1; "Thousands Participate," p. 10.

19. Jackson to Johnson, late June, 1924, Andrew Johnson Papers.

20. Barbour to Johnson, July 2, 1924, Andrew Johnson Papers.

21. Rath, *Early Ford County*, p. 85; Schmidt, "It's Worth Remembering: Last Survivor," sec. 1, pp. 11, 15.

22. [Johnson], "Adobe Walls Survivor," p. 10.

23. "Adobe Walls Celebration on Thursday: Re-Burial of Colonel Billy Dixon to Be Feature of Historic Event," *Amarillo Daily News*, June 26, 1929, p. 1; "Adobe Walls Ceremony Plans June 27 Completed," *Miami Chief*, June 13, 1929, p. 1; "Billy Dixon Remains to Be Buried near Scene of Battle," *Amarillo Daily News*, May 6, 1929, p. 3; "Billy Dixon Rites to Feature Adobe Walls Celebration," *Amarillo Globe*, June 27, 1929, pp. 1, 2; "Col. Billy Dixon Gets Last Wish; Buried at Site of Adobe Walls," *Amarillo Daily News*, June 28, 1929, pp. 1, 15; A. B. McDonald, "The Recent Re-Burial in Texas of 'Billy' Dixon Recalls the Indian Fight at 'Dobe Walls," *Kansas City Star*, July 7, 1929, C-1; "Remove Body of Col. Dixon from Texline; Remains of Famed Indian Fighter to Be Reburied at Adobe Walls Today," *Amarillo Daily News*, June 27, 1929, pp. 1, 15.

24. "Adobe Walls Celebration to Be at Borger," *Amarillo Globe*, June 19, 1934, p. 1; "Adobe Walls Fete Is Set for Holiday: Historic Battle Recalled as Veterans Prepare to Assemble," *Amarillo Daily News*, June 11, 1934, p. 2; "Adobe Walls Fete Slated on July 4," *Amarillo Daily News*, May 16, 1934, p. 4; "'Indians!' Cries Billy Dixon to Comrades and 'Dobe Walls Fight Began—60 Years Ago Today," *Amarillo Daily News*, June 27, 1934, pp. 1, 11; Harry Montgomery, "Red Warriors Routed in 'Dobe Walls Fight 59 Years Ago Tuesday," *Amarillo Daily News*, June 28, 1933, p. 12; "Today Is Anniversary of Adobe Walls Battle," *Amarillo Globe*, June 27, 1934, p. 2; "Tomorrow Is Anniversary," p. 1.

25. "Comanche Indian Braves Want to Visit Historic Adobe Walls Battle Site; Only

Four Survive," *Amarillo Daily News*, Jan. 16, 1931, p. 8; "Comanches Here to Arrange for Three Lone Survivors of Adobe Walls to See Site," *Amarillo Daily News*, Feb. 12, 1931, p. 2; Hill, *Panhandle-Plains Historical Society*, p. 123; "Indian Survivors of Dobe Walls to Visit Old Scene," *Dodge City Daily Globe*, Jan. 20, 1931, p. 1; Riddle, "Indian Survivors," pp. 1, 13; Sargent, "War-Paint Off," pp. 1, 3; Jenna V. Stephenson, "History Professor Is Carried away by Indian Warriors," *Prairie*, May 9, 1939, pp. 1, 4.

26. "Adobe Walls Ceremonials' Success Assured as Merchants Back What Should Be Profitable Annual Event," *Borger Daily Herald*, Oct. 8, 1941, pp. 1, 2; "Adobe Walls Ceremonies Being Staged by Director of Coronada [*sic*] Entrada," *Borger Daily Herald*, Oct. 13, 1941, p. 1; "Adobe Walls Pageantry of Yester-Year Re-Enacted: Borger Jammed for Gala Event," *Amarillo Daily News*, Oct. 18, 1941, p. 10; "Borger Takes on a Gala Appearance as Intensive Preparations Get under Way for Big Indian Celebration Next Week," *Borger Daily Herald*, Oct. 10, 1941, p. 1; "Cast of 200 Indians to Appear in Adobe Walls Pageantry," *Amarillo Daily News*, Oct. 3, 1941, p. 7; "Celebration Is Advertised over Entire State," *Borger Daily Herald*, Oct. 8, 1941, p. 14; "Chief Baldwin Parker, Son of Quanah Parker, Will Bring His Family to Borger Celebration," *Borger Daily Herald*, Oct. 10, 1941, p. 2; Olive K. Dixon, "Indians Visit Adobe Walls Battle Site," *Amarillo Sunday News-Globe*, Apr. 20, 1941, sec. 1, p. 5; "Gala Ceremonies at Borger Today," *Amarillo Sunday News-Globe*, Oct. 19, 1941, sec. 1, p. 1; Mark Hamilton, *1941 Adobe Walls Indian Ceremonials: Drama from the Historical Cavalcade of the Frontier West, Borger, Texas, October 17–18–19, Huber Stadium, 8:00 P.M.*, n.p.; "Hutchinson County Fair Association Sponsors Adobe Walls Ceremonials," *Borger Daily Herald*, Oct. 5, 1941, sec. 1, p. 6; "Indian War Whoops Will Ring out in Borger for Adobe Walls Party," *Amarillo Daily News*, Oct. 16, 1941, p. 16; "Indians Arrive at 'Dobe Walls,'" *Amarillo Daily News*, Oct. 17, 1941, p. 1; "Indians Arrive Today in Preparation for Borger's Most Colorful Celebration," *Borger Daily Herald*, Oct. 16, 1941, pp. 1, 5; "Indians Confer Here for Pageant Plans," *Borger Daily Herald*, Oct. 7, 1941, p. 1; "Indians Ready for Adobe Walls Ceremonials Opening on Friday," *Amarillo Daily News*, Oct. 15, 1941, p. 11; "Indians Receive Enthusiastic Reception on Trips Advertising Big Adobe Walls Ceremonials," *Borger Daily Herald*, Oct. 14, 1941, pp. 1, 6; "Motor Caravans to Advertise Indian Pageant," *Borger Daily Herald*, Oct. 8, 1941, p. 2; "Survivor of First Adobe Walls Fight Here for Pageant," *Borger Daily Herald*, Oct. 19, 1941, sec. 1, p. 1; "Tentative Plans Are Mapped for Adobe Walls Celebration," *Amarillo Sunday News-Globe*, Aug. 31, 1941, p. 8; "Thousands Here for Indian Ceremonials: Colorful Parade Launches Three Day Celebration," *Borger Daily Herald*, Oct. 17, 1941, pp. 1, 2; "Tom-Toms, War Whoops and Indians Give Children Thrill of a Lifetime," *Borger Daily Herald*, Oct. 12, 1941, p. 1.

27. Bill Freemon, "Impressive Rites Dedicate Adobe Walls Monument," *Amarillo Daily News*, Oct. 20, 1941, pp. 1, 9; "Indian Ceremonials End Stamped Definite Success," *Borger Daily Herald*, Oct. 20, 1941, pp. 1, 2; "Indian Ceremonials End Today: Dedication at Adobe Walls Site, Pageant Slated," *Borger Daily Herald*, Oct. 19, 1941, pp. 1, 5.

28. John H. Bass, "In the Land of the Comanches," TS, n.d., pp. 1–14, John H. Bass Papers; "Battle of Adobe Walls 74 Years Ago Today," *Amarillo Sunday News-Globe*, June 27, 1948, sec. 2, p. 21; Don Chadsey, "Mark 75th Anniversary of Adobe Walls Fight," *Amarillo Sunday News-Globe*, June 26, 1949, sec. 2, p. 17; Margaret Kirk, "82nd Anniversary of 'Adobe Walls Battle' Observed Wednesday," *Borger News-Herald*, June 24, 1956, p. 17; *Souvenir of Trek to Adobe Walls, 100th Anniversary, June 27th 1874, Trip from Dodge City, Kansas, to Spearman and Adobe Walls, Texas*, handbill.

29. Frank Tolbert, "At Adobe Walls," *Dallas Morning News*, June 30, 1979, A-35.

30. George Turner, "Scientists Digging into Buffalo Hunter Lifestyle," *Amarillo Sunday News-Globe*, Aug. 10, 1975, D-1, 2.

NOTES TO PART 2
Notes to Chapter 7

1. U.S. Department of the Interior, Geological Survey, *Amarillo, Texas, NI 14–1, 1:250,000*, 1 lf.; U.S. Department of the Interior, Geological Survey, *Perryton, Texas; Oklahoma; Kansas, NJ 14–10, 1:250,000*, 1 lf.; U.S. Department of the Interior, Geological Survey, *Tucumcari, New Mexico; Texas, NI 13–3, 1:250,000*, 1 lf.

2. Hutchinson County, Tex., Deed Records, 26:332.

3. U.S. Department of the Interior, Geological Survey, *Adobe Creek, Tex., N3552.5–W10107.5/7.5*, 1 lf.

4. Ibid.; Billy R. Stringer, *Soil Survey of Hutchinson County, Texas*, pp. 5–24, plates 16, 21.

5. Stringer, *Soil Survey*, pp. 31–33; J. E. Weaver and F. W. Albertson, *Grasslands of the Great Plains: Their Nature and Use*, pp. 267–83.

Notes to Chapter 8

1. Hutchinson County, Tex., Deed Records, 26:332.

2. For a discussion of the construction of the buildings at Adobe Walls, see Part 1 of this study.

3. For background on the 1874 and 1929 burials at the site, see Part 1 of this study.

4. Robert G. Chenhall, *Nomenclature for Museum Cataloging: A System for Classifying Man-Made Objects*.

Notes to Chapter 9

1. Oringderff, *True Sod*.

2. John Francis McDermott, Jr., *The French in the Mississippi Valley*, pp. 26–35.

3. Bruce D. Dickson and William Westbury, *Archaeological Research at Fort Richardson State Park, Summer 1975*, Texas A&M University, Anthropology Laboratory, Report No. 28, pp. 5–25; Anne A. Fox, *Archaeological Investigations at Fort Griffin State Historic Park, Shackelford County, Texas*, Center for Archaeological Research, Archaeological Survey Report No. 23, pp. 13, 18; Herbert M. Hart, *Old Forts of the Southwest*, pp. 119, 154, 166.

4. Oringderff, *True Sod*, pp. 21–77, 104–22; Roger L. Welsch, *Sod Walls: The Story of the Nebraska Sod House*, pp. 21–117.

5. W. Ellis Groben, *Adobe Architecture: Its Design and Construction*, pp. 1–36; John O. West and Roberto Gonzales, "Adobe: Earth, Straw, and Water," in *Built in Texas*, ed. Francis Edward Abernethy, Publications of the Texas Folklore Society 42 (1979), pp. 60–77.

6. Drury Blakeley Alexander, *Texas Homes of the 19th Century*, p. 236, plate 13; Marshall Gettys and Alicia Hughes-Jones, "Vertical Log Construction in Oklahoma," *Outlook in Historic Conservation*, July/Aug. 1981, n.p.; McDermott, *The French*, pp. 26–35; Willard B. Robinson, *Gone from Texas: Our Lost Architectural Heritage*, pp. 18, 22–24, 48.

7. McDermott, *The French*, pp. 19–23; Oringderff, *True Sod*, pp. 78–103.

8. Hathaway, "Adventures of Buffalo Hunter," p. 130.

9. Ibid.

10. It is extremely doubtful that additional excavation of the corral fence area would produce sufficient information or artifacts to warrant the cost.

11. [Dixon], *Life and Adventures*, p. 196; Little, "Battle of Adobe Walls," p. 76; Rye, *Quirt and Spur*, p. 320; Van Sickel, *A Story of Real Life*, p. 14.

12. Most of the larger stove pieces must have been removed by visitors through the years. One such person wrote to Johnson in 1924: "I went all over the ground looking for specimens & relics for my already big collection," adding, "I got the top off the old wood burner at the store." Jackson to Johnson, [late June, 1924], Andrew Johnson Papers.

13. Farnsworth to Field Adjutant, Sept. 23, 1874, Consolidated File 2815–1874.

14. For an account of the establishment of the Rath and Company store, see Part 1 of this study.

15. Unless otherwise indicated, measurements given for the Rath and Company store are based on the inside dimensions of the building. The north-to-south length, however, is computed from exterior measurement minus the approximate wall thickness because the Dixon grave and the presence of the bastion prevented interior measurement.

16. Connelley, "In Relation to the Visit," pp. 3–4; Andrew Johnson, sworn deposition, Oct. 10, 1892, pp. 38, 40; Parker, *Personal Experiences*, p. 59; Charles Rath, sworn deposition, Oct. 10, 1892, pp. 11¼ to 11½; [Untitled plan of 1874 Adobe Walls trading post].

17. [Johnson], "Adobe Walls Survivor," p. 10; Johnson, "The Battle of Adobe Walls," pp. 2, 5–6.

18. Andrew Johnson, a principal workman in the construction of the Rath and Company complex, noted in 1892, "We had part of a stockade, [but] we did not have it finished. We had not worked on it for several days before that attack." Andrew Johnson, sworn deposition, Oct. 10, 1892, p. 35.

19. [Dixon], *Life and Adventures*, p. 222.

20. Coulter, "Adobe Walls Fight," p 2; Johnson, "The Battle of Adobe Walls," p. 1; J. Wright Mooar to Haley, interviews, Nov. 25, 1927, and Jan. 4, 1928, p. 7, J. Evetts Haley Papers.

21. Dickson and Westbury, *Archaeological Research at Fort Richardson*, p. 32.

22. Robert M. Herskovitz, *Fort Bowie Material Culture*, Anthropological Papers of the University of Arizona No. 31, pp. 116–17.

23. Sears, Roebuck and Company, Chicago, *Sears, Roebuck, and Co., Incorporated, Cheapest Supply House, Consumers Guide Catalogue No. 104*, n.p.

24. Dessamae Lorrain, "An Archaeologist's Guide to Nineteenth Century American Glass," *Historical Archaeology* 2 (1968): 37.

25. Sears, Roebuck, and Company, n.p.

Notes to Chapter 10

1. Herskovitz, *Fort Bowie Material Culture*, pp. 34–35.

2. *Lamps & Other Lighting Devices 1850–1906*, p. 14; *Meriden City Directory for 1873–74*, pp. 15, 103; Edward Miller and Company, Meriden, Conn., *Price List of Edward Miller & Co. . . .* , pp. 1–23; *Price, Lee & Co.'s Meriden Directory for 1876*, pp. 95,

118; Catherine M. V. Thuro, *Oil Lamps: The Kerosene Era in North America*, pp. 41, 44, 65. For perhaps the best general nineteenth-century guide to kerosene lamps, see John Jonesbury, Jr., *Lamp Primer, or Lamp Light and Lamps, and How to Care for Them*.

3. *Lamps & Other Lighting Devices*, p. 14; Plume and Atwood Manufacturing Company, Waterbury, Conn., *The Plume and Atwood Manufacturing Company Illustrated Catalogue of Kerosene Oil Burners, Gas and Oil Lamp Trimmings, Lamps, Oil Heaters, Etc.*, pp. 1–78; *Price, Lee & Co.'s Waterbury Directory for 1877*, p. 156 and p. viii of front advertising section; Thurow, *Oil Lamps*, pp. 40, 44, 60, 77.

4. *Lamps & Other Lighting Devices*, pp. 14–15.

5. U.S. Department of the Interior, Patent Office, Patent No. 106,303, Aug. 16, 1870, Benjamin Franklin Adams, lamp burner.

Notes to Chapter 11

1. For representative guides to animal shoes and the work of farriers, see G. Fleming, *Practical Horseshoeing*, and Robert F. Wiseman, *The Complete Horseshoeing Guide*, 2nd ed. The animal shoes recovered at Adobe Walls were identified and classified by Dick Stotts of Amarillo, Tex., a well-known farrier and blacksmith in the area. Stotts donated to the Panhandle-Plains Historical Museum a large and valuable collection of animal shoes, many examples from which are analogous to specimens recovered at Adobe Walls.

2. Jack T. Hughes and Patrick S. Willey, *Archeology at Mackenzie Reservoir*, Texas Historical Commission, Office of State Archeologist, Archeological Survey Report 24, pp. 20–21; Vance T. Holliday and Curtis M. Welty, "Lithic Tool Resources of the Eastern Llano Estacado," *Bulletin of the Texas Archeological Society* 52 (1981): 207–208.

3. James Austin Hanson, *Metal Weapons, Tools, and Ornaments of the Teton Dakota Indians*, pp. 26–31.

4. Holliday and Welty, "Lithic Tool Resources," p. 207; J. B. Shaeffer, "The Alibates Flint Quarry, Texas," *American Antiquity* 24, no. 2 (Oct., 1958): 189–91; Kirk Bryan, *Flint Quarries—The Sources of Tools and, at the Same Time, the Factories of the American Indian*, Papers of the Peabody Museum of American Archaeology and Ethnology, Harvard University, XVII, no. 3, pp. 14–15.

5. Norm Flayderman, *Flayderman's Guide to American Firearms and Their Values*, pp. 519–20.

6. Panhandle-Plains Historical Museum, Artifact Nos. 34/3 and 1200/9 (Spencer carbines).

7. Ibid.

8. Panhandle-Plains Historical Museum, Artifact No. 1200/5 (1850s octagon barrel muzzle-loading rifle).

9. Panhandle-Plains Historical Museum, Artifact No. 1909/4 (powder flask).

10. Warren Ripley, *Artillery and Ammunition of the Civil War*, p. 233.

11. Frank Sellers, *Sharps Firearms*, p. 347.

12. Cator receipts.

13. Frank C. Barnes, *Cartridges of the World*, ed. John T. Amber, p. 305.

14. Cator receipts.

15. [Dixon], *Life and Adventures*, p. 248; C. E. (Ed) Jones to L. F. Sheffy, interview, Dec. 31, 1929, p. 3, C. E. Jones Papers; J. E. McAllister to Haley, interview, July 1, 1926, p. 2, J. E. McAllister Papers.

16. Cator receipts.

17. Ibid.

18. Ibid.

18. Ibid.

19. Ibid.

20. James H. Cator, sworn deposition, Oct. 10, 1892, p. 23; [Dixon], *Life and Adventures*, pp. 183, 212; William B. Masterson, sworn deposition, June 24, 1893, p. 2; "Texas Frontier Veteran," p. 7.

21. Cator receipts.

22. Andrew Johnson, sworn deposition, Oct. 10, 1892, pp. 37, 44; James H. Cator, sworn deposition, Oct. 10, 1892, p. 23; Charles Rath, sworn deposition, Oct. 10, 1892, p. 8.

23. Harry B. Harris, "Coffee Mills," in *The Antique Trader Annual of Articles for 1973*, pp. 149–50; Sears, Roebuck and Company, n.p.

24. Donald Blake Webster, *Decorated Stoneware Pottery of North America*, pp 55–57, 60.

25. Shirley J. Shepherd, "Ball Collectibles for Fun and Profit," in *The Antique Trader Annual on Antiques Volume VIII*, pp. 260–63.

26. Edward Clarke succeeded Bridgwood and Clarke in operating the Phoenix Works at Tunstall about 1865, continuing its operation until 1877, when he moved it to Burslem. The firm existed until it was acquired by A. J. Wilkinson in 1887. J. P. Cushion, *Pocket Book of English Ceramic Marks and Those of Wales, Scotland and Ireland*, p. 54; J. P. Cushion, *Pocket Book of British Ceramic Marks Including Index to Registered Designs 1842–83*, 3rd enlarged ed., p. 101; Geoffrey A. Godden, *Encyclopedia of British Pottery and Porcelain Marks*, pp. 147–48.

27. James Edwards and Son operated a pottery works at Burslem from 1851 to 1882, succeeding James Edwards and being succeeded by Knapper and Blackhurst. Godden, *Encyclopedia of British Pottery*, pp. 230–31; Thomas M. Ormsbee, *English China and Its Marks*, p. 60.

28. John Edwards commenced producing pottery at Longton about 1847, moving to Fenton about 1853, where his firm produced china and earthenware until 1900. His products from the mid-nineteenth century bear a variety of impressed and printed marks of differing designs, some of them ca. 1873–79 having "& Co." added. Godden, *Encyclopedia of British Pottery*, p. 231.

29. Thomas Hughes operated pottery works at Burslem from 1860 to 1894, being succeeded by Thomas Hughes and Son (Ltd.) in 1895. Cushion, *Pocket Book of British Ceramic Marks*, p. 109; Godden, *Encyclopedia of British Pottery*, p. 339.

30. The specimen of ironstone china from Adobe Walls bearing the royal arms and the words "IRONSTONE CHINA MEAKIN & CO COBRIDGE" must have been produced by Henry Meakin, who operated the Abbey Pottery at Cobridge from 1873 to 1876. He is the only known Meakin operating in Cobridge during the 1870s and is known to have used the royal arms mark on his products. Godden, *Encyclopedia of British Pottery*, p. 426.

31. J. and G. Meakin operated both the Eagle Pottery and the Eastwood Works in Hanley beginning in 1851; the company exists today. The royal arms appear in many of the nineteenth-century marks from this important manufacturer. Cushion, *Pocket Book of British Ceramic Marks*, p. 162; Godden, *Encyclopedia of British Pottery*, p. 427.

32. Powell and Bishop were manufacturers of china and earthenware at Hanley from 1867 to 1878, succeeding Livesley, Powell and Company and later being succeeded by Powell, Bishop and Stonier. Cushion, *Pocket Book of British Ceramic Marks*,

p. 160; J. P. Cushion and W. B. Honey, *Handbook of Pottery and Porcelain Marks*, p. 300; Godden, *Encyclopedia of British Pottery*, p. 509.

33. Francis C. Eames with various partners imported china, earthenware, glassware, and related items to the United States at least from the 1860s to the 1880s, starting in Leavenworth, Kans., and later moving his business to Kansas City, Mo. Collins, comp., *Collins' City Directory*, pp. 76, 99; *Hoye's Kansas City Directory for 1882*, pp. 158, 550.

34. Kerr's China Hall (James K. Kerr and Brothers) was a known importer of china, earthenware, and glassware at Philadelphia in the mid-1870s. *Boyd's Business Directory of Over One Hundred Cities and Towns in Pennsylvania*, p. 484; Isaac Costa, comp., *Gospill's Philadelphia Business Directory for 1874*, p. 132.

35. Sears, Roebuck and Company, n.p.

36. Ibid.

37. James A. Watson, "Battle of Adobe Walls," p. 72.

38. Herskovitz, *Fort Bowie Material Culture*, p. 71.

39. Buffalo Scale Company, *Illustrated Catalogue of United States Standard Scales Manufactured by Buffalo Scale Co., Buffalo, N.Y.*, p. 11.

40. James A. Hanson to Billy R. Harrison, interview, July 16, 1976, Adobe Walls—Material Culture—Tacks file, Adobe Walls research files.

Notes to Chapter 12

1. Sears, Roebuck and Company, n.p.

2. Ibid.

3. Towana Spivey, ed., *A Historical Guide to Wagon Hardware & Blacksmith Supplies*, Contributions of the Museum of the Great Plains No. 9, p. 11.

Notes to Chapter 13

1. Chenhall, *Nomenclature for Museum Cataloging*, pp. 37–38.

2. Ketchum, *A Treasury*, pp. 94, 97, 99–102; Richard Watson, *Bitters Bottles*, pp. 13–16.

3. Cator receipts.

4. Ed Bartholomew, *1001 Bitters Bottles*, pp. 116–17; Lynn Blumenstein, *Bottle Rush U.S.A.*, pp. 40–41; Ketchum, pp. 97, 99; John C. Tibbitts, *1200 Bottles Priced: A Bottle Price Guide and Classification System*, p. 14; Richard Watson, *Bitters Bottles*, p. 274; Bill Wilson and Betty Wilson, *Western Bitters*, p. 82.

5. Stewart H. Holbrook, *The Golden Age of Quackery*, pp. 157–66; Ketchum, *A Treasury*, pp. 101–102; Ronald R. Switzer, *The Bertrand Bottles: A Study of 19th Century Glass and Ceramic Containers*, U.S. Department of the Interior, National Park Service, Publications in Archeology No. 12, pp. 30–31, 33–36, 72–73; Rex L. Wilson, *Bottles on the Western Frontier*, ed. Edward Staski, pp. 23–25.

6. Bartholomew, *1001 Bitters Bottles*, p. 82; Graydon La Verne Freeman [James H. Thompson, pseud.], *Bitters Bottles*, p. 47; *The Lockport City Directory, for the Years 1874–75 . . .* , pp. 96, 115, 119; McKearin and Wilson, *American Bottles*, pp. 137–44, 303, 308–309; *The New York State 1874 Business Directory . . .* , p. 324; Richard Watson, *Bitters Bottles*, pp. 204–205.

7. Ballenger and Howe, *Ballenger & Howe, Fourth Annual City Directory*, p. 66; Collins, comp., *Collins' City Directory*, p. 75; *Kansas State Gazetteer . . . 1878*, p. 476; *Merwin's Leavenworth*, p. 34.

8. Herskovitz, *Fort Bowie Material Culture*, pp. 7–9; Wilson, *Bottles on the Western Frontier*, p. 114, 124.

9. Cator receipts.

10. Baldwin, *A Collector's Guide*, pp. 338–39; Ed Bartholomew, *1200 Old Medicine Bottles*, pp. 32–33; Richard E. Fike, *Handbook for the Bottle-ologist*, p. 25; *Lockport City Directory*, pp. 73, 115, and advertisement on outside front cover; McKearin and Wilson, *American Bottles*, pp. 139, 141; John T. Yount, *Bottle Collector's Handbook and Pricing Guide*, p. 41.

11. Holbrook, *Golden Age of Quackery*, pp. 12, 107, 149–56; Wilson, *Bottles on the Western Frontier*, p. 44.

12. *Boyd's Business Directory*, p. 464; Fike, *Handbook for Bottle-ologist*, p. 42; Wilson and Wilson, *19th Century*, pp. 42, 119.

13. Herskovitz, *Fort Bowie Material Culture*, pp. 12–14; Wilson, *Bottles on the Western Frontier*, pp. 43–44, 136.

14. Joseph K. Baldwin, *A Collector's Guide*, p. 85; Costa, comp., *Gospill's*, pp. 164, 167; *Boyd's Business Directory*, p. 399; Wilson and Wilson, *19th Century*, pp. 42, 119; Wilson, *Bottles on the Western Frontier*, p. 136.

15. Joseph K. Baldwin, *A Collector's Guide*, p. 222; Beck, *Bottle Collecting*, p. 63; Kay Denver, *Patent Medicine Picture*, pp. 41–42; Larry Freeman, *Grand Old American Bottles*, p. 428.

16. Wilson, *Bottles on the Western Frontier*, pp. 46, 55, 139.

17. Holbrook, *Golden Age of Quackery*, p. 247.

18. For a review of liquor bottles common in the West during the second half of the nineteenth century, see Wilson, *Bottles on the Western Frontier*, pp. 13–18.

Notes to Chapter 14

1. Chenhall, *Nomenclature for Museum Cataloging*, pp. 43–44.

2. For studies of American Indian trade beads, see William C. Orchard, *Beads and Beadwork of the American Indians: A Study Based on Specimens in the Museum of the American Indian, Heye Foundation*, Museum of the American Indian, Heye Foundation, Contributions 11; Janet D. Spector, "The Interpretive Potential of Glass Trade Beads in Historic Archeology," *Historical Archeology* 10 (1976): 17–27; Arthur Woodward, *The Denominators of the Fur Trade: An Anthology of Writings on the Material Culture of the Fur Trade*, pp. 15–23.

3. John C. Ewers, "Hair Pipes in Plains Indian Adornment: A Study in Indian and White Ingenuity," *Bureau of American Ethnology Bulletin* 164 (1957): 41; Orchard, *Beads and Beadwork*, pp. 59–61; Woodward, *Denominators of the Fur Trade*, p. 30.

4. Ewers, "Hair Pipes," pp. 42–46, 62–64.

5. Edward H. Knight, *Knight's American Mechanical Dictionary*, II, 962–63.

6. For background on shoe and boot types as well as shoemaking techniques of the 1870s, see ibid., III, 2158–64; Adrienne Anderson, "The Archeology of Mass-Produced Footwear," *Historical Archeology* 2 (1968): 56–65; Fred A. Gannon, *A Short History of American Shoemaking*; Herskovitz, *Fort Bowie Material Culture*, pp. 122–27.

7. Erik Oberg and Franklin D. Jones, *Machinery's Handbook: A Reference Book for the Mechanical Engineer, Draftsman, Toolmaker and Machinist*, pp. 1338–40.

8. Anderson, "Archeology of Mass-Produced," pp. 58, 60–61, 64. The Goodyear welt entered general production only in the mid-1870s.

9. For general guides to button manufacture and identification, see Lillian Smith

Albert and Jane Ford Adams, *The Button Sampler*; Grace Horney Ford, *The Button Collector's History*; and Sally C. Luscomb, *The Collector's Encyclopedia of Buttons*.

10. Studies of buttons give their sizes variously in millimeters, inches, and lignes (lines), the last a system of measurement applied only to buttons. Because of its precision in measuring small objects, the metric system is used for indicating the button sizes presented in this study. 1 inch = 25.4 mm = 40 lignes.

11. This type of glass button has several names, among them milk glass, small chinas, white glass, cryolite, and fusible porcelain. For this study, both white and colored examples are identified by the general term "milk glass."

12. Perhaps more is known about the Goodyear patent rubber buttons than about any of the other nonmilitary buttons recovered at Adobe Walls. Among the sources of information on these buttons: Albert and Adams, *Button Sampler*, pp. 135–37; *Boyd's New Jersey State Directory, 1874*, p. 318; Erwina Chamberlin and Minerva Miner, *Button Heritage*, pp. 138–141; Ford, *Button Collector's History*, pp. 192–93.

13. Herskovitz, *Fort Bowie Material Culture*, p. 41.

14. For information on U.S. Army general service buttons and their makers, see, for example: Alphaeus H. Albert, *Record of American Uniform and Historical Buttons with Supplement*, pp. 39–40; Luis Fenolossa Emilio, *The Emilio Collection of Military Buttons . . .* , pp. 28–29, plate 2; Herskovitz, *Fort Bowie Material Culture*, pp. 38–42; David F. Johnson, *Uniform Buttons: American Armed Forces 1784–1948* I, 65–67, II, Plates 22–23; William F. McGuinn, *American Military Button Makers & Suppliers: Their Backmarks & Dates*, pp. 50–53; *Price, Lee & Co., 1877*, p. 145 and p. xiv of front advertising section. The garment from which six coat buttons and eight vest or cuff buttons came appears to have been left in the northwest bastion of the Myers and Leonard corral. The excavators found cloth impressions in the soil where the buttons were found, but the impressions were insufficiently clear to identify the type of garment.

15. Herskovitz, *Fort Bowie Material Culture*, pp. 38, 41.

16. Daniel J. Crouch, *Archaeological Investigations of the Kiowa and Comanche Indian Commissaries, 34–Cm–232*, Contributions of the Museum of the Great Plains No. 7, pp. 151, 156.

17. Sears, Roebuck and Company, n.p.

18. William H. Emmons, George A. Thiel, Clinton R. Stauffer, and Ira S. Allison, *Geology: Principles and Processes*, p. 26; Edward Henry Kraus, Walter Fred Hunt, and Lewis Stephen Ramsdell, *Mineralogy: An Introduction to the Study of Minerals and Crystals*, pp. 389–90; H. Geiger Omwake, "Analysis of 19th Century White Kaolin Pipe Fragments from the Mero Site, Door County, Wisconsin," *Wisconsin Archeologist* 46, no.2 (June, 1965): 125–39; Rex L. Wilson, "Tobacco Pipes from Fort Union, N. Mexico," *El Palacio* 73, no. 1 (spring, 1966): 33–34.

19. Knight, *Knight's American Mechanical Dictionary* III, 2583–84.

20. Wilson, "Tobacco Pipes," p. 37.

21. Rex L. Wilson, *Clay Tobacco Pipes from Fort Laramie National Historic Site and Related Locations*, pp. 50–51, 80.

22. The English specimen was purchased by co-author T. Lindsay Baker from London antique tobacco pipe dealer Peter Adams on Apr. 28, 1979, and subsequently given by Baker to the Panhandle-Plains Historical Museum. T. Lindsay Baker, "Notes Concerning Victorian Clay Pipes Recovered from the Thames River, London, England, Donated to the Panhandle-Plains Historical Museum by T. Lindsay Baker, 30 May 1979," May 30, 1979, Accession Record File No. 1979–103/15.

23. Omwake, "Analysis of 19th Century White Kaolin," pp. 131, 133, 136, 138.

24. For a detailed study of the Pamplin area pipes, see Henry W. Hamilton and Jean Tiree Hamilton, "Clay Pipes from Pamplin," *Missouri Archaeologist* 34, nos. 1–2 (Dec., 1972): 1–47.

25. Herskovitz, *Fort Bowie Material Culture*, p. 88; W. W. Newcomb, Jr., "An Historical Burial from Yellowhouse Canyon, Lubbock County," *Bulletin of the Texas Archeological Society* 26 (1955): plate 25.

26. *The Encyclopedia of Collectibles* IV, 140; Herskovitz, *Fort Bowie Material Culture*, pp. 132–33.

27. Herskovitz, *Fort Bowie Material Culture*, pp. 132–33.

28. The handle was probably at least 3/8 inch longer before its end was fragmented.

29. R. S. Yeoman, *A Guide Book of United States Coins*, pp. 92–93.

Bibliography

T his bibliography lists materials consulted in both the historical and archeological phases of this study. The authors have arranged the bibliography according to the types of materials: manuscripts, interviews, books, and articles.

A number of sources deserve particular attention. Among these are a number of little-known or heretofore unknown manuscript sources. In later years perhaps the most reliable informant on the Adobe Walls story was Andrew Johnson, the Swedish immigrant laborer who worked at the post for Rath and Company for almost the entire period of its occupancy. His personal correspondence, numerous unpublished reminiscences concerning the post, and published remembrances constitute one of the most valuable sources of information on Adobe Walls history.

In the 1890s three cases were argued before the U.S. Court of Claims when the former partners of Rath and Company and of Myers and Leonard as well as the two Cator brothers sued for the recovery of losses they had suffered as a result of Indian hostilities at the time of the Adobe Walls fight. Attorneys attempted to secure sworn depositions from all individuals who might have knowledge of the events of 1874. Preserved in the National Archives we have the sworn testimony of such men as William Dixon, James Langton, W. B. "Bat" Masterson, James H. Cator, Robert M. Wright, and Andrew Johnson, testimony regarding both the trading post and its history. As the testimony taken was under oath and was recorded only about two decades after the events, it may be considered generally reliable, although the claims of losses by the merchants are somewhat inflated.

Another unpublished source on the Adobe Walls story that heretofore has lain unused is the original typescript for Olive K. Dixon's biography of her husband, the *Life and Adventures of "Billy" Dixon*, today preserved in the papers of her editor, Frederick S. Barde. Using this material, one can determine the changes Barde made in the manuscript before its publication in 1914, when it became for many years the standard account.

A number of unpublished first-person accounts of the Adobe Walls fight either have been used ineffectively or have been unknown until recently. Among these are the reminiscences of J. W. McKinley, Frederick J. Leonard, and Quanah. The last is particularly interesting, as the remembrances were noted by General Hugh Scott of Fort Sill during an 1897 interview that he had with Quanah concerning the Adobe Walls fight. This interview, however, is not the sole Indian interview containing Adobe Walls data. The Oklahoma Historical Society preserves in its Indian-Pioneer Papers several important first-person accounts of the Adobe Walls fight as seen from the Indian perspective, as do the research files of Wilbur S. Nye at Fort Sill.

A handful of books hold considerable amounts of information on Adobe Walls, but probably the most notable is the *Life and Adventures of "Billy" Dixon* prepared by his widow. Another significant and virtually unknown version of the story comes from S. S. Van Sickel in a rare fifty-page booklet published about 1890; it recounts his arrival at the post just after the 1874 battle.

The standard articles surveying the history of Adobe Walls are those written by G. Derek West and J'Nell Pate, but they are merely among the most recent of many articles on the subject. Perhaps the first article on the Adobe Walls fight as a historical event, and one of the best, was written by John Coulter and published in several Kansas newspapers in 1877. Numerous other newspapers in the 1870s printed articles on Adobe Walls and the battle there, notable examples being "From the Front" published in the Topeka *Commonwealth* on August 8, 1874, and articles reporting the fight in the *Leavenworth Daily Times* of July 10, 1874, and in the *Leavenworth Daily Commercial* of July 26, 1874.

From early in this century, Edward Campbell Little's article in *Pearson's Magazine* presents one of the best early syntheses of events on the Canadian River in 1874. It is complemented by such twentieth-century articles as Seth Hathaway's reminiscences published in *Frontier Times* in 1931 and those of Frederick J. Leonard entitled "Texas Frontier Veteran" in the *Salt Lake Tribune*.

Because the materials used in preparing this study came from a large number of repositories and because many of them are unique items, the authors have provided a code that identifies the repositories where the individual materials were found. This by no means represents a guide to all the locations where individual items may be preserved, but it does document where they were examined at the time this book was written. The coding system, which follows, modifies the symbols of American libraries developed by the Library of Congress.

CCmL   Personal library of Fred U. Leonard, Costa Mesa, Calif.

CU–LM   Lowie Museum of Anthropology, University of California, Berkeley, Calif.

CoC   Penrose Public Library, Colorado Springs, Colo.

CoD Western History Department, Denver Public Library, Denver, Colo.
CoDAr Division of State Archives and Public Records, Denver, Colo.
CoHi Colorado Historical Society, Denver, Colo.
CoLake Office of County Clerk and Recorder, Hinsdale County Courthouse, Lake City, Colo.
CoPsB Personal library of Mrs. Mabel Bennett, Pagosa Springs, Colo.
CtY Beinecke Library, Yale University, New Haven, Conn.
DLC Library of Congress, Washington, D.C.
DNA National Archives and Records Service, Washington, D.C.
DP U.S. Patent and Trademark Office, Washington, D.C.
ICF Field Museum of Natural History, Chicago, Ill.
IHi Illinois State Historical Society, Springfield, Ill.
IU University of Illinois, Urbana, Ill.
IdHi Library and Archives, Idaho State Historical Society, Boise, Idaho
KDcB Historical Files, Boot Hill Museum, Inc., Dodge City, Kans.
KDcKhc Kansas Heritage Center, Dodge City, Kans.
KHi Kansas State Historical Society, Topeka, Kans.
MB Boston Public Library, Boston, Mass.
MBSpnea Society for the Preservation of New England Antiquities, Boston, Mass.
MH–BA Baker Library, Graduate School of Business Administration, Harvard University, Boston, Mass.
MnU University of Minnesota, Minneapolis, Minn.
NhD College Library, Dartmouth College, Hanover, N. H.
OAkF Firestone Archives, Firestone Tire and Rubber Company, Akron, Ohio
OBgU University Library, Bowling Green State University, Bowling Green, Ohio
OkFsA U.S. Army Field Artillery and Fort Sill Museum, Fort Sill, Okla.
OkHiamd Archives and Manuscripts Division, Oklahoma Historical Society, Oklahoma City, Okla.
OkHirl Research Library, Oklahoma Historical Society, Oklahoma City, Okla.
OkU Western History Collections, University Library, University of Oklahoma, Norman, Okla.
TxAm Amarillo Public Library, Amarillo, Tex.
TxBor Hutchinson County Library, Borger, Tex.
TxCM University Library, Texas A&M University, College Station, Tex.
TxCaP Research Center, Panhandle-Plains Historical Museum, Canyon, Tex.
TxCaW Cornette Library, West Texas State University, Canyon, Tex.
TxDaHi Dallas Historical Society, Dallas, Tex.
TxE Southwest Collection, El Paso Public Library, El Paso, Tex.
TxEU University of Texas at El Paso, El Paso, Tex.
TxF Fort Worth Public Library, Fort Worth, Tex.
TxLT University Library, Texas Tech University, Lubbock, Tex.

TxLTswc Southwest Collection, Texas Tech University, Lubbock, Tex.

TxMH Nita Stewart Haley Memorial Library, Midland, Tex.

TxPlW Wayland University, Plainview, Tex.

TxSa San Antonio Public Library, San Antonio, Tex.

TxSaDrt Daughters of the Republic of Texas Library, San Antonio, Tex.

TxSaU University Library, University of Texas at San Antonio, San Antonio, Tex.

TxSaW Library, Witte Memorial Museum, San Antonio, Tex.

TxSt Office of County Clerk, Hutchinson County Courthouse, Stinnett, Tex.

TxUAr University of Texas Archives, University of Texas at Austin, Austin, Tex.

TxWicM George Moffett Library, Midwestern University, Wichita Falls, Tex.

UU Marriott Library, University of Utah, Salt Lake City, Utah

UkCrJ Personal Library of Robert Jones, South Croydon, England

ViWC Curatorial Library, Colonial Williamsburg, Inc., Williamsburg, Va.

WHi State Historical Society of Wisconsin, Madison, Wis.

WyU American Heritage Center, University of Wyoming, Laramie, Wyo.

Manuscript Materials

"Adobe Walls. Beeson Museum. April 15, 1935." TS. April 15, 1935. Adobe Walls vertical file, KDcB.

"The Adobe Walls Fight." TS. n.d. 4 lvs. W. S. Campbell Papers, OkU.

Alexander, R. T., to Dr. J. A. Hill, July 1, 1954. R. T. Alexander Papers, TxCaP.

[Archambeau, Ernest R.], to Col. Wilbur Sturtevant Nye, February 20, 1961. Ernest R. Archambeau Papers, TxCaP.

———, to Col. Wilbur Sturtevant Nye, January 18, 1967. Ernest R. Archambeau Papers, TxCaP.

———, to Col. Wilbur Sturtevant Nye, February 4, 1967. Ernest R. Archambeau Papers, TxCaP.

———, to Col. Wilbur Sturtevant Nye, February 17, 1967. Ernest R. Archambeau Papers, TxCaP.

———, to Col. Wilbur Sturtevant Nye, March 31, 1967. Ernest R. Archambeau Papers, TxCaP.

"At Rest." Unidentified newspaper clipping. 1894. CoPsB.

Attebury, Mrs. Clyde. "The Birth of the Panhandle." TS. n.d. 6 lvs. Mrs. Clyde Attebury Papers, TxCaP.

Baker, T. Lindsay. "Notes Concerning Victorian Clay Pipes Recovered from the Thames River, London, England, Donated to the Panhandle-Plains Historical Museum by T. Lindsay Baker, 30 May 1979." TS. May 30, 1979. 1 lf. Accession Record File No. 1979–103/15, Office of Registrar, TxCaP.

———. "Notes on Time Required to Run and Walk between Buildings at the Adobe Walls Archaeological Site." TS. August 28, 1979. 1 lf. Adobe Walls research files, TxCaP.

Baldwin, Frank Dwight. Diary Transcript for August 19–20, 1874. MS. Ca. February 20, 1890. 5 lvs. Adobe Walls vertical file, KDcB.

——, to George W. Baird, February 20, 1890. Maj. George W. Baird Papers, KHi.

Barbour, Jim, to Andy Johnson, July 2, 1924. Andrew Johnson Papers, KDcB.

Bass, John H. "In the Land of the Comanches." TS ditto copy. Ca. 1960. 17 lvs. John H. Bass Papers, TxCaP.

"Bat Masterson." TS. n.d. 3 lvs. William Barclay Masterson vertical file (B–M393–wb), WyU.

"'Bat' Masterson Is Dead." Unidentified newspaper clipping. 1921. 1 lf. William Barclay Masterson vertical file (B–M393–wb), WyU.

"Bat Masterson's Career. He Is a Square Sport and a Renowned 'Shooter.'" Unidentified newspaper clipping. Ca. 1888. 1 lf. Bat Masterson vertical file, KDcB.

"Battle of Adobe Walls Made History." Indian Depredations and Battles Scrapbooks, IV, 131–34, KHi.

Beeson, Merritt L. "Adobe Walls Fight, June 27, 1874" [plans showing structures at the 1874 Adobe Walls trading post]. MS. n.d. 2 lvs. Andrew Johnson Papers, KDcB.

Bennett, Mrs. Mabel L., to T. Lindsay Baker, November 28, 1978. Henry Born Papers, TxCaP.

——, to T. Lindsay Baker, April 18, 1980. Henry Born Papers, TxCaP.

Born, Henry, to Charles A. Siringo, July 6, 1920. Charles Siringo Papers, TxCaP.

Born, Mrs. Henry, to Charles A. Siringo, December 20, 1923. Charles Siringo Papers, TxCaP.

Branham, Dr. G. H., to R. N. Richardson, February 16, 1937. TS. 11 lvs. "Buffalo, the Frontier, the Indians" Notebook, pp. 282–92, Carl Coke Rister Papers, Box 10, TxLTswc.

Breaden, Susannah W., to T. Lindsay Baker, March 26, 1980. Langton—James file, Adobe Walls research files, TxCaP.

Brown, Frank, to Andy Johnson, June 24, 1923. Andrew Johnson Papers, KDcB.

Brown, W. C. "Tribute to Maj. Gen. Frank D. Baldwin, U.S.A., Retired." Offprint from *Army and Navy Register*. Ca. 1923. 1 lf. Frank Dwight Baldwin Papers, CoHi.

"Buffalo Hunter Speaks." Unidentified newspaper clipping. Ca. 1935. 1 lf. J. Wright Mooar Papers, TxCaP.

Bussell, Dick. "Hunting Buffalo in the Panhandle." TS. Ca. 1925. 4 lvs. Dick Bussell Papers, TxCaP.

"Came to Dodge from Sweden." Unidentified newspaper clipping. n.d. Scrapbook no. 1782, p. 23, KDcB.

Campbell, W. S., to Mrs. Olive K. Dixon, March 22, 1950. W. S. Campbell Papers, OkU.

——, to Stuart N. Lake, March 14, 1951. W. S. Campbell Papers, OkU.

"Caroline Markley Rath (Bainbridge)." TS. 1976. 1 lf. Caroline Markley Rath vertical file, KDcB.

"Cator Bros. Account." MS. February, 1878. 3 lvs. Robert H. Cator Papers, TxCaP.

Cator, James Bertie, to Robert H. Cator and James H. Cator, July 27, 1874. Robert H. Cator Papers, TxCaP.

———, to Robert H. Cator and James H. Cator, October 18, 1874. Robert H. Cator Papers, TxCaP.

———, to Robert H. Cator and James H. Cator, December 6, 1874. Robert H. Cator Papers, TxCaP.

———, to Robert H. Cator and James H. Cator, September 29, 1874. Robert H. Cator Papers, TxCaP.

———, to Robert H. Cator and James H. Cator, March 2, 1874. Robert H. Cator Papers, TxCaP.

———, to Robert H. Cator and James H. Cator, June 21, 1874. Robert H. Cator Papers, TxCaP.

Cator, James H. Sworn deposition prepared at Wichita, Kans., October 10, 1892, in the case of Charles Rath and Company v. the United States and the Cheyenne, Kiowa, and Comanche Indians. MS. 13 lvs. U.S. Court of Claims, Indian Depredation Case Files. Case 4593, Charles Rath and Company Claimants. Record Group 123, DNA.

———. Sworn deposition prepared at Wichita, Kans., October 11, 1892, in the case of James H. Cator and Arthur J. L. Cator v. the United States and the Cheyenne, Kiowa, and Comanche Indians. MS. 19 lvs. U.S. Court of Claims, Indian Depredation Case Files. Case 4601, James H. Cator and Arthur J. L. Cator Claimants. Record Group 123, DNA.

Cator, Louie, to James Cator, September 23, 1874, and October 17, 1874. Robert H. Cator Papers, TxCaP.

Cator Receipts. Robert H. Cator Papers, TxCaP.

"Charles Rath, an Early Merchant of Dodge City, Did Business in Partnership with Robert M. Wright, under the Name of Charles Rath & Co." MS and TS. n.d. 1 lf. Charles Rath vertical file, KDcB.

"Chas. Rath and Company." TS. n.d. 1 lf. Charles Rath vertical file, KDcB.

"Charles Rath 12 Yrs in 1848 Born 1836 Died 1902." MS and TS. n.d. 1 lf. Charles Rath vertical file, KDcB.

Clark, O. S., to Plains Panhandle Historical Society [*sic*], August 18, 1936. L. F. Sheffy Papers, TxCaP.

Clarke, L. E. "Map of Adobe Walls." MS. Ca. 1938. 1 lf. Laura V. Hamner Papers, TxCaP.

Coffee, H. C., to C. B. McClure, February 5, 1949. H. C. Coffee Papers, TxCaP.

Collar, Jacob, and Company, to Bob Cator, November 1, 1874. Robert H. Cator Papers, TxCaP.

———, to Bob Cator, November 2, 1874. Robert H. Cator Papers, TxCaP.

Collar, M., and Company, to R. Cator, November 1, 1874. Robert H. Cator Papers, TxCaP.

Collinson, Frank, to Harold Bugbee, January 17, 1935. Harold Bugbee Papers, TxCaP.

————, to Bruce Gerdes, December 16, 1937. Bruce Gerdes Papers, TxCaP.

————, to L. F. Sheffy, March 12, 1930. Frank Collinson Papers, TxCaP.

————. "Jim Greathouse or Whiskey Jim." TS. n.d. 12 lvs. Frank Collinson Papers, TxCaP.

[————.] "Some Hunters I Knew. Others I Heard Of." TS. n.d. 11 lvs. Frank Collinson Papers, TxCaP.

Combs, Jno. W., to [brother-in-law] Josiah Wright Mooar, January 24, 1872. John Wesley Mooar Papers, TxLTswc.

Connelley, William E. "In Relation to the Visit of Tom Stauth of Dodge City, Kansas to the Site of the Battle of Adobe Walls, on the Canadian in the Panhandle of Texas." TS. March 10, 1923. 5 lvs. History—Adobe Walls file, Manuscript Department, KHi.

Curtis, William T.S., to James H. Cator, June 17, 1899. Robert H. Cator Papers, TxCaP.

Davidson, J. W., to Assistant Adjutant General, July 7, 1874. U.S. Department of War, Army, Department of Texas, Letters Received 2723 D Texas 1874 "Indian File." Record Group 393, DNA.

"Dedication of Monument Will Feature Fiftieth Anniversary Celebration on Site of Historic Adobe Walls Battle." Unidentified newspaper clipping. Kansas History Scrapbooks, VI, 164–66, KHi.

Dixon, Olive King, to Hattie M. Anderson, December 26, 1922. Olive K. Dixon Papers, TxCaP.

————, to Frederick S. Barde, April 12, 1913. W. S. Campbell Papers, OkU.

————, to Andrew Johnson, October 22, 1919. Andrew Johnson Papers, KDcB.

————, to Andrew Johnson, May 8, 1923. Andrew Johnson Papers, KDcB.

————, to Andrew Johnson, May 15, 1923. Andrew Johnson Papers, KDcB.

————, to Andrew Johnson, December 6, 1923. Andrew Johnson Papers, KDcB.

————, to Andrew Johnson, May 25, 1924. Andrew Johnson Papers, KDcB.

————, to Andrew Johnson, August 19, 1924. Andrew Johnson Papers, KDcB.

————, to Andrew Johnson, September 15, 1924. Andrew Johnson Papers, KDcB.

————, to Andy Johnson, January 15, 1923. Andrew Johnson Papers, KDcB.

————, to Joseph G. Masters, February 20, 1935. Joseph Masters Collection, Manuscript Department, KHi.

————. "Adobe Walls." TS. January 16, 1942. 2 lvs. Lilly Larsen Papers, TxCaP.

————. "Adobe Walls Indian Fight." TS. Ca. 1923. 4 lvs. Adobe Walls manuscript file, TxCaP.

————. "Adobe Walls Indian Fight." TS. Ca. 1923. 7 lvs. Adobe Walls manuscript file, TxCaP.

————. "The Battle of Adobe Walls." TS. June 21, 1927. 6 lvs. Adobe Walls manuscript file, TxCaP.

————. "The Battle of Adobe Walls." TS. July 15, 1939. 12 lvs. Adobe Walls manuscript file, TxCaP.

———. "The Celebration at Adobe Walls." TS. Ca. June, 1924. 3 lvs. Adobe Walls manuscript file, TxCaP.

[———.] "Life and Adventures of William ("Billy") Dixon of Adobe Walls, Texas Panhandle." TS. 1913. 119 lvs. Battle of Adobe Walls file, Frederick S. Barde Collection, OkHirl.

"Dixon to Rest at Adobe Walls: Rites for Reinterment of the Famous Western Scout Will Be Thursday." Unidentified newspaper clipping. [Ca. June 27, 1929.] 1 lf. Billy Dixon vertical file, KDcB.

Dixon, William, to James H. Cator, August 11, 1903. Robert H. Cator Papers, TxCaP.

———. Sworn deposition prepared at Panhandle, Tex., July 25, 1898, in the case of Frederick J. Leonard and A. C. Myers, trading as Myers and Leonard, v. the United States and the Kiowa, Comanche, and Cheyenne Indians. MS. 7 lvs. U.S. Court of Claims, Indian Depredation Case Files. Case 10102, Frederick J. Leonard and A. C. Myers Claimants. Record Group 123, DNA.

"Dodge Citian Recounts Battle of Adobe Walls." Unidentified newspaper clipping. Ca. June, 1923. Scrapbook no. 1768, p. 36, KDcB.

"Dodge City Daily Globe 4–14–1924." MS and TS. n.d. 3 lvs. Tom Nixon vertical file, KDcB.

Douglas, H., to Commanding General of the Division of the Missouri, January 13, 1867. U.S. President, *Difficulties with Indian Tribes. Message from the President of the United States in Answer to a Resolution of the House of the 7th Ultimo, Asking for Information Relative to Difficulties with Various Tribes of Indians*, pp. 46–48. 41st Congress, 2nd Session, House Executive Document No. 240. Washington, D.C.: Government Printing Office, 1870.

Dunn, F. L., Mayor of the City of Wichita, Kansas, to All to Whom These Presents Come, June 20, 1924. Wichita, Kans., Manuscript File, TxCaP.

"'Dutch Henry' and James Watts Were Treed by a Bear near Rose's Cabin in the San Juan." Unidentified newspaper clipping. Will C. Ferrill Scrapbooks, 1890–1893, III, 71, CoD.

"'Dutch Henry' Born 1849–1921." TS. Ca. 1921. 1 lf. CoPsB.

"Dutch Henry. (Henry Borne.)" TS. n.d. 4 lvs. Dutch Henry Borne vertical file, KDcB.

Eagan, Robert E. "James Hanrahan: Early Day Character of Dodge City." TS. n.d. 7 lvs. James Hanrahan vertical file, KDcB.

Eschiti, James. Document transferring title to certain Indian artifacts to the Panhandle-Plains Historical Museum. TS and MS. June 22, 1963. 1 lf. Mr. and Mrs. Howard Hampton donor file, Office of Registrar, TxCaP.

Evans, Andrew W., to Acting Assistant Adjutant General, Head Quarters Company, January 23, 1869. MS. 38 lvs. U.S. Department of War, Army, Office of the Adjutant General, Letters Received, Item No. M 1560/6 (1869), Report of Maj. Andrew W. Evans on Canadian River Expedition. Record Group 94, DNA.

Evans, R. W., to Cater [*sic*], November 23, 1874. Robert H. Cator Papers, TxCaP.

———, to Robert Cater [*sic*], October 1, 1874. Robert H. Cator Papers, TxCaP.

"'Farmer Jones,' First White Settler in Oklahoma Panhandle, Buffalo Hunter Dies." TS. Ca. 1935. 1 lf. Charles Edward Jones Papers, TxCaP.

Farnsworth, Henry Joseph, to Field Adjutant, Battalion 8th Cavalry, September 23, 1874. U.S. Department of War, Army, Office of Adjutant General, Letters Received Relating to "Campaign against Hostile Indians in the Indian Territory," Consolidated File 2815–1874. Record Group 94, DNA.

———, Commanding Company "H," 8th U.S. Cavalry, to Field Adjutant, Wingate Battalion, 8th Cavalry, November 7, 1874. U.S. Department of War, Army, Office of Adjutant General, Letters Received Relating to "Campaign against Hostile Indians in the Indian Territory," Consolidated File 2815–1874. Record Group 94, DNA.

Field Museum of Natural History, Chicago, Ill. Accession Card No. A 15335 Acc. 870. Office of Registrar, ICF.

Ford County, Kans. Power of Attorney from Peter Johnson, Matilda Johnson, Ava Puolsen, Nelson Puolsen, Augusta Olsen, Lars Olsen, and Andreas Johnson to Andrew Johnson, June 9, 1890. MS. 2 lvs. Andrew Johnson Papers, KDcB.

Ford, Karin E., to T. Lindsay Baker, January 30, 1979. Hanrahan—James file, Adobe Walls research files, TxCaP.

Fowlston, C. J., to T. Lindsay Baker, February 23, 1981. Adobe Walls—Battle—Subsequent Years—1930's file, Adobe Walls research files, TxCaP.

Glenn, Willis Skelton. "Shelton [*sic*] Glenn Buffalo Hunt Manuscript." TS. Ca. 1910. 428 lvs. in various paginations. Special Collections, TxEU.

"Glenwood Sketches. The Man Called Dutch Henry Gives a Page of His Life." Dawson Scrapbooks, 72: 3, CoHi.

Goodnight, Charles, to Mrs. Olive Dixon, April 9, 1913. W. S. Campbell Papers, OkU.

———, to M. S. Seymour, September 2, 1919. Letters C. Goodnight to M. S. Garretson bound TS volume, pp. 67–69, TxMH.

Griffis, Joseph K., to J. [*sic*] F. Sheffy, June 26, 1940. L. F. Sheffy Correspondence, TxCaP.

Hampton, Howard, to C. Boone McClure, September 10, 1961. Mr. and Mrs. Howard Hampton donor file, Office of Registrar, TxCaP.

———, to C. Boone McClure, February 4, 1964. Mr. and Mrs. Howard Hampton donor file, Office of Registrar, TxCaP.

[Harrison, Billy R.] "# of and Calibers of Armament from Adobe Walls." MS. January 25, 1979. 4 lvs. Adobe Walls—Material Culture—Ammunition file, Adobe Walls research files, TxCaP.

Haworth, J. M., to P. E. Smith, Commissioner [of] Indian Affairs, September 1, 1874. U.S. Department of the Interior, Secretary, *Report of the Secretary of the Interior* 1: 527–30. 43rd Congress, 2nd Session, House Executive Document No. 1, Part 5. Washington, D.C.: Government Printing Office, 1874.

"Hero of Adobe Walls Dead: Heart Disease Fatal to 'Billy' Dixon, Indian Fighter." Unidentified newspaper clipping. Ca. 1913. 1 lf. Dixon, Billy vertical file, OkHirl.

Hinsdale County, Colorado. County Commissioners' Court Proceedings. MS. CoLake.

[Hobart, Timothy Dwight] to Mr. and Mrs. J. D. Jackson, October 4, 1927. Timothy Dwight Hobart Papers, TxCaP.

Hobble, F. A. "Dodge City Pioneers and Buffalo Hunters." TS. n.d. 3 lvs. File K 978.1–F75 Mss. Manuscript Department, KHi.

Hull, W. H., to Andy Johnson, September 2, 1924. Andrew Johnson Papers, KDcB.

Hunt, George, to Capt. W. S. Nye, May 6, 1940. "Bad Medicine and Good" correspondence file, "Bad Medicine and Good" research notes, W. S. Nye Collection, OkFsA.

Hutchinson County, Texas. Deed Records. 26: 332, TxSt.

Iseeo. "Iseeo Account" [of 1874 Battle of Adobe Walls]. Ms. Interview with Hugh Scott ca. 1897. "H. L. Scott Material" notebook, pp. 58–60. "Bad Medicine and Good" research notes, W. S. Nye Collection, OkFsA.

———. "Kit Carson's Fight." MS. Interview with Hugh Scott ca. 1897. Ledgerbook, II, 79–80. Hugh Scott Collection, OkFsA.

"Items Purchased 6/22/63 by Mr. & Mrs. Howard Hampton from James Eschiti, Comanche, of Walters, Okla." TS. 1963. 1 lf. Mr. and Mrs. Howard Hampton donor file, Office of Registrar, TxCaP.

Jackson, Albert. "Experiences of Joseph K. Griffis." TS. Ca. 1940. 7 lvs. Albert Jackson Papers, TxCaP.

Jackson, Charles H., to Andy Johnson, June, 1924. Andrew Johnson Papers, KDcB.

"James Langton." TS. n.d. 1 lf. James Langton vertical file, KDcB.

Johnson, Andrew. "Andrew Johnson." TS. March 19, 1913. 7 lvs. Andrew Johnson Papers, KDcB.

———. "The Battle of Adobe Walls." TS. June 27, 1924. 7 lvs. Adobe Walls manuscript file, TxCaP.

[———.] "Six Survivors of 'Dobe Walls' Fight: Buffalo Hunters from Dodge Were Attacked by 500 Savages: In Texas Back in 1874: Graphic Story of Battle Told by Andy Johnson of Dodge." Unidentified newspaper clipping. n.d. 1 lf. Indians—Indian Fights—Adobe Walls (Battles) clipping file, TxSaDrt.

———. Sworn deposition prepared at Wichita, Kans., October 10, 1892, in the case of Charles Rath and Company v. the United States and the Cheyenne, Kiowa, Comanche Indians. MS. 20 lvs. U.S. Court of Claims, Indian Depredation Case Files. Case 4593, Charles Rath and Company Claimants. Record Group 123, DNA.

———. Sworn deposition prepared at Wichita, Kans., October 11, 1892, in the case of James H. Cator and Arthur J. L. Cator v. the United States and the

Cheyenne, Kiowa, and Comanche Indians. MS. 3 lvs. U.S. Court of Claims, Indian Depredation Case Files. Case 4601, James H. Cator and Arthur J. L. Cator Claimants. Record Group 123, DNA.

[Jones, Bill.] "James H. Jones & Esther T. Clarke Family List." TS. Ca. 1981. 1 lf. Charles Edward Jones Papers, TxCaP.

Jones, Charles Edward, to L. F. Sheffy, January 27, 1930. Charles Edward Jones Papers, TxCaP.

[Jones, Philip, and James Jones.] Genealogical record of the family of James Jones (1778–1822). MS. In end papers of *The Christian's Complete Family Bible Containing the Sacred Text of the Old and New Testament*. Manchester: J. Harrop, 1804. The family Bible of the family of James Jones of Chester, England, UkCrJ.

Jones, Robert, to T. Lindsay Baker, January 10, 1982. John Thomson Jones file, Adobe Walls research files, TxCaP.

————. "The Family and Forbears [*sic*] of Philip Jones & Robina Agnes Thomson." MS. 1980. 1 lf. UkCrJ.

Kansas State Historical Society, Topeka, Kans. Artifact Documentation File 21.45. MS. 1921. 5 lvs. Office of Registrar, KHi.

————. Artifact Documentation File 23.6. TS. Ca. 1923. 1 lf. Office of Registrar, KHi.

Kiser, Edwin L. "The Adobe Walls Community: Background History and Buffalo Business." TS. 1976. 66 lvs. Pamphlet files, TxCaP.

————. "Written Discrepancies of Adobe Walls, 1874." TS. Ca. 1976. 17 lvs. Edwin L. Kiser Papers, TxCaP.

Lake, Stuart N., to W. S. Campbell, March 14, 1951. W. S. Campbell Papers, OkU.

————, to W. S. Campbell, March 20, 1951. MS. 4 lvs. W. S. Campbell Papers, OkU.

————, to W. S. Campbell, April 16, 1951. MS. 3 lvs. W. S. Campbell Papers, OkU.

Langton, James. Sworn deposition prepared at Salt Lake City, Utah, January 28, 1896, in the case of Charles Rath and Company v. the United States and the Cheyenne, Kiowa, and Comanche Indians. MS. 10 lvs. U.S. Court of Claims, Indian Depredation Case Files. Case 4593, Charles Rath and Company Claimants. Record Group 123, DNA.

Lefebre, E. C., to John D. Miles, Agent for Cheyennes and Arapahoes, June 14, 1874. Microfilm Roll CAA 24 (Cheyenne and Arapahoe Agency—Depredations 1878–1927), "Cheyenne and Arapahoe Agency: Military Relations and Affairs 1869–1932," OkHiamd.

————, to John D. Miles, Agent for Cheyennes and Arapahoes, June 27, 1874. Microfilm Roll CAA 24 (Cheyenne and Arapahoe Agency—Depredations 1878–1927), "Cheyenne and Arapahoe Agency: Military Relations and Affairs 1869–1932," OkHiamd.

[Leonard, Frederick J.] "Memorandum on the Adobe Walls trading post and the Battle of Adobe Walls." TS and MS. n.d. 2 lvs. CCmL.

Lobenstine, William Christian. Diaries 1851–58. MS. 2 vols. CoD.

"Lone Wolf." TS. n.d. 1 lf. "Buffalo, the Frontier, the Indians" Notebook, p. 322. Carl Coke Rister Papers, TxLTswc.

Long, J. J. "My Indian Expeditions." TS. n.d. 2 lvs. J. J. Long Papers, TxCaP.

Lowie Museum of Anthropology, Berkeley, Calif. Accession Record Card No. 2–4899. Office of Registrar, CU–LM.

──────. "Scott Collection." TS. Ca. 1901. 4 lvs. Office of Registrar, CU–LM.

Lumpkin, Cynthia. "The Turkey Track Ranch." TS. n.d. 8 lvs. Cynthia Lumpkin Papers, TxCaP.

[Maiden, Robert R.] Untitled reference list on Colorado sheriffs. TS. Ca. 1967. CoDAr.

Masterson, William Barclay, to Frederick S. Barde, October 13, 1913. W. S. Campbell Papers, OkU, and William Barclay Masterson Collection, Manuscript Department, KHi.

──────. Sworn deposition prepared at Denver, Colo., June 24, 1893, in the case of Charles Rath and Company v. the United States and the Cheyenne, Kiowa, and Comanche Indians. MS. 8 lvs. U.S. Court of Claims, Indian Depredation Case Files. Case 4593, Charles Rath and Company Claimants. Record Group 123, DNA.

McClure, C. Boone, to Mr. and Mrs. Howard Hampton, February 7, 1964. Mr. and Mrs. Howard Hampton donor file, Office of Registrar, TxCaP.

McKinley, J. W. "J. W. McKinley's Narrative (by Himself)." TS. n.d. 10 lvs. J. W. McKinley Papers, TxCaP.

Mead, Ben Carlton. "Plan of Adobe Walls drawn on the site under Mrs. Billy Dixon's direction, by Ben Mead in 1930. This arrangement based on low mounds of earth, apparently scanty ruins of the 'dobe buildings, and partly on memory descriptions by Dixon and by Andy Johnson." Photocopy of MS drawing. 1930. 1 lf. Ben Carlton Mead Papers, TxCaP.

"Memorandum of Military Services of Brigadier General Frank D. Baldwin, U.S. Army." TS. n.d. 56 lvs. Frank Dwight Baldwin Papers, CoHi.

"Memories." TS. Ca. January, 1921. 1 lf. CoPsB.

Miles, Jno. D., to Enoch Hoag, Superintendent of Indian Affairs, September 1, 1873. U.S. Department of the Interior, Secretary, *Report of the Secretary of the Interior* I, 588–91. 43rd Congress, 1st Session, House Executive Document No. 1, Part 5. Washington, D.C.: Government Printing Office, 1873.

──────, to Edw. P. Smith, Commissioner of Indian Affairs, Washington, D.C., September 30, 1874. U.S. Department of the Interior, Secretary, *Report of the Secretary of the Interior*, 1: 540–44. 43rd Congress, 2nd Session, House Executive Document No. 1, Part 5. Washington, D.C.: Government Printing Office, 1874.

Miles, Nelson A., to Assistant Adjutant General, Department of the Missouri, December 5, 1874. U.S. Department of War, Army, Office of Adjutant General, Letters Received Relating to "Campaign against Hostile Indians in the Indian Territory," Consolidated File 2815–1874. Record Group 98, DNA.

———, to Assistant Adjutant General, Department of the Missouri, March 4, 1875. MS. U.S. Department of War, Army, Office of Adjutant General, Letters Received Relating to "Campaign against Hostile Indians in the Indian Territory," Consolidated File 2815–1874. Record Group 98, DNA.

[Mooar, John Wesley], to Dear Sister, July 7, 1874. John Wesley Mooar Papers, TxLTswc.

Mooar, Josiah Wright, to John Wesley Mooar, February 22, 1872. John Wesley Mooar Papers, TxLTswc.

———, to Andy Johnson, January 20, 1923. Andrew Johnson Papers, KDcB.

———. "Dobe Walls as Sketched by J. Wright Mooar April 11, 1936." MS. April 11, 1936. 1 lf. J. W. Mooar interview file, TxMH.

———. "Dobie [*sic*] Walls as Drawn by J. Wright Mooar, July, 1937." MS. July, 1937. 1 lf. J. W. Mooar interview file, TxMH.

Mooar, Lydia Louise. "The Mooar Brothers and Adobe Walls." TS. n.d. 76 lvs. Mooar Family Papers, TxLTswc.

Mooar, Miss Louise, to Walter Campbell, July 7, 1952. MS. 5 lvs. W. S. Campbell Papers, OkU.

Mooney, James, to D. C. Davis, Field Columbian Museum, May 28, 1904. Department of Anthropology, ICF.

———, U.S. Ethnologist, to Andrew Johnson, July 3, 1903. Andrew Johnson Papers, KDcB.

———, U.S. Ethnologist, Bureau of American Ethnology, Smithsonian Institution, to Andrew Johnson, August 29, 1903. Andrew Johnson Papers, KDcB.

———, U.S. Ethnologist, to Andrew Johnson, February 9, 1904. Andrew Johnson Papers, KDcB.

———, U.S. Ethnologist, to Andrew Johnson, February 22, 1904. Andrew Johnson Papers, KDcB.

Munson, William Benjamin, to Laura V. Hamner, June 29, 1921. W. B. Munson Papers, TxCaP.

Myers, A. C., to Robert Cator, June 6, 1874. Robert H. Cator Papers, TxCaP.

———, to Robert Cator and Company, April 8, 1874. Robert H. Cator Papers, TxCaP.

———, to Wilson and Cator, March 3, 1874. Robert H. Cator Papers, TxCaP.

———, to Wilson and Cator, April 5–May 14, 1874. Robert H. Cator Papers, TxCaP.

———, to Wilson and Cator, May 21, 1874. Robert H. Cator Papers, TxCaP.

Myers and Leanard [*sic*], to Cator and Company, September 5, 1874. Robert H. Cator Papers, TxCaP.

———, to Robert Cator, December 21, 1874. Robert H. Cator Papers, TxCaP.

———, to Robert Cator and Company, December 6, 1874. Robert H. Cator Papers, TxCaP.

Norick, Frank A., Principal Museum Anthropologist, Lowie Museum of Anthropology, University of California, Berkeley, to T. Lindsay Baker, January 28, 1981. Quanah file, Adobe Walls research files, TxCaP.

Nye, Wilbur Sturtevant, to Ernest R. Archambeau, March 2, 1961. Ernest R. Archambeau Papers, TxCaP.

———, to Ernest R. Archambeau, March 20, 1961. Ernest R. Archambeau Papers, TxCaP.

———, to Ernest R. Archambeau, February 21, 1962. Ernest R. Archambeau Papers, TxCaP.

———. "H. L. Scott Material" spiral notebook, "Bad Medicine and Good" research notes, W. S. Nye Collection, OkFsA.

———. "A Red-Haired Indian. Who was Tehan? The Mystery of Tehan." MS. 3 lvs. "Bad Medicine and Good" research notes, W. S. Nye Collection, OkFsA.

Osborn, Thomas A., to Rail Road Agent, Dodge City, Kans., July 9, 1874. T. A. Osborn Papers, Manuscript Department, KHi.

Otterby, John (Chief Lean Elk). "Early Recollections of the Panhandle." TS. 1940. 6 lvs. John Otterby (Chief Lean Elk) Papers, TxCaP.

Panhandle-Plains Historical Museum, Canyon, Tex. Accession Record Card No. 43/3. TS. n.d. 1 lf. Office of Registrar, TxCaP.

———. Accession Record Card No. 43/6. TS. n.d. 1 lf. Office of Registrar, TxCaP.

———. Accession Record Card No. 43/7. TS. n.d. 1 lf. Office of Registrar, TxCaP.

———. Accession Record Card No. 43/8. TS. n.d. 1 lf. Office of Registrar, TxCaP.

———. Accession Record Card No. 43/9. TS. n.d. 1 lf. Office of Registrar, TxCaP.

———. Accession Record Card No. 1510/165. TS. June 22, 1963. 1 lf. Office of Registrar, TxCaP.

———. Accession Record Card No. 1510/166. TS. June 22, 1963. 1 lf. Office of Registrar, TxCaP.

———. Accession Record Card No. 1510/171. TS. June 22, 1963. 1 lf. Office of Registrar, TxCaP.

Panhandle-Plains Historical Society and Panhandle-Plains Historical Museum, Canyon, Tex. "Archeological Excavation of the Adobe Walls Trading Post: Progress Report, Summer, 1978." TS. 1978. 17 lvs. Adobe Walls manuscript file, TxCaP.

Peters, Lorin T., to Stanley Vestlel [*sic*] [W. S. Campbell], February 2, 1952. MS. 2 lvs. W. S. Campbell Papers, OkU.

"Plan to Honor Anniversary of Indian Battle." Unidentified newspaper clipping. Ca. June, 1934. 1 lf. Indians—Indian Fights—Adobe Walls (Battles) clipping file, TxSaDrt.

"Plow." MS. Ca. October 17, 1921. 3 lvs. Artifact Documentation File 21.45, Office of Registrar, KHi.

Pope, Jno., to Governor Thomas A. Osborne [*sic*], July 8, 1874. T. A. Osborn Papers, Manuscript Department, KHi.

Quanah. "Told in English & Signs & Comanche: Quanah Parker's Account of Adobe Walls Fight." MS. Interview with Hugh Scott 1897. Ledgerbook 1:14–17. Hugh Scott Collection, OkFsA.

Quinn, R. B., to Frederick S. Barde, January 6, 1911. Dixon, Billy vertical file, OkHirl.

Rabineau, Phyllis, Custodian of Collections, Department of Anthropology, Field Museum of Natural History, Chicago, Ill., to T. Lindsay Baker, January 12, 1981. Adobe Walls—Material Culture—Indian Artifacts on Battlefield file, Adobe Walls research files, TxCaP.

Rath, Charles, to James H. Carter [Cator], April 29, 1892. Robert H. Cator Papers, TxCaP.

———, to James H. Cator, August 29, 1892. Robert H. Cator Papers, TxCaP.

———, to Friend James [H. Cator], March 31, 1896. Robert H. Cator Papers, TxCaP.

———, to James H. Cator, May 6, [18]99. Robert H. Cator Papers, TxCaP.

———. Sworn deposition prepared at Wichita, Kans., October 10, 1892, in the case of Charles Rath and Company v. the United States and the Cheyenne, Kiowa, and Comanche Indians. MS. 18 lvs. U.S. Court of Claims, Indian Depredation Case Files. Case 4593, Charles Rath and Company Claimants. Record Group 123, DNA.

———. Sworn deposition prepared at Wichita, Kans., October 11, 1892, in the case of James H. Cator and Arthur J. L. Cator v. the United States and the Cheyenne, Kiowa, and Comanche Indians. MS. 3 lvs. U.S. Court of Claims, Indian Depredation Case Files. Case 4601, James H. Cator and Arthur J. L. Cator Claimants. Record Group 123, DNA.

Rath, Charles and Company, to Mr. Caitor [*sic*], October 19, 1874. Robert H. Cator Papers, TxCaP.

———, to Robert Cater [*sic*] and Company, June 21, 1874. Robert H. Cator Papers, TxCaP.

———, to McCabe and Cater [*sic*], October 1, 1874. Robert H. Cator Papers, TxCaP.

———, and Myers and Leonard, to His Excellency Governor Thomas A. Osborn, [July] 8, 1874. T. A. Osborn Papers, Manuscript Department, KHi.

———, and Myers and Leonard, to Governor Thomas A. Osborn, July 9, 1874. T. A. Osborn Papers, Manuscript Department, KHi.

Raymond, H. H. "Notes on Diary of H. H. Raymond of 1873 by Himself, 1935." TS. 1935. 53 lvs. "Buffalo, the Frontier, the Indians" notebook, pp. 110–62. Carl Coke Rister Papers, Box 10, TxLTswc.

Schofield, Donald Frank. "W. M. D. Lee, Indian Trader." Unpublished M.A. thesis, West Texas State University, Canyon, Tex. 1980. TxCaW.

Sheridan, Philip Henry, to John Pope, August 21, 1874. Philip Henry Sheridan Papers, Manuscript Division, DLC.

————, to Wm. D. Whipple, Assistant Adjutant General, Headquarters of the Army, Saint Louis, Mo., October 1, 1874. U.S. Department of War, Secretary, *Report of the Secretary of War* 1: 22–29. 43rd Congress, 2nd Session, House Executive Document No. 1, Part 2. Washington, D.C.: Government Printing Office, 1874.

Shields, Edith. "James E. May." TS. August 23, 1933. 11 lvs. Edith Shields Papers, TxCaP.

Sieber, Coila. "Trail Maker." TS. n.d. 2 lvs. Charles Edward Jones Papers, TxCaP.

Stauth, Tom, to W. E. Connelley, October 17, 1921. Artifact Documentation file 21.45, Office of Registrar, KHi.

Stephens, Jno. H., to James H. Cator, January 31, 1898. Robert H. Cator Papers, TxCaP.

————, to James H. Cator, February 20, 1898. Robert H. Cator Papers, TxCaP.

Sullivan, Dulcie. "The McAllisters: Panhandle Pioneers." TS. n.d. 6 lvs. Dulcie Sullivan Papers, TxCaP.

Taylor, Joe F., to G. Derek West, February 15, 1960. Correspondence, Joe F. Taylor–Derek West file, Ernest R. Archambeau Papers, TxCaP.

Thoburn, Joseph B., to William E. Connelley, August 26, 1934. Joseph B. Thoburn Papers, Manuscript Department, KHi.

Tilghman, Zoe A., to Captain Ronald G. Baxter, November 24, 1955. TS. 2 lvs. CoPsB.

————, to Merritt Beeson, September 25, 1941. Bill Tilghman vertical file, KDcB.

————, to W. S. Campbell, March 23, 1952. W. S. Campbell Papers, OkU.

————. "The Story of 'Dutch Henry' Borne [*sic*]." TS. 1941. 8 lvs. Dutch Henry Borne vertical file, KDcB.

U.S. Court of Claims. Indian Depredation Case Files, Case 711, Robert M. Wright Claimant. MS. Record Group 123, DNA.

————. Indian Depredation Case Files. Case 1167, Charles Rath Claimant. MS. Record Group 123, DNA.

————. Indian Depredation Case Files. Case 4593, Charles Rath and Company Claimants. MS. Record Group 123, DNA.

————. Indian Depredation Case Files. Case 4601, James H. Cator and Arthur J. L. Cator Claimants. MS. Record Group 123, DNA.

————. Indian Depredation Case Files. Case 10102, Frederick J. Leonard and A. C. Myers, trading as Myers and Leonard, Claimants. MS. Record Group 123, DNA.

————. Indian Depredation Case Files. Case 10316, John W. Mooar Claimant. MS. Record Group 123, DNA.

————. Records of the Court of Claims Section. Indian Depredation Case Files. Case 4593, Charles Rath and Company Claimants. MS. Record Group 205, DNA.

————. Records of the Court of Claims Section. Indian Depredation Case Files. Case 4601, James H. Cator and Arthur J. L. Cator Claimants. MS. Record Group 205, DNA.

————. Records of the Court of Claims Section. Indian Depredation Case Files. Case 10102, Frederick J. Leonard and A. C. Myers, trading as Myers and Leonard, Claimants. MS. Record Group 205, DNA.

U.S. Department of the Interior. Patent Office. Patent No. 106,303. August 16, 1870. Benjamin Franklin Adams, lamp burner. DP.

U.S. Department of the Treasury. Internal Revenue Service. "United States Stamp for Internal Revenue Special Tax, Act of October 1, 1890. Received from Andy Johnson the Sum of Fourteen and 58/100 Dollars for Special Tax on the Business of Retail Liquor Dealer at Dodge City, State of Kansas, for the Period Represented by the Coupon or Coupons Hereto Attached. Dated at Leavenworth, Kansas, December 31, 1901, W. W. Sutton." MS. December 31, 1901. 1 lf. Andrew Johnson Papers, KDcB.

U.S. Department of War. Army. Fifth Infantry. General Orders No. 28. Camp near Fort Sill, Indian Territory, January 24, 1875. MS. 1 lf. William Dixon Papers, TxCaP.

————. Army. Office of the Adjutant General. Letters Received Relating to "Campaign against Hostile Indians in the Indian Territory," Consolidated File 2815–1874. MS. Record Group 94, DNA.

[Untitled drawing of corral gate at 1874 Adobe Walls trading post.] MS. Ca. March 10, 1923. 1 lf. History—Adobe Walls file, Manuscript Department, KHi.

[Untitled plan of 1874 Adobe Walls trading post.] MS. Ca. March 10, 1923. 1 lf. History—Adobe Walls file, Manuscript Department, KHi.

Wayne, Frances. "Denver Visitor Recalls Story of Historic Battle in Texas." Unidentified newspaper clipping. August 20, 1933. 1 lf. Scrapbook No. 1768, p. 29, KDcB.

Wellman, Paul I. "The Battle of Adobe Walls." Wellman Indian Wars Scrapbooks, 1:147–53. KHi.

West, G. Derek, to Joe F. Taylor, March 7, 1960. Correspondence, Joe F. Taylor–Derek West file, Ernest R. Archambeau Papers, TxCaP.

White, Lonnie J., ed. "Andy Johnson's Account of the Adobe Walls Fight." TS. Ca. 1968. 11 lvs. Lonnie J. White Papers, TxCaP.

Wood, Lester, to Ernest R. Archambeau, August 14, 1963. Ernest R. Archambeau Papers, TxCaP.

————, to J. Evetts Haley, January 4, 1947. George Causey interview file, TxMH.

Woodall, Z. T., to William Dixon, January 4, 1899. William Dixon Papers, TxCaP.

Woods, Richard G., Director, Vermont Historical Society, to Mrs. Elizabeth Jaderborg, Secretary, Smoky Valley Historical Association, March 16, 1964. File 970.2 Mss. No. 1, Manuscript Department, KHi.

Wright, R. M., to Cator Brothers, September 23, 1892. Robert H. Cator Papers, TxCaP.

————. Sworn deposition prepared at Wichita, Kans., October 10, 1892, in the case of Charles Rath and Company v. the United States and the Cheyenne, Kiowa, and Comanche Indians. MS. 7 lvs. U.S. Court of Claims, Indian Depredation Case Files. Case 4593, Charles Rath and Company Claimants. Record Group 123, DNA.

————. Sworn deposition prepared at Wichita, Kans., October 11, 1892, in the case of James H. Cator and Arthur J. L. Cator v. the United States and the Cheyenne, Kiowa, and Comanche Indians. MS. 3 lvs. U.S. Court of Claims, Indian Depredation Case Files. Case 4601, James H. Cator and Arthur J. L. Cator Claimants. Record Group 123, DNA.

Zimmerman, F. C., to Robert Cater [*sic*], October 1, 1874. Robert H. Cator Papers, TxCaP.

————, to Robert Cater [*sic*] and Brother, October 19, 1874. Robert H. Cator Papers, TxCaP.

————, to R. Cator, November 23, 1874. Robert H. Cator Papers, TxCaP.

Interviews

Alexander, R. T., to C. Boone McClure at unidentified location, May 10, 1958. R. T. Alexander Papers, TxCaP.

Archambeau, Ernest R., to T. Lindsay Baker at Canyon, Tex., September 6, 1978. Adobe Walls—Geography file, Adobe Walls research files, TxCaP.

Asanap, Herman, to R. B. Thomas at Indiahoma, Okla., October 30, 1937. Interview No. 9041. Indian-Pioneer Papers, Vol. 99, pp. 232–37, OkHiamd.

Baldwin, Frank D., to Thomas F. Dawson at Denver, Colo., March 28, 1922. Frank Dwight Baldwin Papers, CoHi.

Botalye to Wilbur Sturtevant Nye, March 6, 1935. MS notes in note pad no. 16, "Carbine and Lance" research materials, W. S. Nye Collection, OkFsA.

Brown, Lloyd M., to T. Lindsay Baker, June 6, 1979. Arthur Brown file, Adobe Walls research files, TxCaP.

Bussell, Richard, to L. F. Sheffy at Canadian, Tex., December 27, 1929. Richard Bussell Papers, TxCaP.

————, to L. F. Sheffy at Canadian, Tex., n.d. L. F. Sheffy Papers, TxCaP.

Carter, W. S., to Margaret Haley at Amarillo, Tex., December 28, 1945. Margaret Haley Papers, TxCaP.

Co-hay-yah to Wilbur Sturtevant Nye on Blue Beaver Creek, Okla., March 18, 1935. MS notes in note pad no. 16, "Carbine and Lance" research materials, W. S. Nye Collection, OkFsA.

Cox, W. C., to Ronald Davis at Childress, Tex., late June or early July, 1936. In Ronald Davis, ed., "Memoirs of Panhandle Pioneers." July 15, 1936. Ronald Davis Papers, TxCaP.

————, to Ethel McConnell at Childress, Tex., n.d. Ethel McConnell Papers, TxCaP.

Dixon, Olive King, to Willie Newbury Lewis at Amarillo, Tex., July 27, 1935. Willie Newbury Lewis Papers, TxDaHi.

Goodnight, Charles, to J. Evetts Haley at Clarendon, Tex., September 17, 1928.

Goodnight Interview File, Charles Goodnight Collection, J. Evetts Haley Papers, TxMH.

Griffis, Joseph K., to Ernest R. Archambeau at Amarillo, Tex., 1938. Ernest R. Archambeau Papers, TxCaP.

Hanson, James A., to Billy R. Harrison at Canyon, Tex., July 16, 1976. Adobe Walls—Material Culture—Tacks file, Adobe Walls research files, TxCaP.

Henn, Nora, to B. Byron Price at Lincoln, N.M., July 23, 1983. Joseph Kingery file, Adobe Walls research files, TxCaP.

Hopkins, J. H., to L. F. Sheffy, December 31, 1929. J. H. Hopkins Papers, TxCaP.

Jones, C. E. (Ed), to L. F. Sheffy at Woodward, Okla., December 31, 1929. C. E. Jones Papers, TxCaP.

Lieneman, Peter T., to Linnaeus B. Ranck at May, Okla., November 30, 1937. Interview No. 9401. Indian-Pioneer Papers, 109: 210–23, OkHiamd.

McAllister, J. E., to J. Evetts Haley at Channing, Tex., July 1, 1926. J. E. McAllister Papers, TxCaP.

Mooar, J. Wright, to J. Evetts Haley at Snyder, Tex., November 25, 1927, and January 4, 1928. J. Evetts Haley Papers, TxCaP.

————, to J. Evetts Haley at Snyder, Tex., February 11, 1928. J. Evetts Haley Papers, TxCaP.

————, to J. Evetts Haley at Snyder, Tex., April 12, 1936. W. S. Campbell Papers, OkU.

————, to Frank P. Hill, J. B. Slaughter, and Jim Weatherford at Snyder, Tex., May 15, 1936. Frank P. Hill Papers, TxCaP.

————, to Earl Vandale, J. Evetts Haley, and Hervey Chesley at Snyder, Tex., March 2, 3, and 4, 1939. Earl Vandale Collection, TxUAr.

Nelson, Orville Howell, to J. Evetts Haley at Romero, Tex., February 26, 1927. Judge O. H. Nelson Papers, TxCaP.

Poafebitty, Frank Yellow Fish, Felix Cowens, and Several Old Women to Wilbur Sturtevant Nye. MS notes in note pad no. 9, "Carbine and Lance" research materials, W. S. Nye Collection, OkFsA.

Puckett, J. L., to James R. Carselowey at Vinita, Okla., Ca. 1937. Interview No. 7120. Indian-Pioneer Papers, 70: 376–92. OkHiamd.

Rath, Robert M., to Seymour V. Connor at Canyon, Tex., June 26, 1952. Robert M. Rath Papers, TxCaP.

Schneider, Alexander, to J. Evetts Haley at Pampa, Tex., July 15, 1926. Alexander Schneider Papers, TxCaP.

Simpson, George, to Pearl Spaugh at Canadian, Tex., July 27, 1936. Pearl Spaugh Papers, TxCaP.

Stroud, Harry, to Ophelia D. Vestal at Oklahoma City, Okla., January 5, 1938. Interview No. 9606. Indian-Pioneer Papers, 87: 368–408, OkHiamd.

Thomas, Robert, B., to J. S. Clark at Cache, Okla., October 1, 1937. Interview No. 8768. Indian-Pioneer Papers, OkHiamd.

Weills, May McAllister, to Curtis C. Cadenhead at Canyon, Tex., June 12, 1971. May McAllister Weills Papers, TxCaP.

————, to Larry Bobbitt at Amarillo, Tex., June 29, 1974. May McAllister Weills Papers, TxCaP.

White, J. Phelps, to J. Evetts Haley at Roswell, N.M., January 15, 1927. J. Phelps White Papers, TxCaP.

Wilson, Jim P., to J. Evetts Haley at Alpine, Tex., January 1, 1928. Jim B. Wilson Papers, TxCaP.

Wood, Lester, to T. Lindsay Baker, June 20, 1980. Adobe Walls—Battle—Fighting file, Adobe Walls research files, TxCaP.

Books

Albert, Alphaeus H. *Record of American Uniform and Historical Buttons with Supplement.* Boyertown, Pa.: Boyertown Publishing Company, 1973. DLC

Albert, Lillian Smith, and Jane Ford Adams. *The Button Sampler.* New York: M. Barrows and Company, 1951. DLC

Alexander, Drury Blakeley. *Texas Homes of the 19th Century.* Austin: University of Texas Press, 1966. TxCaP

Anderson, Charles G. *In Search of the Buffalo: The Story of J. Wright Mooar.* Seagraves, Tex.: Pioneer Book Publishers, 1974. TxCaP

Baldwin, Frank D. *Memoirs of the Late Frank D. Baldwin, Major General, U.S.A.* Edited by Alice Blackwood Baldwin. Los Angeles: Wetzel Publishing Co., 1929. TxCaP

Baldwin, Joseph K. *A Collector's Guide to Patent and Proprietary Medicine Bottles of the Nineteenth Century.* Nashville: Thomas Nelson, 1973. DLC

Ballenger, J. H., and W. C. Howe. *Ballenger & Howe, Fourth Annual City Directory of the Inhabitants, Institutions, Incorporated Companies, Manufacturing Establishments, Business, Business Firms, Etc., in the City of Leavenworth for 1875.* Leavenworth, Kans.: Commercial Steam Book and Job Printing House, 1875. DLC

Barber, Edwin Atlee. *Marks of American Potters.* Reprint, Southampton, N.Y.: Cracker Barrel Press, n.d. ViWC

Barclay's Business Directory of Leavenworth for 1859. Leavenworth, Kans.: Frank F. Barclay's English, French and German Printing Establishment, 1859. DLC

Barnes, Frank C. *Cartridges of the World.* Edited by John T. Amber. Chicago: Follett Publishing Company, 1965. TxCaP

Bartholomew, Ed. *1001 Bitters Bottles.* Fort Davis, Tex.: Bartholomew House, 1970. DLC

————. *1200 Old Medicine Bottles.* Fort Davis, Tex.: Frontier Book Company, 1970. DLC

Battey, Thomas C. *The Life and Adventures of a Quaker Among the Indians.* Boston: Lee and Shepard; New York: Lee, Shepard and Dillingham, 1875; Reprint, Norman: University of Oklahoma Press, 1968. TxCaP

The Battle of Adobe Walls. Guymon, Okla.: First National Bank of Guymon, Oklahoma, n.d. TxCaP

Baumann, Paul. *Collecting Antique Marbles*. Des Moines, Iowa: Wallace-Homestead Book Company, 1970. TxCaP

Bechdolt, Frederick R. *Tales of the Old-Timers*. New York: Century, 1924. TxCaP

Beck, Doreen. *The Book of Bottle Collecting*. London: Hamlyn Publishing Group Limited, 1973. DLC

Berthrong, Donald J. *The Southern Cheyennes*. Norman: University of Oklahoma Press, 1963. TxCaP

Bligh, R. W., comp. *The New York Herald Almanac and Financial, Commercial and Political Register for 1874*. New York, 1874. TxLT

Blumenstein, Lynn. *Bottle Rush U.S.A.* Salem, Ore.: Old Time Bottle Publishing Company, 1966. DLC

Boyd's Business Directory of Over One Hundred Cities and Towns in Pennsylvania. Syracuse, N.Y.: Andrew Boyd; Pottsville, Pa.: W. Harry Boyd, 1873. DLC

Boyd's New Jersey State Directory, 1874. Syracuse, N.Y.: Andrew Boyd, 1874. DLC

Branch, E. Douglas. *The Hunting of the Buffalo*. New York: D. Appleton and Company, 1929. TxCaP

Bryan, Kirk. *Flint Quarries—The Sources of Tools and, at the Same Time, the Factories of the American Indian*. Papers of the Peabody Museum of American Archaeology and Ethnology, Harvard University, XVII, no. 3. Cambridge, Mass.: Peabody Museum of American Archaeology and Ethnology, 1950. TxCaP

Buffalo Scale Company. *Illustrated Catalogue of United States Standard Scales Manufactured by Buffalo Scale Co., Buffalo, N.Y.* Buffalo: Courier Company Print, 1874. MBSpnea

Campbell, Walter S. [Stanley Vestal, pseud.] *'Dobe Walls: A Story of Kit Carson's Southwest*. Boston: Houghton Mifflin Company, 1929. TxCaP

──────. *Queen of the Cowtowns: Dodge City, "the Wickedest Little City in America" 1872–1886*. New York: Harper & Brothers, 1952. TxCaP

──────. *Warpath and Council Fire: The Plains Indians' Struggle for Survival in War and in Diplomacy*. New York: Random House, 1948. KHi.

Carter, Robert Goldthwaite. *On the Border with Mackenzie: or, Winning West Texas from the Comanches*. Washington, D.C.: Eynon Printing Company, 1935. TxCaP

──────. *The Old Sergeant's Story: Winning the West from the Indians and Bad Men in 1870 to 1876*. New York: Frederick H. Hitchcock, Publisher, 1926. TxCaP

Chamberlin, Erwina, and Minerva Miner. *Button Heritage*. Sherburne, N.Y.: Fay Edward Faulkner Printing Company, 1967. DLC

Chenhall, Robert G. *Nomenclature for Museum Cataloging: A System for Classifying Man-Made Objects*. Nashville: American Association for State and Local History, 1978. TxCaP

Chesley, Hervey E. *Adventuring with the Old-Timers: Trails Travelled—Tales*

Told. Edited by B. Byron Price. Midland, Tex.: Nita Stewart Haley Memorial Library, 1979. TxCaP

Clark, O. S. *Clay Allison of the Washita, First a Cow Man and Then an Extinguisher of Bad Men: Recollections of Colorado, New Mexico and the Texas Panhandle, Reminiscences of a '79er*. N.p.: privately printed, 1932. CoD

Collins, Charles, comp. *Collins' City Directory of Leavenworth*. Leavenworth, Kans.: Charles Collins, 1866. DLC

Collins, Dennis. *The Indians' Last Fight or the Dull Knife Raid*. Girard, Kans.: Press of the Appeal to Reason, ca. 1915. CoD

Conover, George W. *Sixty Years in Southwest Oklahoma or the Autobiography of George W. Conover with Some Thrilling Incidents of Indian Life in Oklahoma and Texas*. Anadarko, Okla.: N. T. Plummer, Book and Job Printer, 1927. CoD

Constructive Action Taken on "Adobe Walls Field" June 27th, 1924. N.p.: 1924. Adobe Walls, Battle of, vertical file, OkHirl

Cook, John R. *The Border and the Buffalo: An Untold Story of the Southwest Plains*. Topeka, Kans.: Crane & Company, 1907. TxCaP

Costa, Isaac, comp. *Gospill's Philadelphia Business Directory for 1874*. Philadelphia: James Gospill, 1874. DLC

Covill, William E., Jr. *Ink Bottles and Inkwells*. Taunton, Mass.: William S. Sullwold Publishing, 1971. DLC

Crouch, Daniel J. *Archaeological Investigations of the Kiowa and Comanche Commissaries, 34—Cm—232*. Contributions of the Museum of the Great Plains No. 7. Lawton, Okla.: Museum of the Great Plains, 1978. TxCaP

Cuffley, Peter. *A Complete Catalogue and History of Oil and Kerosene Lamps in Australia*. Yarra Glen, Victoria, Australia: Pioneer Design Studio Pty., 1973. DLC

Curry, George. *George Curry, 1861–1947: An Autobiography*. H. B. Hening. Albuquerque: University of New Mexico Press, 1958. TxCaP

Cushion, J. P. *Pocket Book of British Ceramic Marks Including Index to Registered Designs 1842–83*. 3rd enlarged ed. London: Faber and Faber, 1976. ViWC

———. *Pocket Book of English Ceramic Marks and Those of Wales, Scotland and Ireland*. Boston: Boston Book & Art Shop, 1962. ViWC

Cushion, J. P., and W. B. Honey. *Handbook of Pottery and Porcelain Marks*. London: Faber and Faber, 1956. ViWC

Day, James M., and Dorman Winfrey, eds. *Texas Indian Papers 1860–1916*. Austin: Texas State Library, 1961. TxCaP

DeArment, Robert K. *Bat Masterson: The Man and the Legend*. Norman: University of Oklahoma Press, 1979. TxCaP

Demmin, Auguste. *An Illustrated History of Arms and Armour from the Earliest Period to the Present Time*. Translated by C. C. Black. London: George Bell & Sons, 1877. TxCaP

Denver, Kay. *Patent Medicine Picture*. Tucson, Ariz.: privately printed, 1968. DLC

Dickson, Bruce D., and William Westbury. *Archaeological Research at Fort Richardson State Park, Summer 1975*. Texas A&M University, Anthropology Laboratory, Report No. 28. College Station: Anthropology Laboratory, Texas A&M University, 1976. TxCM

Dixon, Olive K. *The Fight at Adobe Walls: Extract from Life of "Billy" Dixon by Olive K. Dixon*. Dallas: P. L. Turner Company, Publishers, 1935. Adobe Walls Manuscript File. TxCaP

[――――.] *Life and Adventures of "Billy" Dixon of Adobe Walls, Texas Panhandle*. Edited by Frederick S. Barde. Guthrie, Okla.: Co-Operative Publishing Company, 1914. TxCaP

――――. *Life of "Billy" Dixon: Plainsman, Scout and Pioneer*. Edited by Joseph B. Thoburn. Rev. ed. Dallas: P. L. Turner Company, 1927. TxCaP

Dodge, Richard Irving. *Our Wild Indians: Thirty-Three Years' Personal Experience among the Red Men of the Great West*. Hartford, Conn.: A. D. Worthington and Company, 1882. TxCaP

Drago, Henry Sinclair. *Red River Valley: The Mainstream of Frontier History from the Louisiana Bayous to the Texas Panhandle*. New York: Clarkson N. Potter, 1962. TxCaP

Eble, Jesse G. *The Red Trail*. New York: Henry Harrison, 1931. KHi

Eggenhoffer, Nick. *Wagons, Mules and Men: How the Frontier Moved West*. New York: Hastings House Publishers, 1961. TxCaP

Ellis, Richard N. *General Pope and U.S. Indian Policy*. Albuquerque: University of New Mexico Press, 1970. TxCaP

Emilio, Luis Fenolossa. *The Emilio Collection of Military Buttons: American, British, French and Spanish, with Some Other Countries, and Non-Military in the Museum of the Essex Institute, Salem, Mass.* Salem, Mass.: Essex Institute, 1911. DLC

Emmons, William H., George A. Thiel, Clinton R. Stauffer, and Ira S. Allison. *Geology: Principles and Processes*. 3rd ed. New York: McGraw-Hill Book Company, 1949. TxCaW

The Encyclopedia of Collectibles. 16 vols. Chicago: Time-Life Books, 1978–80. TxCaP

Erickson, John R. *Through Time and the Valley*. Austin: Shoal Creek Publishers, 1978. TxCaP

Fehrenbach, T. R. *Comanches: The Destruction of a People*. New York: Alfred A. Knopf, 1974. TxCaP

Fike, Richard E. *Handbook for Bottle-ologist*. Ogden, Utah: privately printed, 1965. DLC

Flayderman, Norm. *Flayderman's Guide to American Firearms and Their Values*. Chicago: Follett Publishing Company, 1977. TxCaP

Fleming, G. *Practical Horseshoeing*. New York: D. Appleton and Company, 1872. TxCaP

Ford, Grace Horney. *The Button Collector's History*. Springfield, Mass.: privately printed, 1943. DLC

Fox, Anne A. *Archaeological Investigations at Fort Griffin State Historic Park, Shackelford County, Texas*. Center for Archaeological Research, Archaeological Survey Report No. 23. San Antonio: University of Texas at San Antonio, 1976. TxSaU

Freeman, Graydon La Verne [James H. Thompson, pseud.]. *Bitters Bottles*. Watkins Glen, N.Y.: Century House, 1947. DLC

Freeman, Larry. *Grand Old American Bottles*. Watkins Glen, N.Y.: Century House, 1964. DLC

Fulton, Maurice Garland. *History of the Lincoln County War*. Edited by Robert N. Mullin. Tucson: University of Arizona Press, 1968. TxCaP

Gannon, Fred A. *A Short History of American Shoemaking*. Salem, Mass.: privately printed, 1912. NhD

Gard, Wayne. *The Great Buffalo Hunt*. New York: Alfred A. Knopf, 1959. TxCaP

Garrett, I. W., comp. *Official Manual of the State of Idaho for the Years 1895–1896*. N.p.: I. W. Garrett, secretary of state, ca. 1896. IdHi

Godden, Geoffrey A. *Encyclopedia of British Pottery and Porcelain Marks*. New York: Bonanza Books, 1965. TxCaP

Goodyear's India Rubber Glove Manufacturing Co., 205 Broadway, Manufacturers and Wholesale Dealers in Every Description of Rubber Goods, Including Clothing of All Kinds, Gloves and Mittens, Druggist's Articles, Combs, Jewelry, Army Blankets, Air Goods, Stationers' Articles, Fancy Articles, Etc., Etc. New York: Goodyear's India Rubber Glove Manufacturing Company, n.d. OAkF

Gove, Philip Babcock, ed. *Webster's Third New International Dictionary of the English Language Unabridged*. Springfield, Mass.: C. & G. Merriam Company, Publishers, 1971. TxCaW

Griffis, Joseph K. *Tahan, Out of Savagery into Civilization: An Autobiography*. New York: George H. Doran Company, 1915. CoD

Grinnell, George Bird. *The Fighting Cheyennes*. New York: Charles Scribner's Sons, 1915. TxCaP

————. *Pawnee, Blackfoot and Cheyenne*. New York: Charles Scribner's Sons, 1961. TxCaP

Groben, W. Ellis. *Adobe Architecture: Its Design and Construction*. Reprint, Seattle: Shorey Book Store, 1975. TxCaP

Groves, G. I., comp. *Famous American Indians*. Chicago: privately printed, 1944. KHi

Hagan, William T. *United States–Comanche Relations: The Reservation Years*. New Haven: Yale University Press, 1976. TxCaP

Haley, J. Evetts. *Charles Goodnight: Cowman & Plainsman*. Boston: Houghton Mifflin Company, 1936. TxCaP

Haley, James L. *The Buffalo War: The History of the Red River Indian Uprising of 1874*. Garden City, N.Y.: Doubleday & Company, 1976. TxCaP

Hall, Frank. *History of the State of Colorado.* 4 vols. Chicago: Blakeley Printing Company, 1895. KHi

Hamilton, Mark. *1941 Adobe Walls Indian Ceremonials: Drama from the Historical Cavalcade of the Frontier West, Borger, Texas, October 17– 18–19, Huber Stadium, 8:00 P.M.* Borger, Tex.: Hutchinson County Fair Association, 1941. Adobe Walls manuscript file, TxCaP

Hanson, James Austin. *Metal Weapons, Tools, and Ornaments of the Teton Dakota Indians.* Lincoln: University of Nebraska Press, 1975. TxCaP

Harris, H. G. *Collecting and Identifying Old Clocks.* Buchanan, N.Y.: Emerson Books, 1977. TxCaP

Hart, Herbert M. *Old Forts of the Southwest.* Seattle: Superior Publishing Company, 1962. TxCaP

Hecht, Arthur, comp. *Postal History in the Texas Panhandle.* Canyon, Tex.: Panhandle-Plains Historical Society, 1960. TxCaP

Heitman, Francis B., comp. *Historical Register and Dictionary of the United States Army, from Its Organization, September 29, 1789, to March 2, 1903.* 2 vols. Washington, D.C.: Government Printing Office, 1903. TxCaP

Herskovitz, Robert M. *Fort Bowie Material Culture.* Anthropological Papers of the University of Arizona, No. 31. Tucson: University of Arizona Press, 1978. TxCaP

Hill, Joseph A. *The Panhandle-Plains Historical Society and Its Museum.* Canyon, Tex.: West Texas State College Press, 1955. TxCaP

Historical and Biographical Record of the Cattle Industry and the Cattlemen of Texas and Adjacent Territory. St. Louis: Woodward & Tiernan Printing Company 1895. TxCaP

Holbrook, Stewart H. *The Golden Age of Quackery.* New York: Macmillan Company, 1959. TxCaW

Hoye's Kansas City Directory for 1882. Kansas City, Mo.: Hoye City Directory, 1882. DLC

Huckabay, Ida Lasater. *Ninety-four Years in Jack County 1854–1948.* Austin: Steck Company, 1949. TxCaP

Hughes, Jack T., and Patrick S. Willey. *Archeology at Mackenzie Reservoir.* Office of the State Archeologist, Archeological Survey Report No. 24. Austin: Texas Historical Commission, 1978. TxCaP

Hyde, George. *Life of George Bent Written from His Letters.* Edited by Savoie Lottinville. Norman: University of Oklahoma Press, 1967. TxCaP

Idaho Senate. *Journal of the Senate of the State of Idaho Third Session* . . . Boise, Idaho: Statesman Printing Company, 1895. IdHi

Jackson, Jack. *Comanche Moon: A Picture Narrative about Cynthia Ann Parker, Her Twenty-Five Year Captivity among the Comanche Indians— and Her Son, Quanah Parker, the Last Chief of the Comanches.* San Francisco: Rip Off Press, Inc., and Last Gasp Eco-Funnies, 1979. TxCaP

Johnson, David F. *Uniform Buttons: American Armed Forces 1784–1948.* 2 vols. Watkins Glen, N.Y.: Century House, 1948. TxCaP

Jones, Douglas C. *The Treaty of Medicine Lodge: The Story of the Great Treaty*

Council as Told by Eyewitnesses. Norman: University of Oklahoma Press, 1966. TxCaP

Jonesbury, John, Jr. *Lamp Primer, or Lamp Light and Lamps, and How to Care for Them*. Columbus, Ohio: Harrop & Company, Publishers, 1893. DLC

Kansas State Gazetteer and Business Directory Including a Complete Business Directory of Kansas City, Mo. 1884–5. Chicago: R. L. Polk & Company, and A. C. Danser, 1884. DLC

Kansas State Gazetteer and Business Directory Including also a Complete Business Directory of Kansas City, Mo. 1878. Detroit: R. L. Polk & Company, and A. C. Danser, 1878. DLC

Kansas State Gazetteer and Business Directory, Including a Complete Business Directory of Kansas City, Mo. 1888–9. Detroit: R. L. Polk & Company, 1888. DLC

Kansas State Gazetteer and Business Directory. Including a Complete Business Directory of Kansas City, Mo. 1882–3. St. Paul, Minn.: R. L. Polk & Company, and A. C. Danser, 1882. DLC

Kappler, Charles J. comp. *Indian Affairs. Laws and Treaties*. 5 vols. Washington, D.C.: Government Printing Office, 1904–1941. TxCaW

Keleher, William A. *Violence in Lincoln County 1869–1881*. Albuquerque: University of New Mexico Press, 1957. TxCaP

Kemper-Paxton Mercantile Company. *Kemper-Paxton Mercantile Co., the House That Saves You Money, Price Book No. 20, Year 1906–7*. Kansas City, Mo.: Kemper-Paxton Mercantile Company, 1906. TxCaP

Ketchum, William C., Jr. *A Treasury of American Bottles*. Indianapolis: Bobbs-Merrill, 1975. DLC

Knight, Edward H. *Knight's American Mechanical Dictionary*. 3 vols. New York: Hurd and Houghton; Cambridge, Mass.: Riverside Press, 1876. TxCaP

Kovel, Ralph M., and Terry H. Kovel. *Dictionary of Marks—Pottery and Porcelain*. New York: Crown Publishers, 1953. ViWC

Kraus, Edward Henry, Walter Fred Hunt, and Lewis Stephen Ramsdell. *Mineralogy: An Introduction to the Study of Minerals and Crystals*. 4th ed. New York: McGraw-Hill Book Company, 1951. TxCaW

Lake, Stuart N. *Wyatt Earp: Frontier Marshal*. Boston: Houghton Mifflin Company, 1931. TxCaP

Lamps & Other Lighting Devices 1850–1906. Princeton, N.J.: Pyne Press, 1972. DLC

Lavender, David. *Bent's Fort*. Garden City, N.Y.: Doubleday & Company, 1954. TxCaP

Leckie, William H. *The Military Conquest of the Southern Plains*. Norman: University of Oklahoma Press, 1963. TxCaP

Lewis, Alfred Henry. *The Sunset Trail*. New York: A. S. Barnes & Company, 1905. TxCaP

Lewis, Willie Newberry [*sic*]. *Between Sun and Sod*. Clarendon, Tex.: Clarendon Press, 1938. TxCaP

Lobenstine, William Christian. *Extracts from the Diary of William C. Loben-*

stine December 31, 1851–1858; Biographical Sketch by Belle W. Loben-stine. New York: privately printed, 1920. CoD

The Lockport City Directory, for the Years 1874–75. . . . Rochester, N.Y.: Fitzgerald & Dillon, Publishers, 1874. DLC

Logan, Herschel C. *Cartridges: A Pictorial Digest of Small Arms Ammunition.* New York: Bonanza Books, 1959. TxCaP

Logue, Roscoe. *Under Texas and Border Skies.* Amarillo, Tex.: Russell Stationery Company, 1935. CoD

Lowther, Charles C. *Dodge City, Kansas.* Philadelphia: Dorrance and Company Publishers, 1940. KHi

Ludlum, Stuart D., ed. *Great Shooting Stories.* Garden City, N.Y.: Doubleday & Company, 1947. KHi

Luscomb, Sally C. *The Collector's Encyclopedia of Buttons.* New York: Crown Publishers, 1967. TxCaP

Mayhall, Mildred P. *Indian Wars of Texas.* Waco, Tex.: Texian Press, 1965. TxCaP

_____. *The Kiowas.* Norman: University of Oklahoma Press, 1962. TxCaP

McCarty, John L. *Adobe Walls Bride: The Story of Billy and Olive King Dixon.* San Antonio: Naylor Company, 1955. TxCaP

McDermott, John Francis, Jr., ed. *The French in the Mississippi Valley.* Urbana: University of Illinois Press, 1965. TxCaP

McGinnis, Edith B. *The Promised Land.* Boerne, Tex.: Topperwein Publishing Company, 1947. TxLTswc

_____. *The Promised Land.* 2nd ed. Ann Arbor, Mich.: Cushing-Mallory, 1959. TxLTswc

McGuinn, William F. *American Military Button Makers & Suppliers: Their Backmarks & Dates.* McLean, Va.: privately printed, 1978. DLC

McKearin, Hellen, and Kenneth M. Wilson. *American Bottles & Flasks and Their Ancestry.* New York: Crown Publishers, 1978. DLC

McNeal, T. A. *When Kansas Was Young.* Topeka, Kans.: Capper Publications, 1922. KHi

Meriden City Directory for 1873–74. Hartford, Conn.: Nathan Fenn and Company, 1873. DLC

Merwin's Leavenworth City Directory for 1870–71. Leavenworth, Kans.: Herman Merwin, Publisher, 1870. DLC

Methuin, J. J. *Andele, or the Mexican-Kiowa Captive: A Story of Real Life among the Indians.* Louisville, Ky.: Pentecostal Herald Press, 1899. KHi

Miles, Nelson A. *Personal Recollections and Observations of General Nelson A. Miles, Embracing a Brief View of the City War; or, from New England to the Golden Gate, and the Story of His Indian Campaigns with Comments on the Exploration, Development and Progress of Our Great Western Empire.* Chicago: Werner Company, 1896. TxCaP

Edward Miller and Company. *Price List of Edward Miller & Co., Meriden, Conn., Manufacturers of Coal Oil Burners, Lamp Trimmings, Tinmen's Hardware, Machine Oilers.* . . . Hartford, Conn.: Case, Lockwood & Brainard, Printers, Book Binders and Paper Dealers, 1868. MH–BA

Miller, Nyle H., and Joseph W. Snell. *Why the West Was Wild: A Contemporary Look at the Antics of Some Highly Publicized Kansas Cowtown Personalities.* Topeka: Kansas State Historical Society, 1963. KHi

Milner, Joe E., and Earle R. Forrest. *California Joe: Noted Scout and Indian Fighter.* Caldwell, Idaho: Caxton Printers, 1935. KHi

Mooney & Morrison's General Directory of the City of San Antonio, for 1877–78. Galveston, Tex.: [Mooney & Morrison] Printed at the Book and Job Office of the Galveston News, 1877. TxSaW

The New York State 1874 Business Directory, Containing the Names, Business and Address of All Merchants, Manufacturers and Professional Men throughout the State. Boston: Sampson, Davenport, & Company, 1874. DLC

Nye, Wilbur Sturtevant. *Bad Medicine & Good: Tales of the Kiowas.* Norman: University of Oklahoma Press, 1962. TxCaP

—————. *Carbine & Lance: The Story of Old Fort Sill.* 2nd ed. Norman: University of Oklahoma Press, 1943. TxCaP

—————. *Plains Indian Raiders: The Final Phases of Warfare from the Arkansas to the Red River.* Norman: University of Oklahoma Press, 1968. TxCaP

Oberg, Erik, and Franklin D. Jones. *Machinery's Handbook: A Reference Book for the Mechanical Engineer, Draftsman, Toolmaker and Machinist.* 19th ed. New York: Industrial Press; Brighton, England: Machinery Publishing Company, 1974. TxCaW

O'Connor, Richard. *Bat Masterson.* Garden City, N.Y.: Doubleday & Company, 1957. TxCaP

Orchard, William C. *Beads and Beadwork of the American Indian: A Study Based on Specimens in the Museum of the American Indian, Heye Foundation.* Contributions 11. New York: Museum of the American Indian, Heye Foundation, 1929. TxCaP

Oringderff, Barbara. *True Sod: Sod Houses of Kansas.* North Newton, Kans.: Mennonite Press, 1976. TxCaP

Ormsbee, Thomas H. *English China and Its Marks.* New York: Deerfield Books, 1959. TxCaP

Paddock, B. B., ed. *A Twentieth Century History and Biographical Record of North and West Texas.* 2 vols. Chicago: Lewis Publishing Company, 1906. TxCaP

[Panhandle-Plains Historical Society]. *Don't Miss the Big Celebration June 27–28, 1924[,] 50th Anniversary of the Famous Frontier Battle of Adobe Walls in Which a Few White Men Fought So Valiantly Against an Overwhelming Number of Indians.* [Canyon, Tex.: Panhandle-Plains Historical Society, 1924.] broadside printed on pink newsprint. KDcB, KHi, OkHirl.

Parker, W. Thornton. *Personal Experiences among Our North American Indians from 1867 to 1885.* Northampton, Mass.: privately printed, 1913. KHi

Patten, Lewis B. *The Hide Hunters.* New York: New American Library, 1973. OBgU

Peterson, Harold L. *American Knives: The First History and Collectors' Guide.* New York: Charles Scribner's Sons, 1958. TxCaP

Pettis, George H. *Personal Narrative of the Battles of the Rebellion: Kit Carson's Fight with the Comanche and Kiowa Indians.* Historical Society of New Mexico [Pamphlet] No. 12. Santa Fe: New Mexican Printing Company, 1908. TxLTswc

Plume and Atwood Manufacturing Company. *The Plume and Atwood Manufacturing Company Illustrated Catalogue of Kerosene Oil Burners, Gas and Oil Lamp Trimmings, Lamps, Oil Heaters, Etc.* Waterbury, Conn.: Plume and Atwood Manufacturing Company, ca. 1906. Reprint, Simpson, Ill.: J. W. Courter Enterprises, n.d. TxCaP

Polk's Kansas State Gazetteer and Business Directory. Including a Complete Business Directory of Kansas City, Mo. 1904. Detroit: R. L. Polk & Company, 1904. DLC

Porter, Millie Jones, ed. *Memory Cups of Panhandle Pioneers.* Clarendon, Tex.: Clarendon Press, 1945. TxCaP

Pratt, Richard Henry. *Battlefield and Classroom: Four Decades with the American Indian, 1867–1904.* Edited by Robert M. Utley. New Haven: Yale University Press, 1964. TxCaP

Price, Lee & Co.'s Meriden Directory for 1876. New Haven: Price, Lee & Company, 1876. DLC

Price, Lee & Co.'s Waterbury Directory for 1877. New Haven: Price, Lee & Company, 1877. DLC

Raine, William MacLeod. *Guns of the Frontier: The Story of How Law Came to the West.* Boston: Houghton Mifflin Company, 1940. KHi

Raine, William MacLeod, and Will C. Barnes. *Cattle.* Garden City, N.Y.: Doubleday, Doran & Company, 1930. KHi

Rath, Ida Ellen. *Early Ford County.* 2nd ed. North Newton, Kans.: Mennonite Press, 1964. TxCaP

———. *The Rath Trail.* Wichita, Kans.: McCormick-Armstrong Co., 1961. TxCaP

Rathjen, Frederick W. *The Texas Panhandle Frontier.* Austin: University of Texas Press, 1973. TxCaP

Refbord, Ada D., ed. *Distinguished Alumni, University of Kentucky.* Lexington, Ky.: University of Kentucky Alumni Association, ca. 1966. TxCaP

Richardson, Rupert Norval. *The Comanche Barrier to South Plains Settlement.* Glendale, Calif.: The Arthur H. Clark Company, 1933. TxCaP

Ripley, Warren. *Artillery and Ammunition of the Civil War.* New York: Promontory Press, 1970. TxCaP

Rister, Carl Coke. *Fort Griffin on the Texas Frontier.* Norman: University of Oklahoma Press, 1956. TxCaP

Rivera, Betty, and Ted Rivera. *Inkstands & Inkwells: A Collector's Guide.* New York: Crown Publishers, 1973. TxCaP

R. L. Polk & Co.'s Salt Lake City Directory (biennial and annual vols.). Salt Lake City: R. L. Polk & Co., Publishers, 1891–1927. DLC

Roberts, Ned, and Kenneth L. Waters. *The Breech-Loading Single-Shot Match Rifle*. Princeton, N.J.: D. Van Nostrand Company, 1967. TxWicM

Robinson, Willard B. *Gone from Texas: Our Lost Architectural Heritage*. College Station: Texas A&M University Press, 1981. TxCaP

Russell and Erwin Manufacturing Company, New Britain, Conn. *Illustrated Catalogue of American Hardware of the Russell and Erwin Manufacturing Company*. New York: Francis Hart & Company, Printers, 1865; Reprint, n.p.: Association for Preservation Technology, 1980. TxCaP

Rye, Edgar. *The Quirt and the Spur: Vanishing Shadows of the Texas Frontier*. Chicago: W. B. Conkey Company Publishers, 1909. CoD

Salt Lake City Directory for 1890. Salt Lake City: R. L. Polk & Company, Publishers, 1890. DLC

Sandoz, Mari. *The Buffalo Hunters: The Story of the Hide Men*. New York: Hastings House, 1954. TxCaP

Schofield, Donald F. *W. M. D. Lee, Indian Trader*. Panhandle-Plains Historical Review, 54. Canyon, Tex.: Panhandle-Plains Historical Society, 1981. TxCaP

Sears, Roebuck and Company, Chicago. *Sears, Roebuck and Co., Incorporated, Cheapest Supply House, Consumers Guide Catalogue No. 104*. Chicago: Sears, Roebuck and Company, 1897. Reprint. Edited by Fred L. Israel. New York: Chelsea House Publishers, 1968. TxCaP

Seger, John H. *Early Days among the Cheyenne and Arapahoe Indians*. Edited by W. S. Campbell [Stanley Vestal]. Norman: University of Oklahoma Press, 1934. TxCaP

Sellers, Frank. *Sharps Firearms*. North Hollywood, Calif.: Beinfeld Publishing, 1978. TxCaP

Shirley, Glenn. *Buckskin and Spurs: A Gallery of Frontier Rogues and Heroes*. New York: Hastings House, Publishers, 1958. KHi

Souvenir of Trek to Adobe Walls, 100th Anniversary, June 27th, 1874, Trip from Dodge City, Kansas, to Spearman and Adobe Walls, Texas. N.p.: privately printed, ca. 1974. Handbill. Adobe Walls vertical file, KDcKhc

Spivey, Towana, ed. *A Historical Guide to Wagon Hardware & Blacksmith Supplies*. Contributions of the Museum of the Great Plains, No. 9. Lawton, Okla.: Museum of the Great Plains, 1979. TxCaP

Stringer, Billy R. *Soil Survey of Hutchinson County, Texas*. Washington, D.C.: Soil Conservation Service, U.S. Department of Agriculture, 1976. TxCaP

Sutton, Fred E., and A. B. McDonald. *Hands Up! Stories of the Six-Gun Fighters of the Old Wild West*. Indianapolis: Bobbs-Merrill Company Publishers, 1926. KHi

Switzer, Ronald R. *The Bertrand Bottles: A Study of 19th Century Glass and Ceramic Containers*. U.S. Department of the Interior, National Park Service, Publications in Archaeology No. 12. Washington, D.C.: Government Printing Office, 1974. TxCaP

Tanner, Henry, comp. *Directory & Shippers' Guide of Kansas & Nebraska. . . .* Leavenworth, Kans.: T. A. Holland & Company, 1866. DLC

Texas Business Directory, for 1878–9. Austin: Texas Directory Company, 1878. DLC

Thuro, Catherine M. V. *Oil Lamps: The Kerosene Era in North America*. Des Moines: Wallace-Homestead Book Co., 1976. DLC

Tibbitts, John C. *1200 Bottles Priced: A Bottle Price Guide and Classification System*. New rev. ed. Sacramento: Little Glass Shack, 1970. DLC

Tilghman, Zoe A. *Marshal of the Last Frontier: Life and Service of William Matthew (Bill) Tilghman for 50 Years One of the Greatest Peace Officers of the West*. Glendale, Calif.: The Arthur H. Clark Company, 1949. TxCaP

———. *Quanah, the Eagle of the Comanches*. Oklahoma City: Harlow Publishing Corporation, 1938. TxCaP

U.S. Department of the Interior. Geological Survey. *Adobe Creek, Tex., N3552.5-W10107.5/7.5*. Washington, D.C.: U.S. Geological Survey, 1974. TxCaP

———. *Amarillo, Texas, NI 14-1, 1:250,000*. Washington, D.C.: U.S. Geological Survey, 1966. TxCaP

———. *Perryton, Texas; Oklahoma; Kansas, NJ 14-10, 1:250,000*. Washington, D.C.: U.S. Geological Survey, 1966. TxCaP

———. *Tucumcari, New Mexico; Texas, NI 13-3, 1:250,000*. Washington, D.C.: U.S. Geological Survey, 1965. TxCaP

University of Kentucky, Lexington, Ky. *University of Kentucky Centennial Founders Day Convocation*. Lexington, Ky.: University of Kentucky, ca. 1965. TxCaP

Van Sickel, S. S. *A Story of Real Life on the Plains Written by Capt. S. S. Van Sickel, Born Sept. 6, 1826: A True Narrative of the Author's Experience*. N.p.: ca. 1890. CoD, CtY, KHi

Walker, Billy Joe. *Focusing on the Past: Adobe Walls Fight, June 26 [sic], 1874*. N.p.: n.d. Handbill. "Maps" vertical file, TxE

Wallace, Ernest, and E. Adamson Hoebel. *The Comanches: Lords of the South Plains*. Norman: University of Oklahoma Press, 1952. TxCaP

Watson, Richard. *Bitters Bottles*. New York: Thomas Nelson & Sons, 1965. DLC

Weaver, J. E., and F. W. Albertson. *Grasslands of the Great Plains: Their Nature and Use*. Lincoln, Nebr.: Johnsen Publishing Company, 1956. TxCaP

Webster, Donald Blake. *Decorated Stoneware Pottery of North America*. Rutland, Vt.: Charles E. Tuttle Company, 1971. TxCaP

Weems, John Edward. *Death Song: The Last of the Indian Wars*. Garden City, N.Y.: Doubleday & Company, 1976. KHi

Wellman, Paul I. *Death on the Prairie: The Thirty Years' Struggle for the Western Plains*. New York: Macmillan Company, 1934. KHi

Welsch, Roger L. *Sod Walls: The Story of the Nebraska Sod House*. Broken Bow, Nebr.: Purcells, 1968. TxCaP

White, Lonnie J., Jerry Keenan, Stanley R. Davidson, James T. King, and Joe A. Stout, Jr. *Hostiles and Horse Soldiers: Indian Campaigns in the West*. Boulder, Colo.: Pruett Publishing Company, 1972. KHi

Whitlock, V. H. (Ol' Waddy). *Cowboy Life on the Llano Estacado.* Norman: University of Oklahoma Press, 1970. TxCaP

Williams, Harry. *Legends of the Great Southwest.* San Antonio: Naylor Printing Company, 1932. TxSa

Wilson, Bill, and Betty Wilson. *19th Century Medicine in Glass.* Amador City, Calif.: 19th Century Hobby & Publishing Company, 1971. DLC

———. *Western Bitters.* Santa Rosa, Calif., 1969. DLC

Wilson, Rex L. *Bottles on the Western Frontier.* Edited by Edward Staski. Tucson: University of Arizona Press, 1981. TxCaP

———. *Clay Tobacco Pipes from Fort Laramie National Historic Site and Related Locations.* Washington, D.C.: Division of Archeology and Anthropology, Office of Archeology and Historic Preservation, National Park Service, 1971. TxCaP

Wiseman, Robert F. *The Complete Horseshoeing Guide.* 2nd ed. Norman: University of Oklahoma Press, 1973. TxCaP

Woodward, Arthur. *The Denominators of the Fur Trade: An Anthology of Writings on the Material Culture of the Fur Trade.* Pasadena, Calif.: Socio-Technical Publications, 1970. TxCaP

Wright, Robert M. *Dodge City: The Cowboy Capital and the Great Southwest in the Days of the Wild Indian, the Buffalo, the Cowboy, Dance Halls, Gambling Halls and Bad Men.* Wichita, Kans.: Wichita Eagle Press, 1913. TxCaP

Yeoman, R. S. *A Guide Book of United States Coins.* 16th rev. ed. Racine, Wis.: Whitman Publishing Company, 1963. TxCaP

Yount, John T. *Bottle Collector's Handbook and Pricing Guide.* San Angelo, Tex.: privately printed, 1967. DLC

Articles

"Adobe Walls Celebration on Thursday: Re-Burial of Colonel Billy Dixon to Be Feature of Historic Event." *Amarillo Daily News* (Amarillo, Tex.), June 16, 1929, p. 1. TxCaP

"Adobe Walls Celebration Plans Advancing Rapidly as June 27 Approaches." *Amarillo Daily News*, June 8, 1924, Western Weekly Supplement, p. 10. TxAm

"Adobe Walls Celebration Plans Continue; Hope to Get Funds for Monument." *Amarillo Daily News*, May 20, 1923, sec. 2, p. 6. TxAm

"Adobe Walls Celebration to Be at Borger." *Amarillo Globe* (Amarillo, Tex.), June 19, 1934, p. 1. TxCaP

"Adobe Walls Ceremonials' Success Assured as Merchants Back What Would Be Profitable Annual Event." *Borger Daily Herald* (Borger, Tex.), October 8, 1941, pp. 1, 2. TxBor

"Adobe Walls Ceremonies Being Staged by Director of Coronada [*sic*] Entrada." *Borger Daily Herald*, October 13, 1941, p. 1. TxBor

"Adobe Walls Ceremony Plans June 27 Completed." *Miami Chief* (Miami, Tex.), June 13, 1929, p. 1. TxLTswc

"Adobe Walls Fete Is Set for Holiday: Historic Battle Recalled as Veterans Prepare to Assemble." *Amarillo Daily News* (Amarillo, Tex.), June 11, 1934, p. 2. TxCaP

"Adobe Walls Fete Slated on July 4." *Amarillo Daily News*, May 16, 1934, p. 4. TxCaP

"Adobe Walls Fighters Here." *Miami Chief* (Miami, Tex.), December 7, 1922, p. 1. TxLTswc

"Adobe Walls Fund Has Been Half Pledged." *Amarillo Daily News* (Amarillo, Tex.), April 27, 1924, sec. 1, p. 10. TxAm

"The 'Adobe Walls:' Graphic Account of a Bloody Battle with Comanches and Kiowas." *Dallas Morning News* (Dallas, Tex.), March 13, 1888, p. 6. TxCaW

"Adobe Walls Monument and Fiftieth Anniversary Picnic Plans Discussed at Pampa." *Amarillo Daily News* (Amarillo, Tex.), January 27, 1924, sec. 1, p. 1. TxAm

"Adobe Walls Pageantry of Yester-Year Re-Enacted: Borger Jammed for Gala Event." *Amarillo Daily News*, October 18, 1941, p. 10. TxCaP

"Adobe Walls Project Funded." *Medallion* (Austin, Tex.) 15, no. 5 (September–October, 1978): 2. TxCaP

"Adobe Walls, Site of Famous Indian Battle, Will Be Preserved." *Amarillo Daily News*, (Amarillo, Tex.), July 24, 1930, p. 13. TxCaP

"Adobe Walls Survivor Says Fight More Important Than San Jacinto." *Amarillo Daily News*, July 13, 1936, p. 1. TxCaP

"Adobe Wells [sic] Battle Veteran Tells Story." *Sunday Topeka Daily Capital* (Topeka, Kans.), June 17, 1934, sec. B, p. 6. KHi

"Amos Chapman" [published notice of cattle brands and markings]. *Globe Live Stock Journal* (Dodge City, Kans.), September 29, 1885), p. 8. KHi

Anderson, Adrienne. "The Archaeology of Mass-Produced Footwear." *Historical Archaeology* 2 (1968): 56–65. TxCaP

"Andy Johnson, Survivor of Famous Adobe Walls Battle, Passes Away in Dodge City." *Amarillo Globe* (Amarillo, Tex.), June 21, 1925, sec. 2, p. 4. TxAm

"Association Is Formed at Adobe Walls Celebration." *Amarillo Daily News* (Amarillo, Tex.), July 7, 1923, p. 5. TxAm

Atchison Daily Champion (Atchison, Kans.), July 7, 1874, p. 2. CoD

Atchison Daily Champion, July 10, 1874, p. 2. CoD

Aynesworth, Joseph H. "Battle of First Adobe Walls Recalled by Borger Lawyer." *Amarillo Sunday News-Globe* (Amarillo, Tex.), June 24, 1934, sec. 2, pp. 5, 10. TxCaP

————. "Wichita Falls Man Writes about Adobe Walls Battle and Gives Many Side Lights." *Amarillo Daily News* (Amarillo, Tex.), July 13, 1924, sec. 2, p. 4. TxAm

Ballard, L. S. "Bud." "Famous Indian Chiefs of the Southwest." *Wichita Magazine* 7, no. 3 (November 20, 1929): 20. KHi

Bass, Henry B. "Quanah Parker's Bonnet." *The War Chief of the Indian Territory Posse of Oklahoma Westerners* 4, no. 3 (December, 1970): 3–6. CoD

"Bat Masterson Was in Adobe Walls Fight." *Randall County News* (Canyon, Tex.), November 17, 1921, [p. 7]. TxCaP

"Battle of Adobe Walls." *Winners of the West* 7, no. 4 (March 30, 1930): 7. KHi

"Battle of Adobe Walls 74 Years Ago Today." *Amarillo Sunday News-Globe* (Amarillo, Tex.), June 27, 1948, sec. 2, p. 21.

"Battle of 'Dobe Walls, Five-Day Fight with Comanche Band, Thrilling Remembrance of John Clinton, Abilene's Pioneer Police Chief." *Fort Worth Star-Telegram* (Fort Worth, Tex.), September 24, 1916, n.p. TxF

"Battled Indians in Western Texas." *Frontier Times* 2, no. 10 (July, 1925): 23–24. TxCaP

Berry, Mrs. C. B. "Scout's Wife." *Amarillo Sunday News-Globe* (Amarillo, Tex.), August 14, 1938, sec. A, p. 30. TxCaP

"Big Celebration Is to Mark Fiftieth Anniversary of Big Indian Battle of Adobe Walls." *Amarillo Daily News* (Amarillo, Tex.), June 22, 1924, p. 10. TxAm

"Billy Dixon[,] Hero of Adobe Walls and Buffalo Wallow[,] One of Nation's Noted Indian Fighters." *Amarillo Daily News*, September 12, 1927, p. 10. TxCaP

"Billy Dixon Remains to Be Buried near Scene of Battle." *Amarillo Daily News*, May 6, 1929, p. 3. TxCaP

"Billy Dixon Rites to Feature Adobe Walls Celebration." *Amarillo Globe* (Amarillo, Tex.), June 27, 1929, pp. 1, 2. TxCaP

Bishop, Curtis. "Red Lightning Struck." *True West* 10, no. 2 (November–December, 1962): 15–16. CoD

Blalock, Fred Frank. "J. Wright Mooar and the Decade of Destruction." *Real West* 17, no. 123 (January, 1974): 50–57. CoD

"Borger Takes on a Gala Appearance as Intensive Preparations Get Under Way for Big Indian Celebration Next Week." *Borger Daily Herald* (Borger, Tex.), October 10, 1941, p. 1. TxBor

Breihan, Carl W. "Horse Thief Deluxe." *Real West* 18, no. 137 (April, 1975): 28–33. CoD

————. "This Time the Cavalry Couldn't Come to the Rescue: The Second Fight at Adobe Walls." *Big West* 4, no. 4 (April, 1970): 50–56, 58. Adobe Walls vertical file, KDcKhc

"'Brick' Bond First Meat Salesman." *Dodge City Daily Globe* (Dodge City, Kans.), March 29, 1939, sec. B, p. 5. KHi

Brininstool, E. A. "Billy Dixon, a Frontier Hero." *Hunter-Trader-Trapper* 50, no. 3 (March, 1925): 11–13; 50, no. 4 (April, 1925): 15–17. TxCaP

"Brothers Meet for First Time in Many Years." *Amarillo Daily News* (Amarillo, Tex.), June 29, 1924, p. 10. TxAm

Brown, George W. "Life and Adventures of George W. Brown: Soldier, Pioneer, Scout, Plainsman and Buffalo Hunter." Edited by William E. Connelley. *Collections of the Kansas State Historical Society* 17 (1926–1928): 98–139. TxCaP

"Buffalo Hunters Resent Slight to Prowess." *Dodge City Daily Globe* (Dodge City, Kans.), November 8, 1933, p. 4. KHi

"Buffalo Wallow Battle Survivor Has Passed Away." *Amarillo Daily News* (Amarillo, Tex.), July 26, 1925, p. 9. TxCaP

Burroughs, Jean M. "Chief Satanta and His Bugle." *Southwest Heritage* 4, no. 4 (Summer, 1974): 21–28. TxCaP

Cable, Ernest, Jr. "A Sketch of the Life of James Hamilton Cator." *Panhandle-Plains Historical Review* 6 (1933): 12–23. TxCaP

Campbell, Charles E. "Down among the Red Men." *Collections of the Kansas State Historical Society* 17 (1926–1928): 623–91. TxCaP

Carlson, Paul H. "Panhandle Pastores: Early Sheepherding in the Texas Panhandle." *Panhandle-Plains Historical Review* 53 (1980): 1–15.

"Cast of 200 Indians to Appear in Adobe Walls Pageantry." *Amarillo Daily News* (Amarillo, Tex.), October 3, 1941, p. 7. TxCaP

"Cator First Judge Hansford County." *Amarillo Daily News*, February 20, 1921, sec. 6, p. 6. TxCaP

"Celebration Is Advertised over Entire State." *Borger Daily Herald* (Borger, Tex.), October 14, 1941, p. 1. TxBor

Chadsey, Don. "Mark 75th Anniversary of Adobe Walls Fight." *Amarillo Sunday News-Globe* (Amarillo, Tex.), June 26, 1949, sec. 2, p. 17. TxCaP

"Cheyenne Dancers to Attend Ceremonials." *Amarillo Daily News* (Amarillo, Tex.), October 8, 1941, p. 14. TxCaP

"Chief Baldwin Parker, Son of Quanah Parker, Will Bring His Family to Borger Celebration." *Borger Daily Herald* (Borger, Tex.), October 10, 1941, p. 2. TxBor

Coleman, Max. "Transformation of the Llano Estacado." *Frontier Times* 13, no. 9 (July, 1936): 476–81. TxCaP

Collins, Ellsworth. "Roman Nose: Chief of the Southern Cheyennes." *Chronicles of Oklahoma* 42, no. 4 (Winter, 1964–65): 429–57. TxCaP

"Col. Billy Dixon Gets Last Wish; Buried at Site of Adobe Walls." *Amarillo Daily News* (Amarillo, Tex.), June 28, 1929, pp. 1, 15. TxCaP

"Comanche Indian Braves Want to Visit Historic Adobe Walls Site; Only Four Survive." *Amarillo Daily News*, January 16, 1931, p. 8. TxCaP

"Comanches Here to Arrange for Three Lone Survivors of Adobe Walls to See Site." *Amarillo Daily News*, February 12, 1931, p. 2. TxCaP

Compton, Lawrence V. "The First Battle of Adobe Walls." In *Great Western Indian Fights*. Edited by B. W. Allred, J. C. Dykes, Frank Goodwyn, and D. Harper Simms. Washington, D.C.: Potomac Corral of the Westerners, 1960. TxCaP

Cook, John R. "Incidents of the Buffalo Range." *Frontier Times* 20, no. 9 (June, 1943): 161–63. TxLTswc

Coulter, John. "The Adobe Walls Fight." *Dodge City Times* (Dodge City, Kans.), November 24, 1877, p. 8. KHi

———. "The Adobe Walls Fight." *Leavenworth Daily Times* (Leavenworth, Kans.), November 17, 1877, [p. 2]. KHi

Coyle, Clarence C. "Stories of Quanah Parker." *Texas Magazine* 4, no. 4 (August, 1911): 30–32; 4, no. 5 (September, 1911): 64–66. TxSaW

Crane, R. C. "Bat Masterson Never Killed Men Needlessly." *Amarillo Sunday News-Globe* (Amarillo, Tex.), August 14, 1938, sec. D, p. 18. TxCaP

———. "First Battle of Adobe Walls." *Amarillo Sunday News-Globe*, August 14, 1938, sec. C, pp. 2–4. TxCaP

———. "Greatest Indian Battle Fought at Adobe Walls." *Dallas Morning News*, (Dallas, Tex.), March 30, 1930, sec. 3, p. 12. TxCaW

———. "King of Them All: Mooar Followed the Lost Herds." *Amarillo Sunday News-Globe* (Amarillo, Tex.), August 14, 1938, sec. D, pp. 1, 4, 5. TxCaP

———. "Old Man Keeler." *West Texas Historical Association Year Book* 4 (1928): 100–104. TxCaP

———. "The Settlement in 1874–5 of Indian Troubles in West Texas." *West Texas Historical Association Year Book* 1 (1925): 3–14. TxCaP

———. "Some Early History of the Panhandle-Plains Region of Texas." *Panhandle-Plains Historical Review* 8 (1935): 88–100. TxCaP

———. "Some Neglected Facts in Frontier History." *Frontier Times* 16, no. 5 (February, 1939): 208–13. TxCaP

———. "Texan Tells Story of Indian Fights in Western Texas: Two Adobe Walls Battles Recalled." *Dallas Morning News* (Dallas, Tex.), May 26, 1925, p. 21. TxCaW

———. "The Unsung Hero of Adobe Walls." *Frontier Times* 5, no. 12 (September, 1928): 458–59. TxCaP

Crimmins, M. L. "General Nelson A. Miles in Texas." *West Texas Historical Association Year Book* 23 (1947): 36–45. TxCaP

Crisler, B. R. "Saga of an Unvanished American." *New York Times*, February 11, 1940, sec. 9, p. 4. TxCaW

Cunningham, Eugene. "Out of the Dawn They Rode: Painted Horde Repulsed at Battle of Adobe Walls." *Amarillo Sunday News-Globe* (Amarillo, Tex.), August 14, 1938, sec. D, pp. 17–18. TxCaP

Daily Conservative (Leavenworth, Kans.), September 16, 1864, [p. 1]. KHi

Daily Express (San Antonio, Tex.), July 17, 1874, p. 1. TxLT

"Death Comes to O. A. Bond, Noted Dodge Pioneer." *Dodge City Daily Globe* (Dodge City, Kans.), May 9, 1927, p. 1. KHi

"Death Takes Tom Stauth." *Dodge City Daily Globe*, May 24, 1960, p. 1. KHi

Debo, Angie. "An English View of the Wild West." *Panhandle-Plains Historical Review* 6 (1933): 24–44. TxCaP

"Desperate Fighting at Adobe Walls." *Frontier Times* 1, no. 12 (September, 1924): 1–4. TxCaP

Dickinson, John P. "On a Government Survey in the Early '70s." *Trail* 10, no. 7 (December, 1917): 14–22. KHi

Dixon, "Billy." "A Story of Adobe Walls When Indians and Buffaloes Roamed in Texas." *Denver Times* (Denver), June 9, 1902, p. 4. CoD

Dixon, Olive K. "Archaeologists Visit Miami." *Miami Chief* (Miami, Tex.), June 17, 1920, p. 1. TxLTswc

———. "The Battle of Adobe Walls." *Frontier Times* 1, no. 9 (June, 1924): 1. TxCaP

————. "The Battle of Adobe Walls." *Santa Fe Magazine* 28, no. 8 (July, 1934): 15–21. KHi

————. "Early Days in Hutchinson County." *Frontier Times* 5, no. 7 (April, 1928): 316–17. TxCaP

————. "Fifty-Three Years Ago Today Battle of Adobe Walls Fought between Indians and White Men." *Amarillo Daily News* (Amarillo, Tex.), June 27, 1927, p. 3. TxCaP

————. "Indians Visit Adobe Walls Battle Site." *Amarillo Sunday News-Globe*, April 20, 1941, sec. 1, p. 5. TxCaP

————. "June 27 Commemorated as Anniversary of Adobe Walls[;] Act of Providence Saves Pioneer Who Battled with Indians in Panhandle 59 Years Ago." *Amarillo Daily News*, June 26, 1930, p. 8. TxCaP

————. "A Long, Useful Life Ended." *Frontier Times* 3, no. 2 (November, 1925): 33. TxCaP

"Dodge Citizens Find Grave at Adobe Walls: History of Old Plains Battle Recalled by Comrades after Finding Bones." *Miami Chief* (Miami, Tex.), January 18, 1923, p. 8. TxLTswc

Dodge City Messenger (Dodge City, Kans.), June 25, 1874, pp. 2, 3. KHi

"Dodge City Residents Find Grave at Adobe Walls; Old Plains Battle Is Recalled." *Amarillo Daily News* (Amarillo, Tex.), January 28, 1923, sec. 4, p. 1. TxAm

Dodge City Times (Dodge City, Kans.), October 14, 1876, to January 4, 1879. KHi

"Dodge Man Is Survivor of 'Dobe Walls Battle." *Topeka Daily Capital* (Topeka, Kans.), June 28, 1914, sec. B, p. 10. KHi

"Dodge Men Find the Long Lost Grave of an Adobe Walls Victim[;] Texas Historical Society Failed in Long Search[;] Bodies of William Olds and 'Billy' Dixon Will Rest in Memorial Park on Battle Site." *Dodge City Daily Globe* (Dodge City, Kans.), January 2, 1923, pp. 1, 7. KHi

"Dodge to Adobe Walls Once a 9-Day Trip." *Dodge City Daily Globe*, May 10, 1933, p. 5. KHi

Dubbs, Emanuel. "Personal Reminiscences." Pp. 29–99 of *Pioneer Days in the Southwest from 1850 to 1879: Thrilling Descriptions of Buffalo Hunting, Indian Fighting and Massacres, Cowboy Life and Home Building.* Guthrie, Okla.: State Capital Company, 1909. TxCaP

————. "Pioneer Days in the Panhandle." *Frontier Times* 2, no. 4 (January, 1925): 4–7. TxCaP

————. "Trials and Tribulations of a Buffalo Hunter." *Frontier Times* 28, no. 11 (August, 1951): 324–27. TxCaP

"'Dutch Henry,' the Chief of the Outlaws of the Western Plains Overtaken at Trinidad[;] Some of the Exploits of the Greatest Horse Thief in the West[;] the Man with a Secret." *Daily Denver Tribune* (Denver), March 1, 1879, p. 4. CoHi

Dykes, J. C. "The Second Battle of Adobe Walls." In *Great Western Indian Fights,* edited by B. W. Allred, J. C. Dykes, Frank Goodwyn, and D. Harper

Simms. Washington, D.C.: Potomac Corral of the Westerners, 1960. TxCaP

Eames, Francis C. "Francis C. Eames, Importer and Jobber of China, Glass and Earthenware, Looking Glasses, Silver Plated and Britannia Ware, Belgian and Bohemian Glassware, Lava Ware, Etc." [advertisement]. *Collins' City Directory of Leavenworth*, compiled by Charles Collins. Leavenworth, Kans.: Charles Collins, 1866. DLC

Emporia News (Emporia, Kans.), July 17, 1874, p. 2; August 21, 1874, p. 2. KHi

Englert, Steve. "The Guns of Marshal Bill Tilghman." *Arms Gazette* 4, no. 10 (June, 1977): 12–15, 44–45, 48. TxCaP

Ewers, John C. "Hair Pipes in Plains Indian Adornment: A Study in Indian and White Ingenuity." *Bureau of American Ethnology Bulletin* 164 (1957): 29–85. TxCaW

"Famous Adobe Walls Fight Lives Again: Fiftieth Anniversary of Heroic Contest When 28 Whites Held 700 Indians at Bay." *New York Times*, June 3, 1924, sec. 8, p. 3. TxCaW

"First Wheeler Judge." *Frontier Times* 9, no. 10 (July, 1932): 448. TxCaP

Fontana, Bernard L., and J. Cameron Greenleaf. "Johnny Ward's Ranch: A Study in Historic Archaeology." *Kiva* 28, nos. 1–2 (October–December, 1962): 1–115. TxCaP

Ford Motor Company. "Ford[,] $295 F.O.B. Detroit[,] an Exceptional Value!" [advertisement]. *Randall County News* (Canyon, Tex.), April 10, 1924, [p. 6]. TxCaP

Fort Scott Daily Monitor (Fort Scott, Kans.), July 9, 1874, [p. 4]. KHi

"Fred J. Leonard." *Salt Lake Tribune* (Salt Lake City), August 8, 1928, p. 6. UU

Freeman, Larry. "Fate Brought Battle of Adobe Walls Instead of Massacre by Indians." *Hutchinson Herald* (Hutchinson, Kans.), November 17, 1929, p. 17. KHi

Freemon, Bill. "Impressive Rites Dedicate Adobe Walls Monument." *Amarillo Daily News* (Amarillo, Tex.), October 20, 1941, pp. 1, 9. TxCaP

"From the Front." *Commonwealth* (Topeka, Kans.), August 8, 1874, p. 2. KHi

"Frontier Sketches." *Field and Farm* (Denver) 27, no. 1375 (June 8, 1912): 8. CoD

"Frontier Sketches." *Field and Farm* 27, no. 1403 (December 21, 1912): 8. CoD

"Frontier Tales." *Field and Farm* 8, no. 417 (December 30, 1893): 6. CoD

"Frontier Tales." *Field and Farm* 10, no. 472 (January 19, 1895): 6 CoD

"Funeral of Pioneer Buffalo Hunter to Be Conducted Friday." *Denver Post* (Denver), August 29, 1935, p. 19. CoD

"Funeral Service for 'Brick' Bond to Be on Friday." *Dodge City Daily Globe* (Dodge City, Kans.), May 11, 1927, p. 1. KHi

"Gala Ceremonies at Borger Today." *Amarillo Sunday News-Globe* (Amarillo, Tex.), October 19, 1941, sec. 1, p. 1. TxCaP

Gard, Wayne. "The Mooar Brothers, Buffalo Hunters." *Southwestern Historical Quarterly* 63, no. 1 (July, 1959): 31–45. TxCaP

"General Frank D. Baldwin, 81, Famed Warrior of Old Indian Fighting Days in West, Dies." *Rocky Mountain News* (Denver), April 23, 1923, pp. 1–2. CoD

"General Nelson A. Miles Coming to Adobe Walls Next Spring." *Randall County News* (Canyon, Tex.), September 6, 1923, [p. 3]. TxCaP

"General Nelson A. Miles May Attend Adobe Walls Celebration Next Summer." *Amarillo Daily News,* (Amarillo, Tex.), December 2, 1923, sec. 2, p. 1. TxAm

Gettys, Marshall, and Alicia Hughes-Jones. "Vertical Log Construction in Oklahoma." *Outlook in Historic Conservation* (State Historic Preservation Office, Oklahoma City, Okla.), July/August, 1981, n.p.

Glenn, W. S. "The Recollections of W. S. Glenn, Buffalo Hunter." Edited by Rex W. Strickland. *Panhandle-Plains Historical Review* 22 (1949): 15–64. TxCaP

Godfrey, E. S. "Medicine Lodge Treaty Sixty Years Ago." *Frontier Times* 5, no. 3 (December, 1927): 102–103. TxCaP

Goodnight, Charles. "Pioneer Outlines Sketch of Quanah Parker's Life." *Amarillo Sunday News-Globe* (Amarillo, Tex.), August 8, 1926, sec. 2, p. 14. TxCaP

———. "True Sketch of Quanah Parker's Life." *Frontier Times* 4, no. 2 (November, 1926): 5–7. TxCaP

———. "True Sketch of Quanah Parker's Life." *Southwest Plainsman* (Amarillo, Tex.), August 7, 1926, p. 1. Charles Goodnight Papers. TxCaP

Goolsby, William F. "Battle of 'Adobe Walls' Marked the Passing of Plains Indians: Early Oklahoma's Most Deadly Gunmen Baptised in Fire There." *Tulsa World* (Tulsa, Okla.), January 10, 1932, sec. 5, pp. 1, 3. Grant Foreman Collection. OkHiamd

"The Great Battle of Adobe Walls." *Frontier Times* 28, no. 6 (March, 1951): 168–72. TxCaP

Grinnell, George Bird. "Bent's Old Fort and Its Builders." *Collection of the Kansas State Historical Society* 15 (1919–21): 42–91. TxCaP

Grossman, Max R. "Ninety-Year-Old Indian Chief Tells Why He Fought White Men." *Boston Sunday Post* (Boston, Mass.), December 3, 1939, Color Feature Section, pp. 3, 6. MB

Hagan, William T. "Quanah Parker." Pp. 175–91 of *American Indian Leaders: Studies in Diversity*. Edited by R. David Edmunds. Lincoln: University of Nebraska Press, 1980. TxCaP

Haley, J. Evetts. "Jim East—Trail Hand and Cowboy." *Panhandle-Plains Historical Review* 4 (1931): 39–61. TxCaP

Hamilton, Henry W., and Jean Tiree Hamilton. "Clay Pipes from Pamplin." *Missouri Archaeologist* 34, nos. 1–2 (December, 1972): 1–47. TxCaP

Harris, Harry B. "Coffee Mills." Pp. 149–50 of *Antique Trader Annual of Articles for 1973*. Dubuque, Iowa: Antique Trader, 1973. TxCaP

Harrison, Lowell R. "Adobe Walls, Frontier Enterprise." *West Texas Historical Association Year Book* 46 (1970): 14–24. TxCaP

———. "Damage Suits for Indian Depredations in the Adobe Walls Area, 1874." *Panhandle-Plains Historical Review* 36 (1963): 37–60. TxCaP

———. "Indians vs Buffalo Hunters at Adobe Walls." *American History Illustrated* 2, no. 1 (April, 1967): 18–27. TxCaP

———. "The Two Battles of Adobe Walls." *Texas Military History* 5, no. 1 (Spring, 1965): 1–11. TxCaP

Hathaway, Seth. "The Adventures of a Buffalo Hunter," edited by John P. Wilson. *Frontier Times* 9, no. 3 (December, 1931): 105–12, 129–35. TxCaP

Henderson, James C. "Reminiscences of a Range Rider." *Chronicles of Oklahoma* 3, no. 4 (December, 1925): 253–88. TxCaP

"Historical Andirons Made by Pioneer Blacksmith to Be Used in Decorating Adobe Walls Fort." *Amarillo Globe*, July 24, 1930, p. 7. TxCaP

Holliday, Vance T., and Curtis M. Welty. "Lithic Tool Resources of the Eastern Llano Estacado." *Bulletin of the Texas Archeological Society* 52 (1981): 201–14. TxCaP

Holt, Daniel D. "Lieutenant Frank D. Baldwin and the Indian Territory Expedition of 1874." *Trail Guide* 10, no. 3 (September, 1965): 1–20. CoD

Hughes, Jack T. "Lake Creek: A Woodland Site in the Texas Panhandle." *Bulletin of the Texas Archeological Society* 32 (1961): 65–84. TxCaP

Hughes, Pollyanna B. "Adobe Walls May Rise Again." *Texas Parade* 15, no. 5 (October, 1954): 34–36. TxCaP

Hunt, Fred A. "The Adobe Walls Argument." *Overland Monthly* 53, no. 6 (May, 1909): 382–90. CoD

Hunt, George. "The Annual Sun Dance of the Kiowa Indians," edited by Wilbur Sturtevant Nye. *Chronicles of Oklahoma* 12, no. 3 (September, 1934): 340–58. TxCaP

Hunter, J. Marvin, Sr. "The Battle of Adobe Walls." *Frontier Times* 24, no. 7 (April, 1947): 380–83. CoD

———. "John W. Mooar, Successful Pioneer." *Frontier Times* 29, no. 12 (September, 1952): 331–37. TxCaP

———. "Quanah Parker, Chief of the Comanches." *Frontier Times* 24, no. 9 (June, 1947): 448–51. TxCaP

"Hutchinson County Fair Association Sponsors Adobe Walls Ceremonials." *Borger Daily Herald* (Borger, Tex.), October 5, 1941, sec. 1, p. 6. TxBor

Hutchinson, W. H. "Billy Dixon and 'Big Fifty.'" *Westerners New York Posse Brand Book* 10, no. 14 (1963): 73–74, 92–94. KHi

"Indian Ceremonials End Stamped Definite Success." *Borger Daily Herald* (Borger, Tex.), October 20, 1941, pp. 1, 2. TxBor

"Indian Ceremonials End Today: Dedication at Adobe Walls Site, Pageant Slated." *Borger Daily Herald*, October 19, 1941, pp. 1, 5. TxBor

"Indian Dances Are Portrayed by Boy Scouts." *Amarillo Daily News* (Amarillo, Tex.), June 29, 1924, p. 10. TxAm

"Indian Fighter Dead." *Pagosa Journal* (Pagosa Springs, Colo.), January 13, 1921, p. 1. CoHi

"Indian Survivors of Dobe Walls to Visit Old Scene." *Dodge City Daily Globe* (Dodge City, Kans.), January 20, 1931, p. 1. KHi

"Indian War Whoops Will Ring out in Borger for Adobe Walls Party." *Amarillo Daily News* (Amarillo, Tex.), October 16, 1941, p. 16. TxCaP

"Indians Arrive at 'Dobe Walls.'" *Amarillo Daily News*, October 17, 1941, p. 1. TxCaP

"Indians Arrive Today in Preparation for Borger's Most Colorful Celebration." *Borger Daily Herald* (Borger, Tex.), October 16, 1941, pp. 1, 5. TxBor

"Indians Confer Here for Pageant Plans." *Borger Daily Herald*, October 7, 1941, p. 1. TxBor

"'Indians!' Cries Billy Dixon to Comrades and 'Dobe Walls Fight Began—60 Years Ago Today." *Amarillo Daily News* (Amarillo, Tex.), June 27, 1934, pp. 1, 11. TxCaP

"Indians Ready for Adobe Walls Ceremonials Opening on Friday." *Amarillo Daily News*, October 15, 1941, p. 11. TxCaP

"Indians Receive Enthusiastic Reception on Trips Advertising Big Adobe Walls Ceremonials." *Borger Daily Herald* (Borger, Tex.), October 14, 1941, pp. 1, 6. TxBor

Isaacs, Mrs. Sam. "Billy Dixon: Pioneer Plainsman." *Frontier Times* 16, no. 8 (June, 1939): 372–74. TxCaP

"James Langton Hurled to Death." *Deseret Evening News* (Salt Lake City), July 21, 1913, p. 13. UU

"James Langton Meets Death in Auto Accident." *Salt Lake Tribune* (Salt Lake City), July 21, 1913, pp. 1, 12. UU

"Jim Barbour, 86, Adobe Walls Survivor, Dies in Kansas." *Amarillo Sunday News-Globe* (Amarillo, Tex.), September 5, 1937, sec. 1, p. 19. TxCaP

"Jim Barbour, Oldtimer Visits in Miami." *Miami Chief* (Miami, Tex.), September 11, 1924, p. 1. Adobe Walls Manuscript File, TxCaP

"J. K. Griffis Named Father of Year by Son's Marine Unit." *Enterprise and Vermonter* (Vergennes, Vt.), July 31, 1952, pp. 1–2, 7. Elizabeth Jaderborg Collection, Microfilm. KHi

[Johnson, Andrew]. "Adobe Walls Survivor Tells about Fight: Andrew Johnson Relates Details of Indian Battle." *Amarillo Daily News* (Amarillo, Tex.), June 29, 1924, p. 10. TxCaP

————. "Andy Johnson, Blacksmith, Wagonmaker and Repairer" [advertisement]. *Globe Live Stock Journal* (Dodge City, Kans.), September 29, 1885, p. 6. KHi

————. "The Facts Concerning Indian Fight at the 'Dobe Wall." *Oklahoma City Times* (Oklahoma City, Okla.), August 13, 1911, Sturm's Magazine Section, p. 1. KHi

————. "The Fight at 'Dobe Walls." *Kansas City Star* (Kansas City, Mo.), August 6, 1911, sec. A, p. 5. KHi

————. "Tells of Battle." *Topeka Daily State Journal* (Topeka, Kans.), August 19, 1911, p. 3. KHi

————. "What Really Happened at the Famous Frontier Fight Which Is Known in History as the Battle of 'Dobe Walls." *Dodge City Globe* (Dodge City, Kans.), August 8, 1911, p. 4. KHi

Johnson, T. E. "Many Visit Adobe Walls: 2-Day Event Opens with Picnic and Barbecue." *Amarillo Daily News* (Amarillo, Tex.), June 15, 1923, pp. 1, 5. TxAm

"J. W. McKinley's Narrative." *Panhandle-Plains Historical Review* 36 (1963): 61–69. TxCaP

"J. Wright Mooar." *Frontier Times* 5, no. 12 (September, 1928): 449–53. TxCaP

"Kansas Gets Historic Plow That Turned the Sod at Adobe Walls." *Topeka Capital* (Topeka, Kans.), October 28, 1921, p. 16. KHi

"A Kansas Killer. 'Bat' Masterson, the Noted Frontiersman, Interviewed." *Topeka Daily Capital* (Topeka, Kans.), June 26, 1888, p. 5. KHi

Kauffman, Harlan B. "Hunting the Buffalo." *Overland Monthly* 66, no. 2 (August, 1915): 165–70. KHi

Keck, Nan, and Katherine Albers. "Mile-Long Shot Ends Indian Siege." *Amarillo Daily News* (Amarillo, Tex.), August 18, 1980, sec. C, p. 1. TxCaP

Kirk, Margaret. "82nd Anniversary of 'Adobe Walls Battle' Observed Wednesday." *Borger News-Herald* (Borger, Tex.), June 24, 1956, p. 17. TxBor

Knox, Bill. "When the Sharps Wrote History." *Amarillo Sunday News-Globe* (Amarillo, Tex.), June 26, 1966, sec. D, p. 1. TxCaP

Kountz, Nita. "The First Judge in the Panhandle." *Frontier Times* 4, no. 7 (April, 1927): 5–8. TxCaP

Lake, Stuart N. "The Buffalo Hunters." *Saturday Evening Post* 203, no. 17 (October 25, 1930): 12–13, 81–82, 84–85. TxCaW

"Langton & Walker" [published notice of cattle brands and markings]. *Globe Live Stock Journal*, July 15, 1884, p. 8. KHi

"Last Man Who Took Part in Adobe Walls Indian Fight Is Dead at Salt Lake City." *Dodge City Daily Globe* (Dodge City, Kans.), August 9, 1928, p. 7. KHi

"Last Survivor of Indian Fight in Texas Dies: Manager of Cullen Hotel for Past Eighteen Years Victim of Arthritis." *Salt Lake Tribune* (Salt Lake City), August 5, 1928, p. 20. UU

Leavenworth Daily Commercial (Leavenworth, Kans.), July 11, 1874, p. 1; July 26, 1874 [p. 2]. KHi

Leavenworth Daily Times (Leavenworth, Kans.), July 8, 1874 [p. 1]; July 10, 1874 [p. 4]; July 19, 1874 [p. 6]. TxCaP

Leckie, William H. "The Red River War 1874–1875." *Panhandle-Plains Historical Review* 29 (1956): 78–100. TxCaP

Lee, John. "California Man Says He Was Trapped with 27 at Adobe Walls by Indians." *Amarillo Daily News* (Amarillo, Tex.), August 27, 1925, p. 7. TxCaP

Leonard, H. B. "In the Fight at 'Dobe Walls. H. B. Leonard's Brother Was One of

28 Who Whipped 500 Indians." *Kansas City Star* (Kansas City, Mo.), July 21, 1911, Special Late Edition, p. 7. KHi

Lewis, Alfred Henry. "Inez of the 'Dobe Walls." *Kansas City Times* (Kansas City, Mo.), July 19, 1911, p. 6. IU

————. "William Barclay Masterson: An Adventure Story with a Live Hero." *Colorado Springs Gazette* (Colorado Springs, Colo.), December 22, 1912, pp. 10–11. CoC

————. "William Barclay Masterson: An Adventure Story with a Live Hero." *Texas Magazine* 7, no. 5 (March, 1913): 370–81. TxSaW

Linton, Ralph. "The Comanche Sun Dance." *American Anthropologist* 37, no. 3 (July–September, 1935): 420–28. TxCaW

Little, Edward Campbell. "The Battle of Adobe Walls." *Pearson's Magazine* 19, no. 1 (January, 1908): 75–85. MnU

Lorrain, Dessamae. "An Archaeologist's Guide to Nineteenth Century American Glass." *Historical Archaeology* 2 (1968): 35–44. TxCaP

Mabry, W. S. "Early West Texas and Panhandle Surveys." *Panhandle-Plains Historical Review* 2 (1929): 22–42. TxCaP

MacCarthy, Donald F. "The Adobe Walls." *Frontier Times* 7, no. 9 (June, 1930): 410–15. TxCaP

"Magazine Article Stirs Memories of Adventurous Life on Plains." *Dodge City Daily Globe* (Dodge City, Kans.), February 14, 1927, p. 1. KHi

Maiden, R. R. "Marshal Maiden Compiles Succession of Sheriffs for Colorado Counties." *Colorado Sheriff and Peace Officer* 2, no. 11 (November, 1962): 7–9. CoD

"Many Speakers to Be Features at Adobe Walls." *Amarillo Daily News* (Amarillo, Tex.), June 10, 1923, p. 1. TxCaP

Masterson, "Bat." "In the Indian Days." *Sunday Inter Ocean* (Chicago), February 27, 1898, sec. 4, p. 35. IHi

"Masterson's Death Brings Recollections: Famous Sports Writer in Battle of Adobe Walls." *Amarillo Daily News* (Amarillo, Tex.), November 5, 1921, sec. 1, p. 6. TxCaP

McCarty, John L. "Veteran of Adobe Walls Battle Can Clog Dance at 77." *Amarillo Sunday News-Globe* (Amarillo, Tex.), April 29, 1928, sec. 1, p. 6. TxCaP

McClure, C. B., ed. "The Battle of Adobe Walls 1864." *Panhandle-Plains Historical Review* 21 (1948): 18–65. TxCaP

McDonald, A. B. "The Recent Re-Burial in Texas of 'Billy' Dixon Recalls the Indian Fight at 'Dobe Walls." *Kansas City Star* (Kansas City, Mo.), July 7, 1929, sec. C, p. 1. KHi

McFadden, Thompson. "Thompson McFadden's Diary of an Indian Campaign, 1874," edited by Robert C. Carriker. *Southwestern Historical Quarterly* 75, no. 2 (October, 1971): 198–232. TxCaP

McGregor, Stuart. "He Killed an Indian 1,200 Yards Away: The Courage of Frontiersman Who Opened up the Panhandle Is a Glory of Texas History."

Dallas Morning News (Dallas, Tex.), June 19, 1927, sec. 7, p. 5. TxCaW

"Members of the Western Stock Growers' Association." *Globe Live Stock Journal*, July 15, 1884, p. 6. KHi

Meyer, Sophia. "Society." *Amarillo Daily News* (Amarillo, Tex.), September 30, 1914, p. 3. TxCaP

Miller, Nyle H., and Joseph W. Snell. "Some Notes on Kansas Cowtown Police Officers and Gun Fighers." *Kansas Historical Quarterly* 27, no. 3 (Autumn, 1961): 383–447. KHi

Montgomery, Harry. "Billy Dixon's Medal to Museum; Story of Battle Is Recalled." *Amarillo Sunday News-Globe* (Amarillo, Tex.), March 19, 1933, p. 10. TxCaP

————. "Red Warriors Routed in 'Dobe Walls Fight 59 Years Ago Tuesday." *Amarillo Daily News* (Amarillo, Tex.), June 28, 1933, p. 12. TxCaP

Montgomery, Wayne. "Amos Chapman: An Early Journey of the Hero of the Buffalo Wallow Fight." *Frontier Times* 46, no. 3 (April–May, 1972): 26–28, 44, 46–47. KHi

"Monument to Heroes of Adobe Walls Battle." *Topeka Daily Capital* (Topeka, Kans.), June 22, 1924, sec. B, p. 6. KHi

Mooar, J. Wright. "Buffalo Days," edited by James Winford Hunt. *Holland's, the Magazine of the South* 52, no. 1 (January, 1933): 13, 24; no. 2 (February, 1933): 10, 44; no. 3 (March, 1933): 8, 24, 28; no. 4 (April, 1933): 5, 22; no. 5 (May, 1933): 11–12; no. 7 (July, 1933): 10, 30; no. 9 (September, 1933): 14. TxCaW

————. "The First Buffalo Hunting in the Panhandle." *West Texas Historical Association Year Book* 6 (1930): 109–11. TxCaP

————. "Frontier Experiences of J. Wright Mooar." *West Texas Historical Association Year Book* 4 (1928): 89–92. TxCaP

————. "Some Observations on the Cattle Industry." *West Texas Historical Association Year Book* 5 (1929): 134–36. TxCaP

Mooney, James. "Calendar History of the Kiowa Indians." *Seventeenth Annual Report of the Bureau of American Ethnology to the Secretary of the Smithsonian Institution*. 2 vols. Washington, D.C.: Government Printing Office, 1898. KHi

"Motor Caravans to Advertise Indian Pageant." *Borger Daily Herald* (Borger, Tex.), October 8, 1941, p. 2. TxBor

"Mrs. Dixon Lauds Move to Restore Old Adobe Walls." *Amarillo Daily News* (Amarillo, Tex.), June 28, 1935, p. 1. TxCaP

Newcomb, W. W., Jr. "An Historical Burial from Yellowhouse Canyon, Lubbock County." *Bulletin of the Texas Archeological Society* 26 (1955): 186–99. TxCaP

New York Times, July 14, 1874, p. 5; July 21, 1874, p. 4; July 31, 1874, p. 1; August 8, 1874, p. 4. TxCaW

"New York Times Carries Story on Adobe Walls; Detailed Report Given." *Amarillo Daily News* (Amarillo, Tex.), June 13, 1923, p. 12. TxAm

"Noted Officer Visits Friends at Celebration." *Amarillo Daily News* (Amarillo, Tex.), June 29, 1924, p. 10. TxAm

"Old Indian Wants to Meet His Foes of 'Dobe Walls." *Dodge City Daily Globe* (Dodge City, Kans.), November 28, 1933, p. 1. KHi

"Old Scout Fights for Panhandle." *Amarillo Globe* (Amarillo, Tex.), September 3, 1937, pp. 1, 2. TxCaP

Omwake, H. Geiger. "Analysis of 19th Century White Kaolin Pipe Fragments from the Mero Site, Door County, Wisconsin." *Wisconsin Archeologist* 46, no. 2 (June, 1965): 125–39. WHi

"Panhandle Photoplay Is Being Considered." *Amarillo Daily News* (Amarillo, Tex.), October 9, 1914, p. 8. TxCaP

"Panhandle Pioneer Will Lecture Here." *Amarillo Daily News*, June 8, 1912, p. 8. TxCaP

"Panhandle Postal History." *Panhandle-Plains Historical Review* 33 (1960): 122–25. TxCaP

Pate, J'Nell. "The Battles of Adobe Walls." *Great Plains Journal* 16, no. 1 (Fall, 1976): 2–44. TxCaP

Payne, W. E. "Dutch Henry's Raid near Fort Elliott." *Frontier Times* 1, no. 4 (January, 1924): 24–27. TxCaP

Pettis, George H. "Kit Carson's Fight with the Comanche and Kiowa Indians." *Weekly New Mexican* (Santa Fe, N.M.), March 22, 1879, p. 1; March 29, 1879, p. 1; April 5, 1879, p. 1. CoD

Phillips, C. J. "The Battle of Adobe Walls." *Hunter-Trader-Trapper* 57, no. 6 (December, 1928): 19, 32, 34. KHi

"Picnic and Barbecue at Adobe Walls on June 14 and 15." *Randall County News* (Canyon, Tex.), May 24, 1923 [p. 3]. TxCaP

"Pioneer Passes Away." *Creede Candle* (Creede, Colo.), January 22, 1921, p. 1. CoHi

"Plan Celebration of Anniversary of 'Dobe Walls Battle." *Dodge City Journal* (Dodge City, Kans.), November 8, 1923, p. 1. KHi

Posey, Sheryl. "The Battle of Adobe Walls, 1874." *West Texas Historian* 4, no. 1 (January, 1973): 1–12. TxPlW

"Quantrill Hero Dead: Fred Leonard also Took Part in Indian Fight." *Topeka Daily Capital* (Topeka, Kans.), August 10, 1928, p. 5. KHi

Rath, Charles. "Charles Rath, Dealer in General Merchandise, Mobeetie, Texas" [advertisement]. *Globe Live Stock Journal*, July 15, 1884, p. 1. KHi

———. "Notice." *Globe Live Stock Journal*, September 29, 1885, p. 5. KHi

Raymond, Henry Hubert. "Diary of a Dodge City Buffalo Hunter, 1872–1873," edited by Joseph W. Snell. *Kansas Historical Quarterly* 31, no. 4 (Winter, 1965): 345–95. TxCaP

"Remarkable Life Story of Quanah Parker." *Frontier Times* 1, no. 1 (October, 1923): 28–30. TxCaP

"Remove Body of Col. Dixon from Texline: Remains of Famed Indian Fighter to Be Reburied at Adobe Walls Today." *Amarillo Daily News* (Amarillo, Tex.), June 27, 1929, pp. 1, 15. TxCaP

Renfroe, Charles. "Trader's Quest for Wealth Led to Site of Early Adobe Walls Fight." *Amarillo Sunday News-Globe*, August 14, 1938, sec. C, p. 2. TxCaP

Richardson, Rupert N. "The Battle of Adobe Walls, 1874." Pp. 171–89 in *Battles of Texas*. Waco, Tex.: Texian Press, 1967. TxLTswc

———. "The Comanche Indians and the Fight at Adobe Walls." *Panhandle-Plains Historical Review* 4 (1931): 24–38. TxCaP

Riddle, Roy. "Indian Survivors of Adobe Walls Visit Site 65 Years after Fight." *Amarillo Daily News* (Amarillo, Tex.), April 26, 1939, pp. 1, 13. TxCaP

"Robert Cator & Bro." [published notice of cattle brands and markings]. *Globe Live Stock Journal*, July 15, 1884, [p. 6]. KHi

"Robert M. Wright Dead." *Dodge City Kansas Journal* (Dodge City, Kans.), January 8, 1915, p. 1. KHi

"Robert M. Wright, Dodge Pioneer Merchant, Died This Morning." *Dodge City Daily Globe* (Dodge City, Kans.), January 4, 1915, p. 1. KHi

"Robt. M. Wright Noted Pioneer Passes Away." *Amarillo Daily News* (Amarillo, Tex.), January 8, 1915, p. 8. TxCaP

Rocky Mountain News (Denver), January 3, 1879, p. 1; March 1, 1879, p. 4; March 2, 1879, p. 4. CoD

Rodgers, Walter. "XIT Ranch Formed about 20 Years after Famous Battle in Panhandle." *Sunray News* (Sunray, Tex.), August 5, 1965, p. 2. "Texas—History—1846–1950 (Adobe Walls)" vertical file, TxCaW

Sargent, Joe. "War-Paint Off, Comanches Return to Scene of Second Battle of Adobe Walls." *Hutchinson County Herald* (Stinnett, Tex.), April 29, 1939, pp. 1, 3. Adobe Walls Manuscript File, TxCaP

Schmidt, Heinie. "Chapman's Life Is History of Frontier Scout." *High Plains Journal* (Dodge City, Kans.), March 15, 1956, pp. 2–3. "Amos Chapman" vertical file, KDcB

———. "It's Worth Remembering: The Last Survivor of Adobe Walls." *High Plains Journal*, August 3, 1950, sec. 1, pp. 11, 15. "It's Worth Repeating" Scrapbooks, pp. 222–23, KHi

———. "It's Worth Repeating: Adobe Walls, June 27, 1874." *High Plains Journal*, June 30, 1949, sec. 2, pp. 4, 8. "It's Worth Repeating" Scrapbooks, pp. 108–110, KHi

———. "It's Worth Repeating: O. A. (Brick) Bond, Buffalo Hunter." *Dodge City Journal* (Dodge City, Kans.), February 5, 1948, p. 2. KHi

"Semi-Centennial of the Battle of Adobe Walls." *Chronicles of Oklahoma* 2, no. 4 (December, 1924): 402–404. TxCaP

Schaeffer, J. B. "The Alibates Flint Quarry, Texas." *American Antiquity* 24, no. 2 (October, 1958): 189–91. TxCaW

Shepherd, Shirley J. "Ball Collectibles for Fun and Profit." In *The Antique Trader Annual on Antiques Volume VIII*. Dubuque, Iowa: Antique Trader, 1978. TxCaP

Simms, D. Harper. "Battle of the Bugles at the Adobe Walls." *Corral Dust, Potomac Corral of the Westerners* (Washington, D.C.) 2, no. 3 (September, 1957): 19. CoD

"Sitler & Langton" [published notice of cattle brands and markings]. *Globe Live Stock Journal*, July 15, 1884 [p. 8]; October 6, 1885 [p. 8]. KHi

Sneed, John. "Monument at Adobe Walls Battleground, One of Two Survivors of Historic Fight and Officer Slain after Picture Taken." *Dallas Morning News* (Dallas, Tex.), April 26, 1925, sec. 4, p. 10. TxCaW

Spector, Janet D. "The Interpretive Potential of Glass Trade Beads in Historic Archaeology." *Historical Archaeology* 10 (1976): 17–27. TxCaP

Stark, Dolores. "Terror at Adobe Walls!" *Gasser* 20, no. 10 (October, 1963): 7–10. TxCaP

Steele, Aubrey L. "Lawrie Tatum's Indian Policy." *Chronicles of Oklahoma* 22, no. 1 (Spring, 1944): 83–98. TxCaP

Stephenson, Jenna V. "History Professor Is Carried away by Indian Warrior." *Prairie* (Canyon, Tex.), May 9, 1939, pp. 1, 4. TxCaW

"Survivor of Famous Indian Fight at Dobe Walls Has Lived in the Community for More Than 50 Years." *Dodge City Daily Globe* (Dodge City, Kans.), June 28, 1921, p. 1. KHi

"Survivor of First Adobe Walls Fight Here for Pageant." *Borger Daily Herald* (Borger, Tex.), October 19, 1941, sec. 1, p. 1. TxBor

Swett, Morris. "Sergeant I-See-O, Kiowa Indian Scout." *Chronicles of Oklahoma* 13, no. 3 (September, 1935): 340–54. TxCaP

Syers, Ed. "Adobe Walls Site of Historic Single Long Range Shot." *San Antonio Express* (San Antonio, Tex.), December 2, 1971, sec. B, p. 8. Indians— Indian Fights—Adobe Walls (Battles) clipping file, TxSaDrt

———. "History's Greatest Shot by Indian Fighter Dixon." *San Antonio Evening Sun* (San Antonio, Tex.), November 8, 1963, sec. B, p. 7. Indians— Indian Fights—Adobe Walls (Battles) clipping file, TxSaDrt

Taylor, Joe F., comp. and ed. "The Indian Campaign on the Staked Plains, 1874–1875: Military Correspondence from War Department Adjutant General's Office, File 2815–1874." *Panhandle-Plains Historical Review* 34 (1961): 1–216; 35 (1962): 215–368. TxCaP

"Tentative Plans Are Mapped for Adobe Walls Celebration." *Amarillo Sunday News-Globe* (Amarillo, Tex.), August 31, 1941, p. 8. TxCaP

"Texas Frontier Veteran Is Salt Laker: Tells of History-Making Indian Fights: Ridgepole on Saloon Building Credited with Saving Lives of Twenty-Nine." *Salt Lake Tribune* (Salt Lake City), February 11, 1923, p. 7. UU

"Thousands Here for Indian Ceremonials: Colorful Parade Launches Three Day Celebration." *Borger Daily Herald* (Borger, Tex.), October 17, 1941, pp. 1, 2. TxBor

"Thousands Participate in Fiftieth Anniversary of the Famous Adobe Walls Fight." *Amarillo Daily News* (Amarillo, Tex.), June 29, 1924, pp. 1, 10. TxAm

Tilghman, Zoe A. "My Husband Helped Tame the West." *True* 46, no. 20 (May 18, 1959): 105–106, 109–12. TxCaP

"Today Is Anniversary of Adobe Walls Battle." *Amarillo Globe* (Amarillo, Tex.), June 27, 1934, p. 2. TxCaP

Tolbert, Frank. "At Adobe Walls." *Dallas Morning News* (Dallas, Tex.), June 30, 1979, sec. A, p. 35. TxCaW

"Tomorrow Is Anniversary of Battle at Adobe Walls." *Amarillo Globe* (Amarillo, Tex.), June 26, 1935, p. 1. TxCaP

"Tom-Toms, War Whoops and Indians Give Children Thrill of a Lifetime." *Borger Daily Herald* (Borger, Tex.), October 12, 1941, p. 1. TxBor

"'Tough Indians' of 1874 Presents Savage's Tale: 'Tahan' Spreads Gospel Now But Danced to Dixon's Lead." *Amarillo Sunday News-Globe* (Amarillo, Tex.), June 30, 1940, p. 2. TxAm

Traylor, Champ. "Attack on 'Adobe Walls:' Disastrous Results of Advice Given Panhandle Indians by a Comanche 'Medicine Man.'" *Dallas Morning News* (Dallas, Tex.), February 7, 1904, p. 14. TxCaW

Turner, George. "Comanche Firebrand for Freedom Turned to Peace: Quanah Parker's Mighty Medicine Lost at Adobe Walls." *Amarillo Sunday News-Globe* (Amarillo, Tex.), March 19, 1972, sec. D, p. 1. TxCaP

————. "Scientists Digging into Buffalo Hunter Lifestyle." *Amarillo Sunday News-Globe*, August 10, 1975, sec. D, pp. 1, 2. TxCaP

"Twenty Beeves Are Barbecued to Feed Crowd." *Amarillo Daily News*, June 29, 1924, p. 10. TxAm

"Unveiling Adobe Walls Monument Planned June 27." *Amarillo Daily News*, May 20, 1924, p. 8. TxAm

"Unveiling of Monument to Adobe Walls Indian Fighters to Be Celebration Feature." *Amarillo Daily News*, June 27, 1924, pp. 1, 3. TxAm

Utley, Robert M. "Kit Carson and the Adobe Walls Campaign." *American West* 2, no. 1 (Winter, 1965): 4–11, 73–75. TxCaP

Vickers, Paul T. "Adobe Walls Heroes Get Recognition at Last." *Amarillo Daily News* (Amarillo, Tex.), March 2, 1924, Western Weekly Supplement, p. 4. TxAm

Watson, Elmo Scott. "The Battle of Adobe Walls." *Weekly Register-Call* (Central City, Colo.), June 8, 1934, p. 2. CoD

Watson, James A. "The Battle of Adobe Walls: A Survivor of One of the West's Last Great Indian Battles Tells Some Previously Unwritten American History," edited by Edwin V. Burkholder. *True* 16, no. 93 (February, 1945): 36–37, 72–76. CoD

Wellman, Paul I. "Some Famous Kansas Frontier Scouts." *Kansas Historical Quarterly* 1, no. 4 (August, 1932): 345–59. KHi

West, G. Derek. "The Battle of Adobe Walls—1874." *English Westerners' Brand Book* 4, no. 2 (January, 1962): 1–12. TxCaP

————. "The Battle of Adobe Walls (1874)." *Panhandle-Plains Historical Review* 36 (1963): 1–36. TxCaP

West, John O., and Roberto Gonzales. "Adobe: Earth, Straw, and Water." In *Built in Texas*, edited by Francis Edward Abernethy. Publications of the Texas Folklore Society 42. Waco, Tex.: E-Heart Press, 1979. TxCaP

White, Edwin J. "Magazine Article Stirs Memories of Adventurous Life on

Plains." *Dodge City Daily Globe* (Dodge City, Kans.), February 14, 1927, p. 1. KHi

White, Lonnie J. "Indian Battles in the Texas Panhandle, 1874." *Journal of the West* 6, no. 2 (April, 1967): 278–309. KHi

———. "New Sources Relating to the Battle of Adobe Walls, 1874." *Texas Military History* 8, no. 1 (1969): 1–12. TxCaP

———, ed. "Kansas Newspaper Items Relating to the Red River War of 1874–1875." *Panhandle-Plains Historical Review* 36 (1963): 72–88. TxCaP

Wilson, Rex L. "Tobacco Pipes from Fort Union, N. Mexico." *El Palacio* 73, no. 1 (Spring, 1966): 32–40. TxCaP

Wright, Robert M. "Early Days in Dodge City." *Frontier Times* 26, no. 12 (September, 1949): 317–22. TxCaP

[———.] "Notable Indian Fight of Plains." *Amarillo Daily News* (Amarillo, Tex.), September 27, 1914, p. 19. TxCaP

———. "Personal Reminiscences of Frontier Life in Southwest Kansas." *Transactions of the Kansas State Historical Society* 7, (1901–1902): 47–83. TxCaP

Wright, Mrs. Robert M. "Inez Not the Heroine." *Kansas City Star* (Kansas City, Mo.), July 19, 1911, Special Last Edition, p. 7. KHi

"Writer Visits Battleground: J. G. Masters of Omaha Is Gathering Material for New Book." *Amarillo Daily News* (Amarillo, Tex.), August 2, 1935, p. 3. TxCaP

Wyatt, M. K. "Battle of Adobe Walls: Twenty-Eight White Men and One Woman Against 800 Indians." *Drummond Times* (Drummond, Okla.), June 18, 1926, Magazine Section, p. 2. "Adobe Walls, Battle of" vertical file. OkHirl

Index

Welsh, Mike, 51, 87, 328 n.26
Wert, Henry, 91
Wertz, Henry, 91, 328 n.26
West Texas Historical Association, 69
West Texas State Teachers College, 115;
  band, 116
West Virginia, 8
whale oil lamps, 176
Wheeler County, Tex., 89
wheel nuts, 233–34
wheels, 23, 36, 226, 234, 236
whetstones, 218–21, 293
Whirlwind (Indian), 41, 70, 72
whiskers, 5
whiskey, 27, 39, 42, 103, 112, 250
whiskey peddlers, 42, 78, 103
White, J. Phelps, 98
White Eagle. *See* Isatai
White Goose (Indian), 32
White Oaks, N. Mex., 77
whitewash, 139
White Shield (Indian), 41
White Wolf (Indian), 46, 48
Wichita Indians, 45
wick (lamp), 181
wick holder (lamp), 181
wick wheel (lamp), 180–81
wild game as food, 26, 202–205
Wild Horse (Indian), 120
Wilkes, George, 328 n.26
Williams, Jack, 328 n.26
willow trees, 137
Wilson, Lem. *See* Wilson, Lemnot T.
Wilson, Lemnot T., 34, 36, 307 n.140
Wilson, Sam, 308 n.140
wind, 156, 168
windowpanes, 16, 22, 94, 144, 158–59,
  164, 168, 170–73, 281, 291, 294
windows of buildings: blocked during
  battle, 53; broken during battle, 94;

burned by Indians, 107, 144–45, 158,
  171–73, 190, 226; evidence of perma-
  nency planned for trading post, 291;
  fragments, 168–73; installed by Andrew Johnson, 294; mess hall, 150;
  Myers and Leonard store, 144–45,
  147, 171–72; open for ventilation at
  night, 50; in picket buildings, 139; Rath
  and Company store, 158–59, 171, 173,
  190, 201, 226; saloon, 102, 140; in
  sod buildings, 138; used during battle,
  54, 62
Wing, Ira, 92
wire, 261, 267, 269–70, 281–82
Wisconsin, 7
Wise (Indian), 32
Wizard Oil. *See* Hamlin's Wizard Oil
Wolf Creek, 33, 58
Wolf Shit. *See* Isatai
wolves, 87, 129, 250
women on the buffalo range, 110,
  329 n.37. *See also* Olds, Hannah
Woods, J. E., 92
woodworking tools and supplies, 182,
  223–31
World War I, 79
World War II, 120
Worthington, George, Company, 237
wrenches, 233, 235–37
Wright, Charles, 328 n.26
Wright, Robert Marr, 18–20, 56, 81, 90,
  99, 103, 132, 300 n.52, 321 n.16, 343
Wyatt, M. K., 92

Yellowfish (Indian), 48–49, 52, 118–20
Yellow Horse (Indian), 119
Yorkshire, England, 5

zoological artifacts, 287–88